'This remarkably well-curated book offers us tremendous insight into the horrors of our planet, ranging from authoritarianism and anti-Semitism to racism and colonialism. The esteemed editors and contributors have provided us with much depth-psychological wisdom and have reminded us of the importance of studying the core concepts of critical theory and psychoanalysis. Every politician should read this text!'
> **Professor Brett Kahr**, *Senior Fellow, Tavistock Institute of Medical Psychology, London, and Honorary Director of Research, Freud Museum, London*

'Comprised of scintillatingly eloquent essays, this volume ranges from philosophically nuanced accounts of the place of psychoanalysis within Critical Theory, penetrating discussions of the concept of transgenerational transmission of trauma and illuminating analyses of the growing propensity towards authoritarianism in certain quarters of the Left, to critical, yet nuanced and judicious, encounters with contemporary critical race theory, whiteness studies, and much more besides. It's essential reading for anyone seriously interested in understanding and appreciating the rich and enduring theoretical legacy of the sophisticated synthesis of Marx and Freud forged by members of the Frankfurt School in the early decades of the previous century, after the moment to "realize philosophy" was missed.'
> **Samir Gandesha**, *Professor of Humanities and Director of the Institute for the Humanities, Simon Fraser University, Vancouver, Canada*

'The papers collected in *Critical Theory and Psychoanalysis* demonstrate the continuing relevance of the Frankfurt School by applying their synthesis of Marxism and psychoanalysis to show the richness of their confluence; and how key thinkers in the tradition appropriated psychoanalysis in their critical social theory, engagement with Freud, and the social and political issues of the day. These original papers exhibit the vibrancy and timeliness of the Frankfurt School's appropriation of Freud to key issues of contemporary psychoanalytic and social theory.'
> **Douglas Kellner**, *Distinguished Research Professor of Education, UCLA*

Critical Theory and Psychoanalysis

Critical theory has traditionally been interested in engaging classical psychoanalysis rather than addressing postclassical thought. For the first time, this volume brings critical theory into proper dialogue with modern developments in the psychoanalytic movement and covers a broad range of topics in contemporary society that revisit the Frankfurt School and its contributions to psychoanalytic social critique.

Theoretical, clinical, and applied investigations in social pathology are explored in relation to new directions in critical cultural discourse from a variety of psychoanalytic perspectives. In this volume, internationally acclaimed social political theorists, philosophers, psychoanalysts, cultural critics, and scholars of humanities examine contemporary issues in social critique that address a myriad of topics.

Critical Theory and Psychoanalysis will be of interest to philosophers, psychoanalysts, political scientists, cultural theorists, sociologists, psychologists, religious studies, academe, and those generally interested in the humanities and social sciences.

Jon Mills, PsyD, PhD, ABPP, is a Canadian philosopher and psychoanalyst. He is an honorary professor, Department of Psychosocial and Psychoanalytic Studies, University of Essex, UK, and is on faculty in the postgraduate programs in psychoanalysis and psychotherapy, Adelphi University, and the New School for Existential Psychoanalysis, USA.

Daniel Burston, PhD, PhD, is an associate professor of psychology at Duquesne University in Pittsburgh and the author of numerous books and journal articles on psychoanalysis and critical theory. His most recent book is titled *Anti-Semitism and Analytical Psychology: Jung, Politics and Culture* (Routledge, 2021).

Philosophy & Psychoanalysis Book Series
Series Editor
Jon Mills

Philosophy & Psychoanalysis is dedicated to current developments and cutting-edge research in the philosophical sciences, phenomenology, hermeneutics, existentialism, logic, semiotics, cultural studies, social criticism, and the humanities that engage and enrich psychoanalytic thought through philosophical rigor. With the philosophical turn in psychoanalysis comes a new era of theoretical research that revisits past paradigms while invigorating new approaches to theoretical, historical, contemporary, and applied psychoanalysis. No subject or discipline is immune from psychoanalytic reflection within a philosophical context including psychology, sociology, anthropology, politics, the arts, religion, science, culture, physics, and the nature of morality. Philosophical approaches to psychoanalysis may stimulate new areas of knowledge that have conceptual and applied value beyond the consulting room reflective of greater society at large. In the spirit of pluralism, *Philosophy & Psychoanalysis* is open to any theoretical school in philosophy and psychoanalysis that offers novel, scholarly, and important insights in the way we come to understand our world.

Titles in this series:

The Emergent Container in Psychoanalysis
Experiencing Absence and Future
Ana Martinez Acobi

Critical Theory and Psychoanalysis
From the Frankfurt School to Contemporary Critique
Edited by Jon Mills and Daniel Burston

For more information about this series, please visit: www.routledge.com/Philosophy-and-Psychoanalysis/book-series/PHILPSY

Critical Theory and Psychoanalysis

From the Frankfurt School to Contemporary Critique

Edited by Jon Mills and Daniel Burston

LONDON AND NEW YORK

Designed cover image: "Leave of Absence" State of the Arts
© Bob Omar Tunnoch, bobomartunnoch.com

First published 2023
by Routledge
4 Park Square, Milton Park, Abingdon, Oxon OX14 4RN

and by Routledge
605 Third Avenue, New York, NY 10158

Routledge is an imprint of the Taylor & Francis Group, an informa business

© 2023 selection and editorial matter, Jon Mills and Daniel Burston; individual chapters, the contributors

The right of Jon Mills and Daniel Burston to be identified as the authors of the editorial material, and of the authors for their individual chapters, has been asserted in accordance with sections 77 and 78 of the Copyright, Designs and Patents Act 1988.

All rights reserved. No part of this book may be reprinted or reproduced or utilised in any form or by any electronic, mechanical, or other means, now known or hereafter invented, including photocopying and recording, or in any information storage or retrieval system, without permission in writing from the publishers.

Trademark notice: Product or corporate names may be trademarks or registered trademarks, and are used only for identification and explanation without intent to infringe.

British Library Cataloguing-in-Publication Data
A catalogue record for this book is available from the British Library

Library of Congress Cataloging-in-Publication Data
Names: Mills, Jon, 1964– editor. | Burston, Daniel, 1954– editor.
Title: Critical theory and psychoanalysis : from the Frankfurt school to contemporary critique / edited by Jon Mills and Daniel Burston.
Description: Abingdon, Oxon ; New York, NY : Routledge, 2023. | Series: Philosophy and psychoanalysis | Includes bibliographical references and index.
Identifiers: LCCN 2022028685 | ISBN 9781032104287 (hardback) | ISBN 9781032104270 (paperback) | ISBN 9781003215301 (ebook)
Subjects: LCSH: Social sciences and psychoanalysis. | Critical theory.
Classification: LCC BF175.4.S65 .C75 2023 | DDC 150.19/5—dc23/eng/20220824
LC record available at https://lccn.loc.gov/2022028685

ISBN: 978-1-032-10428-7 (hbk)
ISBN: 978-1-032-10427-0 (pbk)
ISBN: 978-1-003-21530-1 (ebk)

DOI: 10.4324/9781003215301

Typeset in Times New Roman
by Apex CoVantage, LLC

Contents

About the Contributors — ix
Preface — xiii
DANIEL BURSTON

1 **Psychoanalysis and the Frankfurt School** — 1
   JOEL WHITEBOOK

2 **Communism and Ambivalence: Freud, Marxism, and Aggression** — 26
   ADRIAN JOHNSTON

3 **Recapitulation and the Vicissitudes of Progress, From Freud to the Frankfurt School: "The Germ of the Regression"** — 66
   FRANK PITTENGER

4 **Analytical Psychology and the Dialectic of Enlightenment** — 95
   PAUL BISHOP

5 **Dysrecognition and *Pathos*** — 115
   JON MILLS

6 **Critical Theory and Anti-Semitism: Implications for Politics, Education, and Psychoanalysis** — 131
   BENJAMIN B. STROSBERG

7 **Critical Theory, Left-Wing Authoritarianism, and Anti-Semitism** — 158
   DANIEL BURSTON

8   The Evolutionary Anthropology of Erich Fromm:
    The Frankfurt School, Second Nature, and the Existential
    Crisis of Consciousness   185
    GARY CLARK

9   Colonizing the American Psyche: Virtue and the Problem
    of Consumer Capitalism   211
    JOHN R. WHITE

10 No Sex Without Coffee: The One Nature and Its
    Superstructures: Elements of Freudian Materialism   231
    ROBERT PFALLER

11 Shrinking Vistas: Critical Theory, Psychoanalysis,
    and the Postmodern Mire   247
    KURT JACOBSEN

12 Mapping the White Unconscious: Critical Race Theory,
    Whiteness Studies, and Psychoanalysis   264
    DANIEL BURSTON

13 Critical Theory and Contemporary Psychoanalysis   287
    JON MILLS

    Index   303

About the Contributors

Paul Bishop is William Jacks Chair of Modern Languages at the University of Glasgow and has published on various topics relating to analytical psychology and intellectual history. His most recent publications include *Ludwig Klages and the Philosophy of Life* (Routledge, 2019), and he is currently co-editing with Leslie Gardner and Terence Dawson a volume on the archaic and the abyss for Routledge.

Daniel Burston has a PhD in social and political thought and a PhD in psychology, both from York University in Toronto. He is Associate Professor of Psychology at Duquesne University in Pittsburgh and the author of numerous books and journal articles on psychoanalysis and critical theory, ranging from *The Legacy of Erich Fromm* (Harvard University Press, 1991) to *Psychoanalysis, Politics and the Postmodern University* (Palgrave McMillan, 2020). His most recent book is titled *Anti-Semitism and Analytical Psychology: Jung, Politics and Culture* (Routledge, 2021). Burston is a member of Cheiron – the International Society for the History of the Behavioral and Social Sciences, and a lifetime supporter of the Nexus Institute.

Gary Clark, PhD, is an Australian writer and researcher. He is currently a visiting research fellow in the University of Adelaide Medical School. His research focus is in paleoanthropology and the evolution of music, language, and human ritual life. He has a particular interest in situating Jungian psychology in the context of current debates in evolutionary neuroscience.

Kurt Jacobsen, PhD, is co-editor of the UK-based journal *Free Associations* and a research associate in the Political Science Department at the University of Chicago. He is author or editor of 11 books, including

Freud's Foes: Psychoanalysis, Science and Resistance; *International Politics and Inner Worlds: Masks of Reason under Scrutiny*; *Pacification and Its Discontents*; and the forthcoming coedited (with R. D. Hinshelwood), *Psychoanalysis, Science and Power: Essays in Honour of Robert Maxwell Young*. He also is a regular contributor to the international press and is an award-winning documentary filmmaker.

Adrian Johnston, PhD, is Distinguished Professor in the Department of Philosophy at the University of New Mexico at Albuquerque and a faculty member at the Emory Psychoanalytic Institute in Atlanta. He is the author of *Time Driven: Metapsychology and the Splitting of the Drive* (2005), *Žižek's Ontology: A Transcendental Materialist Theory of Subjectivity* (2008), *Badiou, Žižek, and Political Transformations: The Cadence of Change* (2009), and *Prolegomena to Any Future Materialism, Volume One: The Outcome of Contemporary French Philosophy* (2013), all published by Northwestern University Press. He also is the author of *Adventures in Transcendental Materialism: Dialogues with Contemporary Thinkers* (Edinburgh University Press, 2014). He is the co-author, with Catherine Malabou, of *Self and Emotional Life: Philosophy, Psychoanalysis, and Neuroscience* (Columbia University Press, 2013). His most recent books are *Irrepressible Truth: On Lacan's "The Freudian Thing"* (Palgrave Macmillan, 2017); *A New German Idealism: Hegel, Žižek, and Dialectical Materialism* (Columbia University Press, 2018); and *Prolegomena to Any Future Materialism, Volume Two: A Weak Nature Alone* (Northwestern University Press, 2019). With Todd McGowan and Slavoj Žižek, he is a co-editor of the book series *Diaeresis* at Northwestern University Press.

Jon Mills, PsyD, PhD, ABPP, is a philosopher, psychoanalyst, and retired clinical psychologist. He is Honorary Professor, Department of Psychosocial and Psychoanalytic Studies, University of Essex, Colchester, UK; Faculty member in the Postgraduate Programs in Psychoanalysis and Psychotherapy, Gordon F. Derner School of Psychology, Adelphi University, NY, and the New School for Existential Psychoanalysis, CA; and is Emeritus Professor of Psychology and Psychoanalysis, Adler Graduate Professional School, Toronto, Canada. Recipient of numerous awards for his scholarship, including four Gradiva Awards, he is the author and/or editor of over 30 books in psychoanalysis, philosophy, psychology, and cultural studies, including most recently *Psyche, Culture, World: Excursions in Existentialism and Psychoanalytic Philosophy*. In 2015 he was given the Otto Weininger Memorial Award for Lifetime Achievement by the Canadian Psychological Association.

Robert Pfaller is Professor of Philosophy at the University of Art and Industrial Design in Linz, Austria. Founding member of the Viennese psychoanalytic research group "stuzzicadenti," he received the Paul Watzlawick Ring of Honor in 2020, awarded by the Viennese Medical Chamber (Ärztekammer Wien), and "The Missing Link" award by Psychoanalytisches Seminar Zurich, Switzerland, in 2007. His many works include *Interpassivity: The Aesthetics of Delegated Enjoyment* (Edinburgh University Press, 2017) and *The Pleasure Principle in Culture: Illusions without Owners* (Verso, 2014), which was awarded the American Board and Academy of Psychoanalysis Book Prize for best book in 2015.

Frank Pittenger, PhD, is a clinical psychologist in private practice and Clinical Assistant Professor of Psychology at the University of Tennessee. He received his PhD in clinical psychology from Duquesne University and holds degrees in religious studies from Florida State University and Haverford College. His doctoral thesis, "The Anxiety of Atavism," addressed the history and afterlife of biogenetic recapitulationism within psychoanalysis and evolutionary psychology. His contribution to this volume is part of a broader reappraisal of the place of the biogenetic law within psychoanalysis and social theory.

Benjamin B. Strosberg is a PhD candidate in clinical psychology at Duquesne University. His research focuses on the continued relevance of Frankfurt School Critical Theory for psychology and psychoanalysis. He has published on topics such as teletherapy, phenomenology, anti-Semitism, racism, and Lacanian theory.

John R. White, PhD, Jungian Diplomate, is a practicing Jungian psychoanalyst and licensed mental health counselor. His original training was in philosophy. He completed his doctorate in philosophy at the International Academy of Philosophy and subsequently taught philosophy at three different institutions over the span of 20 years. His publications are mainly in continental philosophy, ethics, environmental philosophy, and the philosophy of psychoanalysis. He is currently a scholar-in-residence at the Simon Silverman Phenomenology Center, Duquesne University, Pittsburgh, PA. He obtained his masters in mental health counseling and his diploma as a Jungian psychoanalyst from the Inter-Regional Society of Jungian Analysts. He is a member of the Pittsburgh Society of Jungian Analysts and of the Board of Directors of the Pittsburgh Psychoanalytic Center. He is the author of *Adaptation and Clinical Practice: Robert Langs' Adaptive Psychotherapy in the Light of Analytical Psychology*.

Joel Whitebook received his PhD in philosophy from the New School for Social Research, a PhD in clinical psychology from the City University of New York (CUNY), and received his psychoanalytic training at the New York Freudian Society. He has been in private practice for decades and has taught at the New School, Columbia University, as well as in a number of clinical settings. He is currently on the faculty of Columbia's Center for Psychoanalytic Training and Research and is the former director of its Psychoanalytic Studies Program. His books include *Perversion and Utopia: A Study in Psychoanalysis and Critical Theory* and *Freud: An Intellectual Biography*.

Preface

We live in dangerous times. Almost everywhere we look, climate change, income inequality, corruption, and the erosion of democratic norms and institutions undermine the stability of civil society. As a result, xenophobia, nativism, and hostility to immigrants have grown alarmingly, propelling far-right nationalist and populist governments to power in Russia, India, the United States, Brazil, Poland, Hungary, Italy, Turkey, the Philippines, and elsewhere. Moreover, parties that embrace and espouse hostile attitudes to "outsiders" are steadily gaining popularity, posing serious electoral challenges to ruling parties and governing coalitions throughout Europe and Scandinavia.

Meanwhile, income inequality jeopardizes the living standards and future prospects of the middle and working classes, diminishing trust in mainstream politicians and fueling the proliferation of wild conspiracy theories and extremism on both sides of the political spectrum. In many parts of the world, rising sea levels, prolonged droughts, and catastrophic weather events are causing rising prices and chronic shortages of food, water, and fuel. These conditions are already feeding into violent conflicts in Africa, the Middle East, Asia, and Latin America, sending large waves of refugees to Europe and the United States seeking asylum. These sources of global anxiety and uncertainty are only compounded by North Korea's development of intercontinental ballistic missiles, China's support for Russia and its menacing stance toward Taiwan and Australia, ongoing turmoil in Israel/Palestine, and Iran's proxy wars with its Sunni neighbors. Worse yet, Vladimir Putin's brutal and senseless invasion of Ukraine on February 24, 2022, provoked what promises to be a new nuclear arms race, a seismic shift in international defense postures and policies, all conjured up by the specter of yet another world war.

In the midst of these burgeoning crises, the Far Right exploits the sense of victimization felt by middle and working class people by providing them with scapegoats who are depicted as dangerous or expendable, rather than as vulnerable human beings who are entitled to dignity and human rights. Anti-Semitism is a prominent feature of many of these movements, which often use hostility to immigrants and minorities as their primary recruiting tool. Many have scripted George Soros, a Jewish billionaire, in the role of a demonic Jewish adversary who is using his wealth to flood their respective countries with immigrants and criminals. He is accused of undermining national sovereignty and traditional values through his support of liberal civic organizations. This idea is expressed repeatedly in the official media in Victor Orban's Hungary. And we heard a variation on the same message (in abbreviated form) among the neo-Nazis who marched in the Unite the Right rally in Charlottesville in August 2017, chanting, "The Jews will not replace us!"

The Far Left's narrative about Jews is quite different, of course. In the United States, many left-wing activists now insist that Jews enjoy all the perks of White privilege and therefore "uphold" rather than oppose White supremacy, the very thing Far Right activists insist Jewish people are secretly intent on destroying. Despite the recent uptick in anti-Semitism in communities of color, and the enduring influence of Louis Farrakhan, many activists still claim that anti-Semitism is just a "White on White" issue that has nothing to do with White supremacy or systemic racism and is therefore not worthy of their attention or concern. Unlike right-wing extremists, who abhor multiculturalism and promote Islamophobia, the Far Left espouses a strange brand of multiculturalism that typically excludes and devalues Jewish experience but often *embraces* Islamist movements and organizations in what it imagines is a progressive, anti-imperialist coalition.

As democracy falters and authoritarianism spreads, some aspects of our current crises resemble the situation in the years preceding WWII. For example, racism and conspiracy theories abound, and Jewish people and institutions are now targeted by mobs and vigilantes much as they were in the 1930s across Europe and the United States, when Father Charles Coughlin and industrialist Henry Ford spread their anti-Semitic venom all across this continent. However, as illuminating and disturbing as these parallels may be, it is important to remember that Jews are merely the proverbial canaries in the coal mine, that the scale and severity of the chaos already unfolding in our backyards will soon engulf everybody and have a far more damaging impact on our planet than the two world wars that ravaged the twentieth century.

Strange as it sounds, in the midst of these worrisome developments, many conservative pundits nowadays blame critical theory for our current societal malaise and, more specifically, for spawning something called "cultural Marxism," which ostensibly threatens our cultural cohesion. But what is cultural Marxism, actually? A term coined by the Norwegian mass murderer Anders Breivik, adopted by White supremacist Kevin MacDonald and conspiracy theorist Alex Jones (Braune, 2019). Despite its inauspicious derivation, the term "cultural Marxism" shows up with surprising regularity in the podcasts and publications of more mainstream media personalities like Christopher Rufo and Jordan Peterson, among others, who repeat the popular mantra that proclaims that Marxism begat critical theory, which begat postmodernism, which (supposedly) begat cultural Marxism.

The problem with this narrative is that it is simply not true. It is a straw man, which only seems plausible if you cherry-pick and decontextualize ideas from these various schools of thought, something Christopher Rufo is particularly skilled at doing. Unfortunately, this popular mythology about critical theory and cultural Marxism encourages a kind of smug, know-it-all attitude that masks intellectual laziness and complacency among many contemporary conservatives, who crafted this oversimplified narrative to assure themselves that they are right to mistrust and dismiss all critical social theory. There is also something ahistorical and conspiratorial about this line of thinking, as if the radical thinkers of today are simply putting old wine into new bottles, instead of putting forward genuinely new ideas of their own in response to new social and political realities. In truth, however, there are profound differences between Marxism and critical theory, and between critical theory and postmodernism. In order to grasp them clearly, one has to understand the social and historical contexts in which these movements arose.

To put these reflections in context, please consider the following. In 1794, Nicholas de Condorcet (1743–1794) wrote a book titled *Sketch for a Historical Picture of the Progress of the Human Mind*. Condorcet was a leading figure in the French Enlightenment who depicted progress as a slow but inexorable process that would eventually dispel ignorance and superstition through the development of science and confer previously undreamed-of moral and material benefits on all humankind, ending poverty, abolishing slavery, and granting women full legal and political equality with men, etc.

At its inception, Marxism was really a radical extension of the French Enlightenment project, predicated on a belief in progress and a program for universal human emancipation. Marx shared the Enlightenment's belief in equality but stipulated that progress is not a simple, easy, or linear process. On the contrary, it is marked by oppression and exploitation, class conflict, and class struggle. He called his analysis of capitalism and his program for the transformation of society *historical materialism* and believed that the working class had a special role to play in transforming society and would soon acquire "class consciousness," working together across national boundaries to inaugurate a classless society, promoting the emancipation of all humanity and not just the bourgeoisie.

Unfortunately, this never happened. On the contrary, when World War I broke out, the working classes in England, France, Germany, and Austria rallied to the defense of their respective countries, participating actively in what V. I. Lenin condemned as an imperialistic war designed to benefit the ruling class alone. Because capitalist modes and methods of production had not yet penetrated the vast Russian Empire, Russia lacked an industrial proletariat, and as a result, the Russian revolution of 1917 resulted from a collaboration between alienated members the intelligentsia (mostly professionals, like Lenin himself) and the Russian peasantry. Once the Bolsheviks seized power, Russia withdrew from the conflict, and Lenin swiftly banished or killed the Social Democrats (or Mensheviks) who had helped him and his followers overthrow the Czar.

Not surprisingly, the fact that Russia underwent a revolution despite the absence of a strong working class obligated Lenin to rework certain features of Marxist theory. One upshot was the theory of revolutionary vanguardism, which stipulated that the Communist Party represents the interests of the working class and, in the interests of creating a centralized and unified movement, must adopt an organizational structure known as democratic centralism. Unfortunately, despite its name, democratic centralism stifled dissent within its own ranks, and after the death of Lenin in January of 1924, a power struggle ensued between the followers of Leon Trotsky and those of Joseph Stalin. Stalin won and modified Marx's ideas and program even more profoundly than Lenin had, creating an ideology known as "dialectical materialism" by its proponents and "vulgar

Marxism" by its critics, an ideology that was used to justify a bloody reign of terror.

Then, in 1929, the stock market crashed – the biggest crisis of capitalism to that point – and contrary to expectation among Western Marxists, the European proletariat did not mobilize on cue to mount the revolution that Marx had predicted should eventually ensue. Indeed, critical theory arose primarily as a response to the failure of Marx's predictions at this historical juncture. Granted, the first director of the Frankfurt Institute for Social Research was an orthodox Marxist. But his successor, Max Horkheimer, who took over in 1930, was not. Horkheimer and associates rejected revolutionary vanguardism and claimed that the European and British working class were failing in their historic mission because of social psychological processes that orthodox Marxism was not equipped to elucidate or address. So with the help of Erich Fromm, the only analyst working among the institute's faculty, Horkheimer and associates attempted to develop a Marx-Freud synthesis that would account for the failure of the working class to lead the transition to a classless society.

In addition to integrating psychoanalytic perspectives on social psychology, critical theorists deviated from orthodox Marxism by rejecting economic determinism and promoting interdisciplinarity, integrating ideas and insights from a wide range of non-Marxist theorists in sociology, anthropology, philosophy, and literature. In the process, as Perry Anderson observed, their emphasis shifted away from the pragmatics and exigencies of class struggle toward a critique of social factors that Marx had deemed to be "superstructural," notably, literature, the arts, radio and cinema, popular music, and propaganda, which they deemed to be more consequential than Marx had ever imagined in perpetuating the status quo (Anderson, 1983).

Finally, remember that Marx shared the Enlightenment's enthusiasm for technological innovation, nowadays called *technophilia*. He believed that new technologies were intrinsically liberating and should be welcomed because they dramatically altered social conditions and power relations between classes of people, hastening the crisis of capitalism that would set the stage for the proletariat to seize the means of production from the capitalist class and effect a more equitable distribution of goods, services, and opportunities for education and personal self-expression.

Though they still clung to Enlightenment ideals, Horkheimer and Adorno et al. had witnessed the galloping Nazification of Germany at close quarters before they fled Germany in 1935. As a result, they were quite critical of the concept of progress, arguing that scientific and technological progress often masked and facilitated a collective regression to barbarism, culminating in the Holocaust (Horkheimer and Adorno, 1947). This led to a rather gloomy philosophy of history, very unlike Marx's, which anticipated a "happy ending" (or a new beginning) for humankind after the revolution. Indeed, critical theory's attitude toward the Enlightenment could only be described as profoundly ambivalent, sharing the Enlightenment's aspirations for human emancipation and equality but lacking any faith in the ability of relentless scientific and technological innovation to bring it all about.

That being so, it is probably no coincidence that in 1930 – one year after the stock market crash and the same year Horkheimer became director of the Frankfurt Institute for Social Research – Sigmund Freud published *Civilization and Its Discontents*. Freud believed in progress but stipulated that it always comes with a hefty price tag attached. According to Freud, progress is only achieved through the domestication and secondary transformation of our instinctual drives, creating a good deal of sexual privation and anguish, rendering everyone "an enemy of civilization" in the depths of their unconscious. He also noted that scientific and technological progress have given us godlike powers undreamed of by our ancestors, but that the very same discoveries that confer power over nature can be harnessed in the service of our innate aggression. Indeed, he warned that unless or until we learn to harness or deflect our instinctive aggression, we are menaced by the prospect of technologically mediated self-extinction in the not-too-distant future. Nowadays, of course, the prospect of species-wide extinction is far more than a theoretical possibility. On the contrary, it is a specter that haunts each and every human being alive today, and few informed observers would now dispute that Freud's words in 1930 were somewhat prophetic. But in 1930, orthodox Marxists were scandalized that the Frankfurt School incorporated Freudian ideas and perspectives into their work, not least because Freud was a fierce critic of the Soviet Union.

Unlike critical theory, which was born in Weimar, postmodernism arose in response to the mass protests that roiled France, and above all Paris, in May of 1968. Following in the wake of yet another failed revolution, it wrestled with the theoretical problems and possibilities bequeathed to French intellectuals by the structuralist movement initiated earlier that decade by Claude Levi-Strauss (Anderson, 1983). Furthermore, unlike critical theory, which has its roots in Marx and Freud, postmodernism borrows extensively from anti-Enlightenment thinkers like Friedrich Nietzsche and Martin Heidegger. This was an odd and unprecedented move for Left-leaning intellectuals, because Nietzsche and Heidegger had nothing but contempt for the masses and no interest whatsoever in promoting a program of universal human emancipation. Indeed, Nietzsche argued forcefully for the continuation of slavery, while Heidegger was an unrepentant Nazi. That being so, this gradual migration of intellectual capital from right-wing philosophers to left-wing theorists in the Cold War era is one of the strangest episodes in the history of philosophy (Burston and Frie, 2006).

Generally speaking, postmodernists and post-structuralists are dismissive of historical materialism and the very idea of progress, which they regard as just one more "grand narrative" that is vacuous, self-serving, or ripe for deconstruction. And unlike Marx and Freud, they claim that there is nothing like a universal human nature that all people share, which renders it possible for us to empathize with the experience of someone whose cultural context is radically different from our own. On reflection, then, the differences between Marxism, critical theory, and postmodernism are pretty clear and pivot largely around their attitudes toward the Enlightenment. Marx was unabashedly enthusiastic about the Enlightenment, while Critical Theory, informed by Freud, waxed ambivalent toward it. Postmodernism and post-structuralism, by contrast, are generally quite dismissive or derisive in their appraisals of Enlightenment thought. Besides, Marx stressed the primacy of *praxis*, labor, and economics in the shaping of society, while Freud and his followers stressed the primacy of instincts and their vicissitudes, or "the economics of the libido." By contrast with both Marx and Freud, postmodernists and post-structuralists generally stress the primacy of language, which they often maintain is culture constitutive.

Despite the gravity of our current situation, the essays in this volume attest to the continuing vitality and relevance of critical theory today, but they do so in different ways and from differing perspectives. When we circulated our call for papers, we deliberately solicited contributions from relative newcomers as well as from well-established scholars. In that, we succeeded. Moreover, rather than seeking to promote uniformity of opinion, we welcomed the efforts of scholars who have engaged seriously with the legacy of the Frankfurt School but without attempting to minimize or ignore their differences. The result is a collection of essays whose subject matter converge and overlap in many ways but without giving anyone "the final word." So for example, Joel Whitebook's chapter relates how three generations of critical theorists have fruitfully engaged with psychoanalysis. The papers of Adrian Johnston and Robert Pfaller probe some of the subtler, far-reaching implications of Freud's brand of materialism and ponder the extent to which it was (or could be rendered) compatible with a more Marxist understanding of (historical) materialism. Kurt Jacobsen's paper takes aim at what he describes as the quietist and stoic implications of Lacanian theory. Three other papers – those of Benjamin B. Strosberg, Paul Bishop, and John R. White – delve deeply into the substance of Horkheimer and Adorno's book *The Dialectic of Enlightenment* and its relevance to contemporary social thought. Frank Pittenger's delightful essay dwells on problems in Freud's metapsychology and its impact on Adorno and Marcuse, while Gary Clark offers us a refreshing new look at Erich Fromm's contributions to critical theory and his intellectual development after leaving the Frankfurt School. Daniel Burston's papers apply the lens of critical theory to the study of left-wing authoritarianism and the impact of critical race theory and whiteness studies on contemporary psychoanalytic discourse. Finally, Jon Mills's two papers address the prevalence of dysrecognition in contemporary culture and offers a critique of Axel Honneth's recent reflections on the relationship between psychoanalysis and critical theory.

As our planetary crises deepen, right-wing populism and ethnonationalism pose the gravest threats to democracy, not critical theory, and certainly not the mythical boogeyman manufactured by conservative pundits. Evidence for this, if any is needed, was furnished by the insurrection on Capitol Hill on January 6, 2021, and more recently by Putin's brutal and senseless invasion of Ukraine. But with that said, there are some worrisome developments on the Left that should be addressed as well. In Chapter 16 of *Grand Hotel Abyss: The Lives of the Frankfurt School*, Stuart Jeffries notes that the concept of left-wing authoritarianism – which Habermas dubbed "Left Fascism" – only arose in critical theory circles long after the publication of *The Authoritarian Personality*, and more specifically, in 1967–1968, when aggrieved students occupied the Institute for Social Research and disrupted Theodor Adorno's lectures, which were thronged by noisy students attempting to de-platform him for not lending his unqualified support to their movement (Jeffries, 2017). While Adorno never published anything on this topic, he did discuss it (with considerable bitterness) in his correspondence with Herbert Marcuse shortly before his death. And in an article titled "The Authoritarian Personality Reconsidered: The Phantom of 'Left Fascism,'" Gandesha points to more recent developments of an even more disturbing nature. He writes as follows:

> Today, we possibly see some of the very tendencies identified by Adorno . . . afoot in certain quarters of the Left both in the contemporary university and beyond it. We have seen ample evidence of the Left's reluctance to tolerate dissent within its own ranks. For example, we have seen it in the students' demands at Evergreen College in Olympia, Washington, for the resignation of tenured professors who made principled objections to political actions that they understood as re-instituting forms of segregation in the name of combatting it (Hartocollis, 2017). We've seen it in the case of a letter signed by over 800 academics (see Vigo and Garano, 2017), demanding the retraction of an article on "trans-racialism" by a young assistant professor, Rebecca Tuvel (2017), in the feminist philosophy journal Hypatia. . . . Beyond the university, we've seen it in the demand made by British New York-based artist, Hannah Black (2017), that "non-Black" artist, Dana Shultz's (2017) painting of Emmett Till, not simply be criticized but . . . actually . . . destroyed. Perhaps more consequentially, sections of the Left have defended figures like Milosevic, Vladimir Putin, Baathist regimes of Saddam Hussein and Bashar al-Assad, (despite evidence that all of these regimes brutally suppressed and murdered their own people) (Al Yafai (2017), under the banner of anti-imperialism on the basis of the logic of "my enemy's enemy is my friend" (Hensman, 2018). Moreover, recently Steve Bannon, former advisor to Donald J. Trump and architect of a new fascist international recently shared pleasantries with left-wing firebrand George Galloway.
>
> (Gandesha, 2019, pp. 602–603)

So if Gandesha is right – and we believe he is – left-wing authoritarianism poses a less potent and immediate threat to democracy than right-wing authoritarianism but remains a significant longer-term threat because it has infiltrated our universities. In fact, many accomplished scholars and gifted teachers are *already* leaving higher education for other careers because they feel that their departments or universities have been thoroughly captured or compromised by the new activist *Zeitgeist*. So while cultural Marxism is indeed a myth, cancel culture is not (German, K. and Lukianoff, G., 2022). Indeed, we have many friends and colleagues in academia who live in fear of losing their livelihoods, or being "cancelled" for saying or doing something that offends the activist sensibilities of their colleagues and students. The resulting self-censorship places invisible constraints on academic freedom. It is therefore detrimental to the basic functioning of the university. And let's not kid ourselves. Thriving democracies actually *need* intact universities to foster critical thinking and an informed and responsive citizenry. Absent these qualities, citizens devolve into mere consumers and conformists who lack the judgment, resolve, and the sense of solidarity with others to mobilize in defense of their increasingly fragile freedoms.

Sadly, the crisis in our universities is also compounded by the astonishing growth of the managerial caste in the last four decades. While the numbers of administrators in universities and colleges grows in leaps and bounds, the number of tenured professors is shrinking steadily, and those that remain have been drastically de-professionalized. Rather than treating them as colleagues and respected professionals, university administrators frequently treat faculty as mere employees who should meekly forgo any meaningful role in the governance of the university and accept their decisions without question (Burston, 2020). Indeed, even tenured faculty are increasingly regarded as expendable and certainly not worthy of the increasingly extravagant salaries and bonuses administrators routinely award themselves. Worse yet, this trend toward administrative bloat was accompanied by the precipitous decline of the liberal arts and the explosive growth of diversity, equity, and inclusion programs, which are now an $8 billion industry in the United States, although evidence for their long-term effectiveness is vanishingly scarce. So why do university administrators insist on them? To boost enrollments? Certainly. But promoting DEI programming of various kinds is also a vehicle for collective virtue signaling, helping administrators cultivate an image of themselves as good people who are genuinely concerned about social justice, even though they are too timid or indifferent to come to the defense of faculty who are unjustly accused and harassed, and increasingly happy to dismiss them for trivial offenses, without just cause or due process.

We conclude with a quote from Max Horkheimer, who addressed the student activists of the 1960s and 1970s in a preface to an earlier collection of essays on critical theory as follows:

> An open declaration that even a dubious democracy, for all its defects, is always better than . . . dictatorship seems necessary for the sake of truth. . . . Rosa Luxemburg, whom many students venerate, said fifty years ago that "the remedy of Trotsky and Lenin have found, the elimination of democracy as such, is worse than the disease it is supposed to cure." To protect, preserve and where possible, to extend the ephemeral freedom of the individual in the face of the growing threat to it is a far more urgent a task than to issue abstract denunciations of it or endanger it by actions that have no hope of success.
> (Horkheimer, 1972, p. viii)

Horkheimer then went on to characterize much of the Left as "pseudo-revolutionary" and to chastise the radical Right for being "pseudo-conservative." Why? In his own words, because

> a true conservatism which takes man's spiritual heritage seriously is more closely related to the revolutionary mentality, which does not simply reject that heritage but absorbs it into a new synthesis than it is to the radicalism of the Right which seeks to eliminate them both.
> (Horkheimer, 1972, p. ix)

Sadly, according to Horkheimer's criteria, genuine conservatives are quite rare nowadays, while "pseudo-conservatives" are plentiful, and for now, at least, still backing Donald Trump. For all our sakes, let's hope that thoughtful American conservatives rally to their senses, repudiate Trump and Trumpism, and reject the other toxic demagogues in their midst. And if the Left can rein in or repudiate the authoritarians in their own ranks, we may yet manage to restore a measure of sanity to our political discourse, as we prepare to confront the grim realities that lie ahead.

Daniel Burston

References

Al Yafai, F. 2017. "The cult of Bashar extends from the far right to the far left." Retrieved from www.thenational.ae/opinion/the-cult-of-bashar-extends-from-the-far-right-to-the-far-left.-1.621909.

Anderson, P. 1983. *In the Tracks of Historical Materialism*. London: Verso.

Black, H. 2017 (March 21). "'The painting must go': Hannah Black pens open letter to the Whitney about controversial biennial work." *Art News*. Retrieved from www.artnews.com/2017/03/21/the-painting-must-go-hannah-black-pens-an-open-letter-to-the-whitney-about-controversial-biennial-work/.

Braune, J. 2019. "Who's afraid of the Frankfurt school? 'Cultural marxism' as an anti-semitic conspiracy theory." *Journal of Social Justice*, vol. 9, pp. 1–25.

Burston, D. 2020. *Psychoanalysis, Politics and the Postmodern University*. Cham: Palgrave MacMillen.

Burston, D. and Frie, R. 2006. *Psychotherapy as a Human Science*. Pittsburgh: Duquesne University Press.

Gandesha, S. 2019. "The 'authoritarian personality' reconsidered: The phantom of 'left fascism'." *The American Journal of Psychoanalysis*, vol. 79, pp. 601–624.

German, K. and Lukianoff, G. 2022 (March 25). "Don't stop using the term 'cancel culture'." *The Daily Beast*. Retrieved from <thedailybeast.com>.

Hartocollis, A. 2017 (June 16). "A campus argument goes viral. Now the campus is under siege." *New York Times*. Retrieved from www.nytimes.com/2016/06/16/us/evergreen-state-protests.html.

Hensman, R. 2018. *Indefensible: Democracy, Counter-Revolution and the Rhetoric of Anti-Imperialism*. Chicago, IL: Haymarket Books.

Horkheimer, M. 1972. *Critical Theory: Selected Essays*. New York: Continuum Books.

Horkheimer, M. and Adorno, T. 1947. *The Dialectic of Enlightenment*, translated by Edmund Jephcott. Stanford: Stanford University Press, 2002.

Jeffries, S. 2017. *Grand Hotel Abyss: The Lives of the Frankfurt School*. London: Verso.

Shultz, D. 2017. *Open Casket* [Painting]. New York: Whitney Museum.

Tuvel, R. 2017 (March 29). "In defense of trans-racialism." *Hypatia*. Retrieved from https://doi.org/10/11/11/hypa.1237.

Vigo, J. and Garano, L. 2017. "Open letter on the *hypatia* controversy." *Feminist Current*. Retrieved from www.feministcurrent.com/2017/05/25/open-letter-hypatia-controversy/.

Chapter 1

Psychoanalysis and the Frankfurt School

Joel Whitebook

Introduction

In the 1930s, the philosophers and social scientists of the Institute for Social Research were the first members of the conservative German academy to not only treat the disreputable avant-garde new discipline of psychoanalysis seriously – whose membership was almost entirely Jewish – but also to accord Freud the same stature as the titans of the philosophical tradition. The radicalism of psychoanalysis fit with the radicalism of the position they were attempting to develop, and the appropriation of psychoanalysis provided one of the pillars on which critical theory was constructed (Jay 1973: 86–112).

In addition to the theoretical affinity between the Frankfurt School and psychoanalysis, the relationship between the two intellectual movements was also practical. The Institute for Social Research and the Frankfurt Psychoanalytic Institute shared a building, in which they held their classes in the same rooms, and jointly sponsored public lectures by such eminent analysts as Anna Freud, Paul Federn, Hans Sachs, and Siegfried Bernfeld. Indeed, the connection between the two organizations went even further. Max Horkheimer, the director of the Institute for Social Research, sat on the board of the analytic institute, while Eric Fromm – a trained analyst and member of both groups – helped the critical theorists educate themselves about the workings of psychoanalysis.

A major concern that led the critical theorists to turn to psychoanalysis was a deficit in Marxian theory: it lacked a so-called subjective dimension and tended to treat subjectivity simply as an epiphenomenon, that is, as a reflection of the material base. With the economic crisis of the 1930s, this concern became especially pressing. Objective conditions obtained that Marxian theory predictions should have produced the radicalization of the working class. But just the opposite was happening: a large portion of the European proletariat was turning to fascism instead. Max Horkheimer, Eric Fromm, and Herbert Marcuse, among others, undertook *Studies in Authority and the Family* to account for this supposedly anomalous fact (Horkheimer 1936; Jay 1973: 113–142; Wiggershaus 1994: 149–156).

In one sense, the study was groundbreaking for, along with Wilhelm Reich's work, it represented the first attempt to incorporate psychoanalysis into Marxian theory. But in another sense, its innovations remained limited. *Studies on Authority and the Family* still remained Marxist – albeit, of highly heterodox sort – insofar as it retained the general framework of political economy. Furthermore, the work drew on the less radical theories in the Freudian *corpus*, for example, those pertaining to character formation, rather than Freud's late, more scandalous cultural texts, which Horkheimer and Adorno turned to in conjunction with their reconstitution of critical theory in the 1940s.

After immigrating to California, Adorno joined with colleagues outside of the institute to conduct another psychoanalytically oriented interdisciplinary research project that returned to many of the same themes contained in *Studies on Authority and the Family*. Their findings were published in *The Authoritarian Personality: Studies in Prejudice* (Adorno 1982). Despite its initial influence, the work was later criticized on methodological grounds and fell out of fashion. But as Peter Gordon has recently suggested, with the election of Donald Trump and the rise of authoritarian leaders around the world, revisiting *The Authoritarian Personality* might be in order (Gordon 2017).

Max Horkheimer and Theodor Adorno

"Beneath the known history of Europe," Horkheimer and Adorno observe, "there runs a subterranean one [that] consists of the fate of the human instincts and passions repressed and distorted by civilization" (Horkheimer and Adorno 2002: 192). It can be argued that for these two philosophers, the sustained excavation of this subterranean history, as well as a focus on the body in general, constitutes a condition *sine qua non* of their position – as distinguished from what Horkheimer referred to as traditional theory (Horkheimer 1972). This orientation, moreover, comprised an essential aspect of the materialist perspective – of the "preponderance of the object," as Adorno called it – that they sought to maintain (Adorno 1973: 183).

When Horkheimer and Adorno received news that the Nazis had set the final solution into motion and that their colleague Walter Benjamin had committed suicide while trying to escape the Gestapo on the Spanish frontier, they concluded that it was necessary to radicalize their theory in order to do justice to the enormity of the catastrophe that was unfolding in Europe (Rabinbach 1997). That catastrophe, as they saw it, involved more than the failure of the proletariat to fulfill its historical task. It resulted from the self-destruction of the project of Enlightenment itself. "Why," they asked, was "humanity . . . sinking into a new kind of barbarism" precisely at the point where, according to the (Baconian) Enlightenment, the material conditions had been created that could produce a "truly human state" (Horkheimer and Adorno 2002: xiv)?

The radicalization of critical theory consisted in a move from the critique of political economy to the philosophy of history centering on the domination of nature (Jay 1973: 253–280). In addition to Freud, the two philosophers drew on Nietzsche, Weber, Mauss, as well as others to write a depth-psychological and depth-anthropological *Urgeschichte* or primal history of civilization. The new position was articulated in *Dialectic of Enlightenment*, which became the defining text of the Frankfurt School during its classical phase. Where the domination of nature in general – as opposed to economic exploitation and class struggle – became the overarching theme of the new philosophy of history, the idea of the domination of inner nature provided the specific link through which Horkheimer and Adorno incorporated Freud into their new theory.

For the mature Freud, the reality principle, understood as *Ananke* or *Atropos* (necessity or the ineluctable), defined the human condition (Whitebook 2017: Chapter 10). It designated the price that nature inevitably exacted from us finite transient beings, in the form of physical suffering and decay, loss, and ultimately death. By reading Marx's theory of exchange back into prehistory, Horkheimer and Adorno sought to integrate his economic theory with Freudian anthropology. They maintained that the law of equivalence – the principle that everything that happens must pay for having happened – governed mythical thought, and they saw the capitalist principle of exchange as the latest and most complete instantiation of the law of equivalence. The practice of sacrifice, which aims at mitigating the law's effects, follows from it. For example, the sacrifice that our so-called primitive ancestors performed to placate the gods after a successful hunting expedition constituted an attempt to control the price they would have to pay for their good fortune by offering an advanced propitiatory payment.

According to Horkheimer and Adorno, enlightenment consists in the attempt to escape mythic fate and sacrifice. Deploying his cunning, which was the precursor of instrumental reason, Odysseus, who is the prototype of the enlightened individual, sought to outsmart the law of equivalence through "the introversion of sacrifice." Rather than sacrificing a piece of external nature, for example, the hindquarter of an ox, Odysseus sacrificed a piece of his inner nature, which is to say, renounced a piece of his unconscious-instinctual life. By repressing his inner nature in order to form a purposeful, autocratic, virile, and rational (qua calculating) ego, Odysseus believed he could dominate external nature, thereby escaping its dangers, outsmart mythical fate, and evade the law of equivalence. Horkheimer and Adorno argue, however, that the strategy was flawed. Their thesis is that "the denial of nature in human beings," which constitutes "the core of all civilizing rationality," contains "the germ cell of proliferating mythic irrationality" out of which the dialectic of enlightenment ineluctably unfolds (Horkheimer and Adorno 2002: 42).

An erroneous Baconian assumption, which was taken over by Marx, underlies the program of the domination of nature: namely, its demand for renunciation is justified for, in the long run, the domination of nature will create the material conditions that are the prerequisite for what Bacon called "the relief of man's estate" – or the emancipation of the humanity, to put it in Marxian terms. But there is a hitch in this program, and it generates the self-defeating logic of the dialectic of enlightenment. Because it represents "the introversion of sacrifice," the renunciation of inner nature, which seeks to escape sacrifice, remains a form of sacrifice, albeit a displaced one. And as such, it is still subject to the law of equivalence. The math, Adorno and Horkheimer maintain, does not work: "all who renounce give away more of their life than is given back to them, more than the life they preserve" (Horkheimer and Adorno 2002: 43).

More concretely, the faulty math produces a calamitous result. In order to carry out the domination of nature, the subject must form a purposive calculating self by repressing its unconscious-instinctual life. It thereby reifies itself at the same time and to the same degree that it reifies external nature. It follows that at the point that nature has been thoroughly reified and dominated in order to produce the presumptive material preconditions for emancipation – which Horkheimer and Adorno assume had been approximated by the first half of the twentieth century – the self will have been thoroughly reified as well. In the process of creating the preconditions for its emancipation, the subject has, in short, so deformed itself – has so "annihilated" itself – that it is in no condition to appropriate those preconditions and create a better form of life. Hence, the self-defeating logic of the dialectic of enlightenment: "[w]ith the denial of nature in humans, not only the *telos* of the external mastery of nature, but also the *telos* of one's one life becomes opaque and confused." Instead of emancipation, barbarism results. It should be noted that, for Horkheimer and Adorno, "nature in the human being" constitutes that which is sacrificed in the process of dominating nature, as well as (in some unspecified fashion) that for the sake of which the entire process is pursued (Horkheimer and Adorno 2002: 42).

Because of their anti-Hegelian opposition to all modes of final reconciliation and their thesis of a totally administered world, Horkheimer and Adorno opposed all utopian solutions, indeed, positive solutions as such. Nevertheless, logically there is an unthematized utopian implication of their hyperbolic analysis – which they would surely have rejected had it been explicitly presented to them: that only the cessation of renunciation *in toto*, only the emancipation of inner nature and unfettered fulfillment, could prevent the dialectic of enlightenment from unfolding. Short of this implicit utopian solution, the most that Horkheimer and Adorno do is hint at one other possible way out of the dialectic's fateful logic, namely, "the remembrance of nature within the subject" (Horkheimer and Adorno 2002: 32). But they do not provide the idea with much content.

After the war, however, there was one place where Adorno might have speculated on non-reified forms of subjectivity. But his prohibition against speculating on positive conceptions of the self prevented him from pursuing this path (Adorno 1968; Jay 1984: Chapter 5; Whitebook 1996: 152–164). Despite his reservations about false reconciliation, in his aesthetic theory, Adorno allows himself to speculate about non-reified forms of synthesis – different relations between part and whole, particular and universal. Borrowing an idea from Kant, he argues that the truly advanced work of avant-garde art exhibits "a non-violent togetherness of the manifold" that provides a glimpse of what a non-reified world might be like. But Adorno stopped there, refusing to extrapolate from his aesthetic theory in order to envision less violent and more desirable forms of the togetherness of the self, that is, of ego-integration.

Herbert Marcuse

But in an effort to break out of the *Dialectic of Enlightenment*, Herbert Marcuse did play the utopian card, first as a theoretical exercise, then as a concrete theoretical program. In the midst of the seemingly closed world of the 1950s, which appeared to confirm Horkheimer and Adorno's prognosis, Marcuse's *Eros and Civilization* attempted to provide a philosophical demonstration that a "nonrepressive civilization" – that is, a civilization in which the sacrifice-repression of inner nature was no longer necessary so that it could be liberated – was possible. But it was just that, philosophical. At the time, Marcuse did not advocate an attempt to realize that society (Marcuse 1955: 5; Whitebook 1996: 26–41, 2004: 82–89).

In *Eros and Civilization*, Marcuse undertakes an immanent critique of Freud, whose "own theory," he argues, "provides reasons for rejecting the identification of civilization with repression" (Marcuse 1955: 4). Marcuse's strategy is to historicize Freud's basic framework. Where Freud presented the fundamental opposition between the reality principle and pleasure principle as transhistorical and therefore immutable, Marcuse, with the aid of Marx, attempts to "de-ontologize" it by historicizing the Reality Principle. His entire argument rests on this central move.

As mentioned earlier, the mature Freud understood the reality principle as *Ananke* (necessity) or *Atropos* (the ineluctable). But in what amounts to a Marxifying sleight of hand, Marcuse alters the meaning of that principle and reconceptualizes it in economic terms. Instead of transhistorical necessity, *Ananke* is recast as historically variable *Lebensnot* (scarcity) and is defined in terms of "struggle for existence" (Marcuse 1955: 132). The term now refers to the metabolism between humanity and nature that will exist in any conceivable society and to the amount of toil that, to one degree or another, will be necessary to extract the means of existence from the natural environment at a particular level of economic development. Toil requires unpleasure, that is, frustration, delayed gratification, and the repression of the pleasure principle. Thus, insofar as the reality principle refers to the quantum of toil that is necessary in a given society, it also refers to the degree of repression of the pleasure principle – of inner nature – that is required to carry it out.

The redefinition of *Ananke* allows Marcuse to introduce another distinction that is obviously modeled on Marx's distinction between necessary and surplus labor, that is, between basic or necessary repression on the one hand and surplus repression on the other. Necessary repression denotes the ineliminable quantum of repression that will be required in any conceivable society in virtue of the fact that we are embodied beings who will, to one degree or another, always have to extract the means of existence from nature. Surplus repression, as the name suggests, refers to the excess repression beyond the basic repression that could be eliminated in a given society on the basis of the development of its scientific and technological means of production. Marcuse's thesis is that surplus repression is largely exploitative and is enforced in the interests of the dominant class. Indeed, the difference between necessary and surplus repression can be taken as a measure of the degree of exploitation in a given society.

Marcuse maintains that surplus repression comprises the largest portion of repression in advanced capitalist societies, and he refers to the particular historical instantiation of it that obtains in them as the performance principle. His claim is that the performance principle – which is maintained in the economic interest of the capitalist ruling class – is perpetuated by the endless creation of false consumerist needs in the population and through capitalism's perpetual production of (often useless) commodities that can fulfill them.

There is, however, if not an outright contradiction, at least a serious tension lurking in this configuration. The advanced state of the means of production, according to Marcuse, generates the potential and therefore the pressure for a qualitatively different socioeconomic order in which surplus repression could in principle be eliminated. And this potential is at odds with an arrangement where the performance principle is artificially enforced. Given a differently constituted system of needs – one not based on the incessant multiplication of false needs – advanced science and technology could be employed to vastly reduce the amount of toil necessary to produce the material requirements not only for existence but also for the satisfaction of true needs that were not artificially inflated. The tension between the existing state of affairs and the potential of advanced science and technology might, Marcuse suggests, contribute to the motivation for a radical transformation of society.

Reinterpreting Marx's notion of the transition from the realm of necessity to the realm of freedom in psychoanalytic terms, Marcuse attempts to envisage a utopian transformation of society. If the highly developed means of production in the advanced world were to be properly appropriated, a social transformation could be affected that would drastically reduce the amount of toil necessary for securing the necessities of life. With the elimination of scarcity, surplus repression could also be eliminated. This, in turn, would make it possible to establish a nonrepressive society – that is, one in which only the minimal amount of basic repression remained – and to emancipate inner nature.

Marcuse draws on the psychoanalytic theory of perverse sexuality to provide content for the vision of a utopian society beyond "the established reality principle" (Marcuse 1955: 129). His rather questionable reasoning is this: because the sexual perversions have somehow eluded, indeed, rebelled against the Oedipally structured historical reality principle, they can offer an indication of what form a different arrangement of human sexuality might assume. Marcuse goes so far as to claim that primary narcissism constitutes not only a stage of preoedipal psychosexual development but also that the concept contains "ontological implications" that point "at another mode of being" – one that would be reconciled with external nature (Marcuse 1955: 107 and 109). What Marcuse fails to appreciate is that perverse sexuality, whatever that may mean in today's context, does not constitute an unalloyed expression of the pleasure principle, but is, like all psychical productions, multiply determined. (In a similar romantic vein, the young Foucault made a related mistake when he maintained that madness contained a privileged form of truth that had escaped contamination by normalizing rationality [Whitebook 2002, 2005].)

Freud never denied that the reality principle contained an economic component. This is especially true in *The Future of an Illusion*, his most Marxist book, which progressives regularly cite. But to reduce the concept to economic scarcity is to substantially diminish its philosophical depth. Paul Ricoeur has argued that the mature Freud's introduction of the term *Ananke* to denote the reality principle indicated a transformation of the concept from a "principle of 'mental regulation'" into "a cypher of possible wisdom . . . beyond illusion and consolation" (Ricoeur 1970: 262 and 325). Freud was staunchly anti-utopian, and his tragic wisdom consisted in the resignation to *Ananke*, that is, the disconsolate acceptance of the fact that human reality is constituted by transience and inevitably permeated with loss and death (Whitebook 2017: 329).

But Marxists typically dismiss Freud's tragic vision as the ideological prejudice of a *fin-de-siècle bourgeois* patriarch whose world and worldview were crumbling. And it cannot be denied that a number of the questionable anthropological assumptions upon which Freud's political pessimism is based must be criticized. Nevertheless, even in an emancipated society – however one conceives of it – this tragic dimension should not be eliminated. On the contrary, whereas the tragic register is systematically denied in the infantilism of mass consumerist society and the culture industry, in an emancipated society, it would be actively engaged as it was in most pre-capitalist societies. To accept *Ananke* is to accept our finitude, and the acceptance of our finitude is not reactionary hogwash but an essential component of a truly human society. These themes are not entirely lost on Marcuse, and he attempts to confront them (as well as the theme of destructiveness). But his discussion of "the defeat of time," while interesting, remains unconvincing (Marcuse 1955: 232–237).

Whereas in the 1950s Marcuse treated the idea of a nonrepressive society merely as a philosophical possibility, in the 1960s, it not only became a plausible political program but also a necessary one. He argued that the creation of a post-scarcity society, in which the species' relationship to its inner and outer nature had been radically transformed, was necessary to prevent the world from slipping into a new form of barbarism and to avoid the destruction of the earth's ecosystem.

During the heady days of the 1960s, Marcuse published two provocatively titled articles. One, "The End of Utopia," maintained that insofar as the concept of utopia literally meant "no place" – a *topos* that could never be occupied – it had become obsolete (Marcuse 1970b: 62–83). Far from constituting an unrealistic fantasy, the establishment of an emancipated nonrepressive society, based on "the achievements of the existing societies, especially their scientific and technical achievements," had not only become realistic but historically necessary. The argument of the other paper, "The Obsolescence of the Freudian Concept of Man," was in line with his thesis in *Eros and Civilization* (Marcuse 1970a: 44–61). Because Freud's anthropology was predicated on the false ontologization of the opposition between the pleasure principle and the reality principle, and because it was now possible to transcend the historical performance principle, Freud's concept of man, Marcuse argued, had also become obsolete (Marcuse 1969: 22).

Like Horkheimer and Adorno, Marcuse subscribed to a version of the totally administered society (Marcuse 1964: xxxvi). As we saw, he argued that through the uninterrupted generation and fulfillment of false (consumerist) needs, the system could integrate all opposition and perpetuate itself indefinitely. A break in this fateful process – which meant a Great Refusal that rejected the false system of needs and the creation of a "new sensibility" embodying an alternative to them – was a necessary condition for the transformation of the established order and the creation of new form of life (Marcuse 1969: 23–48). As opposed to Adorno, Marcuse guilelessly and enthusiastically celebrated the countercultural and radical political movements of the 1960s as an expression of that new sensibility, at least in an incipient form (Adorno and Marcuse, "Correspondence" 1999: *New Left Review* I/233, January – February).

But as those movements receded further and further into the past, his position increasingly appeared hopelessly and perhaps even embarrassingly naive. Ronald Reagan and Margaret Thatcher's Counter-Revolution successfully quashed the 1960's vision of the good life and succeeded in reinstating the pursuit of wealth as the *summum bonum*. The entrepreneur in a pinstriped suit replaced the civil rights worker in overalls as the new culture hero. Moreover, with the collapse of communism and the triumphant ascendance of liberal political theory, the discussion of the good as opposed to the right was often condemned as illicit. Indeed, it was sometimes suggested that to countenance the distinction between true and false needs, as Marcuse emphatically did, was to begin down the slippery slope to totalitarianism. The liberal turn in political theory, in short, appeared to exclude the notion of a new sensibility from legitimate discourse and to limit its parameters to a consideration of rights.

But "after the brief interlude of liberalism," which, one can argue, lasted from the fall of the Berlin Wall to the economic crisis of 2008, the idea of a new sensibility may not seem so daft (Horkheimer and Adorno 2002: 68). It might be the case that a rights-oriented politics cannot adequately address the rapacious dynamics of the globalized capitalism – the system's incessant and methodical "colonization of the lifeworld" and the environment – and its lethal effects on the global ecosystem (Habermas 1989: 332–372). Furthermore, where liberal and postmodern critics tend to dismiss Adorno and Horkheimer's theory of the cultural industry as elitist, the two critical theorists were, in fact, diagnosing embryonic tendencies that have now developed beyond their wildest imagination. The capacity of today's social media and celebrity culture to deflect, disarm, and confuse critical thinking, while simultaneously creating a simulacrum of popular debate, has surpassed their worst fears. As unlikely as the emergence of a new sensibility might seem given our current conditions, it is difficult to imagine how, from a purely logical point of view, a social and political movement that can address the problems that are confronting us can be formed without one. On this point, Marcuse may not have been that naive after all.

Jürgen Habermas

Because it occurred at the beginning of his career, Habermas's only sustained *Auseinandersetzung* with Freud is conflicted and difficult to sort out. At the time, Habermas had one foot planted in the psychoanalytically informed materialism of the first generation of the Frankfurt School. But with the other, he was stepping into the world of linguistified Kantianism that came to define him. Although the early Habermas tried on the mantle of the first generation of critical theorists for size, because he possessed substantially different pre-theoretical intuitions, he was never entirely at home in it and therefore moved beyond it relatively quickly (Rabinbach 1997: 168–170).

The first generation's experience, which was shaped by Weimar, emigration, the war, Nazism, Stalinism, and the Holocaust, resulted in the choice between hyper-radical utopianism and quietist resignation. Habermas's experience was different. As someone who, as an adolescent, had been glued to the radio listening to the broadcasts of the Nuremburg Trials and who entered adulthood as the Federal Republic was being established, the either/or of quietism versus revolution was unacceptable. Possessing the instincts of a radical reformer, Habermas placed the solidification, cultivation, and defense of German democracy at the top of his political agenda. And he cannot be commended enough for his exemplary career as a public intellectual and for the many courageous political stances he has taken. At the same time, however, it must also be admitted that his resolute defense of democracy has often been coupled with excessive progressivist Whiggishness. This has not only led him to deny the darker antisocial forces in human nature documented by Freud, but it has also prevented him from effectively addressing the irrational forces that are so evident in today's politics around the globe. For example, while progressive Protestants or reformed Jews might find his position on religion congenial, he sidesteps the really hard problem: how to address fundamentalism. For someone with a fundamentalist mindset would find the position he is advocating well-nigh unfathomable. How does one enter into a rational dialogue with someone who has not cathected the idea of rational dialogue?

In the 1960s, Freud was required reading for a budding critical theorist, and it is clear from *Knowledge and Human Interests* that Habermas's *Auseinandersetzung* with the psychoanalyst's work was comprehensive and deep (Habermas 1971). But he did not share the first generation's elective affinity with the founder of psychoanalysis. As Thomas McCarthy observes, Habermas's "orientation to Freud's work" was less substantive and "more methodological than was theirs" (McCarthy 1978: 195). Furthermore, this methodological orientation was one aspect of a larger point of difference separating their younger colleague from the authors of *Dialectic of Enlightenment*. Horkheimer and Adorno were prepared to resign themselves to the self-referential implication that followed from their analysis: namely, that they could not elucidate their own theoretical standpoint. They therefore abstained in principle from any attempt to clarify the methodological foundations of critical theory. At best, they dialectically circled them.

For Habermas, this abstention was unacceptable on theoretical as well as political grounds. Still situating himself within a Marxist vein, he drew on the new working-class theory current at the time and argued that after the Second World War, science and technology had come to occupy a new strategically decisive position in the productive apparatus of the capitalist economy. Therefore, if critical theory hoped to influence a progressive transformation of advanced capitalist society, it would have to engage members of scientific and academic communities. To do so, it would be necessary for critical theorists to clarify and defend the methodological foundations of their position in a way that was acceptable to those communities of investigators. If the representatives of the first generation of the Frankfurt School sometimes (and somewhat disingenuously) made a fetish of being outsiders, Habermas wanted to challenge the academic community on its own terms, forcing its members to reflect on the dogmatic assumptions underlying their positions.

Where Horkheimer, Adorno, and Marcuse were attracted to psychoanalysis because of its scandalousness, Habermas wanted to use it to make the project academically legitimate and critical at the same time. Strange as it may sound today when the field is in such disrepute, in the 1960s, he believed that psychoanalysis provided a model of a social science that was not simply successful but successful qua reflective and critical. "Psychoanalysis is relevant to us," he wrote, because it is "the only tangible example of science incorporating methodological self-reflection" (Habermas 1971:

124). He believed that the discipline provided a model case from which general methodological (and normative) principles for a critical theory of society could be extrapolated. To accomplish this task – and to rectify what he, like Lacan, mistakenly saw as Freud's biologism – Habermas sought to apply the findings of the linguistic turn, which was in full force at the middle of the twentieth century, to psychoanalysis. He reinterpreted neurosis and ideology as two structurally homologous forms of false consciousness and conceptualized them as forms of systematically distorted communication.

It is at this point that the serious tensions emerge in Habermas's position. (A) On the one hand, he continues to not only use the language of the first generation's materialistically inflected interpretation of Freud but also to gesture toward the substance of that interpretation. (B) On the other hand, however, this strain of his argument is at odds with the linguistifying and transcendentalizing dynamic that he introduces with the notion of systematically distorted communication.

Regarding (A): when, for example, Habermas set out to refute Nietzsche's Darwinian reductionism, he deployed Freud's instinct theory (*Triebtheorie*) – a theory which, if he did not totally repudiate, he radically altered and diluted under the linguistifying pressures of his program. Habermas responds to Nietzsche's claim that reason is nothing but "an organ of adaptation for men just as claws and teeth are for animals" in the following way. He grants Nietzsche's claim that reason is a natural organ of self-preservation, but over the course of evolution, he argues, it also develops into something more than nature. And Habermas uses the concept of libido to explain that something more, that is to say, the "cultural break with nature." Human drives are excessive – superabundant – in that they overshoot the requirements of self-preservation, of mere life. "Along with the tendency to realize natural drives," Habermas claims that the cultural formations that have *emerged* over the course of evolution "have incorporated the tendency toward release from the constraint of nature," latent in the excessiveness of the drives (Habermas 1973: 312).

At this point, Habermas bursts into a downright Marcusean panegyric to the utopian significance of *Eros*: "an enticing natural force, present in the individual as libido, has detached itself from the behavioral system of self-preservation and urges toward utopian fulfillment" (Habermas 1973: 312). Habermas also enlists Marcuse's distinction between necessary repression and surplus repression as a means for elucidating the critique of ideology and as a device for measuring the amount of exploitation in a given society

(Whitebook 1996: 27–29). He argues, moreover, that the degree of repression obtaining in a given society determines the extent to which it restricts the public expression of libidinally based wishes. According to him, the wishes that are excluded and repressed at a given level of economic development tend to find alternative modes of fulfillment in pathological symptoms, fantasies, illusions, and ideologies, which are structurally homologous formations. And insofar as these phenomena constitute disguised forms of wish fulfillment, they "harbor Utopia" (Habermas 1971: 280).

Also in keeping with the vocabulary and sensibility of the first generation of critical theorists, Habermas borrows Adorno's notion of "exact fantasy" to formulate a normative theory in psychoanalytic terms. (It should be noted that, as opposed to his later normative theory, this earlier iteration of it is primarily concerned with the substantive question of the good rather than with the procedural question of justification.) "The 'good,'" he writes, "is neither a convention nor an essence, but rather the result of fantasy." It must, however, be "fantasized so exactly that it corresponds to and articulates a fundamental interest . . . in that measure of emancipation that is objectively historically possible" (Habermas 1971: 228).

Regarding (B): the linguistic turn, however, took hold of Habermas's argument and led to a radical alteration of Freudian theory that is most apparent in his account of repression and of the unconscious. Though Freud's approach contains an important interpretative dimension, it does not comprise a pure hermeneutics. At its core, it is psychodynamic, which means it combines the language of meaning with the language of force (Ricoeur 1970: 65–67). Every psychoanalytically pertinent idea (*Vorstellung*) has an affective charge attached to it and a pressure (*Drang*) behind it. To be clinically effective, a psychoanalytic intervention requires more than interpretation – the explication of meaning through meaning. As Ricoeur insisted, it requires technique: that is, the ability to assess the psychodynamic forces at work in a given situation and to successfully intervene in them (Ricoeur 1974). For Freud, moreover, the source of psychical forces is somatic. They emanate from the drives which he describes

- as a "frontier" concept lying "between the mental and the somatic,"
- as "the psychical representative [*psychischer Repräsentant*] of the stimuli originating within the organism" that reaches "the mind,"
- "as a measure of the demand made upon the mind for work in consequence of its connection with the body" (Freud 1915: 121–122).

To be sure, Habermas registers the right points in his discussion of Freud's clinical practice. He acknowledges the necessity of the dynamic point of view and even cites the relevant *aperçu* from Freud. To simply present patients with accurate information about the content of their unconscious without addressing the psychodynamics of their resistances, Freud wryly observes, would "have as much influence on the symptoms of nervous illness as a distribution of menu-cards in a time of famine has upon hunger" (Freud 1910: 225). Habermas also recognizes that the force of the defenses and resistances encountered in the clinical setting requires that one posit a force-like, which is to say, a nature-like (*naturwüchsig*), phenomenon at work in the human psyche. As a result, to apprehend these phenomena theoretically, psychoanalysis must, in addition to hermeneutical concepts, employ causal-explanatory ones similar to those used in the natural sciences. Indeed, these considerations have led the anti-positivist Habermas to observe that Freud's scientific self-understanding is not "entirely unfounded" (Habermas 1971: 214).

But the linguistifying imperatives of his program have caused Habermas to undo his correct observations concerning Freud's clinical practice. In his theoretical reflections on those practices – in his metapsychology, as it were – Habermas equates repression with excommunication. Developmentally, he argues, repression arises in situations where children feel it is too dangerous to express certain wishes publicly, that is, in the intersubjective grammar of ordinary language (secondary processes). Because of the weakness of their egos and the superior power of the parental figures populating their environment, children are compelled to repress those wishes. They do this by excommunicating them from the public domain – including the internal public domain of consciousness – and banishing them to the private realm that, for Habermas, comprises the unconscious. The excommunication is accomplished by de-grammaticizing those dangerous wishes. Their representations are thereby expelled from the grammar of ordinary language and relocated in the de-grammaticized realm of the unconscious. (The alogical mentation of the unconscious is the way that Habermas understands primary processes.)

Habermas's argument for the claim that repression is an entirely intralinguistic affair, consisting in the excommunication of forbidden ideas from the intersubjective realm of ordinary language, borders on a tautology. From the fact that repression can be reversed through the talking cure, he wants to infer that it was a purely linguistic process to begin with. But as we have seen in his discussion of clinical practice, he acknowledges that the undoing of repression is more than an interpretative enterprise. It also involves the force-like phenomena of resistance that must be opposed with the counterforce deployed by clinical technique.

Habermas denies a canonical distinction of Freudian psychoanalysis: "the distinction between word-presentations and symbolic ideas," he declares *ex cathedra*, "is problematic," and "the assumption of a nonlinguistic substratum, in which these ideas severed from language are 'carried out,' is unsatisfactory" (Habermas 1971: 241; Whitebook 1996: 179–196). The distinction between word-presentations and thing-presentations, however, is a linchpin for Freud's entire construction. It is intended to mark the difference between conscious, rational, and what one may call diurnal thought and a radically different form of archaic mental functioning – the language of the night.

And it is also meant to mark the essential division of the self. To deny the existence of a "nonlinguistic" unconscious and to redefine it is as merely protolinguistic – which means it can be translated into consciousness without the special effort required by psychoanalysis – is to deny the radical alterity of the ego's "internal foreign territory" and to substantially soften the essentially divided and conflicted nature of the self (Freud 1933: 57). It is also to substantially domesticate the Freudian project. Furthermore, this is one symptom of the general difficulty Habermas has accommodating the "nonlinguistic" – the "nonconceptual," as Adorno calls it – in his theory.

Habermas's compulsion to think everything in terms of language is so strong that his own position ends up as a variant of linguistic monism that is difficult to distinguish from the Gadamerian hermeneutics he claimed to oppose (Habermas 1980; Lafont 1999: 55–124). The thesis that repression is a purely linguistic affair *ipso facto* excludes the extralinguistic, that is, the extralinguistic forces that act on language and distort it. And it also leaves out the body, for, as we have seen, the body is the source of the forces that impinge on the psyche and "mutilate" its symbolic texts. Indeed, for Freud, the thing-representations of the unconscious are the mental representations of somatic forces that lie just on the other side of the frontier separating soma and psyche.

A political motive also leads Habermas to reject the distinction between word-representations and thing-representations. It is based on a mistaken presupposition that he shares with many thinkers on the Left: namely, that to defend a progressive position, one must maintain it is society or language all the way down – that "the self is socially constituted through and through" (Habermas 1992: 183). Given the reactionary uses for which biology has often been employed in discussions of race and gender – epitomized in the slogan "biology is destiny" – one can understand the skepticism toward it among progressives. Nevertheless, as Jean Laplanche has pointed out, sociologism is every bit as much in error as biologism, and both forms of one-sidedness must be avoided (Laplanche 1989: 17ff).

The linguistic strain and the transcendental strain converged in Habermas's theory and steadily moved him away from the psychoanalytic materialism he had flirted with in *Knowledge and Human Interests*. The idea of systematically distorted communication that Habermas introduced to elucidate Freud's theory of neurosis funneled his thinking into the increasingly transcendental channel that he followed for the remainder of his career. The concept of systematically distorted communication can be compared to Descartes's notion of totalized delusion, resulting from the machinations of a malevolent genius, that the founder of modern philosophy employed in his philosophical construction. And just as Descartes required an Archimedean point outside the totalized delusionary cosmos, so Habermas must locate a standpoint outside the structure of systematically distorted communication. On purely logical grounds, systematically distorted communication requires a concept of undistorted communication from which its distortions can be recognized as distortions and corrected. As Habermas observes,

> If the interpretation I have suggested is true, the psychoanalyst must have a "prenotion," or rough (sic) understanding, of the structure of undistorted ordinary-language communication in order to be able at all to trace systematic distortions of language back to a confusion of two developmentally distinct stages of prelinguistic and linguistic organization.
>
> (Habermas 1975: 184)

To elucidate the notion of systematically distorted communication, Habermas, in the wake of *Knowledge and Human Interests*, posited the notion of an ideal speech situation. It consisted in a counterfactual, distortion-free location from which the systematic distortions of actual communication can be illuminated as distorted.

The postulation of an ideal speech situation represented the first of many attempts in which Habermas sought to delineate a (quasi-)transcendental standpoint to ground his position while avoiding the pitfalls of a full-blown transcendental theory. It is often said that Aristotle is the philosopher of the equivocal, of the "in some sense," and what one makes of Aristotle often depends on what one makes of his notion of the equivocal. Something similar can be said of Habermas. At different points in the development of his theory, he has employed prefixes like "quasi-," "soft-," or "post-" to characterize his brand of modified transcendental theorizing. How the success of Habermas's philosophical program as a whole is evaluated depends in no small part on what one makes of his use of these prefixes. Are they question-begging devices, or do they do the conceptual work he claims they do?

Habermas maintains that he has de-transcendentalized his position by formulating it in terms of the philosophy of language rather than of the philosophy of consciousness. But he fails to recognize a fundamental point: his linguistically formulated "quasi"-transcendental position remains every bit as much an instance of what Adorno calls "constitutive subjectivity" as Kant's paradigmatic rendering of transcendental philosophy that was formulated in terms of the philosophy of consciousness (Adorno 1973: xx). Transcendental intersubjectivity is still transcendental subjectivity. *The only difference is that the subject is plural rather than singular. One might say that Habermas's position is one of "constitutive intersubjectivity,"* and as such, it not only retains some of the fundamental difficulties with transcendental philosophy but also hypostatizes the "primacy of language" over the "primacy of the object," which, as we saw, was Adorno's way of referring to materialism.

In the same vein, Habermas's transcendental quest not only led him away from Freud in general but also resulted in one particular consequence: all references to the body virtually disappeared from his thinking. Because Habermas's "investigation of the basic structures of intersubjectivity is directed exclusively to an analysis of rules of speech," Axel Honneth observes, "the bodily dimension of social action no longer comes into view." Consequently, "the human body, whose historical fate Adorno [and Horkheimer] had drawn into the center of their investigation . . . loses all value within critical social theory" (Honneth 1991: 281).

Axel Honneth and Joel Whitebook

In the third generation of the Frankfurt School, Axel Honneth and I have continued the attempt to integrate psychoanalysis and critical theory (Honneth 1996: 92–237, 2012: 101–231; Honneth and Whitebook 2016; Whitebook 1996, 2004, 2017). However, despite the fact that we have both drawn on the preoedipal turn in psychoanalysis, our positions differ in substantial ways. For Honneth, psychoanalysis plays a subsidiary role and is only one element of his larger theory of recognition. Moreover, he has moved in the direction of relational psychoanalysis, which, he believes, avoids the putative biologism and anthropological pessimism of Freudian drive theory and provides support for his intersubjectivist position. For me, on the other hand, psychoanalysis does not only retain a central role in my thinking, but I have also remained closer to the classical Freudian position and the way in which the first generation appropriated it.

Perhaps the major difference in our positions is this. Honneth, like many other progressives who have taken up psychoanalysis, has turned to infant research and the relational school to elucidate the pro-social forces in psychic life and combat Freud's postulation of "primary mutual hostility [between] human beings." I too want to do justice to the pro-social aspects of our psychological inheritance, which, to be sure, were often overlooked in the Freudian tradition. I do not want to accomplish this, however, by minimizing the antisocial forces – most notably, destructiveness and omnipotence – that are also part of that same inheritance. In my opinion, Honneth, no less than Habermas, is guilty of that mistake. The task of accurately elucidating the relation between the pro-social and antisocial forces inherent in the human psyche, as I see it, is located high on the contemporary psychoanalytic agenda.

Hegel, the philosopher of the World Spirit, and Donald Winnicott, the theorist of the teddy bear, may strike one as an unlikely twosome. Nevertheless, as Jessica Benjamin had done before him, Honneth brings the two thinkers together in an attempt to develop his version of critical theory (Benjamin 1988). He sees their convergence as consisting in the fact that both thinkers wanted to overcome a monadic starting point and maintained that the self is a product of interaction. Thus, Hegel's way of exiting the philosophy of consciousness was to introduce the struggle for recognition. And Winnicott – who famously stated that "there is no such thing as baby without a mother" – attempted to overcome Freud's one-person psychology, which began with primary narcissism, by introducing the notion of transitional phenomena (Winnicott 1960: 587, n. 1).

In turning to the relational analysts, however, Honneth inherited three difficulties that are characteristic of their position. First, he tends to share their implicit and erroneous assumption that to demonstrate that the self is a product of interaction – a claim that nobody would deny today – is to demonstrate that the self is *ipso facto* sociable (Whitebook 2008: 382). Second, like the Freud Left tradition in general, he tends to assume that antisocial phenomena like destructiveness and omnipotence are not intrinsic features of psychic life but are reactive, that is, the result of environmental failure. The implication is that they could be avoided through better familial arrangements and child-rearing practices. And third, like the relational analysts, he tends to make selective use of Winnicott. It is true that Winnicott is a preeminent two-person psychologist and that, with his theory of transitional phenomena, he has made an essential contribution to the field. But it is also true that the British analyst posits a state of omnipotence – of complete "illusionment" – at the beginning of life and argues the mother's task is to disillusion the infant. *Indeed, the whole purpose of the transitional object is to make that disillusionment possible.* The notion of transitional phenomena would not make sense without the assumption of an original state of omnipotence. By minimizing or denying the role of omnipotence in psychic life, Honneth provides us with an overly socialized account of the human animal and, despite his differences with Habermas, also, domesticates psychoanalytic theory (Honneth and Whitebook 2016: 176).

In my estimate, in order to advance the integration of psychoanalysis and critical theory, three difficulties have to be avoided: Adorno and Horkheimer's impasse and political quietism, Marcuse's utopianism, and Habermas's domestication of psychoanalysis, which excluded the body and denied the radical alterity of the unconscious. My program has been to draw on the work of the psychoanalyst Hans Loewald and the philosopher, psychoanalyst, and social theorist Cornelius Castoriadis, to return to Horkheimer and Adorno's notion of "the remembrance of nature within the subject" in an attempt to provide it with content (Castoriadis 1984: 3–118, 1987: 101–114 and 273–339; Loewald 2000).

Before pursuing that program, however, a preliminary task is in order: Horkheimer and Adorno's (as well as Marcuse's) notion of a totally administered world has to be contested. I agree with Habermas that the claim of totalized untruth is not only theoretically untenable but that it also denies the very real empirical advances in individual freedom, morality, legality, and democracy that have been achieved in modernity.

Once the concept of a totally administered world has become cleared away, it becomes possible to return to another of Adorno's concepts: the nonviolent togetherness of the manifold. As we saw, because of his claim that "the whole is the false," Adorno prohibited himself from advancing any positive formulations concerning the individual or society (Adorno 2006: 50). He maintained that, in an untrue world, any such formulation necessarily constitutes false reconciliation. But as we also saw, there was one place where Adorno allowed himself to relax this prohibition, that is, with regard to truly advanced works of art. In works of Arnold Schoenberg or Samuel Beckett, for example, Adorno maintained that a new form of the non-reified synthesis of the manifold could be observed and that it constituted an alternative to the forced integration that characterizes instrumental reason.

Where Adorno stopped at this point, Albrecht Wellmer did not. He extended Adorno's analysis, speculating that the form of non-reifying integration observable in the advanced work of art might provide a glimpse into the mode of social integration that would be obtained in an emancipated society (Wellmer 1985: 48; Whitebook 2004: 57–80). This, however, was the point at which Wellmer brought his investigation to a halt. He did not attempt to extend his analysis to a consideration of the modes of psychological synthesis – of the integration the self – that might be obtained in a free society.

And this became my point of departure. (It should be pointed out that the new formations of post-conventional identity and the "neosexualities" that emerged from the movements of the 1960s provided the sociocultural context for his analysis [McDougall 2103: Chapter 11]). I drew on the preoedipal turn in psychoanalysis, the feminist critique of the field, infant research, and attachment theory to contest the official Freudian, patricentric, and Oedipal conception of maturity – which was seen as connected with the classical bourgeois individual and its supposed counterpart, the classical neurotic.

To be sure, there are "unofficial" countervailing tendencies in Freud's thinking. But his "official" Oedipal notion of "maturity," that is to say, of optimal development, consists in what Castoriadis has called a "power grab," in which the more "advanced" strata of the psyche dominate the more "primitive" – the ego dominates the id, consciousness dominates the unconscious, realistic thinking dominates fantasy thinking, cognition dominates affect, activity dominates passivity, and the civilized part of the personality dominates unconscious-instinctual life (Castoriadis 1987: 104; Whitebook 2017). Indeed, Freud's official notion of maturity led to one of his more objectionable formulations where he likened the work of analysis (and the work of civilization) to "the draining of the Zuider Zee." On this view, maturity consists in a state where all the "primitive" sludge of inner nature had been dredged out of mental life (Freud 1933: 80).

Like Loewald and Castoriadis, I reject Freud's "official" conception of maturity and attempt to provide an alternative conception of a desirable integration of the psyche, that is, of the felicitous togetherness of the psychic manifold. Maturity must no longer be understood as the domination of the supposedly more advanced strata of the psyche over the supposedly more archaic. Rather, it must be reconceptualized, as Castoriadis observes, as involving "another relation between" them (Castoriadis 1987: 104). Likewise, Loewald maintains that "the so-called fully developed, mature ego is not one that has become fixated at the presumably highest or latest stages of development, having left the other behind it." Instead, it is one that "integrates its reality in such a way that the earlier and deeper levels of ego-reality integration remain alive as dynamic sources of higher organization" (Loewald 2000: 20).

What is more, this form of psychic integration is not, Castoriadis argues, "an attained state" but an ongoing "active situation," in which the individual is "unceasingly involved in the movement of taking up again" the contents of inner nature and reworking them into richer and more differentiated synthetic configurations. In other words, it does not comprise a state of "'awareness' achieved once and for all," in which the ego has established its dominance over unconscious-instinctual life. The goal, rather, is to institute

> another relation between the conscious and the unconscious, between lucidity and the function of the imaginary . . . another attitude of the subject with respect to himself or herself, in a profound modification of the activity-passivity mix, of the sign under which this takes place, of the respective place of the two elements that compose it.
>
> (Castoriadis 1987: 104)

Far from constituting the "dictatorship of reason" that Freud unfortunately advocated at one point, what is being suggested is a less violent organization of the psyche, that is, a more propitious integration of the psychic manifold (Freud 1933: 215). And this active form of integrating the self can be understood as a living and ongoing remembrance of "nature within the subject."

References

Adorno, T.W., (1968), "Sociology and Psychology," *New Left Review* 47: 79–97.
Adorno, T.W., (1973), *Negative Dialectics*, New York: Seabury Press.
Adorno, T.W., (1982), *The Authoritarian Personality: Studies in Prejudice*, New York: W.W. Norton & Company.
Adorno, T.W., (2006), *Minima Moralia: Reflections on a Damaged Life*, New York: Verso.
Adorno, T.W. and H. Marcuse, (1999), "Correspondence," *New Left Review* I(233), January–February: 124–135.
Benjamin, J., (1988), *The Bonds of Love: Psychoanalysis, Feminism, & the Problem of Domination*, New York: Pantheon.
Castoriadis, C., (1984), *Crossroads in the Labyrinth*, Cambridge, MA: The MIT Press.
Castoriadis, C., (1987), *The Imaginary Institution of Society*, Cambridge, MA: The MIT Press.
Freud, S., (1910), "'Wild' Psycho-Analysis," In *The Standard Edition of the Complete Psychological Works of Sigmund Freud*, Vol. 10, London: The Hogarth Press.
Freud, S., (1915), "Instincts and Their Vicissitudes," In *The Standard Edition of the Complete Psychological Works of Sigmund Freud*, Vol. 14, London: The Hogarth Press.
Freud, S., (1933), "New Introductory Lectures on Psycho-Analysis," In *The Standard Edition of the Complete Psychological Works of Sigmund Freud*, Vol. 22, London: The Hogarth Press.
Gordon, P.E., (2017), "The Authoritarian Personality Revisited: Reading Adorno in the Age of Trump," *Boundary* 44(2): 31–56.
Habermas, J., (1971), *Knowledge and Human Interests*, Boston, MA: Beacon Press.
Habermas, J., (1973), "Between Philosophy and Science – Marxism as Critique," In *Theory and Practice*, Boston, MA: Beacon Press.
Habermas, J., (1975), "A Postscript to Knowledge and Human Interests," *Philosophy of the Social Sciences* 3(2): 157–189.
Habermas, J., (1980), "The Hermeneutic Claim to Universality," In *Contemporary Hermeneutics: Hermeneutics as Method*, Boston, MA: Routledge and Kegan Paul.

Habermas, J., (1989), *The Theory of Communicative Action, Volume 2: Lifeworld and System: A Critique of Functionalist Reason*, Boston, MA: Beacon Press.

Habermas, J., (1992), "Individuation Through Socialization: On Mead's Theory of Subjectivity," In *Postmetaphysical Thinking*, Cambridge, MA: The MIT Press.

Honneth, A., (1991), *The Critique of Power: Reflective Stages in a Critical Theory of Society*, Cambridge, MA: The MIT Press.

Honneth, A., (1996), *The Struggle for Recognition: The Moral Grammar of Social Conflicts*, Cambridge, MA: The MIT Press.

Honneth, A., (2012), *The I in We: Studies in the Theory of Recognition*, Malden MA: Polity Press.

Honneth, A. and J. Whitebook, (2016), "Omnipotence or Fusion? A Conversation Between Axel Honneth and Joel Whitebook," *Constellations* 23(2): 170–179.

Horkheimer, M. (ed.), (1936), *Studien über Autorität und Familie*, Paris: Alacan.

Horkheimer, M., (1972), "Traditional and Critical Theory," In *Critical Theory: Selected Essays*, New York: Seabury Press.

Horkheimer, M. and T.W. Adorno, (2002), *Dialectic of Enlightenment: Philosophical Fragments*, Stanford, CA: Stanford University Press.

Jay, M., (1973), *The Dialectical Imagination: A History of the Frankfurt School and the Institute for Social Research, 1923–1950*, New York: Little Brown.

Jay, M., (1984), *Adorno*, Cambridge, MA: Harvard University Press.

Lafont, C., (1999), *The Linguistic Turn in Hermeneutic Philosophy*, Cambridge, MA: The MIT Press.

Laplanche, J., (1989), *New Foundations of Psychoanalysis*, New York: Blackwell.

Loewald, H., (2000), *The Essential Loewald: Collected Papers and Monographs*, Hagerstown, MD: University Publishing Group.

Marcuse, H., (1955), *Eros and Civilization: A Philosophical Inquiry into Freud*, Boston, MA: Beacon Press.

Marcuse, H., (1964), *One Dimensional Man: Studies in the Ideology of Advanced Industrial Society*, Boston, MA: Beacon Press.

Marcuse, H., (1969), *An Essay in Liberation*, Boston, MA: Beacon Press.

Marcuse, H., (1970a), "The Obsolescence of the Freudian Concept of Man," In *Five Lectures*, Boston, MA: Beacon Press.

Marcuse, H., (1970b), "The End of Utopia," In *Five Lectures*, Boston, MA: Beacon Press.

McCarthy, T., (1978), *The Critical Theory of Jürgen Habermas*, Cambridge, MA: The MIT Press.

McDougall, J., (2013), *Theaters of the Mind: Illusion and Truth on the Psychoanalytic Stage*, New York: Routledge.

Rabinbach, A., (1997), "The Cunning of Unreason: Mimesis and the Construction of Anti-Semitism in Horkheimer and Adorno's *Dialectic of Enlightenment*," In *The Shadow of Catastrophe*, Berkeley: University of California Press.

Ricoeur, P., (1970), *Freud and Philosophy: An Essay in Interpretation*, New Haven, CT: Yale University Press.

Ricoeur, P., (1974), "Technique and Nontechnique in Interpretation," In *The Conflict of Interpretations*, Evanston, IL: Northwestern University Press.
Wellmer, A., (1985), "Reason, Utopia and the *Dialectic of Enlightenment*," In R. J. Bernstein (ed.) *Habermas and Modernity*. Cambridge MA, The MIT Press, pp. 35–66.
Wellmer, A., (1991a), "The Dialectic of Modernism and Postmodernism: The Critique of Reason Since Adorno," In *The Persistence of Modernity*, Cambridge, MA: The MIT Press.
Wellmer, A., (1991b), "Truth, Semblance and Reconciliation: Adorno's Aesthetic Redemption of Modernity," In *The Persistence of Modernity*, Cambridge, MA: The MIT Press.
Whitebook, J., (1996), *Perversion and Utopia: A Study in Psychoanalysis and Critical Theory*, Cambridge, MA: The MIT Press.
Whitebook, J., (2002), "Michel Foucault: A Marcusean in Structuralist Clothing," *Thesis Eleven* 71: 52–70.
Whitebook, J., (2004), "Weighty Objects: Adorno's Kant-Freud Interpretation," In T. Huhn (ed.) *The Cambridge Companion to Adorno*, New York: Cambridge University Press, pp. 51–78.
Whitebook, J., (2005), "Against Interiority: Foucault's Struggle with Psychoanalysis," In *The Cambridge Companion to Foucault*, New York: Cambridge University Press.
Whitebook, J., (2008), "First Nature and Second Nature in Hegel and Psychoanalysis," *Constellations* 15(3): 382–389.
Whitebook, J., (2017), *Freud: An Intellectual Biography*, New York: Cambridge University Press.
Wiggershaus, R., (1994), *The Frankfurt School: Its History, Theories and Political Significance*, Cambridge, MA: The MIT Press.
Winnicott, D.W., (1960), "The Theory of the Parent-Infant Relationship," *The International Journal of Psycho-Analysis* 41: 585–595.

Further Reading

Castoriadis, C., (1987), *The Imaginary Institution of Society*, Cambridge, MA. Part 6 (A Crucial Contribution to the Left Psychoanalytic Tradition).
Homans, P., (1989), *The Ability to Mourn*, Chicago, IL: University of Press (An Important Attempt to Integrate Weberian and Freudian Theory).
Loewald, H., (2000), *The Essential Papers: Collected Papers and Monographs*, Hagerstown, MD: University Publishing Group (Loewald Was a Student of Heidegger and His Work Represents Some of the Deepest Psychoanalytic Theorizing After Freud).
Ricoeur, P., (1970), *Freud and Philosophy: A Study in Interpretation*, New Haven, CT: Yale University Press (Perhaps the Major Text on Freud and Philosophy).
Ricoeur, P., (1974), *The Conflict of Interpretations: Essays and Hermeneutics*, Evanston, IL (Contains a Continuation of the Investigations Ricoeur Began in *Freud and Philosophy*).

Chapter 2

Communism and Ambivalence
Freud, Marxism, and Aggression

Adrian Johnston

Two major historical developments run parallel to each other during the late 1910s and early 1920s: the Bolshevik Revolution of October 1917, with its protracted aftermath, and an interlinked set of fundamental shifts in Freud's ideas, involving both his topography of the psychical apparatus as well as his account of drives (*Triebe*). Moreover, Freud, during this pivotal period in the evolution of his psychoanalytic thinking, sees fit to reflect upon these contemporaneous political events transpiring in Russia. Although obviously no communist – as Russell Jacoby observes, "Freud's subversiveness is derived from his concepts and not from his stated political opinions"[1] – Freud's manners of bringing analytic concepts to bear on the Soviets' project during this time provide openings not only for exploring the intersections between Marxism and psychoanalysis but also for reworking each of these theoretical orientations.

The first and most famous of Freud's remarks upon Bolshevism occur in 1930's *Civilization and Its Discontents*. This widely read book by the later Freud centrally involves redeploying the relatively new theory of the death drive (*Todestrieb*) first introduced a decade earlier in *Beyond the Pleasure Principle* (1920). *Civilization and Its Discontents* focuses on those dimensions of the *Todestrieb* associated with aggression, with destructiveness as directed by human beings against each other. For this Freud, the death drive as aggression poses the greatest permanent threat to the very existence of civilization (*Kultur*) qua cohesive human social groupings enjoying historical endurance. In this vein, he signals his sympathy with one of the most un-Marxist of worldviews, namely, Thomas Hobbes's political philosophy according to which human beings are naturally (in the supposed "state of nature") isolated selfish predators preying on each other. Freud joins Hobbes in repeating Plautus's *"homo homini lupus."*[2]

DOI: 10.4324/9781003215301-2

In *Civilization and Its Discontents*, immediately after endorsing man being a wolf to man via the hypothesis of a naturalized aggression (i.e., an innate *Todestrieb*), Freud turns his attention to revolutionary Russia. He begins by attributing to "communists" a crude Rousseauian vision having it that "man is wholly good and is well-disposed to his neighbour; but the institution of private property has corrupted his nature."[3] Ironically, Antonio Gramsci, in a letter roughly contemporaneous with *Civilization and Its Discontents*, accuses Freudian psychoanalysis of promoting a new version of the Rousseauian myth of the " 'noble savage' corrupted by society, that is to say, by history."[4] That noted, whether Karl Marx's own conception of human nature (*als Gattungswesen*) as essentially linked to social laboring requires disavowing aggression, evil, viciousness, selfishness, and the like, as Freud charges, is highly debatable. What is more, Marx emphatically rejects all forms of the "state of nature" myth, whether Hobbesian, Rousseauian, or any other permutation. Freud appears to be relying more on Soviet propaganda for his image of communism than on a careful consideration of the actual textual basis of Marxism (just as Gramsci appears to be relying on popular misperceptions of Freud in hurling at psychoanalysis the same accusation of Rousseauian romanticism that Freud, with equal unfairness, hurls at "communists").

Freud promptly proceeds to attack what he takes to be communists' beliefs in a lost-but-recoverable original goodness purportedly lying at the historically eclipsed basis of human nature. After admitting his lack of qualifications for assessing the economic feasibility and desirability of implementing a Marxist approach to political economy,[5] he asserts apropos Marxism that "the psychological premisses (*Voraussetzung*) on which the system is based are an untenable (*haltlose*) illusion."[6] He then warns that "in abolishing private property (*Privateigentums*) we deprive the human love of aggression (*menschlichen Aggressionslust*) of one of its instruments, certainly a strong one, though certainly not the strongest."[7] One should note in passing Freud's admission that property is neither the unique nor the most important conduit for channeling aggression. That noted, Freud goes on to argue that aggression, both phylogenetically and ontogenetically, precedes the emergence of the institution of private property.[8] He even worries about an imagined communist "free love" ethos stoking explosively violent rivalries in the field of human sexual relationships.[9]

One obvious Marxist rebuttal of Freud's line of criticism in this context is to draw attention to the crucial distinction between private property and personal possessions. When Marx speaks of "private property" (*Privateigentum*), he does not thereby designate the trans-historical category of any object of ownership and this ownership's attendant claims or rights. By "private property," Marx instead designates means of production intended to serve as surplus-value-generating capital and held by individual capitalists as members of one class among several within specifically capitalist societies.

Marx does not envision depriving individuals of their personal possessions. Socialism and communism would not require whole groups to share the same communal toothbrush, for example. Hence, the Marxist abolition of private property is not equivalent to the abolition of personal possessions. Rather, it amounts to the abolition of property as capital specifically. This already takes some of the sting out of Freud's previously noted objections to "the communists." Although sizable inequalities between personal possessions indeed would be problematic for socialism/communism – these would be inequalities sufficient to recreate class-like social stratifications – differences in possessions, and the very having of personal possessions as not capital qua private property strictly speaking, are not of real concern for socialist/communist political economics.

In the context of these reflections on Bolshevism in *Civilization and Its Discontents*, Freud makes another observation that packs greater critical punch thanks to its resonance with the tragic realities of Stalinism. He remarks,

> It is intelligible that the attempt to establish a new, communist civilization in Russia should find its psychological support in the persecution of the bourgeois. One only wonders, with concern, what the Soviets will do after they have wiped out their bourgeois.[10]

The Stalinist purges of Kulaks (and "sub-Kulaks"), old-guard Bolsheviks (including former members of V.I. Lenin's Politburo), and numerous others seem sadly and amply to justify Freud's concern. Yet Freud's naturalistic eternalization of the death drive as aggression implies that Stalin's reign of terror, with its show trials, gulags, executions, and assassinations, was an inevitable, preordained outcome of the October Revolution. Obviously, whether Stalinism was or was not a necessary consequence of

Leninism remains one of the biggest unsettled questions left by the history of the Soviet experience. And whether the viciousness of a naturalized *Todestrieb* settles the matter is open to vigorous debate.

Several chapters later in *Civilization and Its Discontents*, Freud briefly picks back up the thread of his discussion of Bolshevism. Whether intentionally or not, he accentuates an ambivalent tone already detectable in his prior remarks regarding this subject. Apropos dealing with "aggressiveness" as "a potent obstacle to civilization,"[11] Freud states,

> I too think it quite certain (*unzweifelhaft*) that a real change in the relations of human beings to possessions (*Besitz*) would be of more help in this direction than any ethical commands; but the recognition of this fact among socialists has been obscured and made useless for practical purposes by a fresh idealistic misconception of human nature.[12]

It seems that Freud, in this passage, softens and qualifies his critique of Marxism (as socialism, communism, and/or Bolshevism). Earlier in *Civilization and Its Discontents*, he appeared, as seen, to assert that Marxist-type changes of wealth distribution either would fail to defuse or even further aggravate aggression between people. Now, Freud instead concedes that economically egalitarian redistributions of possessions (*als Besitz*) or property (*als Eigentum*) indeed are "quite certain" (*unzweifelhaft*) to result in some genuine progress in the history of societies' struggles to tame and domesticate the destructive side of the death drive – and this by contrast with mere ethical admonishments of a "Love thy neighbor as thyself" sort.[13]

Within the pages of *Civilization and Its Discontents*, Freud's stance regarding Marxist political economics abruptly shifts from denying it will be of any assistance against aggression to admitting that it promises real help on this front. His reservation becomes one concerning the management (or lack thereof) of expectations. Now, instead of denying the anti-aggression efficacy of combatting material inequality, Freud simply warns against expecting too much progress along these lines from socialist or communist economic changes.

Jacques Lacan's ambivalent engagements with Marx – the later Lacan teases his audience by saying that they cannot tell whether his Marx-related remarks are "ringing on the left or on the right" (*vient de droite ou de gauche*) of their ears[14] – sometimes convey the same Freudian message. Lacan cautions that crushing disappointment and traumatizing disillusionment await those overoptimistic leftists anticipating paradise on the other side of a political-economic revolution, should one come to pass,[15] with the later Lacan expressing his pessimism about such an eventuality[16] (although at one point, in 1972, he describes consumer capitalism as in overt crisis and doomed soon to implode[17]). Already in *Seminar VI* (*Desire and Its Interpretation* [1958–1959]), Lacan puts forward his metapsychological category of impossible-to-satisfy desire (*désir*) as the key "discontent in civilization" (*malaise dans la culture*) to be managed by all societies, post-revolutionary Marxist ones included.[18] The twenty-first seminar (*Les non-dupes errent* [1973–1974]) features a Lacanian neologism signaling a problematic tendency for revolutionaries to be excessively hopeful utopians: "*rêve-olution*," in which "*révolution*" is made to contain the word "*rêve*" (dream).[19] Similarly, Lacan did not think that the Soviet Union had gotten very far along truly revolutionary lines.[20]

After *Civilization and Its Discontents*, on two occasions published in 1933, Freud returns to the topic of Marxism. He addresses it both in the *New Introductory Lectures on Psycho-Analysis* (primarily in his lecture on "The Question of a *Weltanschauung*") as well as in the exchange with Albert Einstein titled "Why War?" Both of these texts from 1933 contain reiterations of Freud's 1930 objection to Marxism, according to which socialist/communist economic policies are powerless to tamp down the *Todestrieb* as an aggression inherent to an incorrigible human nature.[21] The myth of a future Soviet "New Man" is fated to remain just that, namely, a mere fiction of hopelessly utopian propaganda.

However, in 1933, Freud adds further points and nuances to his considerations of Marxism not to be found in *Civilization and Its Discontents*. To begin with, in the *New Introductory Lectures on Psycho-Analysis*, he proffers an ambivalent assessment of what he takes to be the essence of historical materialism as a conceptual framework. Therein, Freud praises Marx for discovering the previously un- or under-appreciated influences of economic forces and factors on societies and the human beings shaped by them.[22]

Yet Freud qualifies this praise of Marxian historical materialism with two caveats. First, he argues against the idea that the entirety of more-than-economic superstructure can be reduced wholly and completely to a mere reflection of whatever constitutes the current infrastructure (i.e., the economic base constituted by a society's given mode of production). With the concept of the super-ego in view, Freud comments,

> A child's super-ego is in fact constructed on the model not of its parents but of its parents' super-ego; the contents which fill it are the same and it becomes the vehicle (*Träger*) of tradition and of all the time-resisting (*zeitbeständigen*) judgements of value which have propagated themselves in this manner from generation to generation. . . . It seems likely that what are known as materialistic views of history sin in under-estimating this factor. They brush it aside with the remark that human "ideologies" are nothing other than the product and superstructure of their contemporary economic conditions. That is true, but very probably not the whole truth. The past, the tradition of the race and of the people, lives on in the ideologies of the super-ego, and yields only slowly to the influences of the present and to new changes; and so long as it operates through the super-ego it plays a powerful part in human life, independently of economic conditions.[23]

Already in *Civilization and Its Discontents*, Freud speaks of a "cultural super-ego" (*das Kultur-Über-Ich*).[24] However, this passage from the *New Introductory Lectures on Psycho-Analysis* indicates that this phrase is a pleonasm. The super-ego is by metapsychological definition inherently cultural qua an internalization of sociohistorical forms and contents transmitted primarily via the family unit.

Faced with this just-quoted Freud, the very first thing that any Marxist worth his/her salt ought to do is point out the oversimplification of historical materialism relied upon in this quotation. Perhaps taking certain more vulgar Marxists as accurately representing the core commitments of Marxism, Freud's stated remarks reveal that, as he understands it, historical materialism posits that the entirety of a given society's superstructure springs wholly out of that same society's infrastructure (qua mode of production). This sort of superstructure therefore would contain no surviving traces of earlier historical periods tied to different modes of production.

Such classical Marxist moments as Friedrich Engels's October 27, 1890 letter to Conrad Schmidt, in which Engels clarifies that historical materialism insists on economic determination as a matter of "in the last instance," warn that neither Marx nor Engels espouse a crudely simplistic doctrine according to which a single economic base generates each and every more-than-economic dimension and detail of society contemporaneous with this base[25] (A. R. Luria, citing this same Engels, points out a sad parallel between the unjustified charge of economic reductionism against Marx and the equally unjustified charge of sexual reductionism against Freud[26]). Hence, Freud is wrong to assume that historical materialism presupposes or posits a one-and-only linear causal relationship between a particular infrastructure as cause and a corresponding superstructure, in its entirety, as effect of this, and exclusively this, particular infrastructure. Incidentally, Freud belatedly, in 1937, comes to concede that his pre-1937 criticisms of Marx and Engels involving recourse to the analytic theory of the super-ego were ill-informed and invalid.[27]

Furthermore, Marxist questions can and should be raised about whether and how much "the ideologies of the super-ego" really are "independent of economic conditions." If Freud is willing to concede that "contemporary economic conditions" influence "human 'ideologies,'" then why would past economic conditions not have influenced "the tradition of the race and of the people" that "lives on in the ideologies of the super-ego?" If so, then the Freudian super-ego would reflect a lag between the influences of at least two modes of production, one current and one or more preceding ones. But in this case, the super-ego would not be independent of economic conditioning.

There is another Marxist line of response that this Freud would need to take into account. Specifically, how would he respond to the Marxist who, on the one hand, admits that contemporary society contains vestiges of prior social formations while, on the other hand, maintaining that these carryovers from the past are able to persist in the present only if and when they are amenable to being pressed into the service of the present socio-economic system? Would this not indicate an infrastructural mediation, if only an indirect one, by the present mode of production of even those superstructural ghosts originating out of earlier modes of production?

Also, in the preceding 1933 block quotation, Freud employs the German word "*Träger*" ("vehicle") to characterize the super-ego. This is the same word Marx uses to depict individuals as vehicles (or bearers) of class identities and functions (with, for example, the individual capitalist as a bearer for the logic of capital as M-C-M').[28] In this vein, is there not ample evidence in capitalist societies of persons' super-egos operating, at least in part, as vehicles for the productive and/or consumptive demands of capital? Is not one of the appealing aspects of Lacan's linking of the super-ego to the imperative to "enjoy" its ability to capture the injunctions and pressures bearing down upon, and introjected within, psyches immersed in (consumerist) capitalism?[29]

Even if the cultural super-ego contains residues of the pre-capitalist past, it also seems to harbor fragments of the capitalist present too. It indeed would be a false dilemma to insist on a forced choice between either an entirely pre-capitalist or an entirely capitalist super-ego wholly of the past or wholly of the present. Especially for a psyche said by Freud himself to be, at its unconscious base, blithely unconcerned with avoiding contradiction[30] (not to mention indifferent to linear chronological time[31]), such either/or alternatives definitely should be off the table as regards theorizing the super-ego. Indeed, in the *New Introductory Lectures on Psycho-Analysis*, just six pages after the previous quotation concerning communism and the super-ego, Freud mentions that, "The logical laws of thought do not apply in the id, and this is true above all of the law of contradiction."[32]

What is more, the same later Freud who criticizes Marxism along the lines presently under consideration also portrays the type of cultural super-ego typical of his late-nineteenth and early-twentieth-century European cultural milieu as essentially Kantian. That is to say, the super-ego of concern in, for instance, *Civilization and Its Discontents* closely resembles the will and conscience of Immanuel Kant's deontological ethics of pure practical reason, with its categorical imperative and "You can, because you must!" (*Du kannst, denn du sollst*) unconditionality.[33] The *New Introductory Lectures on Psycho-Analysis* continue to associate the super-ego's severity with Kantian ethical rigorism.[34] And in 1923's *The Ego and the Id*, Freud is especially explicit about the connection between Kant's conscience and his super-ego: "the super-ego – the conscience at work in the ego – may . . . become harsh, cruel and inexorable against the ego which is in its charge. Kant's Categorical Imperative is thus the direct heir of the Oedipus complex."[35] And the Kantian metaphysics of morals is itself a barely disguised pseudo-secularization of a Protestant ethical worldview.

Protestantism is born at roughly the same time as European capitalism. Additionally, as both Marx and, after him, Max Weber stress, Protestant Christianity plays a key role in the rise and persistence of industrial capitalism.[36] And of course, Kant and his work are situated in the German-speaking world of late-eighteenth-century Europe. So if the Freudian cultural super-ego is modeled on the subject of Kantian ethics, then, once again, just how "independent" is this super-ego of its surrounding "economic conditions"?

In addition to Freud's just-criticized qualification of historical materialism involving the theory of the super-ego, his 1933 pronouncements on the topic of Marxism also put forward a second caveat tempering his concessions to the (partial) validity of this economically centered political perspective. In the context of lecturing on the topic of *Weltanschauungen*, Freud claims that Marxism, in its atheistic fight against religious worldviews, has itself become another religious worldview. One should bear in mind that, by 1933, Stalinism is in terrifying full swing. Freud states:

> The newly achieved discovery of the far-reaching importance of economic relations brought with it a temptation not to leave alterations in them to the course of historical development but to put them into effect oneself by revolutionary action. Theoretical Marxism, as realized in Russian Bolshevism, has acquired the energy and the self-contained and exclusive character of a *Weltanschauung*, but at the same time an uncanny likeness to what it is fighting against. Though originally a portion of science (*Ursprünglich selbst ein Stück Wissenschaft*) and built up, in its implementation, upon science (*Wissenschaft*) and technology, it has created a prohibition of thought (*Denkverbot*) which is just as ruthless as was that of religion in the past. Any critical examination of Marxist theory is forbidden, doubts of its correctness are punished in the same way as heresy was once punished by the Catholic Church. The writings of Marx have taken the place of the Bible and the Koran as a source of revelation, though they would seem to be no more free from contradictions and obscurities than those older sacred books.[37]

At the start of these remarks, Freud again grants a great deal of validity to historical materialism, with its emphasis on the role of economic dimensions in history. The second sentence of this passage then opens with what appears to be an implicit distinction between the intellectual framework of historical materialism (i.e., "Theoretical Marxism") and its concrete sociopolitical implementation (i.e., "revolutionary action," "as realized in Russian Bolshevism").

Apropos this implicit distinction, it remains unclear here whether Freud considers Bolshevik practice to be a high-fidelity extension of Marx's theory. On the one hand, given Freud's other comments about the Soviet experiment already examined by me, it seems he would have to assume that Bolshevism's practices can be taken to be faithful applications of Marx's theories. And this assumption is quite questionable.

Yet on the other hand, the previous quotation involves Freud distinguishing between an initially scientific (*als wissenschaftlich*) historical materialism as per Marx himself ("originally a portion of science" [*Ursprünglich selbst ein Stück Wissenschaft*]) and a subsequent loss of this scientificity through Marxism's alleged degeneration into just another religious sect, a cult of Marx with its dogmas, deifications, and *Denkverbote*. This narrative of a decline from science to religion suggests that Freud indeed recognizes substantial differences between Marx's theories and the Bolsheviks' practices. If nothing else, Freud's assessments of the Bolsheviks look to be ambivalent, vacillating, and shot through with inconsistencies. At one point in 1933, Freud himself basically admits to his indecision and uncertainty apropos Marx's ideas.[38]

Clearly, the central thrust of the preceding passage from the *New Introductory Lectures on Psycho-Analysis* is the unfavorable comparison of Bolshevism with Catholicism and/or Islam. This comparison should come as no surprise in a lecture titled "The Question of a *Weltanschauung*." As is well-known, Freud is at pains in this particular lecture to deny that psychoanalysis itself constitutes its own worldview. He famously insists that analysis merely borrows or participates in the *Weltanschauung* of modernity's empirical, experimental sciences of nature. This appeal to the scientific worldview brings with it the familiar contrasts between science and religion, reason and faith.[39]

Marx already warns against his work being turned into a fixed and inflexible creed. For example, in replying to the criticisms of *Capital* by the Russian Narodnik Nikolay Mikhailovsky, he denies that his historical materialism amounts to "a general historico-philosophical theory"[40] (a denial akin to that of Freud apropos turning psychoanalysis into a worldview). Other letters involve Marx similarly emphasizing the unpredictably contingent character of social history. Addressing the concerns of Mikhailovsky and another Russian, Vera Sassoulitch, he foregrounds historical materialism's admittance of alternate courses of social development (such as a Russian leap from feudal-agrarian tsarism directly to socialism and communism) other than those mapped out in his mature critique of political economy (with its England-centered analyses seeming to suggest that capitalism is a necessary phase of development between feudalism and socialism/communism).[41] All this to say that this later Marx presents historical materialism as an intellectual framework that can and should be open to modification, revision, and supplementation in relation to various unforeseeable unknowns, especially those regularly served up by the twists and turns of continually unfolding history. In this light, Marx's materialism would appear to be more like science than religion or philosophy.

Finally, there is a real irony to Freud chastising Marxism for allegedly having become just another religion. Beginning already during Freud's own lifetime, and despite his protests against the existence of a psychoanalytic *Weltanschauung*, countless others have accused psychoanalysis of exactly the same sins as Freud here accuses Marxism (or, at least, Bolshevism). The psychoanalytic movement has been depicted time and again by many of its critics as a cult of Freud-the-father in which the texts of the Master are worshipped as infallible Holy Writ. Likewise, a plethora of Freud's detractors would say of his writings what Freud says on this occasion of Marx's writings, namely, that they are filled with "contradictions and obscurities." Freud's attempts to parry such attacks by allying analysis with science (and the scientific *Weltanschauung*) have proven unconvincing to his opponents and are even treated by some of his followers as symptomatic of a grave self-misunderstanding on his part. Various analytic types, including the majority of Lacanians, are skeptical of and/or allergic to Freud's appeals to the natural sciences.

The Marxist tradition has available yet another line of counter-argument against Freud's 1933 denunciation of (Bolshevik) Marxism as a new religion. This line brings together related aspects of Marxism's theories of both knowledge and ideology. In terms of epistemology, Marxism entails an account of the inherent partisanship of knowledge and truth, at least when it comes to social theory. Insofar as all perspectives on class-based societies (i.e., the societies of Marx's "history hitherto"[42]) are themselves tied to and reflective of class positions within these same societies, there is no neutral, nonpartisan perspective on classes and the societies based upon them. Just as there is no sexless view of sexual difference, so too is there no classless view of class difference.

However, one must be careful at this juncture not to lapse into the commonplace conflation of neutrality and objectivity. Recent and contemporary American political journalism is rife with examples of this far-from-innocent conflation. For instance, when reporting on a debate between two opposed politicians in which one of the politicians clearly bests the other, these journalists strain to seem objective by trying to be neutral. They issue statements such as "Both sides had some good points," "Both sides fared badly," or "The debate was too close to call," even though it is glaringly evident that one side won with good points and the other lost with bad points (or that one side at least did less badly than the other). Such fake objectivity insidiously favors types of politics and politicians unable to prevail in the back-and-forth of argument and counter-argument, perhaps due to them being irrational and/or indefensible.

The assumption behind these sorts of journalistic verbal contortions is that the objective truth is inherently nonpartisan (à la the cliché "The truth always lies in-between"). Journalists tying themselves in these knots do so assuming that being objective requires being neutral qua nonpartisan. Yet as the example of the political debate I just mentioned shows, the objective truth (in this case, the reality of one politician besting the other) sometimes is partisan (i.e., one political side really did out-argue the other).

What is worse, one only needs to imagine the disastrous, if not also comic, consequences of applying the erroneous conflation of objectivity with neutrality to fields such as mathematics and natural science. The truth most definitely does not lie in between incompatible judgments such as "$2 + 2 = 4$" and "$2 + 2 = 5$" or "Phlogiston is necessary to explain combustion" and "Oxygen is necessary to explain combustion." The partisans of certain sides in these conflicts have objective truth on their side, and the partisans of other sides do not. As Jacoby proposes apropos an overlap between Marxism and Freudianism, those partisans with objective truth on their side (such as Marxists and Freudians) perhaps should pursue a "liberating intolerance" as regards their opponents and these opponents' falsehoods, an intolerance that frees others from such untruths.[43] And Jacoby's liberating intolerance avowedly is the complementary inverse of Herbert Marcuse's notion of "repressive tolerance,"[44] itself a correlate of Marcusian "repressive desublimation" and "repressive progress."[45] Moreover, Marcuse, in describing the false nonpartisanship tied to the erroneous and insidious conflation of objectivity with neutrality, observes, "It refrains from taking sides – but in doing so it actually protects the already established machinery of discrimination."[46] He soon adds, "Such objectivity is spurious – more, it offends against humanity and truth by being calm where one should be enraged, by refraining from accusation where accusation is in the facts themselves."[47]

For Marxism, the same holds as concerns class-colored social theories as holds with the obvious nonequivalence between objectivity and neutrality in such fields as mathematics and science. The fact that there is no class-neutral perspective on class societies does not mean that social theorizing is a truth-less, relativistic free-for-all lacking in any objectivity (with the objective truth presumed to lie in between clashing class views). Instead, Marxist epistemology wagers on the partisanship of truth, namely, non-neutral objectivity. In capitalist societies, the proletarian perspective, although one class view on capitalism among other capitalist class views, nonetheless uniquely articulates the objective truth of capitalism. Historical materialism is an expression of proletarian class consciousness. But its critique of political economy enjoys a status as objectively true knowledge of the underpinnings of the capitalist mode of production in ways that other partisan perspectives competing with it do not (such as the multiple forms of bourgeois economics, trying to pass themselves off as objectively neutral qua classless/nonpartisan, when, in fact, they amount to ideology masquerading as mathematics).

The preceding reflections on Marxist epistemology, with its partisanship of truth, lead into a couple of manners of responding to Freud's critical linking of Marxism with religions. First, and as I noted a short while ago, psychoanalysis likewise often is treated by its critics as not scientific but, instead, as a dogmatic faith resting on a misguided deification of the figure of Freud. Yet are not defenders of psychoanalysis justified in responding to this line of criticism with evidence and arguments about how and why important objective truths about human mindedness and like-mindedness cannot be grasped without the contested hypothesis of the analytic unconscious and related Freudian concepts? Has not psychoanalysis been an embattled partisan perspective from its beginnings right up through the present?

These questions give rise to still others: why would partisanship on behalf of psychoanalysis be any more or less dogmatic than partisanship on behalf of Marxism? More generally, should any and all passionate commitments to and fierce advocacies of specific intellectual orientations be dismissed as religious-style fanaticism? If so, is not Freud himself vulnerable to this very same dismissal that he has recourse to in response to Marxism? If not, what specific criteria enable Freud to differentiate between his non-neutrality in favor of psychoanalysis from Marxists' non-neutrality in favor of historical materialism?

A second manner of responding to Freud's unfavorable comparison of Marxism with religion made possible by the Marxist idea of the partisanship of truth has to do with the topic of worldviews as ideologies and, hence, with the Marxist theory of ideology. Given Freud's fashion of contrasting science and religion coupled with his attribution of a worldview to modern science itself, he has to admit that something can be a worldview without, for all that, therefore being a religion too. In the prior block quotation, Freud indeed appears to distinguish between Marxism as a scientific *Weltanschauung* (i.e., Marx's original historical materialism) and Bolshevism as a religion departing from this worldview.

Yet interesting questions remain. How would Freud relate the concept-terms "*Weltanschauung*" and "ideology"? Are all worldviews also ideologies? Or are some worldviews (such as, perhaps, scientific ones) not ideological? Furthermore, and apropos the Marxist tradition, if Freud grants that historical materialism is (or participates in) a scientific *Weltanschauung* without being a religion, can the translation of this theory into practice through (revolutionary) sociopolitical action be accomplished in a nonreligious way? Or for Freud, is the alleged morphing of the science of Marxism into the religion of Bolshevism made inevitable by the very nature of the general process of turning ideas into politics? Does the eternal, inescapable innateness of the aggression of the *Todestrieb* cement in place this inevitability? Alas, much of what these questions ask about remains hazy or even unaddressed in Freud's writings.

Certain strains of classical Marxism share in common with Freud an Enlightenment-style inclination to assume or advocate a strict difference-in-kind between science and religion, with the latter but not the former as ideological. In this vein, both Marxist and psychoanalytic outlooks put forward, among other things, critiques of religions specifically and ideologies generally. The sort of traditional Marxist who adopts this Enlightenment stance along with Freud could respond to the latter's 1933 objections to Marxism-become-religion along lines I already suggested: regardless of one's interpretation of the historical case of Russian Bolshevism, why should theoretical and/or practical militancy on behalf of historical materialism be any more or less "religious" than such militancy on behalf of psychoanalysis? This question is particularly pressing if both Marxism and Freudianism participate in scientific worldviews while not being themselves religions.

A less traditional form of Marxism would go even further by problematizing Enlightenment presumptions about ideologies as limited, circumscribed, and surpassable phenomena. Various sorts of classical historical materialism predict an "end of ideologies" with the advent of classless societies. From this perspective, ideologies are necessary only in class-based societies requiring such forms of false consciousness in order to secure the acquiescence primarily of the exploited and oppressed classes. With the abolition of classes and, along with them, relations of exploitation and oppression, the need for ideologies vanishes too. They become superfluous and automatically wither away.

This Enlightenment-type Marxist likewise believes that the historical materialist is he/she from whose eyes the scales of ideologies have fallen. The critic of political economy simply stands outside of ideology, enjoying a pure, uncompromised externality. Freud's notions of scientificity and "the scientific *Weltanschauung*" similarly flirt with suggesting that the scientist (and the scientifically minded psychoanalyst) not only repudiates religiosity but rationally transcends all ideology whatsoever.

But Louis Althusser's recasting of Marxism, to take a nontraditional variant of this orientation, rejects all visions of any end of ideology, Marxist ones included.[48] According to Althusser, all modes of production, even socialist and communist ones, spontaneously secrete ideologies as the "imaginary" (*à la* the Lacanian register of the Imaginary) contents (such as beliefs, categories, concepts, customs, faiths, ideas, ideals, mores, norms, notions, rituals, values, etc.) rendering the "real" of an established social system a livable reality for its subjects. Without ideologies conceived thusly, societies would not seem livable and, hence, would fail to be produced and reproduced. So long as there are societies, up to and including fully communist ones entirely liberated from and free of classes and private property, there will be ideologies. The latter are like the air that is breathed by all social subjects.

One of many upshots to this Althusserian account of ideology is that Marxist theory, although itself a nonideological science, must work with and through nonscientific ideologies (and not just because it is always surrounded by ideology as an omnipresent, unsurpassable feature of social existence). This is particularly necessary, for Althusser, at the level of Marxist political practice. For Marx himself, the superstructures of ideologies are the terrain on which, speaking of class conflict due to crises in relations and modes of production, "men become conscious of this conflict and fight it out"[49] (with this statement from the preface to 1859's *A Contribution to the Critique of Political Economy* being crucial to Gramsci,[50] among others). Following this Marx, Althusser too maintains that, despite his own strict distinction between science and ideology, the practical-political deployment of the scientific theory of historical materialism inevitably will interact with and need to rely upon certain ideologies in its enveloping *Zeitgeist*.

In Freud's eyes, this inevitable commingling of science and ideology in the translation of theory into practice might very well be tantamount to the degeneration of the scientific into the religious. Yet in line with Althusser, is this commingling not requisite for a scientific theory to enjoy actual transformative efficacy at the practical level of real-world politics? Are not phenomena commonly associated with religiosity, including belief, devotion, faith, fervor, and passion, crucial ingredients of any effective political movement? He/she who wishes to avoid dirtying his/her hands with ideologies and anything resembling religious phenomena also wishes to avoid all revolutionary activity. As will be seen shortly, Freud himself comes to concede that what he disapproves of as the religious aspects of Bolshevism may turn out to be indispensable to its quest to usher in a "new social order."

There are two more sets of lengthy remarks Freud makes about communism in his 1933 lecture on "The Question of a *Weltanschauung*" I have yet to address. Both of these portions of this lecture evince a pronounced, explicit ambivalence on Freud's part apropos Marxism and its political implementation in the guise of Bolshevism. Indeed, these two passages from the *New Introductory Lectures on Psycho-Analysis* provide openings for an immanent-critical reworking of Freud's political reflections, a reworking informed by a synthesis of Marxism and psychoanalysis.

Freud dismisses the claims of classical historical materialism to predictive power. However, he values this same historical materialism for its insights into the previously un- or under-appreciated importance of economies for human social existence. In this vein, Freud comments as follows:

> The strength of Marxism clearly lies, not in its view of history or the prophecies of the future that are based on it, but in its sagacious indication of the decisive influence which the economic circumstances of men have upon their intellectual, ethical and artistic attitudes. A number of connections and implications were thus uncovered, which had previously been almost totally overlooked. But it cannot be assumed that economic motives are the only ones that determine the behaviour of human beings in society (*Gesellschaft*). The undoubted fact that different individuals, races and nations behave differently under the same economic conditions is alone enough to show that economic motives are not the sole dominating factors. It is altogether incomprehensible how psychological factors can be overlooked where what is in question are the reactions of living human beings; for not only were these reactions concerned in establishing the economic conditions, but even under the domination of those conditions men can only bring their original instinctual impulses (*ursprünglichen Triebregungen*) into play – their self-preservative instinct (*Selbsterhaltungstrieb*), their aggressiveness (*Aggressionslust*), their need to be loved (*Liebesbedürfnis*), their drive (*Drang*) towards obtaining pleasure and avoiding unpleasure. In an earlier enquiry I also pointed out the important claims made by the super-ego, which represents tradition and the ideals of the past and will for a time resist the incentives of a new economic situation. And finally we must not forget that the mass of human beings who are subjected to economic necessities also undergo the process of cultural development (*Kulturentwicklung*) – of civilization (*Zivilisation*) as other people may say – which, though no doubt influenced by all the other factors, is certainly independent of them in its origin, being comparable to an organic process and very well able on its part to exercise an influence on the other factors. It displaced instinctual aims (*Triebziele*) and brings it about that people become antagonistic to what they had previously tolerated. Moreover, the progressive strengthening of the scientific spirit (*wissenschaftlichen Geistes*) seems to form

an essential part of it. If anyone were in a position to show in detail the way in which these different factors – the general inherited human disposition (*die allgemeine menschliche Triebanlage*), its racial variations and its cultural (*kulturellen*) transformations – inhibit and promote one another under the conditions of social rank, profession and earning capacity – if anyone were able to do this, he would have supplemented Marxism so that it was made into a genuine social science (*einer wirklichen Gesellschaftskunde*). For sociology too, dealing as it does with the behaviour of people in society, cannot be anything but applied psychology. Strictly speaking there are only two sciences (*Wissenschaften*): psychology, pure and applied, and natural science (*Naturkunde*).[51]

A remark by Gramsci is a fitting response to Freud's concerns (ones Freud shares with the likes of Weber[52]) – "Frequently, people attack historical economism in the belief that they are attacking historical materialism."[53] Economistic vulgarizations of historical materialism perpetrated by both the Second International and Stalinism indeed are vulnerable to the sorts of reservations and objections raised by Freud in this passage. However, Marx and Engels, especially given their concessions apropos the role of human mindedness in sociohistorical processes,[54] are far from guilty of the neglect of "psychology" prompting Freud's criticisms here. And of course, almost the entirety of the Western Marxist tradition from Georg Lukács, Karl Korsch, and Gramsci onward amounts to a sustained struggle within Marxism against the crudely reductive economism problematized by Freud. If anything, I believe Western Marxism has too excessively de-emphasized economics in its anti-economism campaigns.

In the quotation in the previous section, Freud also refers back to his employment of the theory of the super-ego against historical materialism's prioritization of the economy (an employment contained in one of the earlier lectures, "The Dissection of the Psychical Personality," in his *New Introductory Lectures on Psycho-Analysis*). Having already responded to this, I will not repeat myself now. I also will leave aside Freud's highly debatable assertion having it that "strictly speaking there are only two sciences (*Wissenschaften*): psychology, pure and applied, and natural science (*Naturkunde*)." I will limit myself to suggesting that this is true only on an exceedingly broad construal of "psychology."

Furthermore, the just-quoted passage from "The Question of a *Weltanschauung*" also involves Freud repeating his now-familiar recourse to the notion of an immutable human nature as an obstacle to the perhaps unrealistic aspirations of socialist/communist sociopolitical programs. He speaks of humanity's "original instinctual impulses" (*ursprünglichen Triebregungen*) as constituting this purportedly incorrigible nature. Yet the very list Freud then furnishes of these *Triebe* provides openings for Marxist lines of response to his charging of Marxism with a hopeless, doomed utopianism.

Freud identifies the following as instances of the "original instinctual impulses" he has in mind when warning Marxists about the impossibility of radically reforming human nature: "their self-preservative instinct (*Selbsterhaltungstrieb*), their aggressiveness (*Aggressionslust*), their need to be loved (*Liebesbedürfnis*), their drive (*Drang*) toward obtaining pleasure and avoiding unpleasure." As seen, both in *Civilization and Its Discontents* and elsewhere in the *New Introductory Lectures on Psycho-Analysis*, Freud focuses exclusively on aggression as the purportedly natural drive threatening to derail Marxist revolutions. On these other occasions of making the human-nature objection to Marxism, Freud does not mention self-preservation, love, and the (un)pleasure principle.

Apart from the issue of aggression, which I will address momentarily, the other "original instinctual impulses" Freud mentions in the preceding block quotation from "The Question of a *Weltanschauung*": one, pose no obstacles to socialism/communism; two, readily could be pressed into the willing service of such new social orders; and/or three, potentially could be encouraged to rebel against really existing capitalism. Apropos the "self-preservative instinct" (*Selbsterhaltungstrieb*), is not today's global capitalism, with its staggering wealth inequality, vulnerable to (and deserving of) being judged an abject failure by the majority of the world's population? Does this capitalism not fail to satisfy even the most basic "self-preservative" needs of the billions of people it abandons to squalid poverty? Does it not turn the bulk of humanity into "the wretched of the earth"? By stark contrast, what about the core promise of socialist and communist political projects to furnish real economic equality and decent material standards of living for everyone? Is not Marxism much more in line with what the enlightened self-interest of most persons' "self-preservative" drives would and should demand?

As regards Freud's postulated "need to be loved" (*Liebesbedürfnis*), there seems to be no reason whatsoever to presume that this drive-level natural impulse can be satisfied only through non-socialist/non-communist social arrangements and/or that such a need cannot be satisfied through socialist/communist social arrangements. One must recall that this same later Freud ties love to a sweeping vision of "Eros" inspired by the ancient Greeks. Starting in 1920's *Beyond the Pleasure Principle*, Eros's life drives, enjoining the individual organism and its psyche to forge links and unite with others, are portrayed by Freud as pushing back against the *Todestrieb*'s inclinations toward hostility, severance, and withdrawal.[55]

This push-and-pull between the centrifugal and constructive life drives and the centripetal and destructive death drive(s) is very different from the uncontested dominance and one-way thrust of virulent, undiluted aggression. Could not the need for love and striving for (social) connectedness be harnessed and bolstered by Marxist revolutionaries? What would prevent them from potentially forging a powerful alliance with Eros? Does Freud, especially when arguing that human aggressiveness will bring to naught all socialist/communist endeavors, simply assume that the *Todestrieb* as aggression will always win in every instance in its conflicts with Eros?

Indeed, elsewhere, including in *Civilization and Its Discontents*, when not objecting to Marxism, Freud describes the struggle between Eros and the *Todestrieb* as open-ended and of uncertain outcome. In *The Ego and the Id*, when entertaining the possibility that the id is "under the domination of the mute but powerful death instincts (*unter der Herrschaft der stummen, aber mächtigen Todestriebe stünde*)," he admits, "perhaps that might be to undervalue the part played by Eros (*aber wir besorgen, doch dabei die Rolle des Eros unterschätzen*)."[56] And the concluding paragraph of the sixth chapter of *Civilization and Its Discontents* draws to a close, after emphasizing the threat posed by innate human aggression to organized sociality itself,[57] with a sweeping vision of the war between Eros and the *Todestrieb* writ large across the entire arc of human history:

> Now, I think, the meaning of the evolution of civilization (*der Kulturentwicklung*) is no longer obscure to us. It must present the struggle between Eros and Death (*Kampf zwischen Eros und Tod*), between the instinct of life (*Lebenstrieb*) and the instinct of destruction (*Destruktionstrieb*), as it works itself out in the human species. This struggle is what all life essentially consists of, and the evolution of civilization

may therefore be simply described as the struggle for life of the human species (*der Lebenskampf der Menschenart*). And it is this battle of the giants (*diesen Streit der Giganten*) that our nurse-maids (*unsere Kinderfrauen*) try to appease with their lullaby about Heaven.[58]

Two closely related features of this passage are important to note in the present context. First, Freud says nothing about the outcome one way or another of "the struggle between Eros and Death." He is silent regarding the future course of this "struggle for life of the human species" (*Kampf als Lebenskampf der Menschenart*). Thus, he by no means forecasts the victory of death over life, of the *Todestrieb* over Eros (nor *vice versa*).

Second, Freud's last sentence in the preceding quotation, with its dismissive reference to "nurse-maids . . . with their lullaby about Heaven," indicates that Freud sees himself as having to labor mightily against the weight of tradition, received wisdom, popular views, and/or persistent illusions serving most of the rest of humanity as defenses against painful truths. Just like other deeply entrenched and widespread defensive prejudices undermined by psychoanalysis, such as those concerning sex, love, and mindedness, faith in the victoriousness and reliability of "the better angels of our nature" cannot but be profoundly shaken by the analytic hypothesis of the *Todestrieb* and its consequences. However, although Freud seeks to bend the stick against rosy or even Pollyannaish pictures of a benevolent human nature (as per any "lullaby about Heaven"), he does not preach a diametrically opposed necessitarian anti-gospel about hell. That is to say, the triumph of love over death is not guaranteed in advance (*contra* nurse-maids' lullabies), but neither is the triumph of aggression (*Todestrieb*) over sociality (Eros). Although Freud is no optimist, neither is he a fatalist.

Then, *Civilization and Its Discontent* concludes by circumnavigating back to the Empedoclean strife pitting life against death drives. This book's final paragraph observes regarding the future fate of humanity:

> The fateful question for the human species (*Die Schicksalsfrage der Menschenart*) seems to me to be whether and to what extent their cultural development (*ihrer Kulturentwicklung*) will succeed in mastering the disturbance of their communal life by the human instinct of aggression and self-destruction (*menschlichen Aggressions- und Selbstvernichtungstrieb*). It may be that in this respect precisely the

present time deserves a special interest. Men have gained control over the forces of nature to such an extent that with their help they would have no difficulty in exterminating one another to the last man. They know this, and hence comes a large part of their current unrest, their unhappiness and their mood of anxiety (*ihrer Angststimmung*). And now it is to be expected that the other of the two "Heavenly Powers" (*himmlischen Mächte*), eternal Eros, will make an effort to assert himself in the struggle with his equally immortal adversary. But who can foresee with what success and with what result?[59]

An editorial footnote points out that the question bringing this book to a close was added in 1931. Again, one should appreciate that, even in the face of the rise of anti-Semitic fascism and species-threatening techno-scientific warfare, Freud insists on the uncertainty as to whether or not the death-drive forces of hatred and annihilation will triumph. This uncertainty is thanks to Eros, namely, what the *New Introductory Lectures on Psycho-Analysis* identifies as both the "self-preservative instinct" (*Selbsterhaltungstrieb*) and the "need to be loved" (*Liebesbedürfnis*) that are, for Freud himself, just as intrinsic to human nature as "aggressiveness" (*Aggressionslust*). In this vein, the very title of Marcuse's 1955 manifesto of Freudo-Marxism, *Eros and Civilization*, is telling. A Marxist engagement with psychoanalysis indeed ought to emphasize the role of Freud's Eros in relation to the conflicts and dangers worrying the author of *Civilization and Its Discontents*.

As I highlighted earlier, Freud tends to play the Hobbesian when pitting himself against Marxism. At such moments, he risks implying, among other things, that the *Todestrieb* as aggression is the exclusive or overriding tendency at the base of human nature and psychical life.[60] But Freud's flirtations with Hobbes court the peril of him falling prey to a profound self-misunderstanding (and encourage the same misunderstanding of him in some of his readers,[61] as reflected, for instance, by Edwin R. Wallace's claim that, "Hobbes . . . was a philosopher after Freud's own heart"[62] and José Brunner's depiction of the Freudian libidinal economy as an intrapsychical version of the Hobbesian state of nature dominated by violence and aggression[63]). Philip Rieff, in his 1959 study *Freud: The Mind of the Moralist*, explains these matters thusly:

Homo homini lupus: the Hobbesian words echo through Freud's social psychology. The natural man is rapacious and self-centered. But Freud

> recognizes as well the natural sociability of man, his permanent emotional need for community. The natural man is instinctually libidinal, a creature born into a hierarchy of love – which goes a long way toward modifying the Hobbesian view. To use Freud's family metaphor, there is not only a sibling rivalry, the model of social divisiveness; there is also a natural love and dependence on the parents. Man is from the beginning a thrall to society, being born into the society of the family. Although so far as Freud stresses the basic component of human aggressiveness he apparently agrees with Hobbes, he complicates the Hobbesian contention that the law of cunning and force is all that obtains in nature. There are force and freedom, Freud agrees. But there are also love and authority. And superior to all is the law of "primal ambivalence," which provides every strong hate with a counterpart of love, and hobbles every act of aggression with a subsequent burden of guilt.[64]

Rieff's "subsequent burden of guilt" is an allusion to the myth of the primal horde in Freud's *Totem and Taboo*.[65] In this myth, although the band of brothers kill the primal father of their horde so as to cast off the yoke of his oppressive tyranny, they afterward are haunted by remorse since, in their "primal ambivalence," they also love and identify with the *Urvater*.[66] In short, the brothers are ambivalent, not purely hostile (and Jean Roy, in his comparative study of Hobbes and Freud, helpfully distinguishes between Hobbes's notion of violence and Freud's concept of aggression as per the theory of the death drive[67]). Incidentally, Althusser suggests that Lacan concurs with Jean-Jacques Rousseau's critique of Hobbes's state of nature as a distorting projection of present social conditions back into a mythical (and via such mythicizing retrojection, thereby falsified) pre-social past.[68] The Marcuse of *Eros and Civilization*, for his part, basically accuses Freud in so many words of lapsing into the Hobbesianism critiqued by Rousseau in Freud's nevertheless justified rubbishing of the Rousseauian romanticized state of nature.[69]

Freud's human is not (wholly) Hobbes's wolf. Instead, he/she is a reluctant, conflicted political animal profoundly ambivalent about his/her inescapable social entanglements with others, but a political animal nonetheless. Perhaps this ambivalence is so profound that a neologism put forward by Lacan to signify the intensity of ambivalence in psychoanalysis, "*hainamoration*"[70] (loosely translatable as "hate-love"), is more suitable in this context. The ambivalent *zoon politikon* of analysis hate-loves sociality.

As is well-known, one of several central fault lines of opposition running through the history of Western political philosophy is that opposing those who conceive of human beings as *zoon politikon* (such as Aristotle, G. W. F. Hegel, and Marx) and those who imagine humans as atomistic individuals (such as Hobbes and others who subscribe to myths about a state of nature preceding any and every social contract). Especially thanks to the introduction of the Eros-versus-*Todestrieb* dual-drive model in *Beyond the Pleasure Principle*, the later Freud's metapsychological speculations, when appreciated in their fullest scope, transform this sociopolitical opposition from a theoretical contradiction into a real one. That is to say, for Freud, human beings and their societies really are split from within by antagonisms between erotic and destructive tendencies. Insofar as humans are internally torn between Eros and the *Todestrieb* right down to their id-level first natures, they are simultaneously both *zoon politikon* (by virtue of Eros) as well as wolves to each other (by virtue of the *Todestrieb*). With this later Freud, what initially appears to be a conflict within the ideality of thinking (i.e., the opposed conceptions of humans as either *zoon politikon* or lone wolves) blocking access to the reality of being (i.e., human nature *an sich*) proves instead to be the key to the latter as the revelation of a conflict internal to the reality of being itself (i.e., human nature really is split from within along Aristotelean-versus-Hobbesian lines). In this way, Freud implicitly repeats Hegel's signature dialectical gesture of transubstantiating various contradictions from epistemological constraints into ontological disclosures.

Rieff, when invoking Eros in the preceding block quotation, twice refers to birth: "born into a hierarchy of love" and "born into the society of the family." Regardless of Rieff's intentions, the topic of birth is linked, in Freudian psychoanalysis, to Freud's emphasis on human beings' species-specific prolonged prematurational helplessness (*Hilflosigkeit*) into which they are thrown at birth.[71] In 1895's *Project for a Scientific Psychology*, Freud posits that, "the initial helplessness of human beings is the *primal source* (Urquelle) of all *moral motives* (moralischen Motive)."[72] Much later, in 1926's *Inhibitions, Symptoms and Anxiety*, Freud revisits this posit and writes thus:

> The biological factor is the long period of time during which the young of the human species is in a condition of helplessness (*Hilflosigkeit*) and dependence (*Abhängigkeit*). Its intra-uterine existence

seems to be short in comparison with that of most animals, and it is sent into the world in a less finished state. As a result, the influence of the real external world upon it is intensified and an early differentiation between the ego and the id is promoted. Moreover, the dangers of the external world have a greater importance for it, so that the value of the object which can alone protect it against them and take the place of its former intra-uterine life is enormously enhanced. The biological factor, then, establishes the earliest situations of danger and creates the need to be loved (*Bedürfnis, geliebt zu werden*) which will accompany the child through the rest of its life.[73]

In 1927's *The Future of an Illusion*, Freud likewise asserts that "the terrifying impression of helplessness in childhood aroused the need for protection (*Schutz*) – for protection through love (*Schutz durch Liebe*) – which was provided by the father"[74] (with this characterization of the father providing a link to the *Urvater* who was loved as well as hated by his sons). Several features of these 1926 and 1927 remarks about uniquely human protracted childhood helplessness deserve attention.

First of all, Freud's reflections bring up the connection between infantile *Hilflosigkeit* and "the need to be loved" (*Bedürfnis, geliebt zu werden*) or "the need for protection (*Schutz*) – for protection through love (*Schutz durch Liebe*)" (or also, as he puts it in a passage from 1933 quoted by me a while ago, the "*Liebesbedürfnis*"). Taking into account Freud's notions of human nature, particularly during this period of his thinking, it seems that both prematurational helplessness and the need for love are conceived by him as biologically innate features of the species *homo sapiens*. Yet how are these two natural factors related to each other? It appears that, according to both *Inhibitions, Symptoms and Anxiety* as well as *The Future of an Illusion* (and perhaps also *Project for a Scientific Psychology*), helplessness is responsible for generating the *Liebesbedürfnis* (as Freud says in 1926 in the block quotation immediately preceding, "The biological factor . . . creates the need to be loved"). However, taking into consideration the later Freud's repeated insistences on the innateness of Eros's life drives without accompanying references to helplessness, it is far from entirely clear whether he would commit to making the need for love dependent on *Hilflosigkeit* or instead would insist on this need being its own biological factor independent of, although abetted by, prematurational helplessness. Maybe for Freud, helplessness as cause transfers its naturalness to the need for love as its direct effect.

Despite any partial obscurity in the *Hilflosigkeit-Liebesbedürfnis* relationship, Freud is neither vague nor ambiguous in asserting that humans' lengthy period of helplessness, itself a biologically innate feature of their organic being, renders them social by nature. Starting with the early total and complete dependence on the *Nebenmensch*-as-helper (usually a caretaking parent or parents), the young subject-to-be is fated/destined (in Freud's sense of "*Schicksal*" as allowing for multiple, but not limitless, possible paths of development) by biology itself to be entangled with and formed by relations with others. One could say that, according to the psychoanalytic account of specifically human helplessness, human beings are naturally inclined to the dominance of nurture (i.e., social mediation via relations with conspecifics) over nature.

Furthermore, *Hilflosigkeit* entails a plasticity of human nature. As Freud indicates, for the psyche rooted in an initially helpless body, "the influence of the real external world upon it is intensified and an early differentiation between the ego and the id is promoted." Of course, the most important features of "the real external world" are social ones, namely, emotionally important others as exerting the decisive influences modulating the nascent subject's id and helping to sculpt its emerging ego. The Freudian psyche, with its plasticity, is naturally preprogrammed by helplessness to be socially reprogrammed.

So not only is Eros substantially empowered by the naturally given and ontogenetically primary couple *Hilflosigkeit-Liebesbedürfnis* – this couple also brings with it a psychical plasticity amounting to the susceptibility of the libidinal economy to being tamed and domesticated by its social milieu. Others' impositions of a social reality principle significantly shape the routes and directions of drives and their derivatives. More specifically, these impositions mold the contours of sublimations. Indeed, social valuations, as determining the substitutive object-choices of libidinal thrusts confronted with social prohibitions, are inherent to the very definition of sublimation as a concept in Freudian psychoanalysis.[75] As Marcuse comments apropos psychoanalytic drive theory, "The 'plasticity' of the instincts which this theory presupposes should suffice to refute the notion that the instincts are essentially unalterable biological substrata."[76]

Hence, the combination of prematurational helplessness and the need for love to which it gives rise renders the psychical-subject-to-be inclined toward socially specified sublimations. Such sublimations, in relation to Freud's 1920-onwards dual drive model, would not be limited exclusively to the side of Eros. Quite the contrary – considering the later Freud's depiction of aggression as much more existentially threatening to societies than sexuality, developing children inevitably are confronted with social regulations demanding sublimations of their aggression.

When, in 1933, Freud mentions humans' "drive (*Drang*) towards obtaining pleasure and avoiding unpleasure" (alongside "their self-preservative instinct" [*Selbsterhaltungstrieb*], "their aggressiveness" [*Aggressionslust*], and "their need to be loved" [*Liebesbedürfnis*]) in the context of criticizing socialism/communism, he is talking not about an individual drive (*Trieb*) or type of drive. Instead, he is speaking of the pleasure principle influencing the operations of all drives. Although the pleasure principle is no longer supreme for the later Freud beginning with 1920's *Jenseits des Lustprinzips*, its influence remains potent and pervasive throughout the psychical apparatus.

All sublimations amount to the pleasure principle continuing successfully to chase pleasure and dodge pain in the face of challenges thrown up to it by external social reality. Indeed, the Freudian reality principle could be defined as the pleasure principle (*Lustprinzip*) once modified in response to this external reality. All societies past, present, and future must generate various sublimations in their subjects. And if the pleasure principle is indeed as powerful as Freud maintains it to be, then no society, including a future communist one, could prevent its pursuit of pleasure (*Lust*) and avoidance of pain (*Unlust*). Moreover, the aggressiveness (*Aggressionslust*) Freud, in the *New Introductory Lectures on Psycho-Analysis*, invokes side by side with the pleasure principle clearly is open to sublimation and other drive-modifying vicissitudes (i.e., Freud's *Triebschicksale*).

According to Freud's own theory, aggression already is a secondary modification of the *Todestrieb*. The latter originally is an intra-psychically-directed self-destructiveness. Extra-psychically-directed destructiveness, aggression toward objects and others in external reality, already is a life-affirming deflection/displacement of this originally life-annulling suicidal tendency. For instance, in the 1933 lecture "Anxiety and Instinctual Life," Freud observes the following:

> We recognize two basic instincts (*zwei Grundtriebe*) and give each of them its own aim (*sein eigenes Ziel*). How the two of them are mingled

in the process of living, how the death instinct (*der Todestrieb*) is made to serve the purposes of Eros, especially by being turned outwards as aggressiveness – these are tasks which are left to future investigation.[77]

In "Why War?" from the same year, he remarks, "There is no question of getting rid entirely of human aggressive impulses (*die menschliche Aggressionsneigung*); it is enough to try to divert them to such an extent that they need not find expression in war."[78] Several things merit noting here. To begin with, Freud indeed treats exogenous aggression as a secondary modification of the death drive's primary endogenous self-destructiveness, with Eros playing a role in bringing about this modification.

However, Freud, in "Anxiety and Instinctual Life," confesses his uncertainty regarding the details of exactly how Eros comes to influence and steer the *Todestrieb*, deflecting it from being self-directed to becoming other-directed. This is an issue to be "left to future investigation." Interestingly, in the very same context, Freud's not-unrelated discussions of the prospects of Marxist revolutionary endeavors similarly leave much to be decided by the unpredictable future of social history. Parallel to the unfinished business of the Eros-*Todestrieb* relationship in psychoanalysis's metapsychological theory, there are the unforeseeable vicissitudes-to-come of this same relationship at the level of Marxism's political practice.

Incidentally, Freud's speculative posit according to which the death drive's exogenous destructiveness already is a secondary detour for its primary endogenous self-destructiveness raises an interesting question in connection with his reservations regarding Marxism's prospects. As seen, Freud frets that the *Todestrieb* as aggression (i.e., exogenous destructiveness) will be resistant to and disruptive of any socialist or communist sociopolitical project. Yet if this aggression is itself a dilution and redirection of a more primordial undercurrent of endogenous self-destructiveness, then could not a Marxist program extolling and enjoining self-sacrifice for the sake of the revolutionary cause appeal to and tap into the foundational, archaic thrust of the death drive prior to its channeling into outwardly directed hostility? Would not the sacrificial self-renunciations demanded by the radical reinvention of society facilitate, perhaps once again with some assistance from Eros, a sort of socialist/communist desublimation tapping back into the original incarnation of the *Todestrieb*? Freud, in his criticisms of Marxism, neither asks nor answers the question: why should one presume, as Freud himself appears to do, that the psyche's libidinal economy always and inevitably would prefer satisfying the death drive(s) through capitalism's selfish economic competition (i.e., sublimated aggression as itself the exogenous destructiveness already deflecting endogenous self-destructiveness) rather than socialism's or communism's self-sacrificial social renewals (i.e., sublimated self-aggression)?

The very last set of Freud's observations about Marxism from 1933's lecture "The Question of a *Weltanschauung*" again speak about the uncertain outcomes *à venir* of the then-new socialist experiment in Russia and the Soviet Union. Freud engages in the following imaginary exchange with the Bolsheviks he has been criticizing intermittently in the *New Introductory Lectures on Psycho-Analysis* (and along lines already spelled out a few years prior in *Civilization and Its Discontents*):

> There is no doubt of how Bolshevism will reply to these objections. It will say that so long as men's nature has not yet been transformed it is necessary to make use of the means which affect them to-day. It is impossible to do without compulsions (*Zwang*) in their education, without the prohibition of thought and without the employment of force to the point of bloodshed; and if the illusions were not awakened in them, they could not be brought to acquiesce in this compulsion. And we should be politely asked to say how things could be managed differently. This would defeat us. I could think of no advice to give. I should admit that the conditions of this experiment would have deterred me and those like me from undertaking it; but we are not the only people concerned. There are men of action, unshakeable in their convictions, inaccessible to doubt (*unzugänglich dem Zweifel*), without feeling for the sufferings of others if they stand in the way of their intentions. We have to thank men of this kind for the fact that the tremendous experiment (*großartige Versuch*) of producing a new order of this kind is now actually being carried out in Russia. At a time when the great nations announce that they expect salvation only from the maintenance of Christian piety, the revolution in Russia – in spite of all its disagreeable details – seems none the less like the message of a better future. Unluckily neither our scepticism (*unserem Zweifel*) nor the fanatical faith (*fanatischen Glauben*) of the other side gives a hint as to how the experiment will turn out. The future will tell us; perhaps it will show that the experiment was undertaken

prematurely (*vorzeitig*), that a sweeping alteration of the social order has little prospect of success until new discoveries have increased our control over the forces of Nature and so made easier the satisfaction of our needs (*die Befriedigung unserer Bedürfnisse*). Only then perhaps may it become possible for a new social order (*eine neue Gesellschaftsordnung*) not only to put an end to the material need of the masses but also to give a hearing to the cultural demands of the individual (*die kulturellen Ansprüche des Einzelnen*). Even then, to be sure, we shall still have to struggle for an incalculable time with the difficulties which the untameable character of human nature (*die Unbändigkeit der menschlichen Natur*) presents to every kind of social community (*sozialer Gemeinschaft*).[79]

Freud, in his extreme intellectual honesty, reaches this point of admitting that his "scepticism" apropos Bolshevism by no means amounts to any knockdown arguments against it and the Marxist tradition of which it is a part. He grants that the October Revolution "seems . . . like the message of a better future," at least by comparison with bourgeois false promises of "salvation only from the maintenance of Christian piety." As for the eventual outcome of the socialist experiment, "The future will tell us."

Freud obviously has in mind the figure of Lenin as epitomizing the sort of Bolshevik he employs in the previous section as an imagined foil for his own doubts about socialism/communism (i.e., "men of action, unshakeable in their convictions, inaccessible to doubt, without feeling for the sufferings of others if they stand in the way of their intentions"). Freud's hypothesis that the future might reveal the October Revolution to have been "premature" echoes certain criticisms of Lenin's politics voiced even from within non-Leninist currents of Marxism (by contemporaneous representatives of the Second International, German Social Democracy, Menshevism, etc.). Likewise, whether Freud realizes it or not, his related speculation that a viable post-capitalist "new social order" balancing collective and individual goods might require an extremely high degree of scientific and technological development (in particular, higher than that achieved in feudal-agrarian Tsarist Russia on the eve of the Bolshevik Revolution) resonates with moments in Marx's writings as well as with the perspectives of certain factions within Marxism. Yet Freud, in the face of what he anticipates by way of the Bolsheviks' self-justification in response to his reservations, concedes that "this would defeat us. I could think of no advice to give." With Freud's many vacillations and hesitations apropos socialism, communism, and Bolshevism, it would be fair to say that he evinces a marked ambivalence *vis-à-vis* Marxism.

But despite Freud's oscillations and inconsistencies in his reactions to Marxism, the final sentence of the prior block quotation amounts to him reiterating his oft-repeated claim that human nature as per psychoanalysis poses a perhaps insurmountable barrier to Marxism's revolutionary political-economic agenda ("we shall still have to struggle for an incalculable time with the difficulties which the untameable character of human nature (*die Unbändigkeit der menschlichen Natur*) presents to every kind of social community (*sozialer Gemeinschaft*)"). James Strachey chooses to render "*Unbändigkeit*" as "untameable character" likely because of this German word occurring in an argumentative context in which Freud is suggesting that "*menschlichen Natur*" will resist efforts to significantly reform or transform it. However, "*unbändig*" could be translated into English as "boisterous" and/or "unrestrained."

As I demonstrated at length in the preceding, the various elements of "human nature" Freud has in mind when criticizing Marxism are not, according to Freud's own psychoanalytic reasoning, "untameable" in the strong sense, namely, utterly impervious to domesticating social influences bringing about sublimations and the like. That is to say, this nature might be boisterous but still not untameable. Analysis indeed provides ample evidence for this boisterousness. Additionally, it also provides ample evidence that this boisterousness can be, and usually is, tamed by external realities, including social ones.

Recall once again the components of human nature Freud lists in the 1933 lecture "The Question of a *Weltanschauung*": human beings' "self-preservative instinct (*Selbsterhaltungstrieb*), their aggressiveness (*Aggressionslust*), their need to be loved (*Liebesbedürfnis*), their drive (*Drang*) towards obtaining pleasure and avoiding unpleasure." As I argued, three out of four of these components – these are self-preservation, the need for love, and the pleasure principle – pose no special resistances specifically to socialism/communism and, at least potentially, could be better served by, and hence be more cooperative with, socialist/communist social orders. Of these four, Freud tends to single out aggression as the key feature of "*die Unbändigkeit der menschlichen Natur*" constituting a major challenge for Marxist politics and its revolutionary socioeconomic ambitions.

Yet *Aggressionslust* and the *Todestrieb* underlying it are not, by Freud's own lights, untameable. Again, aggression itself already is, for Freud, an Eros-assisted taming of the originally self-destructive death drive. Furthermore, I would observe that aggression can be and indeed is sublimated in myriad manners. Freud himself furnishes countless clinical and cultural examples of such sublimations of aggression in the forms of, for instance, sexual practices, ethico-moral stances, professional rivalries, social status aspirations, and so on. Were aggressiveness not so readily tameable (*als bändig*), future socialist and communist societies would not be the only ones to be in trouble – past and present non-socialist/non-communist societies would not have maintained their basic group coherence and would not be able to continue maintaining such coherence in the face of a critical mass of unsublimated individual aggression. Untamed and untameable *Aggressionslust* would be characteristic of the pre/anti-social anarchy of the mythical state of nature, not of any viable social order. The myriad sublimations of aggression testify to its boisterousness but not its untameability.

From a Marxist perspective, I would go even further and assert that capitalist societies foster sublimations of aggression in fashions that help make possible post-capitalist socialist/communist social accommodations of the *Aggressionslust* Freud fears socialist/communist social systems could not accommodate. What I am about to propose is an addition, inspired by a Marxist appreciation of psychoanalysis, to Marxism's inventory of those features of capitalism serving as historical conditions of possibility for the sublation of capitalism via socialism and communism. As with other capitalist phenomena, this is an instance of something that, although superficially appearing to be distant from and/or antagonistic to socialism/communism, actually has the potential to be conducive to such post-capitalist arrangements.

As is common knowledge, competition is central to capitalism. The early stages of capitalist industrialization involved economic sectors in which multiple isolated small producers (for instance, individual factories and their owners) jostled with each other for advantage in given markets. Although such small-producer competition long ago ceased to be a dominant essential feature of capitalist economies, a mythic celebration of such competition continues to live on in capitalist ideologies right up through the present day.

What is more, forms of competition historical materialism would identify as originating at the infrastructural level of capitalist societies have spread like wildfire across the expanses and throughout all the nooks and crannies of the superstructural levels of these same societies. So many of the cultural and political diversions and concerns within capitalism clearly are superstructural sublimations of infrastructural competition, with agonistic competition itself arguably being a sublimation of even more antagonistic and violent aggression. Under capitalism, institutions and spectacles having to do with everything from government and education to sports and games come to be organized as zero-sum, winners-versus-losers competitions, or at least as semblances thereof. Even the sex and love lives of capitalism's subjects are not untouched by subliminatory permutations of cutthroat economic competition. Indeed, as the *Communist Manifesto* already proclaimed in 1848, nothing whatsoever is sacred to capital.[80]

Although historical materialism would propose that superstructural forms of competitiveness originate in capitalism's earlier modes of infrastructural competition, I would venture to posit that, over the subsequent course of capitalist economic history, economic competition has itself been transformed, at least in significant part, into a type of not-immediately-economic competition. Put differently, capitalists' competitiveness about the accumulation of surplus-value, itself a sublimation of aggression as per psychoanalysis,[81] has come to be sublimated in turn by the superstructural sublimations this infrastructural competitiveness initially inspired. In still other words, the riches at stake in the race between capitalists to amass surplus-value primarily in the guise of money come to be more-than-economic signifiers of social status, cultural prestige, political power, and the like. In a reversal resonating with a psychoanalytic sensibility encapsulated in William Wordsworth's "The child is the father of the man," the infrastructural parent (i.e., economic competition) has become the child of its superstructural children (i.e., more-than-economic competition). Perhaps this dynamic of an earlier sublimation being recast in the guise of the later sublimations to which it gives rise should be baptized "retroactive resublimation."

Taking the preceding points apropos competition into account, Freud's worries about aggression specifically as an insuperable difficulty for socialism/communism can be largely, if not completely, laid to rest. In particular, two related lines of counter-argumentation *vis-à-vis* Freud on Marxism-versus-aggressiveness now are available at this juncture. First, capitalism, in fostering the proliferation of superstructural, socio-symbolic sublimations of infrastructural competitiveness (with the latter as already a sublimation of Freud's *Todestrieb-als-Aggressionslust*), provides potential future socialist/communist societies with ample outlets for the aggressive tendencies of these societies' members. Even with the abolition of private property qua capital and, along with it, the wealth disparities of class-stratified social configurations, capitalism leaves behind and bequeaths to its historical successors plenty of more-than-economic opportunities for (competitively) marking differences between persons.

However desirable or not, the sublimated aggression of jockeying for socio-symbolic inequality of recognition and superiority likely will remain after the disappearance of directly material-economic inequality. Twentieth-century experiments in Really Existing Socialism, such as that inaugurated by the Bolsheviks' October Revolution, demonstrated as much. *Contra* the later Freud's expectations, these sociopolitical systems arguably did not fail due to a lack of opportunities for the subliminatory venting of aggression via these systems' subjects jostling with each other for system-acknowledged advantage, influence, and reputation.

Just as socialist/communist societies can and do take over the science, technology, and infrastructural machinery of the capitalist mode of production, with such appropriation being crucial for the viability and success of these post-capitalist orders, so too can such societies also take over the non-economic sublimations of aggression developed by capitalism at its superstructural levels. If, as per Freud, *Aggressionslust* must be satisfied, if only in sublimated manners, then more-than-economic competitiveness ought to do the job effectively enough. By Freud's own criteria, the measure of such sufficiency ought to be whether these sublimations allow for avoiding the unsublimated/desublimated violence of outright war, including the war of all against all, as per the previously quoted remark from "Why War?" about "human aggressive impulses" according to which, "it is enough to try to divert them to such an extent that they need not find expression in war."

I come now to the second line of counter-argumentation with respect to Freud on Marxism-versus-aggressiveness. A moment ago, I described a capitalism-immanent process of economic competitiveness, itself a sublimation of aggression, becoming just one among the more-than-economic permutations of competitiveness (as themselves superstructural sublimations of infrastructural competition-as-sublimation-of-aggression). Especially past a certain threshold in the stacking up of massive amounts of surplus-value, wealth as quotas of quantifiable exchange-value is, for such incredibly affluent capitalists, more about, for example, outranking each other on lists of the most wealthy individuals, garnering greater amounts of media attention, commanding outsize sway over politics, or outdoing one another in socially praised public philanthropy. For such persons as bearers/personifications of capital, money is no longer really about money, if it ever was in the first place.

Hence, the sublimated aggression deep-pocketed capitalists gratify through economic competition, as a competition already about, for these subjects, things different from quantitative wealth alone, is ready-made to be socially re-translated into expressions in terms other than purely monetary ones. Such capitalists' masses of surplus/exchange-values are so far in excess of what could be personally consumed by them and their entourages in tangible qualitative use-values as to reveal that this amassing is not motivated by the desire to consume material riches. The latter subjective motive should be seen here in contrast with the animating logic of capital, M-C-M′, as the self-enhancing, ever-growing spiral of intangible quantitative exchange-values via capital's appropriation of labor-produced surplus-values.

Capitalists appear, at the intersection of Marxism and psychoanalysis, in two distinct but not unrelated lights. From the Marxist angle, they are primarily, in their role as capital's personifications/bearers (*Personifikationen/Träger*), de-psychologized agents of the structural dynamic of M-C-M′. As such, they are concerned, however consciously or not, exclusively with the in-principle infinite accumulation of quantitative surplus- and exchange-values. But from the psychoanalytic angle, they also are more than just such mere personifications/bearers.

As Freud himself would emphasize, capital's agents additionally are, among other things, psychical subjects of enjoyments having to do with socio-symbolic secondary gains exuded from the pure accumulation of capital. Insofar as these secondary gains, as superstructural by-products of capitalism's infrastructural logic, can be generated by strictly superstructural socio-symbolic pursuits, they can be had without the economic category of capitalist private property (i.e., individually owned means of production). Again, the psyches of capital's *Personifikationen/Träger* should be able to satisfy their aggression-tinged libidinal investments in inter- and trans-subjectively recognized prestige, renown, status, etc.

through subliminatory means other than the strictly economic competition associated with the capitalist mode of production. Realizing this goes a long way toward a Marxism that has passed through, rather than simply bypassed, Freud's psychoanalytic reservations about its feasibility.

Notes

1 Russell Jacoby, *Social Amnesia: A Critique of Conformist Psychology from Adler to Laing*, Boston: Beacon Press, 1975, pg. 25.
2 Thomas Hobbes, *The Citizen: Philosophical Rudiments Concerning Government and Society, Man and Citizen* [ed. Bernard Gert], New York: Anchor, 1972, pg. 89–90) Cf. *SE* 21: 111–112; Elmar Waibl, *Gesellschaft und Kultur bei Hobbes und Freud*, Vienna: Löcker, 1980, pg. 19, 27, 35, 40, 63, 78–79, 81; Jean Roy, *Hobbes and Freud* [trans. Thomas G. Osler], Toronto: Canadian Philosophical Monographs, 1984, pg. vii, 17.
3 *SE* 21: 113.
4 Antonio Gramsci, "Letter to Julca Schucht, December 30, 1929," *Letters from Prison, Volume One* [ed. Frank Rosengarten; trans. Raymond Rosenthal], New York: Columbia University Press, 1994, pg. 302.
5 *Standard Edition of the Complete Psychological Works of Sigmund Freud*, trans. J. Strachey, London: Hogarth Press, Vol. 20: 113. Hereafter all references to the Standard Edition will refer to *SE* followed by volume and page number.
6 Sigm. Freud, *Gesammelte Werke: Chronologisch Geordnet*, London: Imago Publishing Co., Vol. 14: 472–473; *SE* 21: 113. Hereafter all references to the *Gesammelte Werke* will refer to *GW* followed by volume and page number.
7 *GW* 14: 473; *SE* 21: 113.
8 *SE* 21: 113.
9 *SE* 21: 113–114.
10 *SE* 21: 115.
11 *SE* 21: 143.
12 *GW* 14: 504; *SE* 21: 143.
13 *SE* 21: 143.
14 Jacques Lacan, *Le Séminaire de Jacques Lacan, Livre XVII: L'envers de la psychanalyse, 1969–1970* [ed. Jacques-Alain Miller], Paris: Éditions du Seuil, 1991, pg. 102; Jacques Lacan, *The Seminar of Jacques Lacan, Book XVII: The Other Side of Psychoanalysis, 1969–1970* [ed. Jacques-Alain Miller; trans. Russell Grigg], New York: W.W. Norton and Company, 2007, pg. 90.
15 Lacan, *The Seminar of Jacques Lacan, Book XVII*, pg. 92, 206–207; Jacques Lacan, "*Acte de fondation*," *Autres écrits* [ed. Jacques-Alain Miller], Paris: Éditions du Seuil, 2001, pg. 237; Jacques Lacan, "*Radiophonie*," *Autres écrits*, pg. 424; Jacques Lacan, "Television" [trans. Denis Hollier, Rosalind Krauss, and Annette Michelson], *Television/A Challenge to the Psychoanalytic Establishment* [ed. Joan Copjec], New York: W.W. Norton and Company, 1990, pg. 30–31.

16 Jacques Lacan, *The Seminar of Jacques Lacan, Book XXIII: The Sinthome, 1975–1976* [ed. Jacques-Alain Miller; trans. A.R. Price], Cambridge: Polity, 2016, pg. 117.
17 Jacques Lacan, "Du discours psychanalytique," *Lacan in Italia, 1953–1978*, Milan: La Salamandra, 1978, pg. 46.
18 Jacques Lacan, *Le Séminaire de Jacques Lacan, Livre VI: Le désir et son interprétation, 1958–1959* [ed. Jacques-Alain Miller], Paris: Éditions de la Martinière, 2013, pg. 486–487.
19 Jacques Lacan, *Le Séminaire de Jacques Lacan, Livre XXI: Les non-dupes errent, 1973–1974* [unpublished typescript], session of March 19, 1974.
20 Jacques Lacan, *Le Séminaire de Jacques Lacan, Livre XIII: L'objet de la psychanalyse, 1965–1966* [unpublished typescript], session of January 12, 1966; Jacques Lacan, *Le Séminaire de Jacques Lacan, Livre XVI: D'un Autre à l'autre, 1968–1969* [ed. Jacques-Alain Miller], Paris: Éditions du Seuil, 2006, pg. 17, 240; (Lacan, *The Seminar of Jacques Lacan, Book XVII*, pg. 206.
21 *SE* 22: 180, 208, 211–212.
22 *SE* 22: 67, 178–179.
23 *GW* 15: 73–74; *SE* 22: 67.
24 *GW* 14: 501–505; *SE* 21: 141–144.
25 Friedrich Engels, "Letter to Conrad Schmidt, October 27, 1890," www.marxists.org/archive/marx/works/1890/letters/90_10_27.htm.
26 A.R. Luria, "Psychoanalysis as a System of Monistic Psychology," *Soviet Psychology*, vol. 16, no. 2, 1977, pg. 41.
27 Jacoby, *Social Amnesia*, pg. 84.
28 Karl Marx, "Karl-Marx-Ausgabe: Werke-Schriften-Briefe, Band IV: Ökonomische Schriften, erster Band [ed. Hans-Joachim Lieber]," *Das Kapital: Kritik der politischen Ökonomie, erster Band*, Darmstadt: Wissenschaftliche Buchgesellschaft, 1962, pg. 147–148; Karl Marx, *Capital: A Critique of Political Economy, Volume One* [trans. Ben Fowkes], New York: Penguin, 1976, pg. 254–255; Karl Marx, *Theories of Surplus-Value, Part One: Volume IV of Capital* [ed. S. Ryazanskaya; trans. Emile Burns], Moscow: Progress Publishers, 1963, pg. 282, 389; Karl Marx, *Theories of Surplus-Value, Part Three: Volume IV of Capital* [ed. S.W. Ryazanskaya and Richard Dixon; trans. Jack Cohen and S.W. Ryazanskaya], Moscow: Progress Publishers, 1971, pg. 296.
29 Jacques Lacan, *The Seminar of Jacques Lacan, Book XX: Encore, 1972–1973* [ed. Jacques-Alain Miller; trans. Bruce Fink], New York: W.W. Norton and Company, 1998, pg. 3, 7–8.
30 *SE* 4: 318; *SE* 5: 596; *SE* 14: 186; *SE* 22: 73–74.
31 *SE* 14: 187.
32 *SE* 22: 73.
33 *SE* 21: 142–143.
34 *SE* 22: 61–62, 163–164.
35 *SE* 19: 167.
36 Karl Marx, *Grundrisse: Foundations of the Critique of Political Economy (Rough Draft)* [trans. Martin Nicolaus], New York: Penguin, 1973, pg. 232; Karl Marx, *A Contribution to the Critique of Political Economy* [ed. Maurice Dobb; trans. S.W. Ryazanskaya], New York: International, 1970, pg. 130; Marx, *Theories of Surplus-Value, Part Three*, pg. 448.

37 *GW* 15: 194–195; *SE* 22: 179–180.
38 *SE* 22: 176–177.
39 *SE* 22: 158–182.
40 Karl Marx, "Letter to Mikhailovsky," *Karl Marx: Selected Writings* [ed. David McLellan], Oxford: Oxford University Press, 1977, pg. 572.
41 Karl Marx, "Letter to Vera Sassoulitch," *Karl Marx*, pg. 576–580; Karl Marx, "Preface to the Russian Edition of the *Communist Manifesto*," *Karl Marx*, pg. 583–584; Karl Marx, "Letters 1863–1881: Marx to Kugelmann, 17 Apr. 1871," *Karl Marx*, pg. 593.
42 Karl Marx and Friedrich Engels, *The Communist Manifesto*, *Karl Marx*, Oxford: Oxford University Press, 1977, pg. 222.
43 Jacoby, *Social Amnesia*, pg. xviii.
44 Herbert Marcuse, "Repressive Tolerance," in *A Critique of Pure Tolerance* [ed. Robert Paul Wolff, Barrington Moore, Jr. and Herbert Marcuse], Boston: Beacon Press, 1969, pg. 81–123; Martin Jay, *The Dialectical Imagination: A History of the Frankfurt School and the Institute of Social Research, 1923–1950*, Boston: Little, Brown and Company, 1973, pg. 97.
45 Herbert Marcuse, *Eros and Civilization: A Philosophical Inquiry into Freud*, Boston: Beacon Press, 1974, pg. 99–101, 224–225; Herbert Marcuse, *One-Dimensional Man: Studies in the Ideology of Advanced Industrial Society*, Boston: Beacon Press, 1964, pg. 72; Herbert Marcuse, *An Essay on Liberation*, Boston: Beacon Press, 1969, pg. 9). (Herbert Marcuse, "Progress and Freud's Theory of Instincts," *Five Lectures: Psychoanalysis, Politics, and Utopia* [trans. Jeremy J. Shapiro and Shierry M. Weber], Boston: Beacon Press, 1970, pg. 38–39; (Herbert Marcuse, "The Obsolescence of the Freudian Concept of Man," *Five Lectures*, pg. 57–58; Herbert Marcuse, *Counterrevolution and Revolt*, Boston: Beacon Press, 1972, pg. 59–60, 76, 80, 113; Marcuse, "Repressive Tolerance," pg. 114–115; Paul A. Robinson, *The Freudian Left: Wilhelm Reich, Geza Roheim, Herbert Marcuse*, New York: Harper & Row, 1969, pg. 240; Martin Jay, "Irony and Dialectics: *One-Dimensional Man* and 1968," *Splinters in Your Eye: Frankfurt School Provocations*, London: Verso, 2020, pg. 140.
46 Marcuse, "Repressive Tolerance," pg. 85.
47 Marcuse, "Repressive Tolerance," pg. 98.
48 Louis Althusser, "Marxism and Humanism," *For Marx* [trans. Ben Brewster], London: Verso, 2005, pg. 232–236; Louis Althusser, *On the Reproduction of Capitalism: Ideology and Ideological State Apparatuses* [trans. G.M. Goshgarian], London: Verso, 2014, pg. 84; Louis Althusser, *Que faire?* [ed. G.M. Goshgarian], Paris: Presses Universitaires de France, 2018, pg. 32–33.
49 Marx, *A Contribution to the Critique of Political Economy*, pg. 21.
50 Antonio Gramsci, *Prison Notebooks, Volume Two* [ed. and trans. Joseph A. Buttigieg], New York: Columbia University Press, 1996, Fourth Notebook, §15 [pg. 157–158], §38 [pg. 184].
51 *GW* 15: 193–194; *SE* 22: 178–179.
52 Max Weber, *The Protestant Ethic and the "Spirit" of Capitalism, the Protestant Ethics and the "Spirit" of Capitalism and Other Writings* [ed. and trans. Peter Baehr and Gordon C. Wells], New York: Penguin, 2002, pg. 13–14, 19, 26, 197; Max Weber, "Remarks on the Foregoing 'Reply'," *The Protestant*

Ethics and the "Spirit" of Capitalism and Other Writings, pg. 233–234, 241–242; Max Weber, "Rebuttal of the Critique of the 'Spirit' of Capitalism," *The Protestant Ethics and the "Spirit" of Capitalism and Other Writings*, pg. 262.
53. Gramsci, *Prison Notebooks, Volume Two*, Fourth Notebook, §38 [pg. 185].
54. Karl Marx, *Economic and Philosophical Manuscripts, Early Writings* [trans. Rodney Livingstone and Gregor Benton], New York: Penguin, 1975, pg. 328–329; Marx, *Capital, Volume One*, pg. 284; (Friedrich Engels, *Ludwig Feuerbach and the Outcome of Classical German Philosophy* [ed. C.P. Dutt], New York: International, 1941, pg. 48–49, 52–53.
55. *SE* 18: 42–43, 50, 52, 60–61, 91–92, 258–259; *SE* 19: 40–47, 56, 159–160, 163–164, 218, 239; *SE* 20: 57, 122, 265; *SE* 21: 108, 210; *SE* 22: 103–104; *SE* 23: 148–151, 197–198, 242–243, 246–247.
56. *GW* 13: 289; *SE* 19: 59.
57. *SE* 21: 122.
58. *GW* 14: 481; *SE* 21: 122.
59. *GW* 14: 506; *SE* 21: 145.
60. Russell Jacoby, *The Repression of Psychoanalysis: Otto Fenichel and the Political Freudians*, New York: Basic Books, 1983, pg. 104; Peter Gay, *Freud: A Life for Our Time*, New York: W.W. Norton and Company, 1988, pg. 546–550; Joel Whitebook, *Perversion and Utopia: A Study in Psychoanalysis and Critical Theory*, Cambridge: MIT Press, 1995, pg. 97; Jean-Marie Vaysse, *L'inconscient des modernes: Essai sur l'origine métaphysique de la psychanalyse*, Paris: Gallimard, 1999, pg. 446–447.
61. Jay, *The Dialectical Imagination*, pg. 105.
62. Edwin R. Wallace, *Freud and Anthropology: A History and Reappraisal*, New York: International Universities Press, 1983, pg. 54.
63. José Brunner, *Freud and the Politics of Psychoanalysis*, London: Transaction Publishers, 2001, pg. 75–76.
64. Philip Rieff, *Freud: The Mind of the Moralist*, Chicago: University of Chicago Press, 1979, pg. 221–222.
65. Paul Ricoeur, *Freud and Philosophy: An Essay on Interpretation* [trans. Denis Savage], New Haven: Yale University Press, 1970, pg. 211; Whitebook, *Perversion and Utopia*, pg. 21–22.
66. *SE* 13: 140–161; Rieff, *Freud*, pg. 222–223.
67. Roy, *Hobbes and Freud*, pg. viii, 59–60.
68. Jean-Jacques Rousseau, *Discourse on the Origin and Foundations of Inequality Among Men (Second Discourse)*, *The First and Second Discourses* [ed. Roger D. Masters; trans. Roger D. Masters and Judith R. Masters], New York: Saint Martin's Press, 1964, pg. 128–131; Louis Althusser, *Psychoanalysis and the Human Sciences* [trans. Steven Rendall], New York: Columbia University Press, 2016, pg. 60–63.
69. Marcuse, *Eros and Civilization*, pg. 147.
70. Lacan, *The Seminar of Jacques Lacan, Book XX*, pg. 90–91; Jacques Lacan, *Le Séminaire de Jacques Lacan, Livre XXII: R.S.I., 1974–1975* [unpublished typescript], session of April 15, 1975.
71. *SE* 1: 318; *SE* 20: 154–155, 167; *SE* 21: 17–19, 30.

72 Sigmund Freud, *Entwurf einer Psychologie, Aus den Anfängen der Psychoanalyse, 1887–1902* [ed. Marie Bonaparte, Anna Freud, and Ernst Kris], Frankfurt am Main: S. Fischer, 1975, pg. 326; *SE* 1: 318.
73 *GW* 14: 186–187; *SE* 20: 154–155.
74 *GW* 14: 352; *SE* 21: 30.
75 Jean Laplanche and Jean-Bertrand Pontalis, *The Language of Psycho-Analysis* [trans. Donald Nicholson-Smith], New York: W.W. Norton and Company, 1973, pg. 431.
76 Herbert Marcuse, "Freedom and Freud's Theory of Instincts," *Five Lectures*, pg. 7.
77 *GW* 15: 115; *SE* 22: 107.
78 *GW* 16: 23; *SE* 22: 212.
79 *GW* 15: 196–197; *SE* 22: 180–181.
80 Marx and Engels, *The Communist Manifesto*, pg. 223–224.
81 Gilles Dostaler and Bernard Maris, *Capitalisme et pulsion de mort*, Paris: Fayard, 2010, pg. 9, 21.

Chapter 3

Recapitulation and the Vicissitudes of Progress, From Freud to the Frankfurt School
"The Germ of the Regression"

Frank Pittenger

> Historical materialism wishes to retain that image of the past which unexpectedly appears to man singled out by history at a moment of danger.
>
> (Benjamin, 1950/1968, pp. 255)

Attentive readers of Freud can attest to his fondness for the long-discredited theory of biogenetic recapitulation, which is best remembered by its defining mantra, "ontogeny recapitulates phylogeny," that is, the idea that the development of any individual organism (or ontogenesis) repeats in compressed, miniaturized form the entire history of its species (or phylogenesis). Indeed, what contemporary readers often find inaccessible or simply bizarre about a work like *Totem and Taboo* coheres abruptly when Freud's commitment to recapitulationism is fully appreciated.

Variously branded the biogenetic principle, the biogenetic law, and biogenetic recapitulationism, the theory enjoyed broad (if not uncontested) acceptance during the early twentieth century. While originally intended to stress the process of phylogenetic improvement, in Freud's (e.g., 1920/1961) hands, recapitulationism tended to function as an explanation for regression, degeneration, and "involution," expressing deep anxiety about the possibilities of social and evolutionary progress (p. 50). While they disregard the original biological referents of the theory, Frankfurt School readings of works in which Freud's recapitulationism was most prominent echo both this anxiety and its use as a vehicle for social critique. This is especially true of *Eros and Civilization*, where Marcuse (1955/1966) bases his critique of Fromm and likeminded neo-Freudians on a subtle but far-reaching reappropriation of Freud's recapitulationism.

DOI: 10.4324/9781003215301-3

Admittedly, with the exception of *Eros and Civilization*, one searches in vain for explicit applications of recapitulationism in the Frankfurt School oeuvre. Instead we find passing references, many of them critical or superficially dismissing – say, Fromm's denunciations of Freud's pessimistic brand of evolutionism, not to mention his early and emphatic repudiation of the (admittedly Haeckelian) Oedipus complex as a template for the study of society (Fromm, 1932/1970; Burston, 1991; Durkin, 2014).[1] For his part, Freud never presented a sustained case for the biogenetic principle, treating it instead as an a priori biological given. That said, the theory of biogenetic recapitulation (and by extension the influence of "archaic heritage" or "archaic inheritance" upon modernity) was but one among several components of Freud's metapsychology, which also presupposed the operation of Lamarckian inheritance within psychic evolution (Marcaggi & Guénolé, 2018; Ritvo, 1990). Still, as historians have long observed (e.g., Dufresne, 2000; Gould, 1977; Sulloway, 1979), the impact of the theory is traceable throughout Freud's clinical and metapsychological writings, amounting to a kind of Rosetta Stone for a subtextual language. As I argue in the following section, the same peripheral influence and critical function are hiding in plain sight within postwar Frankfurt School appeals to psychoanalytic metapsychology.

As is well-known, Freud's recapitulationism grew more pronounced even as the theory itself fell by the wayside among biologists (Otis, 1994; Gould, 1977). Yet sadly, Freud's critics seldom examine the curiously tragic, indeed critical *use* that Freud made of the ostensible parallels between ontogeny and phylogeny. Indeed, even after it had been abandoned as a plausible mechanism of natural selection and individual development, recapitulationism remained invested – or in Freudian terminology, cathected – with a highly moral anxiety. It was this anxiety, centered on the themes of progress and regress, that was amplified in the psychoanalytic speculations of Adorno, Horkheimer, and Marcuse.

That being so, the wholly non-biological appropriation of this concept within the Frankfurt School requires a twofold contextualization. First, I summarize the social and historical dimensions of the biogenetic recapitulationism first introduced by the German biologist Ernst Haeckel (1834–1919), emphasizing the burgeoning contradictions within his commitment to the idea's progressivism ("burgeoning," that is, because Freud seized upon a regressive tendency already latent within Haeckel's theory). Secondly, I discuss the centrality of recapitulationism in Freud's metapsychological writings. Whereas Haeckel understood biogenetic recapitulation as being primarily a vehicle for progress, by the time Freud completed *Beyond the Pleasure Principle*, the idea had come to describe *a bidirectional psychosocial process*, one in which the ontogenetic reenactment of evolution is forever subject to reversal.

First, however, a brief note on terminology is in order. Anyone who wades into the history and "afterlife" of recapitulationism may be forgiven for feeling overwhelmed by a flush of peculiar jargon. Besides being a gifted illustrator, Ernst Haeckel, who systematized the biogenetic law, was an inveterate neologist. As with his evolutionary and social theory, some of his semantic innovations (e.g., "ecology" [*Ökologie*]) have proved more lasting than others.[2] While I try to define his more obscure terms when they appear, the following terms require clarification from the outset.

In brief, "ontogeny" refers to the process of individual development; "psychic ontogenesis," for instance, means the phasic sequence of individual psychological growth from infancy into adulthood. "Phylogeny" refers to the evolutionary history of a species. Thus, Haeckel's (1874/1900) "Phylogeny of the *psyche*" refers to the evolution of the human mind across natural history (vol. 1, p. 23). To say, then, that "ontogeny recapitulates phylogeny" is to say that individual development reenacts or repeats the evolutionary history of its species. Psychologically, this means that in the process of maturation, a child must traverse in compressed form the entire evolutionary history of the mind.

Also, lest we disagree regarding what does and does not qualify as "critical theory," I follow Kieran Durkin's (2019) grouping of the movement's members under the rubric of "a series of *shared axes* and broadly *cognate concerns* that revolve around these axes" (p. 113). In this framework, their positions are "subtly but crucially divergent" but in a dialectical manner that attests to their underlying kinship and ultimately functions to bind them historically. Still, because Marcuse (1955/1966) hazarded the most sustained engagement with the biogenetic principle in his "cryptorevisionist" reading of Freud's concept of archaic inheritance, the lion's share of my discussion here focuses on the reappraisal of the death drive and critique of Fromm found in *Eros and Civilization*.[3]

Ernst Haeckel and Pre-psychoanalytic Recapitulationism

Despite the optimistic, progressive spirit that once animated evolutionary psychologies grounded in recapitulationism, by the time much of the scientific community were won over to "Haeckel's law," the teleology of recapitulationary theory had begun to undergo a directional shift, one that quietly presaged its appropriation first by Freud and later by Adorno, Horkheimer, and Marcuse. While initially presented by Haeckel as a "law" that undergirds the progressive, teleological process of evolution, by the turn of the century, recapitulationism increasingly gave expression to the fears of social and cultural regression or "devolution" that preoccupied psychological theorists in *fin de siècle* Europe and North America.

Such fears found vivid expression in (often explicitly racist) Victorian anxieties surrounding biological degeneration, but their effects could be observed wherever evolutionary thought took root.[4] To many, affirmations of evolutionary progress only served to summon the specter of decline. Even while embracing narratives of developmental progress, a growing number of lay-evolutionists and prominent scientists grew preoccupied with the prospect of degeneration, or the fear that the logic of natural history might pull the human spirit back to its more unsavory, animalistic origins. Freud shared this anxiety of developmental reversal, which, as I discuss in the following section, was already observable in the earliest formulations of "Haeckel's Law."

Initially at least, Ernst Haeckel had no such concerns. In a famous 1863 speech to the Society of German Natural Scientists and Physicians, for instance, he defended evolutionary theory on progressivist grounds, going so far as to argue that "even if we find in particular periods a retrogression, we cannot yet deny progress as a whole." Taking the long view on such matters, Haeckel maintained then that such "progress will not for long be constrained and . . . the whole history of organisms manifests the law of progress" (as cited in Richards, 2008, p. 101).[5]

Yet somewhere between his first encounter with the *Origin of Species* and his later, politically contentious years, Haeckel's view of individual life took on a decidedly tragic cast, even as his defense of the progressivism within evolutionary theory grew ever more strident. This curious inverse relationship – sustained, as it was, by an unwavering commitment to the biogenetic law – is observable in Haeckel's own intellectual development, particularly in his treatments of human psychology. Indeed, Haeckel's increasingly low opinion of *individual* human potential on the one hand, and his steadfast commitment to recapitulationism on the other, amount to more than mere coincidence, setting the stage for the same curious juxtapositions of progress and decline that preoccupied the Frankfurt School.

Much like Freud's theory of the death drive, which emerged in the wake of Freud's (1920/1961) grief for his favorite daughter, Haeckel's most lasting, unwittingly tragic theory crystallized in a moment of profound loss. Following the sudden death of his first wife, Haeckel's mourning transitioned into something of a "creative illness." Working 18-hour days for 12 straight months, in 1866 he produced the magisterial (and still untranslated) two-volume *Generelle Morphologie der Organismen* (Di Gregorio, 2005, pp. 115–145; see also Ellenberger, 1970, p. 890). While replete with extensive, technical discussions that exhaust the lay reader, his newly formulated biogenetic law suffused the entire work, animating the evolutionary treatments of morphology, embryology, and paleontology with all the confidence of a pan-explanatory, unified theory. Of course, Haeckel was not the first to suggest an isomorphic relationship between individual development and natural history. However, he was quite original in at least one respect: more than prior evolutionists (including Darwin), Haeckel insisted that ontogeny was entirely subservient to phylogeny.

From the *Generelle Morphology* onwards, Haeckel never missed a chance to invoke the biogenetic principle and the power differential it implied. The mechanical parallelism of the idea even found its way into the structure of his prose, where, like some rhetorical fractal, it seemed to emerge in concentric echoes, stated and restated *ad infinitum*:

> The history of the Germ is an epitome of the History of the Descent; or, in other words: that Ontogeny is a recapitulation of Phylogeny; or, somewhat more explicitly: that the series of forms through which the Individual Organism passes during its progress from the egg cell to its fully developed state, is a brief, compressed reproduction of the long series of forms through which the animal ancestors of that organism (or the ancestral forms of its species) have passed from the earliest periods of so-called organic creation down to the present time.
> (Haeckel, 1874/1900, vol. 1, pp. 6–7)

To later critics, the orderly systematicity of "Haeckel's law" was the stuff of Teutonic navel-gazing, not natural science. As the Scottish biologist E. S. Russell (1916) wryly observed, one had only to subtract the presumption of historicity "from the biogenetic law – not a difficult matter – and it becomes merely a law of idealistic morphology, applicable to evolution considered as an ideal process, as the progressive development in the Divine thought of archetypal models" (p. 257). Yet for Haeckel, recapitulationism was no idealistic thought project. In his estimation, the biogenetic principle proved that at all levels and in all phenomena – be they living or inorganic – development was animated by a single, dynamic law of progress.

Cracks in the foundation of this progressivism emerged most clearly amidst attempts to account for the presence of degenerative processes. Haeckel, however, treated any appearance of biological or cultural degeneration as so much natural-historical noise. Like the growing number of British Darwinians, he understood descent as a process of incremental improvement and advancement. "By and large," he maintained in the *Generelle Morphologie*,

> the developmental motion of the whole organic world is continuous and everywhere progressive, even though the universally active processes of differentiation on the small and detailed scale necessarily cause numerous and frequently significant regressions in organization alongside the predominant occurrence of progress.
> (as cited Di Gregorio, 2005, p. 163)

In a sense, Haeckel's biogenetic law amounted to a radical resituation of the site and scope of evolutionary progress. One had a law of progressive phylogeny for humanity in the aggregate, and the personal deterioration that it necessarily entailed on the other. Atavistic organs, for instance, "perish during Ontogeny, while others go on growing at their expense," as Haeckel reasoned in typical analogical fashion: "this same phenomenon is met with in human society. In this it is always the case that many individuals perish without effecting anything; while the majority constantly develop more or less steadily" (Haeckel, 1874/1900, vol. 1, p. 163). In other words, an individual person's death was dealt out by phylogeny through its causal control of ontogeny. "Normal death," no more than the conclusion of development, occurred "when the limit of the hereditary term of life is reached," and any actual degeneration occurred only at the inconsequential level of ontogeny (Haeckel, 1904, p. 104).

An individual in this scheme was thus an ephemeral, unremarkable thing, no more or less meaningful than a transitional species along a single branch of a grand *Stammbaum*:

> But it is just as true of the species as of the individual that it lives for itself, and looks above all to self-maintenance. Its existence and "end" are transitory. The progressive development of classes and stems leads slowly but surely to the formation of new species. Every special form of life – the individual as well as the species – is therefore merely a biological episode, a passing phenomenal form in the constant change of life. Man is no exception.
>
> (Haeckel, 1904, p. 403)

And yet Haeckel insisted that the law of biogenesis, which made "transitory" individual development a function of "progressive" evolution, ennobled the human species. That ontogeny was a function of phylogeny also meant that value and meaning were to be located by analogical reference to macrocosmic, broadly progressive processes. The individual was but a fractal instantiation of a far more encompassing concern.

No surprise then that Haeckel's progressive evolutionary psychology accorded minimal importance to individual life. Tellingly, Haeckel's (1868/1883) reasoning in this area appealed to the same analogy that would drive Freud in *Totem and Taboo* – it required one "to study and compare the mental life of wild savages and children" (vol. 2, p. 363). The many parallels that Haeckel drew in this vein reflected the racism typical of nineteenth-century ethnology but did so less to denigrate the subaltern colonial subject than to show that both cultural and child development entail psychological progress. "We are," he concluded, rightly "proud of having so immensely outstripped our lower animal ancestors, and derive from it the consoling assurance that in future also, mankind, as a whole, will follow the glorious career of progressive development, and attain a still higher degree of mental perfection" (Haeckel, 1868/1883, vol. 2, p. 367).

But by the time he published his final popular work, *The Wonders of Life*, Haeckel (1904) wasn't so sure about the human prospect. Industrial progress seemed only to have produced more poverty; "statistics of suicide increase so much in the more civilized communities," and bad luck in heredity boded poorly for many a child of the twentieth century (Haeckel, 1904, p. 116). If ontogenetic recapitulation didn't fully reflect phylogenetic progress in this or that person's life, it would presumably be the height of humanity to allow him to end it himself:

> If then the circumstances of life come to press too hard on the poor being who has thus developed, without any fault of his, from the fertilized ovum – if instead of the hoped-for good, there come only care and need, sickness and misery of every kind – he has the unquestionable right to put an end to his sufferings by death. . . . The voluntary death by which a man puts an end to intolerable suffering is really an act of redemption.
>
> (Haeckel, 1904, pp. 116–117)

Suicide as self-redemption might sound like the cynicism of a deeply disenchanted optimist, but the argument was consistent with the progressivism Haeckel had been advancing all along. According to the unidirectional logic of the biogenetic law in its original form, progress, while certain, was strictly phylogenetic, a property of (or inherent in) the species as a whole. Its history could be observed in the individual's development but not necessarily in the shape or value of her life.

Haeckel's defense of suicide (and elsewhere, euthanasia) seemed to follow logically from the evolutionary doctrine he advanced: in rendering the specimen subservient to the species, the biogenetic law allowed one to maintain a notion of progress at the level of phylogeny, albeit often at the expense of personal meaning or redemption. Worrisome developments or personal misfortune could be explained away as so many bumps along the road, ontogenetic misfortunes absolved or overwritten by "a gradual advance towards perfection" (Haeckel, 1868/1883, vol. 2, p. 456). This, in short, was the tragic dimension of post-Haeckelian recapitulationism: personal tragedy could be freely acknowledged, but only when subsumed within a macrocosmic process that was necessary or beneficial for the species in the long run.

In sum, Haeckel's formulation of the biogenetic law transformed evolutionary progressivism in one distinct, near-paradoxical way: it relied upon individual development to demonstrate evolutionary progress yet required us to treat any instance of individual decline as meaningless in the "big picture." The moral contortions required to maintain this contradiction forced Haeckel to draw some curious and tragic conclusions about the human condition. But when the biogenetic law reappeared *minus* its unidirectional logic, in Freud's reformulation, recapitulationism proved surprisingly useful in explaining ever more troubling developments in individual experience and cultural history.

Freud's Reversal of Recapitulationary Progress

Freud's *use* of the biogenetic principle can be understood as an articulate expression of the tragic, moral anxiety that the once-progressive theory was made to bear. Indeed, in Freud's hands, the (largely latent) ambivalence of Haeckel's law shifted to the surface, and in turn informed the critiques of progress later articulated by Adorno, Horkheimer, and Marcuse. While still a sign of phylogenetic progress, which presumably furnished a normative framework for ontogenetic development, Freud's subtle reworking of the biogenetic principle gave clear and emphatic expression to all those anxieties that lurked in the shadows of the theory's previous iterations. Sometime during the First World War, Freud's application of the biogenetic law underscored the tragic dimensions that previous recapitulationists had considered merely ancillary. In a trend that continued within postwar Frankfurt School thought, the once-progressivist theory became a psychologically weighted vehicle for the expression of anxieties surrounding the direction of Western civilization.

As early as his nineteenth year, Freud (1875/1990) could be found making casual reference to Haeckel as one of "our most modern saints" (p. 96). Though he rarely mentioned the theory's eponym by name, Freud's earliest deployment of recapitulationist ideas emerged amidst his attempts to rework medical theories of "nervous dissolution" within a biogenetic framework. Freud referred to this kind of retrograde development as "involution." Whereas in the *Three Essays on the Theory of Sexuality* and his early case histories Freud (e.g., 1905/1962, p. 43n) used this term in its then-conventional guise (i.e., referring variously to neurological decline and anatomical manifestations of the latency period), by 1915, the term that Strachey translates (and which Freud sometimes used, *in English*) as "involution" had begun to carry a more profound metapsychological meaning.[6]

Six months after the outbreak of the Great War, Freud (1915/1957) found occasion to observe that "a certain extraordinary plasticity of mental developments is not unrestricted as regards direction" (p. 286). In the mind, unlike the body, environmental pressures could just as easily propel the organism downward, toward ostensibly abandoned stages as they could lead upward to "higher" achievements. This, Freud (1915/1957) offered, "may be described as a special capacity for involution [*Rückbildung*] – for regression – since it may well happen that a later and higher stage of development, once abandoned, cannot be reached again. But the primitive stages can always be re-established; the primitive mind is, in the fullest meaning of the word, imperishable" (p. 286).

Thus, for Freud's purposes, the biogenetic law meant that *psychic* recapitulation could proceed along either progressive or regressive lines. Since phylogenetically inherited primitive stages allegedly persist in the unconscious long after they are superceded, the reanimation of atavistic traits or periods could occur at any point in the lifespan. Thus, Freud (1915/1957) argued, "every earlier stage of development persists alongside the later stage which has arisen from it; here succession also involves co-existence" (p. 286). He continued to emphasize this point for the duration of his career, arguing, for example, in *Civilization and Its Discontents* that "only in the mind is such a preservation of all the earlier stages alongside the final form possible. . . . [I]t is rather the rule than the exception for the past to be preserved in mental life" (Freud, 1930/1961b, p. 20).

Yet at some point in the second decade of the new century, Freud also concluded that the biogenetic law was not merely directionally labile, as other psycho-recapitulationists assumed. Prior stages did not simply persist alongside their psychic progeny; they pulled the latter back toward the former, the individual *Ich* back to the ancestral *Es*. As the Great War drew to a close, Freud accorded ever more prominence to the involutionary potential of the human species, especially as regards "group psychology." At the same time, he came to consider the prospects for future progress increasingly dim and fraught with complications and potential reversals. With the previous century's evolutionary optimism now thoroughly compromised, Thanatos gave voice to the devolutionary shadow of the evolutionary *telos*.

Freud, of course, was not alone or altogether original in his growing anxiety about the retrograde tendencies inherent in the descent of man. Yet what ultimately distinguished his thinking on these matters from his nineteenth-century evolutionary and neurological predecessors was his eventual insistence that the evolution-involution dialectic was, by virtue of its chronological priority, always biased toward the latter direction – that, as he would conclude in *Beyond the Pleasure Principle*, "the pleasure principle seems actually to serve the death instincts" (Freud, 1920/1961a, p. 77). Now involution was the rule, not the exception, and this held true for social no less than biological development.

Tracing the development of Freud's involuntionary recapitulationism is a daunting task because it shows up at different periods and in a variety of contexts. Nonetheless, before his legendary pessimism was leveled at political and religious institutions – as it was in *Group Psychology and the Analysis of the Ego* (1921/1959b), *Civilization and its Discontents* (1930/1961b), and *Moses and Monotheism* (1939) – Freud had already delineated the process by which the *telos* of evolution is redirected toward the past.

In the earlier stages of his theory, Freud's recapitulationism functioned more to place psychoanalysis within a biogenetic framework than to modify Haeckel's law. In a later edition of *The Interpretation of Dreams* (1919/1953), for instance, he added a phylogenetic inference to the notion that dreams involve a regression to (the dreamer's) childhood: "behind this childhood of the individual" – behind the ontogenetic component of the dream – "we are promised a picture of a phylogenetic childhood" (p. 548). This "picture of the development of the human race," Freud (1919/1953) speculated, was "in fact an abbreviated recapitulation influenced by the chance circumstances of life" (p. 548). In short, said the early Freud, dreams, like the embryo, contain the buried vestiges of psychic antiquity preserved as in amber. Dream-work and psychoanalysis could therefore claim an honored place among the sciences, particularly those "which are concerned with the reconstruction of the earliest and most obscure periods of the beginnings of the human race" (p. 549).

Even here, however, Freud's recapitulationism was essentially backward-gazing. Rather than illuminating a history of evolutionary advancement or anticipating improvements soon to come, his biogenetic speculations functioned rhetorically to identify everyday processes of involuntionary regression. Dreams and psychopathology amounted to developmental backsliding, momentarily guiding the individual along a reversed recapitulationary sequence. Consistent with early twenty-first-century anthropological opinion on such matters – infused, as such thought was, with a generous dose of racist colonial ideology – Freud's phylogenetic Patient Zero was "primitive man," discernable in the present in the irrational behavior of contemporary children, neurotics, and "savages." Parallels in the development of these three groups – and the implied proximity of savagery to modernity – were emphasized in *Totem and Taboo* (1913/1950), but Freud had been gradually formulating his biogenetic psychology well before he began to apply it to "primitive" cultures.

At times, Freud's nascent preoccupation with phylogenetic parallels prompted him to reframe earlier works along recapitulationist lines. In his 1914 preface to the third edition of the *Three Essays on the Theory of Sexuality*, he all but apologized for the absence of biogenetic interpretations. Such was the nature of psychoanalytic observation, he explained, that "disposition is left in the background, and more weight is attached to ontogenesis than to phylogenesis" – and by "disposition" Freud meant phylogeny, "the precipitate of earlier experience of the species to which the more recent experience of the individual, as the sum of the accidental [or ontogenetic] factors, is super-added" (Freud, 1905/1962, p. xv).

In addition to documenting the increasing prominence of recapitulationism within his thought, Freud's pattern of revisions to previously published texts reflected the degree to which many of his better-known theories involve applications of the biogenetic law. The introduction of the psychosexual stages in the *Three Essays on the Theory of Sexuality* was an especially Haeckelian maneuver. Sandor Ferenczi's student Michael Balint (1896–1970) noted that "the three phases of the psychosexual development of man discovered by Freud correspond to a similar triple gradation in phylogenetic sexual evolution" (Balint, 1930/1965, p. 5). The phase of "*oral incorporation*," Balint observed, recapitulated the development of a single-celled ancestor, with the periods of "*anal evacuation*" and "*genital mating*" each evincing a more phylogenetically recent provenance. Childhood sexuality was "the remnant of a long-vanished epoch; having lost its biological purpose, it is rather like an old paid-off mercenary who willingly offers his services to any bidder" (p. 15).

A similar approach animated Freud's (1920/1961a) argument in *Beyond the Pleasure Principle*, where he became convinced that no amount of cultural progress could do away with the involutionary tendencies of the human species. The combined effect of his study of the war neuroses, the loss of his daughter Sophie, and the general desolation that enveloped interwar Vienna brought Freud back to the Fechnerian psychophysics that had so preoccupied him in the days of his collaboration with Wilhelm Fliess. Moving from a discussion of trauma and an elucidation of the repetition compulsion, Freud "speculated" about the descent of consciousness.

Tellingly, these speculations begin with (and are based on) "embryology, in its capacity as a recapitulation of developmental history" (Freud, 1920/1961a, p. 29). The seat of consciousness, Freud maintained, is located in the cerebral cortex, itself a "baked through," hardened "shield" that mediates external stimulation in much the same manner as an ancestral single cell's "ectoderm" or membrane (p. 27). In the course of human evolution, that cell membrane would have evolved to effectively protect against excessive stimuli from the external world, but not from the internal repository of phylogenetic inheritance. Nonetheless, when the shield of consciousness – itself the result of the recapitulated evolution of the ectoderm – is breached by trauma, the compulsion emerges to repeat the traumatic experience in dreams so that it might be mastered and "undone." Thus, Freud infamously concluded, "There was also a time before the purpose of dreams was the fulfillment of wishes" (p. 38).

Followed to its logical conclusion (or point of origin, if you prefer), this "time before" was the state of inorganic matter. Freud (1920/1961a) realized that this *"urge inherent in organic life to restore an earlier state of things"* was an odd suggestion from a student of evolution like himself (p. 43). "This view of the instincts," he admitted, "strikes us as strange because we have become used to see in them a factor impelling towards change and development, whereas we are now asked to recognize in them the precise contrary" (p. 43). But he justified this about-face by invoking the biogenetic law:

> We are quickly relieved of the necessity for seeking for further examples by the reflection that the most impressive proofs of there being an organic compulsion to repeat lie in the phenomena of heredity and the facts of embryology. We see how the germ of a living animal is obliged in the course of its development to recapitulate (even if only in a transient and abbreviated fashion) the structures of all the forms from which it is sprung, instead of proceeding quickly by the shortest path to its final shape.
>
> (Freud, 1920/1961a, p. 44)

Put differently, the posttraumatic repetition compulsion was, in fact, a derivative form of biogenetic recapitulation. New acquisitions and influences might be added to the old, but development was nonetheless obliged to recapitulate all of phylogeny, albeit now in reverse. The *real*, most phylogenetically ancient drive behind the recapitulationary sequence was inherently (one wants to say "dialectically") negative. Here, then, was the biomechanical determinism in Freud's tragically minded recapitulationism: recapitulation was but a series of detours, manifestly progressive (in the short term) but ultimately involutionary and self-destructive (in the long term).

Instead of seeing development as *potentially* regressive or involutionary, Freud's biogenetic reasoning in *Beyond the Pleasure Principle* maintained that it had always been so. Acquired amidst all the *Sturm und Drang* of human phylogeny, "all the organic instincts" manifest in the recapitulationary repetition of past stages "tend toward the restoration of an earlier state of things" (Freud, 1920/1961a, p. 45). Ontogeny, far from being a record of evolutionary advancement, is actually the result of outside interference, of traumas like the Ice Age that forced the organism to add new traits on top of phylogenetically inherited ones. In truth, Freud reasoned, drives to repeat and develop upward give the "deceptive appearance of being forces tending towards change and progress, whilst in fact they are merely seeking to reach an ancient goal by paths alike old and new" (p. 45). Whatever novelty or creativity as might emerge in ontogeny was at bottom evidence of the fact that "the organism wishes to die only in its own fashion" (p. 47). Even the sexual instincts, to which "alone we can attribute an internal impulse towards 'progress' and towards higher development," only serve to prolong life so that it may be undone in a manner agreeable to the individual (p. 48n).

In an about-face that Marcuse (1955/1966) exploited to his own advantage in *Eros and Civilization*, Freud argued that recapitulationary development ultimately operated in reverse. "There is unquestionably no universal instinct towards higher development observable in the animal or plant world," and what might seem to be higher development in one place is on closer inspection always "balanced or outweighed by involution in another" (Freud, 1920/1961a, pp. 49–50). And lest he appear to have been speaking only of overstimulated ectoderms, Freud made it clear that his law of reverse-recapitulationary involution made all of human civilization the result of so many exogenous detours from degeneration: "what appears in a minority of human individuals as an untiring impulsion toward further perfection can easily be understood as a result of the instinctual repression upon which is based all that is most precious in human civilization" (p. 50). Such repression might forestall the unraveling of "all that is most precious" in the social sphere, but only temporarily. Consequently, the more Freud construed the course of civilization in biogenetic terms, the more he distrusted the direction of its development.

As in *Totem and Taboo*, Freud (1920/1961a) ended *Beyond the Pleasure Principle* with a quotation – an aphoristic afterthought or an epigraph: "what we cannot reach flying we must reach limping. . . . The Book tells us it is no sin to limp" (p. 78). This quote was taken from the nineteenth-century German orientalist Friedrich Rückert's translation of a volume of eleventh-century Arabic prose and provides an apologetic coda for Freud's repeated disavowals of his conclusions and "speculations" in *Beyond the Pleasure Principle*. Rhetorical or not, this cryptic postscript intimates that Freud was shedding what little was left of an earlier, guardedly optimistic sensibility that progressivist evolutionism had originally entailed. Indeed, it is difficult to exaggerate the degree to which Freud reversed Haeckelian recapitulationism in *Beyond the Pleasure Principle* – not because he misrepresented the biogenetic principle, but because he appealed to it in order to demonstrate the involutionary or devolutionary bias of *both* ontogeny *and* phylogeny.

Recall again that the previous century's recapitulationism was construed as a necessary mechanism of heredity and progress. Newer traits could be added onto more ancient and ontogenetically earlier ones. Haeckel's evolutionary principles (i.e., "condensation" and "terminal addition") governed such developments and generally drove them toward advancement and away from degeneration. Freud's use of the concept ultimately functioned to direct the species away from progress and back toward its own nonexistence. From this point forward in his work, Freud's appeals to humanity's "archaic inheritance" exhibited a decidedly tragic character, suffused as they were with the assumption that phylogeny is an essentially autocidal process.

Freud's tragic reversal of the biogenetic law through the death instinct can be counted among the more unusual and more influential instances of intellectual appropriation. The biogenetic metapsychology presented in *Beyond the Pleasure Principle* and subsequent works was at once an application and an inversion of the late nineteenth-century evolutionary progressivism embodied by everyone from Haeckel to G. Stanley Hall. But above all else, perhaps, Freud's dizzying synthesis was also an ambivalent philosophy of history, one which dwelt on the deepening shadows that accompanied the process of progress. Far from the "counter-political triumph" that Carl Schorske once judged it, the doctrine of involution was newly cathected to address Europe at a crossroads (as cited in Spurling, 1989, p. 115). Caught between a half century of post-Enlightenment evolutionary optimism and the increasingly worrisome rise of fascism, Freud's inversion of an outmoded recapitulationist biology had a strong appeal to those living on the edge of the abyss.

Frankfurt School Recapitulationism: Horkheimer, Adorno, Marcuse

"Materialism," Max Horkheimer (1933/2002) famously insisted in the early days of the Institut für Sozialforschung, "requires the unification of philosophy and science" (p. 34). Properly combined, each discipline would be defined by a rejection of both mechanistic reductionism and idealist foundationalism. True "materialist doctrines" would be organized around and situated within economic conditions and social experience; as such, they were anything but "examples of a stable and permanent idea" and contained instead the capacity for internal, self-reflexive critique (p. 45). Curiously, Horkheimer included the "monism of [Ernst] Haeckel" among his examples of "pseudo-materialism" (p. 35). By prioritizing a *Weltanschauung* over "historical practice," Horkheimer argued, Haeckel's evolutionary monism effectively excluded the social from the material, resulting in the worst of both materialism and metaphysics (p. 35; see also Jay, 1973/1996, pp. 52–54).

Yet Horkheimer's distaste for Haeckel's "physicalist materialism" also belied a begrudging acknowledgment of persistent influence, if not continuing relevance.[7] While Haeckel's brand of mechanistic monism was largely discredited by the time of Horkheimer's (1933/2002) writing, the same cannot be said of the former's promulgation of the biogenetic law, whose teleological inversion (in Freud's hands) was amplified and integrated within the broad thrust of Frankfurt School thought, albeit in a thoroughly de-biologized form. The same autocidal tendency that Freud located within individual development's recapitulation of social history was – in the hands Horkheimer and Adorno (1947/2002) no less than

Marcuse (1955/1966) – shifted to the relationship between philosophy, psychology, and political economy. At the twilight of the Second World War, as Horkheimer and Adorno (1947/2002) argued in *Dialectic of Enlightenment*, the Enlightenment had culminated in "the self-destruction of enlightenment" (p. xvi). The very concept of "enlightenment thinking" – including the material and social constituents of that thinking – "already contains the germ of its reversal" (pp. xvi, 254).

While never rendered explicit, *Dialectic of Enlightenment* is replete with loud echoes of Freud's teleological inversion of the biogenetic law. Thus Horkheimer and Adorno (1947/2002) argue that, with the advent of the culture industry, "progress is reverting to regression" (p. xviii). Similarly, National Socialist racism "is a regression to nature as mere violence," and anti-Semitism a series of psychological processes that "recreate moments of biological prehistory" (pp. 138, 148). At times, Horkheimer and Adorno even impose a devolutionary reading where Freud had originally failed to include one. For instance, they reject the alleged psychological parallelism among children, "savages," and neurotics that Freud (1913/1950) introduced in *Totem and Taboo*, insisting that the primitive-child-neurotic's belief in the "omnipotence of thoughts" "applies only to the more realistic form of world domination achieved by the greater astuteness of science" instead (Horkheimer & Adorno, 1947/2002, p. 7; see also pp. 162–163). Rather than a vestige of primitive psychology, neurotic thinking is interpreted as an inevitable feature of the devolutionary process of industrial domination. The disruption or reversal of progress means more than mere fixation or stasis, for paradoxical as it sounds, progress itself is construed as the driving force of phylogenetic regression. "Humanity," they argue, is in this sense

> forced back to more primitive anthropological stages, since, with the technical facilitation of existence, the continuance of domination demands the fixation of instincts by greater repression. Fantasy withers. . . . Adaptation to the power of progress furthers the progress of power, constantly renewing the degenerations which prove successful progress, not failed progress, to be its own antithesis. The curse of irresistible progress is irresistible regression.
>
> (pp. 27–28)

Here, progress is not merely threatened by the possibility of or tendency toward regression (as was the case for Freud, initially). Rather, progress actually *promotes* regression, as it forces a dominated, industrial-era subject to regress toward primitive states.

While *Eros and Civilization* (1955/1966) provided the definitive Frankfurt School appropriation of metapsychological recapitulationism, much of the Institute's earlier critique of Fromm was infused with the peripheral influence of the theory upon the remaining members of the institute. Adorno's (1951/1982) reading of Freud's (1921/1959b) *Group Psychology and the Analysis of the Ego* is more or less representative of this trend. Despite its apparent prescience – the essay enjoyed something of a renaissance during the Trump era – "Freudian Theory and the Pattern of Fascist Propaganda" contains overt invocations of Freud's reverse-recapitulationism, which in turn demonstrate a clear kinship with Marcuse's neo-Marxian revision of biogenetic metapsychology in *Eros and Civilization*.

Adorno (1951/1982) begins the essay with the deceptively simple observation that fascist propaganda does not in fact attempt to persuade its audience or recruit adherents. In practice, the fascist propagandist's real goal is to transform his presumptive audience of free-thinking rational actors into "'rabble,' i.e., crowds inclined to violent action without any sensible aim" (p. 119). This, of course, would be the highly suggestible "horde" or group formation familiar to readers of Freud (1921/1959b), in which the individual's ego-boundaries regressively dissolve through her psychic merger with the group. For Adorno's purposes, however, the strength of Freud's argument was his success in tracing the unseemlier tendencies of *Massenpsychologie* to ontogenetic, intrapsychic processes, ones that Freud "developed within the monadological confines of the individual" (p. 120).

I will return shortly to the tacit recapitulationism in Adorno's (1951/1982) reading of Freud. First, however, a brief précis of *Group Psychology and the Analysis of the Ego* is in order. There, Freud applied his reverse-recapitulationism to modern groups (the stock examples being the army and the Catholic Church), arguing that group formation "resurrects" the primal horde by forcing group members to regress toward a primitive psychological state. So whereas in *Totem and Taboo* Freud (1913/1950) had argued that post-parricidal totemism functions to repress the memory of the primal murder, in *Group Psychology* he maintained that the logic and function of modern groups made them all but identical to the primal horde. In both situations, he observed, the unconscious – in which "all that is evil in the human mind is contained as a predisposition" – is given free reign, impervious to the censorship otherwise exercised by the individual ego

(Freud, 1921/1959b, p. 9). Like the neurotic and the primitive, the group "has a sense of omnipotence; the notion of impossibility disappears for the individual group" (p. 13).

In the group, the otherwise civilized individual undergoes a profound regression that is both ontogenetic and phylogenetic, returning him to his own childhood and the primitive condition of the species, and thereby freeing him of acquired inhibitions. "Thus," Freud (1921/1959b) argues, the modern "group appears to us as a revival of the primal horde. Just as primitive man survives potentially in every individual, so the primal horde may arise once more out of any random collection" (p. 70).[8] Group formation, like hypnosis, is not only "an inherited deposit from the phylogenesis of the human libido"; it is "a direct survival," a social-psychological living fossil (pp. 96–97).[9] Unlike the neurotic-primitive parallelism of *Totem and Taboo*, and crucial to Adorno's (1951/1982) reading, the group amounts to a regressive shortcut.

In many respects, Adorno's later (1951/1982) reading of Freud is similar to that suggested in *Dialectic of Enlightenment*: civilization's regression to barbarism is not an anomaly but an integral feature, the inevitable outcome of the progress of power. Adorno suggests that if anything, modernity can no longer tolerate the concealment of primitive instincts and behaviors. Thus what "is peculiar to the masses is, according to Freud, not so much a new quality as the manifestation of old ones usually hidden" (p. 122).

As was the case in *Dialectic of Enlightenment*, Adorno amplifies what was merely latent or implied in Freud's original analysis, designating fascism as the ultimate referent of Freud's tragic philosophy of history. Ever present within the dynamics of certain group formations, "fascism," Adorno (1951/1982) maintains, "is not simply the reoccurrence of the archaic but its reproduction in and by civilization itself" (p. 122). In this reading, civilization does not simply carry an inherent risk of devolutionary regression; it "reproduces" (in both the Marxian and biological senses) archaic dispositions and primitive social formations like the primal horde. By reawakening the latent, historically transmitted tendency toward regression, the fascist demagogue can instantaneously effect ontogeny's reverse-recapitulation of phylogeny.

Throughout his essay on fascist propaganda, Adorno emphasizes Freud's habit of framing social regression as the rapid acceleration of an otherwise phasic, historical process. In the primal horde and fascist group formation, aggression and libido are not so much cathartically discharged as rediscovered in an automatic devolutionary sequence. In its return, what was repressed is resurrected: "what happens when masses are caught by fascist propaganda is not a spontaneous primary expression of instincts and urges but a quasi-scientific revitalization of their psychology – the *artificial* regression described by Freud in his discussion of organized groups" (Adorno, 1951/1982, p. 135; emphasis mine).

What distinguishes Adorno from Freud here is his ambivalence concerning the degree to which collective regression is actually "artificial." For Freud (1921/1959b), the phenomena of group identification and regression are novel but natural, insofar as they revive the primal horde. Almost literally, the "leader of the group is still the dreaded primal father," demanding obedience and functioning as a surrogate superego (or "ego-ideal," as Freud then styled it) that at once revealed and resurrected ancient phylogenetic experiences (p. 76). Adorno, it appears, found Freud's insistence on the group's instantaneous, recapitulationary regression less convincing. Regression within the group formation was undeniable, but it nonetheless had a somewhat different provenance and a potentially different outcome.

However subtly, Adorno's departure from Freud in this essay hinges on precisely this ambivalence. Again, where Freud saw the potential for sweeping cultural regression in group dynamics, Adorno was less sure. For him, the psychological contradictions required for such a regression were simply unsustainable in the long run. Indeed, the more sweeping the fascist group's "hypnotic spell," the more difficult it becomes for regressed group members to ignore the inherent "phoniness" of their enchantment. At any moment, he suspected (or perhaps merely hoped) that a Benjaminian flash of insight could shatter the hypnotic trance, leading the intensity of the group-based regression to "terminate in sudden awareness of the untruth of the spell, and eventually in its collapse" (Adorno, 1951/1982, p. 137). Certainly, progress contained its own antitheses, but this could just as easily result in the lifting of an ideological veil as initiate a permanent devolutionary regression.

While one could hardly accuse Adorno (1951/1982) of concluding on an optimistic note, his ambivalently hopeful reading of *Group Psychology* presages Marcuse's (1955/1966) separate treatment of *Civilization and Its Discontents* in *Eros and Civilization*. In postwar Frankfurt School writing, a thoroughly de-biologized use of Freud's reverse-recapitulationary pessimism somehow allowed for a cautious optimism, hopeful to the extent that it allowed for the possibility that a devoluationary sequence could be disrupted and new paths forward chosen.

Something quite similar was clearly at work in *Eros and Civilization*. While it was not reflected in his publications until 1955, Marcuse's intellectual engagement with Freud began in the shadow of the Spanish Civil War and the Stalinist show trials (Robinson, 1969). By mid-century, as Fromm was articulating his critique of Freud's pessimistic philosophy of history, Marcuse found himself drawn to its (alleged) critical capacity.

As Marcuse saw it, the error of Fromm's insipid humanism stemmed from a misunderstanding of Freud's biologism. Note that by this, Marcuse does not mean Freud's actual biological claims or assumptions, let alone their seldom acknowledged origins within German Romanticism (cf. Richards, 2002; Ellenberger, 1970). These he chooses to treat as "notions and propositions *implied* in [Freud's theory] only in a reified form, in which historical processes *appear* as natural (biological) processes" (Marcuse, 1955/1966, p. 35; emphasis mine). For Marcuse, Freud's biology was no mere metaphor, but neither was it a straightforward, description of biological reality. Rather, Freud's reverse recapitulationism was simply a hyper-concretized historical sociology, albeit one that faithfully delineated the terrain of the archaic and the unconscious.

Of crucial importance to Marcuse (1955/1966) here was Freud's unwavering commitment to locating an unconscious phylogenetic past within individual psychology and social life. As it happens, this also informs his critique of Fromm et al., which is spelled out in the book's epilogue (which, as Robinson, [1969] observed, would have functioned better as a prologue, considering it appeared in *Dissent* prior to the publication of *Eros and Civilization*). For Marcuse, the neo-Freudians' dismissal of Freud's metapsychology as untenable only demonstrated their misunderstanding of his evolutionary philosophy of history and its social and political applications. That which the revisionists derided as " 'biologism' is social theory in a depth dimension that has been consistently flattened out by the Neo-Freudian schools" (Marcuse, 1955/1966, pp. 5–6). Stripping psychoanalysis of its own archaic heritage, they abandoned what Marcuse deemed the theory's "hidden trend" of social and political critique, ultimately producing little more than an endorsement of the capitalist status quo (pp. 11, 20; see also pp. 273–274).

Arguably, this was the function of Freud's pessimistic appeals to archaic inheritance all along – to transform a theory of progressive development into a critique of progress. And yet Marcuse's secondary goal in this text was to demonstrate the consequences of *not* doing so, of abandoning the unseemly features of Freudian metapsychology in the name of adjustment to industrial society. For one, he argued, Freud's clinical and rhetorical method of moving from the contemporary (or ontogenetic) to the primitive (or phylogenetic) allowed him to push past the veneer of accumulated, repressive ideology:

> This movement was essential for Freud's critique of civilization: only by means of the "regression" behind the mystifying forms of the mature individual and his private and public existence did he discover their basic negativity in the foundations on which they rest. Moreover, only by pushing his critical regression back to the deepest biological layer could Freud elucidate the explosive content of the mystifying forms and, at the same time, the full scope of civilized repression.
> (Marcuse, 1955/1966, p. 273)

In minimizing the biological substrate of Freud's theory, said Marcuse, the revisionists effectively reified an ideological (especially religious) superstructure, devaluing "the sphere of material needs in favor of spiritual needs" (p. 265).

As was the case with Adorno's modifications of Freud's metapsychology, Marcuse (1955/1966) blithely ignored the racist, colonialist, and sexist assumptions embedded in Freud's (e.g., 1921/1959b) notion of "the archaic inheritance" and insisted on attempting to salvage some form of "revolutionary" critique from the very ideas abandoned by the revisionists (e.g., "the most concrete insights into the historical structure of civilization are contained precisely in the concepts that the revisionists reject" [p. 6]). For our purposes here, the cogency of Marcuse's argument in *Eros and Civilization* – including his case for a nonrepressive society and his reorganization of the life and death instincts – is less important than his method. Quite tellingly, this proceeds from an invocation of the then-discredited theory of biogenetic recapitulation.

Drawing on one of Freud's (1911/1959a) earlier discussions of the development of the reality principle, Marcuse (1955/1966) frames his critique in classically recapitulationary terms: "the replacement of the pleasure principle by the reality principle is the greatest traumatic event in the development of man – in the development of the genus (phylogenesis) as well as of the individual (ontogenesis). . . . [T]his event is not unique but recurs throughout the history of mankind and of every individual" (p. 15). Following the standard recapitulationary parallel, Marcuse traces the phylogenetic origins of the reality principle to the primal horde and its ontogenetic development to early childhood. Freud believed that each individual must repeat this process anew; indeed, in his work, both psychic and cultural pathologies are traced back to the ultimately irreconcilable struggle between the pleasure and reality principles. Yet in Marcuse's reading, the perpetual battle between the pleasure and reality principles within ontogenesis transforms neurotic misery into a kind of latent protest. The repressed pleasure principle emerges as an indestructible atavism, giving voice to the demand for "the tabooed aspirations of humanity: the claim for a state where freedom and necessity coincide" (Marcuse, 1955/1966, p. 18). An ever-present relic of that "time before the purpose of dreams was the fulfillment of wishes," here the negatively recapitulated death instinct functions as a repudiation of all the compromises and renunciations demanded in the name of adjustment to industrial society (Freud, 1920/1961a, p. 38).

So in the recapitulationary regression theorized by Marcuse, the unconscious residues of the phylogenetic past begin to serve a critical function and are not just a recurrent leitmotif of development. Marcuse's (1955/1966) unconscious is not a repository of "all that is evil in the human mind" but a means of preserving "the memory of past stages of individual development at which integral gratification is obtained . . . it generates the wish that the paradise be re-created on the basis of the achievements of civilization" (p. 18). This, in fact, is what is meant by Marcuse's paradoxical claim that "regression assumes a progressive function" – a stark inversion of Horkheimer and Adorno's prior assertion that progress promotes regression. In Marcuse's rendering, Freud's appeals to archaic heritage call attention to the lingering influence of phylogeny upon contemporary ontogeny, which in turn redirects the subject away from repetition and toward a constructive future, *minus* the pessimistic resignation that Freud originally demanded (p. 19).

Again, Marcuse's revisionism in *Eros and Civilization* follows Freud's rhetorical appeals to the parallelism of the biogenetic law. He rarely mentions the original biological foundations of "Haeckel's Law" and never dwells on the racist and sexist assumptions that were built into it, appearing instead to have recast the relationship between ontogeny and phylogeny as that between individual and historico-material domination. Surely this step was necessary for his emancipatory and manifestly utopian appropriation of Freud's recapitulationism, which in its original form emphasized the inherently tragic and destructive tendencies of individual and social development.

Still, the basic practice of understanding individual psychology as a reenactment of phylogenetic history remains, only translated into progressive, dialectical-material terms. No less present (if also generously modified) is the devolutionary compulsion of the death instinct, recast here as resistance not to progressive, libidinal drives, but to the instrumentalizing demands of industrial domination. After all, Marcuse argued, alienated, obligatory labor had long required the repression of the drive for non-instrumental pleasure. And yet human phylogeny – at least as Marcuse (1955/1966, pp. 59–77) imagined it – demonstrated that the pleasure principle had not always been subservient to the death instincts; "originally," he elsewhere argues, "the actual difference between the life instinct and death instinct was very small" and reached its current degree of opposition only through the repressive process of exogenous social domination (p. 136). By virtue of its recurrent recapitulation within social relations, the death instinct demonstrated that civilization had failed to fully dominate the subject's endogenous capacity for happiness and social harmony.

As but one of many examples of this curious revision, consider Marcuse's (1955/1966) defense of so-called sexual perversions, which "express rebellion against the subjugation of sexuality under the order of procreation, and against the institutions which guarantee this order" (p. 49). Quietly abandoning the evolutionary assumptions undergirding Freud's theory of perversion, Marcuse's argument is not that non-procreative sexual practices "threaten to reverse the process of civilization which turned the organism into an instrument of work" (p. 50). Thus, all forms of sexuality that resist instrumentalization are auspicious atavisms, roughly analogous to pre-alienated labor. Thus for Marcuse, to the extent that the pleasure principle actually serves the death instincts, it does so in the service of uncoupling both instincts from "the general perversion of the human existence in a repressive culture" (p. 203).

That said, one simply cannot imagine the author of *Beyond the Pleasure Principle* and *Civilization and Its Discontents* approving of the following claim: "the reactivation of prehistoric and childhood wishes and attitudes is not necessarily regression; it may well be the opposite – proximity to a happiness that has always been the repressed promise of a better future" (Marcuse, 1955/1966, p. 203). Then again, Marcuse's argument in *Eros and Civilization* proceeds directly from his case for a thoroughly de-biologized version of Freud's recapitulationism. This, perhaps, explains both his distaste for Fromm's revisionism and the sometimes utopian, cautiously optimistic dimensions of his and Adorno's (1951/1982) appeals to Freud's unambiguously tragic use of the biogenetic law. Even so, differing appraisals of evolutionary theory seem insufficient to explain the ambivalently tragic and utopian uses of psychoanalytic recapitulationism within the Frankfurt circle.

There nonetheless remains a common thread in all Frankfurt School appeals to Freud's recapitulationism, one that goes some length toward explaining the former's cautiously optimistic appropriation of the latter. Recall that for Freud, biology (and not simply anatomy) was destiny. Understanding the psychological operation of the biogenetic law within, say, interwar Germany might strengthen one's critique of worrisome political developments, but such insights could hardly be expected to counteract phylogenetically determined dispositions. And yet when recapitulationary parallelism was used to describe the relationship between society and individual (rather than that between species and specimen), the biogenetic law proved surprisingly useful as a vehicle for historico-material critique. Arguably, in appealing to Freud's recapitulationism while eliding his biologism, Horkheimer, Adorno, and Marcuse amplified the same critical capacity that had animated the biogenetic law all along. Because the by-then discredited theory situated the individual within a historical, macrocosmic process, it proved surprisingly well-suited to both critiques of progress and declarations of decline.

Notes

1 Fromm's rejection of the very notion of drives (in the Freudian sense) in 1937 came three years after his initial rejection of Freud's Oedipal monism, which his colleagues in the Frankfurt School seemed to take in stride at that time. By 1965, he may be found arguing, "Man has no innate 'drive for progress,' but he is driven by the need to solve his existential condition, which arises

again at every new level of development" (Fromm, 1965/1981, p. 39). It is also worth noting that Freud himself did not consider the Oedipus complex to be either evolutionarily determined or developmentally inevitable until mid-1910 (Burston, 1994; Kerr, 1993).
2 In his groundbreaking study, *Ontogeny and Phylogeny*, Stephen Jay Gould (1977) found it necessary to supply readers with a glossary of recapitulationist terminology, though he was addressing an audience that was presumably somewhat familiar with this area's idiosyncratic lexicon (pp. 479–486).
3 The concept of "crypto-revisionism" was introduced by Daniel Burston (1991) to describe followers of Freud who, while "stressing their fidelity to Freud," had a conspicuous habit of making "what are actually major departures from [Freudian] orthodoxy appear as logical extensions or developments of the master's own thought" (p. 3). It seems doubtful that Marcuse, Adorno, and Horkheimer had professional or personal reasons for couching their "innovations" in avowedly filiopietistic terms, insulated as they were from the era's notoriously vicious psychoanalytic institutional culture. Here, a mix of unconscious presentism and creative misprision seems a more plausible explanation of whatever eisegesis they practiced. See also Burston (2020) and Phillips (1988).
4 For summaries of such developments in scientific, medical, and literary quarters, see Pick (1989), Chamberlain (1981), Carlson (1985), and Bowler (1989). On the influence of colonialist notions of racial superiority upon recapitulationary evolutionism and early psychoanalysis, see Brickman (2003) and Weikart (2004).
5 Much of Haeckel's work remains untranslated from the original German. Unless otherwise noted in citations, all translations from secondary sources are those of the relevant author (here, Richards [2008]; R. Richards, personal communication, March 5, 2016).
6 For instance, Freud uses the terms "*evolution and involution*" in English in a 1907 letter to Karl Abraham (as cited in Falzeder, 2001, p. 5). On nineteenth- and early-twentieth-century medical sources for Freud's early theories of degeneration, see Sulloway (1979, pp. 269–273).
7 Amidon (2008) notes that "Haeckel's claims reverberated for decades through German academic natural science and philosophy, and Horkheimer raised them regularly as evidence of the most dominating modes of scientific discourse as social practice" (p. 110).
8 Cf. Freud (1939) in *Moses and Monotheism*: "we must conclude that the mental residue of those primeval times has become a heritage which, with each new generation, needs only to be awakened, not to be reacquired" (p. 170).
9 Freud (1937) later reversed the parallelism of his theory in *Group Psychology*, arguing that it adhered to the same faulty logic as the neurotic individual: "if we consider mankind as a whole and substitute it for the single human individual, we discover that it too has developed delusions which are inaccessible to logical criticism and which contradict reality. If, in spite of this, they are able to exert an extraordinary power over men, investigation leads us to the same explanation as in the case of the single individual. They owe their power to the element of *historical truth* which they have brought up from the repression of the forgotten and primaeval past" (p. 269).

References

Adorno, T. (1982). Freudian theory and the pattern of fascist propaganda. In A. Arato & E. Gebhardt (Eds.), *The essential Frankfurt School reader* (pp. 118–137). New York, NY: Continuum (Original work published 1951).

Amidon, K. S. (2008). "Diesmal fehlt die Biologie!" Max Horkheimer, Richard Thurnwald, and the biological prehistory of German *Sozialforschun*. *New German Critique, 35*(2), 103–137.

Balint, M. (1965). Psychosexual parallels to the fundamental law of biogenetics. In *Primary love and psycho-analytic technique* (2nd ed., pp. 3–30). New York, NY: Liverlight (Original work published 1930).

Benjamin, W. (1968). *Illuminations: Essays and reflections* (H. Arendt, Ed. and H. Zohn, Trans.). New York, NY: Schocken Books (Original work published 1950).

Bowler, P. (1989). Holding your head up high: Degeneration and orthogenesis in theories of human evolution. In J. R. Moore (Ed.), *History, humanity, and evolution: Essays for John C. Greene* (pp. 329–353). New York, NY: Cambridge University Press.

Brickman, C. (2003). *Aboriginal populations in the mind: Race and primitivity in psychoanalysis*. New York, NY: Columbia University Press.

Burston, D. (1991). *The legacy of Erich Fromm*. Cambridge, MA: Harvard University Press.

Burston, D. (1994). Freud, the serpent, and the sexual enlightenment of children. *International Forum of Psychoanalysis, 3*(4), 205–218.

Burston, D. (2020). *Psychoanalysis, politics, and the postmodern university*. Cham, Switzerland: Palgrave Macmillan.

Carlson, E. T. (1985). Medicine and degeneration: Theory and praxis. In J. E. Chamberlain & S. L. Gilman (Eds.), *Degeneration: The dark side of progress* (pp. 121–144). New York, NY: Columbia University Press.

Chamberlain, J. E. (1981). An anatomy of cultural melancholy. *Journal of the History of Ideas, 42*(4), 691–705.

Di Gregorio, M. A. (2005). *From here to eternity: Ernst Haeckel and scientific faith*. Göttingen, Germany: Vandenhoeck & Ruprecht.

Dufresne, T. (2000). *Tales from the Freudian crypt: The death drive in text and context*. Stanford, CA: Stanford University Press.

Durkin, K. (2014). *The radical humanism of Erich Fromm*. New York, NY: Palgrave Macmillan.

Durkin, K. (2019). Erich Fromm and Theodor Adorno reconsidered: A case study in intellectual history. *New German Critique, 46*(1), 103–126.

Ellenberger, H. F. (1970). *The discovery of the unconscious: The history and evolution of dynamic psychiatry*. New York, NY: Basic Books.

Falzeder, E. (Ed.). (2001). *The complete correspondence of Sigmund Freud and Karl Abraham, 1907–1925* (C. Schwarzacher, Trans.). London, UK: Karnac.

Freud, S. (1937). Constructions in analysis. In J. Strachey (Ed. & Trans.), *The standard edition of the complete psychological works of Sigmund Freud* (Vol. 23, pp. 255–270). London, UK: Hogarth Press. Retrieved from www.pep-web.org.

Freud, S. (1939). *Moses and monotheism* (K. Jones, Trans.). New York, NY: Vintage.

Freud, S. (1950). *Totem and taboo* (J. Strachey, Trans.). New York, NY: Norton (Original work published 1913).

Freud, S. (1953). *The interpretation of dreams*. In J. Strachey (Ed. & Trans.), *The standard edition of the complete psychological works of Sigmund Freud* (Vol. 4, pp. ix–627). London, UK: Hogarth Press. Retrieved from www.pep-web.org (Original work published 1900).

Freud, S. (1957). Thoughts for the times on war and death. In J. Strachey (Ed. & Trans.), *The standard edition of the complete psychological works of Sigmund Freud* (Vol. 14, pp. 273–300). London, UK: Hogarth Press. Retrieved from www.pep-web.org (Original work published 1915).

Freud, S. (1959a). Formulations on the two principles of mental functioning. In J. Strachey (Ed. & Trans.), *The standard edition of the complete psychological works of Sigmund Freud* (Vol. 12, pp. 213–226). London, UK: Hogarth Press. Retrieved from www.pep-web.org (Original work published 1915).

Freud, S. (1959b). *Group psychology and the analysis of the ego* (J. Strachey, Trans.). New York, NY: Norton (Original work published 1921).

Freud, S. (1961a). *Beyond the pleasure principle* (J. Strachey, Trans.). New York, NY: Norton (Original work published 1920).

Freud, S. (1961b). *Civilization and its discontents* (J. Strachey, Trans.). New York, NY: Norton (Original work published 1930).

Freud, S. (1962). *Three essays on the theory of sexuality* (J. Strachey, Trans.). New York, NY: Basic Books (Original work published 1905).

Freud, S. (1990). *The Letters of Sigmund Freud to Eduard Silberstein, 1871–1881* (W. Boehlich, Ed. & A. J. Pomerans, Trans.). Cambridge, MA: Harvard University Press.

Fromm, E. (1970). The method and function of an analytic social psychology: Notes on psychoanalysis and historical materialism. In E. Fromm (Ed.), *The crisis of psychoanalysis* (pp. 110–134). New York, NY: Holt (Original work published 1932).

Fromm, E. (1981). The application of psychoanalysis to Marx's theory. In A. Fromm (Ed.), *On disobedience and other essays* (pp. 24–40). New York, NY: Seabury Press (Original work published 1965).

Gould, S. J. (1977). *Ontogeny and phylogeny*. Cambridge, MA: Belknap Press.

Haeckel, E. (1883). *The history of creation: Or the development of the Earth and its inhabitants by the action of natural causes* (Vols. 1–2, E. R. Lankester, Trans.). New York, NY: D. Appleton and Company (Original work published 1868).

Haeckel, E. (1900). *The evolution of man: A popular exposition of the principal points of human ontogeny and phylogeny* (Vols. 1–2, 3rd ed., J. McCabe, Trans.). New York, NY: D. Appleton and Company (Original work published 1874).

Haeckel, E. (1904). *The wonders of life: A popular study of biological philosophy* (J. McCabe, Trans.). London, UK: Watts & Co.

Horkheimer, M. (2002). Materialism and metaphysics. In M. J. O'Connell (Trans.), *Critical theory: Selected essays* (pp. 10–46). New York, NY: Continuum (Original work published 1933).

Horkheimer, M., & Adorno, T. W. (2002). *Dialectic of enlightenment: Philosophical fragments* (E. Jephcott, Trans. & G. S. Noerr, Ed.). Stanford, CA: Stanford University Press (Original work published 1947).

Jay, M. (1996). *The dialectical imagination: A history of the Frankfurt School and the Institute of Social Research, 1923–1950)*. Berkeley, CA: University of California Press (Original work published 1973).

Kerr, J. (1993). *A most dangerous method: The story of Jung, Freud, and Sabina Spielrein*. New York, NY: Knopf.

Marcaggi, G., & Guénolé, F. (2018, June). Freudarwin: Evolutionary thinking as a root of psychoanalysis. *Frontiers in Psychology, 9*, 892. Retrieved from www.frontiersin.org/articles/10.3389/fpsyg.2018.00892/full.

Marcuse, H. (1966). *Eros and civilization: A philosophical inquiry into Freud.* Boston, MA: Beacon Press (Original work published 1955).

Otis, L. (1994). *Organic memory: History and the body in the late nineteenth & early twentieth centuries*. Lincoln, NE: University of Nebraska Press.

Phillips, A. (1988). *Winnicott*. Cambridge, MA: Harvard University Press.

Pick, D. (1989). *Faces of degeneration: A European disorder, c. 1848-c. 1918.* New York, NY: Cambridge University Press.

Richards, R. J. (2002). *The romantic conception of life: Science and philosophy in the age of Goethe*. Chicago, IL: University of Chicago Press.

Richards, R. J. (2008). *The tragic sense of life: Ernst Haeckel and the struggle over evolutionary thought*. Chicago, IL: University of Chicago Press.

Ritvo, L. B. (1990). *Darwin's influence on Freud: A tale of two sciences*. New Haven, CT: Yale University Press.

Robinson, P. A. (1969). *The Freudian left: Wilhelm Reich, Geza Roheim, Herbert Marcuse*. New York, NY: Harper & Row.

Russell, E. S. (1916). *Form and function: A contribution to the history of animal morphology*. London, UK: John Murray.

Spurling, L. (Ed.). (1989). *Sigmund Freud: Critical assessments*. New York, NY: Routledge.

Sulloway, F. (1979). *Freud, biologist of the mind: Beyond the psychoanalytic legend*. New York, NY: Basic Books.

Weikart, R. (2004). *From Darwin to Hitler: Evolutionary ethics, eugenics, and racism in Germany*. New York, NY: Palgrave Macmillan.

Chapter 4

Analytical Psychology and the Dialectic of Enlightenment

Paul Bishop

In a remarkable and unexpected way, the global coronavirus pandemic – still ongoing at the time of writing – has demonstrated the validity of many core theses of critical theory as propounded by Theodor W. Adorno and Max Horkheimer in their book, *Dialectic of Enlightenment* (1944) – as well as of C.G. Jung's analytical psychology. While some of Jung's key tenets were discovered (if the transcriptions of his visions in *The Red Book* are to be believed) against the backdrop of the outbreak of World War I and *Dialectic of Enlightenment* was first published in Amsterdam in the final years of World War II, in this chapter I hope to show the continuing relevance of both intellectual traditions for the post-Covid-19 world and thereby to explore some of the points of affinity between them.

The Totally Administered Society

The argumentational dynamic of *Dialectic of Enlightenment* is clear from the powerful opening words of its first chapter: "Enlightenment," Horkheimer and Adorno (2002) declare, "understood in the widest sense as the advance of thought, has always aimed at liberating human beings from fear and installing them as masters. Yet" – and immediately this project is undermined in the most devastating way – "the wholly enlightened earth is radiant with triumphant calamity" (p. 1). More specifically, they claim, "Enlightenment's program was the disenchantment of the world" – an allusion to Max Weber[1] – for "it wanted to dispel myths, to overthrow fantasy with knowledge" (p. 1). So while they set up an opposition of Enlightenment versus myth, the relation between them is dialectical, for "just as myths already entail enlightenment, with every step enlightenment entangles itself more deeply in mythology" (p. 8).

DOI: 10.4324/9781003215301-4

Thus the dialectic of which Adorno and Horkheimer speak can be approached from the side of Enlightenment or from the side of myth. Here I wish to approach it in relation to analytical psychology from the side of Enlightenment, while noting the possibility of many divergent understandings of myth. After all, while Adorno and Horkheimer claim that "myth is already enlightenment, and enlightenment reverts to mythology" (p. xviii), the anthropologist Bronisław Malinowski (1884–1942) had argued in 1926 that myth is not "an explanation put forward to satisfy curiosity," but rather "the rearising of a primordial [i.e., archetypal] reality in narrative form" (Kerényi, 1969, p. 6; citing Malinowski, 1948, pp. 72–123). And even earlier, Sallust had defined myths (in *On the Gods and the World*, §4) as "things that never happened, but always are" (translated in Murray, 2002, p. 195). Obviously it is precisely such a primordial or archetypal dimension (as found, for instance, in the works of Carl Jung) that the Frankfurt School as a whole and Adorno in particular swiftly rejected.[2]

In seeking to investigate "the self-destruction of enlightenment," Adorno and Horkheimer (2002) argue that "the very concept of [enlightenment thinking], no less than the concrete historical forms, the institutions of society with which it is intertwined, already contains the germ of the regression [*Rückschritt*] which is taking place today" (p. xvi). In other words, "if enlightenment does not assimilate reflection on this regressive moment [*dies rückläufige Moment*], it seals its own fate [*besiegelt . . . ihr eigenes Schicksal*]," and a page or so later they reinforce this point, emphasizing "the necessity for enlightenment to reflect on itself if humanity is not to be totally betrayed" (pp. xvi-xvii). In fact, this is their definition of Fascism itself – that "progress is reverting to regression" (p. xviii). While warning of a "moment of recidivism," Horkheimer and Adorno – in a passage often overlooked by critics – explicitly exonerate myth from responsibility for the collapse of Enlightenment and its "relapse into mythology," the cause of which is said to lie "not so much in the nationalist, pagan, or other modern mythologies concocted specifically to cause such a relapse as in the fear of truth which petrifies enlightenment itself" (p. xvi).

Crucially, both "Enlightenment" and "myth" are held to be ontological equals, as "pertaining not merely to intellectual history but also to current reality" – in German, both are *als . . . real zu verstehen* (p. xvi). Consequently, "truth" (*Wahrheit*) is said to refer not merely to "rational consciousness" (*das vernünftige Bewußtsein*) but equally to "the form it takes in reality" (*dessen Gestalt in der Wirklichkeit*) (p. xvi). For reasons of space, we cannot explore in detail how *Dialectic of Enlightenment* unfolds this argument with its chapters on the concept of Enlightenment, on the culture industry, and on anti-Semitism, and its two excurses on Odysseus, myth, and Enlightenment, and on the Marquis de Sade's pornographic novel *Juliette* and Enlightenment. But this work as a whole and critical theory more generally involve the notion found elsewhere in the writings of Adorno of "the totally administered society" or *die verwaltete Welt*.[3]

The "administered world" refers to the society of late capitalism, in which a new form of fascism has taken root in the form of administration – a self-legitimizing bureaucracy. Drawing on Horkheimer's study of class difference and organized criminality, in which a conspiratorial clique exercises control over the society around it,[4] and developing an analysis that is complementary to Weber's,[5] Adorno offers a chilling analysis of what one might call "structural" or "institutional evil." While the phrase *verwaltete Welt*, or "administered world," is used in various places in Adorno's writings, the concept was given its most extensive treatment in a discussion between Adorno, Horkheimer, and the historian and sociologist Eugen Kogon (1903–1987), transmitted from Frankfurt by Hessischer Rundfunk on September 19, 1959, and broadcast under the title *Die verwaltete Welt*.[6]

In this broadcast, Adorno argues that, as the Austrian writer Ferdinand Kürnberger (1821–1879) put it in his novel *Der Amerikamüde* (1855), "life no longer lives" (*das Leben lebt nicht*) (Adorno, Horkheimer, Kogon, 1959 [2010]). "There is," Adorno maintains, "no longer any life in the sense in which we all use the word life," because there has been "a transition of the entire world, of life as a whole, to a system of administration, to a particular kind of control from above." In particular, he emphasizes that in its most recent forms, bureaucracy serves "to rationalize the irrational," whilst the system of planning conceals a complete lack of real planning.[7]

Agreement with Adorno's view was expressed in this broadcast by Horkheimer, who added that "today human beings still make their own history, it's just that they don't know this"; they can "still make decisions, but they decide to go along with what is happening." For Horkheimer, the present age is the age of psychology and, in particular, psychoanalysis. But on his account, the process of administration can now, thanks to psychoanalysis, be carried on within the individual. Human beings turn themselves into objects and analysis, which used to offer a critical way out of this reified condition, remains part of the reified world.

For his part, Eugen Kogon proposes the view that human beings "still possess an inner freedom" but that our freedom to say yes or no to what is going on in the world around us is not followed by any consequences, which throws us back into our innermost self, so that the increasing administration of the external world is accompanied by a near total loss of what remains of our inner freedom. In *Dialectic of Enlightenment*, Horkheimer and Adorno (2002) describe the consequences of the subsumption of culture to the power of the economic in the following terms:

> The culture industry, the most inflexible style of all, thus proves to be the goal of the very liberalism which is criticized for its lack of style. Not only did its categories and contents originate in the liberal sphere, in domesticated naturalism no less than in the operetta and the revue, but the modern culture combines are the academic area in which a piece of the circulation sphere otherwise in the process of disintegration, together with the corresponding entrepreneurial types, still tenuously survives. In that area people can still make their ways, provided they do not look too closely at their true purpose and are willing to be compliant. Anyone who resists can only survive by being incorporated.
>
> (p. 104)

The question arises: if this is so – if, far from being opposites, mythology and science (or myth and Enlightenment) are dialectically interrelated, each presupposing the other – what should we do about it?

At a crucial point in their argument, Adorno and Horkheimer (2002) speak of the "remembrance of nature in the subject" (*Eingedenken der Natur im Subjekt*) as being the central point at which the Enlightenment is opposed to tyranny. "Through this remembrance of nature within the subject," they write, "a remembrance which contains the unrecognized truth of all culture, enlightenment is opposed in principle to power" (p. 32).

This idea of an inner, primordial nature crops up time and again in the thinking of the first and second generations of the Frankfurt School (who, in their anti-Jungian outlook, attribute it solely to Freud). Indeed, even in the preface to *Dialectic of Enlightenment* Adorno and Horkheimer (2002) write that "the enslavement to nature of people today cannot be separated from social progress" (p. xvii). And their focus in their first excursus on the *Odyssey* on the concepts of sacrifice and renunciation is said to demonstrate "both the difference between and the unity of mythical nature and enlightened mastery of nature" (p. xviii), while the second excursus on Kant, Sade, and Nietzsche is intended to demonstrate "how the subjugation of everything natural to the sovereign subject culminates in the domination of what is blindly objective and natural" (p. xviii).

In his *Theory of Communicative Action* (1981), Jürgen Habermas focuses on this key phrase as part of *his* critique of Adorno's and Horkheimer's critique of instrumental reason. Here Habermas accuses his colleagues of "follow[ing] the (largely effaced) path that leads back to the origins of instrumental reason, so as to *outdo* the concept of objective reason"; thus their theory of mimesis, Habermas (1987) argues, leads them to speak about it "only as they would about a piece of uncomprehended nature [*wie über ein undurchschautes Stück Natur*]" (p. 382). Habermas's judgment on Adorno is particularly severe:

> As opposed as the intentions behind their respective philosophies of history are, Adorno is in the end very similar to Heidegger as regards his position on the theoretical claims of objectivating thought and of reflection: the mindfulness [*Eingedenken*] of nature comes shockingly close to the recollection [*Andenken*] of being.
>
> (p. 385)

(Of course, the shared legacy with Heideigger could alternatively be seen as a *strength*, not a weakness, and as evidence of the global appeal and truth of this *topos*.)

In *Civilization and Its Discontents* (1930), Freud had written that "a piece of unconquerable nature" (*ein Stück der unbesiegbaren Natur*) forms "a part of our own psychical constitution" (Freud, 1961, p. 86). Yet in so writing, Freud was echoing none other than Jung. For Jung, in a paper on "Psychological Types" given at the International Congress on Education held in Territet, Switzerland, in 1923, he had remarked that "the unconscious is the residue of unconquered nature [*das Unbewußte ist der Rest unbezwungener Urnatur*] in us, just as it is also the matrix of our unborn future" (Jung, 1974, para. 907). In a later paper given in Karlsruehe in 1927 titled "Analytical Psychology und *Weltanschauung*," Jung remarks that "hemmed in by rationalistic walls, we are cut off from the eternity of nature [*die Ewigkeit der Natur*]," while insisting that "the fantasy-images of the unconscious which our rationalism has rejected" constitute "part of the nature *in us* [*zur* Natur in uns], which lies buried in our past and against which we have barricaded ourselves behind walls of reason" (Jung, 1969a, para. 739). And in a lecture given to the Alsatian Pastoral Conference at Strasbourg in May 1932, later published as *Die Beziehungen der Psychotherapie zur Seelsorge* and translated as "Psychotherapists or the Clergy," Jung remarked that "the opening up of the unconscious means the outbreak of intense spiritual suffering," and he continued as follows:

> It is as when a flourishing civilization is abandoned to invading hordes of barbarians, or when fertile fields are exposed by the bursting of a dam to a raging torrent. The World War was such an invasion which showed, as nothing else could, how thin are the walls which separate a well-ordered world from lurking chaos. But it is the same with the individual and his rationally ordered world. Seeking revenge for the violence his reason has done to her, outraged Nature only awaits the moment when the partition falls so as to overwhelm the conscious life with destruction [*Hinter seiner vernünftig geordneten Welt wartet rachsüchtig eine durch Vernunft vergewaltigte Natur auf den Augenblick, wo die trennende Wand fällt, um sich verheerend ins bewusste Dasein zu ergiessen*].
>
> (Jung, 1969b, para. 531)

This danger posed to the psyche is, Jung adds, something that humankind has been aware of "since the most primordial and most primitive times" (*seit urältesten und primitivsten Zeiten*) (para. 531). And in his foreword of 1954 to his late, great work *Mysterium coniunctionis* (1955–1956), Jung wrote with even greater urgency – understandably so, in light of the world events of the preceding decade – that

> although contemporary human beings believe that they can change themselves without limit, or be changed through external influences, the astounding, or rather the terrifying, fact remains that despite civilization and Christian education, they are still, morally, as much in bondage to their instincts as an animal, and can therefore fall victim at any moment to the beast within.
>
> (Jung, 1970, p. xviii; trans. modified)

Indeed, the emphasis that we can see in these passages from 1923 to 1954 on the persistence of the archaic – the sense that, like the poor in the gospel, the primordial is always with us – belongs to the major hallmarks of Jungian thought,[8] and the notion of "inner nature" represents an important point of intersection between analytical psychology and critical theory.[9]

Now it is important not to overlook the very real differences of outlook that exist between critical theory and analytical psychology, for instance, in relation to the utility (or otherwise) of astrology![10] Yet the linchpin between these two theoretical approaches is the notion of "inner nature," or "nature in the subject," and the Frankfurt School's insistence on the need for remembrance of nature within the subject is matched by Jung's insistence on the reality of the psyche. In November 1932 Jung gave a lecture at the Kulturbund in Vienna with the suggestive title *Die Stimme des Innern*, that is, "The Voice from Within." (Subsequently Jung published his paper in a revised form as *Vom Werden der Persönlichkeit*, and it has been translated by Stanley M. Dell and by R.F.C. Hull as "The Development of Personality.") "Only the tiniest fraction of the psyche," Jung argued in 1932, is identical with "the conscious mind and its box of magic tricks," that is, instrumental reason, while for the much greater part it is "sheer unconscious *fact*, hard and immitigable as granite, immoveable, inaccessible, yet ready at any time to come crashing down upon us at the behest of unseen powers" (Jung, 1954, para. 302). Nothing can get us around this insight into the psyche as "an objective fact, hard as granite and heavy as lead," something which confronts us as "an inner experience" (para. 303).

Of course, the problem of barbarism is nothing new. Already in 1795, Schiller had asked in his *Letters on the Aesthetic Education of Humankind* (Letter 8, §3–§4), "How is it, then, that we still remain barbarians?," noting that while "reason has accomplished all that she can by discovering the law and establishing it" and has "purged herself of both the illusions of the senses and the delusions of sophistry," nevertheless, "philosophy itself, which first seduced us from our allegiance to Nature, is now in loud and urgent tones calling us back to her bosom" (Schiller, 1982, pp. 49–51). (Tellingly, in his lecture "Analytical Psychologie and *Weltanschauung*," Jung does not urge us to embrace irrationalism. He tells us to do the very opposite: analytical psychology tries to "resolve the resultant conflict not by going 'back to nature' with Rousseau, but by holding on to the level of reason we have successfully reached [*die glücklich erreichte moderne*

Stufe der Ratio], and by enriching consciousness with a knowledge of the spirit of nature [*mit der Erkenntnis des natürlichen Geistes bereichert*]" [Jung, 1969a, para. 739, trans. modified].)

Jung on the Enlightenment

The idea found in Jung's lecture to the Kulturbund in Vienna about the inner voice recalls not just the daimon of Socrates but also the figure of Faust's Mephisto as well as Aesculapius and the Cabir Telesphorus (Jung, 1954, para. 300). While the immediate political context of Jung's remarks was obviously 1932 and the rising influence in Germany of the NSDAP (or, as he put it in 1946, "the year in which Germany's fate was decided" [Jung, 1964, para. 471]), it is hard not to read these remarks today in the light of our own concerns. "The gigantic catastrophes that threaten us today are not elemental happenings of a physical or biological order, but psychic events. To a quite terrifying degree we are threatened by wars and revolutions which are nothing other than psychic epidemics" (Jung, 1954, para. 302).

True, we can only accept these words with some qualification: what we are facing today is a happening of the biological order (in the form of the coronavirus) *and* a psychic epidemic in the form of political polarization, mass shootings and violent extremism. Yet the *biological* dimension of our current crisis should not detract from the force of Jung's warning that "at any moment several millions of human beings may be smitten with a new madness, and then we shall have another world war or devastating revolution," for "instead of being at the mercy of wild beasts, earthquakes, landslides, and inundations, modern humankind is battered by the elemental forces of its own psyche" (Jung, 1954, para. 302).

Analogously to Adorno and Horkheimer, Jung lays the blame for this situation at the feet of the Enlightenment, arguing in *Die Stimme des Innern* in 1932 that "the Age of Enlightenment, which stripped nature and human institutions of gods, overlooked the God of Terror who dwells in the human soul," and adding that, "if anywhere, fear of God is justified in face of the overwhelming supremacy of the psychic" (Jung, 1954, para. 302). Nor was this the only occasion on which Jung offered his own critique of the Enlightenment. Already in *Psychological Types* (1921) Jung had voiced a distinct skepticism toward the confidence expressed in the Enlightenment by Schiller in his *Letters on the Aesthetic Education of*

Humankind when he wrote (in Letter 8, §4) that "our Age is Enlightened; that is to say, such knowledge has been discovered and publicly disseminated as would suffice to correct at least our practical principles" and "the spirit of free inquiry has dissipated those false conceptions which for so long barred the approach to truth, and undermined the foundations upon which fanaticism and deception had raised their throne" (Schiller, 1982, p. 49; cited Jung, 1974, para. 116). While Jung rejects these lines with considerable vigor – "What an overvaluation of the intellect. . . . What rationalism!" (para. 117) – he is nevertheless alert to the ironic dimension of Goethe's figure of the Proktophantasmist in *Faust*, who declares, "Vanish at once, you've been explained away!" (*Faust I*, l. 4159).[11]

The reason for Jung's skepticism about the Enlightenment is founded in the dialectic between freedom and the conflict of instincts as reflected in Schiller's remark in his *Letters* (Letter 7, §3) about how,

> fearful of freedom, which in its first tentative ventures always comes in the guise of an enemy, we shall either cast ourselves into the arms of easy servitude or, driven to despair by a pedantic tutelage, escape into the wild libertinism of the natural state.
> (1982, p. 47; cited in Jung, 1974, para. 115)

For Jung, these statements acquired "a living, albeit bloody background" (*einen ebenso lebendigen als blutigen Hintergrund*) in the form of the French Revolution, contemporaneous with the composition of Schiller's *Letters*: "begun in the name of philosophy and reason, with a soaring idealism, it ended in blood-drenched chaos, from which arose the despotic genius of Napoleon" (para. 115). And so as Jung piquantly puts it, "the Goddess of Reason" – an icon of the Cult of Reason, established in 1793 and represented as a statue in all churches in France, including Notre Dame, in which the symbolic flame of Truth burned on an altar to Liberty – "proved herself powerless against the might of the unchained beast" (para. 116).

In 1794 the Cult of Reason was replaced by the Cult of the Supreme Being and, in turn, in 1802 by the suppression of both cults and the reestablishment of Catholicism by the "Law on Cults of 18 Germinal, year X"; correspondingly, Jung noted the persistence of Judeo-Christianity – and at a deeper level, paganism – despite the Enlightenment. Just as "the religion of the last two thousand years is a psychological attitude, a definite form and manner of adaptation to the world without and within," so "the unconscious was able to keep paganism alive," and Jung points to the Renaissance as an example of "the ease with which the spirit of antiquity springs to life again" and to the early twentieth century (including the First World War) as evidence of "the readiness of the vastly older primitive mentality to rise up from the past can be seen in our own day, perhaps better than at any other epoch known to history" (Jung, 1974, para. 313).

Here Jung articulates the principle that "the more deeply rooted the principle, the more violent will be the attempts to shake it off," citing Voltaire's cry, *Écrasez l'infâme*, as emblematic of the Age of Enlightenment, which heralded "the religious upheaval started off by the French Revolution." Yet this upheaval is said to be "nothing but a basic readjustment of attitude, though it lacked universality," and this problem of a general change of attitude "has never slept since that time," cropping up again "in many prominent minds of the nineteenth century" (Jung, 1974, para. 314). Jung points to the importance in the writings of Goethe of the figure of Prometheus as an example of a dialectical "law," which he describes as follows:

> When an individual meets a difficult task which they cannot master with the means at their disposal, a retrograde movement of libido automatically sets in, i.e., a regression. The libido draws away from the problem of the moment, becomes introverted, and reactivates in the unconscious a more or less primitive analogue of the conscious situation.
>
> (Jung, 1974, para. 314)[12]

Goethe's choice of the figure of Prometheus – equivalent in its significance for Jung's argument to that of Odysseus for Adorno's and Horkheimer's in *Dialectic of Enlightenment* – reflects not simply Goethe's "deep scholarship" but more generally "the classical spirit, which at the turn of the eighteenth century was felt to contain a compensatory value" and had found expression as Philhellenism in aesthetics, philosophy, morals, and politics. "Glorified," Jung says, as *freedom, naivete, beauty*, etc., it was really "the paganism of antiquity" that met "the yearnings of that age," springing from "a feeling of imperfection, of spiritual barbarism, of moral servitude, of drabness" and arising from "a one-sided evaluation of everything Greek, and from the consequent fact that the psychological dissociation between the differentiated and the undifferentiated functions became painfully evident" (Jung, 1974, para. 314). Yet this attempt at "a regressive Renaissance" had been, Jung claims, "still-born," for "the classical solution would no longer work," reflected in the fate of Goethe's "Prometheus Fragment" (1773) and "Pandora" (1807–1808) (para. 315). Because "the intervening centuries of Christianity with their profound spiritual upheavals could not be undone," the *penchant* for antiquity "gradually petered out in medievalism" (para. 315). (Jung points to Goethe's *Faust*, where this problem is "seized by the horns," but it seems that as a problem it remains unresolved, if the *Red Book* is anything to go by.)[13]

In the context of a discussion of *Pragmatism: A New Name for Some Old Ways of Thinking* (1907) by William James (1842–1910), Jung described the contemporary scientific attitude as "exclusively concretistic and empirical" (Jung, 1974, para. 516). On this account, science has "no appreciation of the value of ideas, for facts rank higher than knowledge of the primordial forms in which the human mind conceives them," and Jung describes "this swing toward concretism" as "a comparatively recent development, a relic of the Enlightenment." Its results might be "astonishing," but they are said to have led to "an accumulation of empirical material whose very immensity is productive of more confusion than clarity," and the "inevitable outcome" is "scientific separatism and specialist mythology, which spells death to universality" (Jung, 1974, para. 516) – a situation that sounds very much like the one in which we find ourselves today.

In fact, one of the great strengths of analytical psychology as opposed to critical theory is its interest in its own historical position and in the mechanisms of change. Whereas critical theory relies on the historical dialectics of Marx to do much of its conceptual heavy lifting in this regard, analytical psychology develops a dialectic of progression and regression and is explicit about how it "finds itself in a definite historical setting" (Jung, 1964, para. 22). As a consequence, analytical psychology presents itself (in the introduction and epilogue to *Psychology and Alchemy*) as a program of recovery – above all, recovering a way of thinking that eschews non-ambiguity and non-contradiction as "one-sided and thus unsuited to express the incomprehensible" (Jung, 1968, para. 18).[14] In 1943, Jung wrote that "things have gone pretty rapidly downhill since the Age of Enlightenment, for, once this petty reasoning mind, which cannot endure any paradoxes" – or as the Frankfurt School would put it, instrumental rationality – "is awakened, no sermon on earth can keep down" (para. 19). Unlike critical theory, however, analytical psychology does not rest content with a gesture of lamentation but argues that "a new task then arises: to lift this still undeveloped mind step by step to a higher level and to increase the number of persons who have at least some inkling of the scope of paradoxical truth" (para. 19).

What Jung calls "the upward thrust of evolving consciousness" has reached the point where it has begun to "restore to the psyche that which had been psychic from the beginning" (Jung, 1968, para. 562), and thus one could describe analytical psychology as a project of psychic restitution. "Yet," Jung asks, "ever since the Age of Enlightenment and in the era of scientific rationalism, what indeed was the psyche?," and he answers that it had become synonymous with consciousness, with the ego, with "what I know" (para. 562). In Jungian terminology, a consciousness that is egocentric and conscious of nothing but its own existence is "inflated," initiating "a regression of consciousness into unconsciousness" (para. 563). Such a consciousness is, Jung says, "incapable of leaning from the past, incapable of understanding contemporary events, and incapable of drawing right conclusions about the future," and one of the consequences of this lack of ability was "a war of monumental frightfulness" that had been played out for four years "on the stage of Europe" (i.e., World War I), "a war that *nobody* wanted" – but "nobody dreamed of asking exactly who or what had caused the war and its continuation" (para. 563). For analytical psychology, the causes of the war were ultimately to be found in the Europeans' state of "unconscious possession," something that could only be ended by Europeans distancing themselves from becoming "scared of" their so-called "god-almightiness" (para. 563). The solution, for Jung, lay in recognizing there are contents "which do not belong to the ego-personality" but must rather be ascribed to "a psychic non-ego." In other words, we must recognize the Other, access to which may be found through the "models or *archetypi* that we may well call remedies for both human beings and the times," that is, "the useful and edifying models held up to us by poets and philosophers" (para. 563). Like the Frankfurt School, Jung attaches the highest importance to philosophy and to art. This is the reason for Jung's interest in alchemy – as an "art," since it "[felt] – and rightly so – that it was concerned with creative processes that can be truly grasped only by experience, though intellect may give them a name" (para. §564).

Conclusion

It would be entirely in keeping with the general thrust of critical theory to offer a critique of Adorno's and Horkeimer's critique of the Enlightenment – and of Jung's too. In both analytical psychology and critical theory, the Enlightenment is regarded as something monolithic, whereas Enlightenment is an extraordinarily plural or multiple phenomenon: the French Enlightenment is different from the German *Aufklärung*, which is different from the English Enlightenment (which is different from the Scottish, where there is no separation, for instance, between the domains of rationality and spirituality). In reality there are *many* different forms or varieties of the Enlightenment: a "Rosicrucian" Enlightenment (Frances Yates), a "covert" Enlightenment (Alfred J. Gabay), a "religious" Enlightenment (David Sorkin), and even a "Catholic" Enlightenment (Ulrich L. Lehner). Then again, others have identified *les anti-Lumières* as a tradition linking the eighteenth century and the Cold War (Zeev Sternhell) or described such thinkers as Jean Meslier, La Mettrie, Maupertuis, Helvétius, d'Holbach, and the Marquis de Sade as *les ultras des Lumières* (Michel Onfray).

In particular, the historian Jonathan Israel has distinguished between the "mainstream" of the Enlightenment and its "radical" wing: whereas the "mainstream" or "moderate" Enlightenment is represented by such thinkers as Locke, Voltaire, or Montesquieu, the "radical" Enlightenment is represented by Spinoza and his rationalist materialism (Israel, 2001, 2006, 2011). Whereas "mainstream" or "moderate" Enlightenment was reserved in its critique of laws and social conventions, even to the point of being conservative or timid, the "radical" Enlightenment was much bolder and more confident in asserting its belief in toleration, democracy, and equality. Both critical theory and analytical psychology tend, however, to collapse these different tendencies and even tensions within the Enlightenment into one monolithic entity, failing to distinguish between its radical and non-radical versions.

In fact, Jung was as aware as anyone, including Adorno and Horkheimer, of the historicity of the Enlightenment, that is to say, its specific location in place (Europe) and time (the eighteenth century). In *Mysterium coniunctionis*, Jung reflected on how the growth of empirical science was accompanied by the development of the doctrine of the *lumen naturae* (as found, for example, in Paracelsus).[15] On this account, although the alchemists were "more or less aware that their insights and truths were of divine origin, they knew they were not sacred revelations but were vouchsafed by individual inspiration or by the *lumen naturae*, the *sapientia Dei* hidden in nature" (Jung, 1970, para. 150). Consequently,

> [a]s the West started to investigate nature, till then completely unknown, the doctrine of the *lumen naturae* began to germinate too. Ecclesiastical doctrine and scholastic philosophy had both proved incapable of shedding any light on the nature of the physical world. The conjecture thereupon arose that just as the mind revealed its nature in the light of divine revelation, so nature herself must possess a "certain luminosity" which could become a source of enlightenment.
> (Jung, 1970, para. 425)

As Tatsuhiro Nakajima (2018) has suggested (p. 37), Jung saw the paradigm shift in which the natural philosophy of Aristotle became displaced by the Cartesian philosophy of mind in terms of the "de-psychologization" of "projected psychology" (cf. Jung, 1974, para. 12), and Jung thus plots the emergence of three kinds of "science" or "knowledge" or "[en]light[enment]" – empiricism, revelation, and "natural light" (or *lumen naturae*), and the rise of empirical science is accompanied both by a decline in Aristotelianism and a concomitant resurgence of Hermetic Neoplatonism:

> It is therefore understandable that for those individuals whose particular interest lay in the investigation of natural things the dogmatic view of the world should lose its force as the *lumen naturae* gained in attraction, even though the dogma itself was not directly doubted. The more serious alchemists, if we are to believe their statements, were religious people who had no thought of criticizing revealed truth. There is in the literature of alchemy, so far as I can judge, no attack on dogma. The only thing of this kind is a depreciation of the Aristotelian philosophy sponsored by the Church in favour of Hermetic Neoplatonism.[16]
> (Jung, 1970, para. 425)

Indeed, the alchemists themselves are said by Jung to have been caught up in their own version of the dialectic of enlightenment, for while they believed themselves to be supporting doctrine or dogma, in fact they were undermining it:

> Not only were the old Masters not critical of ecclesiastical doctrine, they were, on the contrary, convinced that their discoveries, real or

imaginary, would enrich the doctrine of the correspondence of heavenly and earthly things, since they endeavoured to prove that the "mystery of faith" was reflected in the world of nature. They could not guess that their passion for investigating nature would detract as much as it did from revealed truth, and that their scientific interests could be aroused only as the fascination of dogma began to pall.

(Jung, 1970, para. 425)

According to Nakajima (2018), Jung's archetypal theory undertakes to compensate for what has gone missing in modern psychology, thanks to the radical break between the Aristotelian soul and the Cartesian mind (p. 37); in other words, to reverse the trend toward nihilism.[17]

Indeed, in some respects, analytical psychology may even be seen to have some advantages over critical theory. For the Frankfurt School is able to analyze the crisis of the Enlightenment but is unwilling (or unable) to offer a solution, hence its pessimistic stance. (One recalls Adorno's "extreme allegiance" to the *Bilderverbot*, and the difficulties that critics have had in disengaging his famous "standpoint of redemption," although the recent work of Sebastian Truskolaski seeks to correct this view of his alleged fatalism.)[18] By contrast, Jung is able to explain the dynamic of historical change in terms of his theory of progression and regression, which opens up at least the possibility of optimism though conceiving regression in terms of a *reculer pour mieux sauter*.

The philosophical and rhetorical sophistication of Adorno and Horkheimer may appear to be opposed to Jung's often plain speaking, but then again one might recall his words from 1932: "But all this is so much abstraction. Everyone knows that the intellect, that clever jackanapes, can put it this way or any other way he pleases" (Jung, 1954, para. 303). In 1941, Jung identified "a peculiar use of language" – namely, when one "wants to speak forcefully in order to impress one's opponent, so one employs a special, 'bombastic' style full of neologisms which might be described as 'power-words'" – as a symptom that was "observable not only in the psychiatric clinic but also among certain modern philosophers" (Jung, 1967, para. 155).[19] Precisely such intellectual abstraction has sadly led to the decline of the Frankfurt School in terms of its cultural influence, whereas the publication of Jung's *Red Book* with its sheer visceral appeal (or repulsion) has reinvigorated the Jungian intellectual tradition (as the series of works edited by Stein & Arzt, 2017,

2018, 2019, suggests). In the end, analytical psychology makes a plea for us to "repudiate the arrogant claim of the conscious mind to be the whole of the psyche, and to admit that the psyche is a reality which we cannot grasp with our present means of understanding" (Jung, 1968, para. 564). In a stunning example of the *topos* of modesty, Jung declares, "I do not call someone who admits their ignorance an obscurantist" (para. 564). Already in the 1950s, Jung was warning that "the danger that faces us today is that the whole of reality will be replaced by words" (Jung, 1964, para. 882). In this respect, it is worthwhile recalling the principle enunciated by Horkheimer and Adorno (2002) that "false clarity is only another name for myth," and that "myth was always obscure and luminous at once," for "it has always been distinguished by its familiarity and its exemption from the work of concepts" (p. xvii).

Where, however, can this recovery and resistance and the "work of concepts" be carried out in a post-Covid-19 world? Not in our universities, as Giorgio Agamben argued in May 2020. For Agamben (in some respects, an inheritor of the critical theory tradition), the decision taken by Italian (and many other European) universities to hold their classes for the 2020–2021 session online was one of huge significance. In his view, the global pandemic was being used as a pretext for "the increasingly pervasive diffusion of digital technologies," reflected in the disappearance of group discussion in seminars. "Part of the technological barbarism that we are currently living through," Agamben (2020) wrote, "is the cancellation from life of any experience of the senses as well as the loss of the gaze, permanently imprisoned in a spectral screen" – or in the classical terms favored by Horkheimer and Adorno, the flickering, post-Homeric underworld of Microsoft Teams and Zoom.

For Agamben, the coronavirus crisis marks the end of a way of life – a way of life he traces back to the *clerici vagantes* and the birth of the universities from student associations in the Middle Ages. On this account, the social dimension of university life is crucial – and its demise, devastating. "All this, which has lasted for almost ten centuries, now ends forever" (Agamben, 2020). In response to this crisis, Agamben made two suggestions: first, those professors who submit to "the new dictatorship of telematics" by holding their courses only online are, in his eyes, "the perfect equivalent of the university teachers who in 1931 swore allegiance to the Fascist regime," and second, students who "truly love to study" should refuse to enroll on such courses and instead constitute in themselves "new *universitates*," as providing the only chance to create something within which – "in the face of technological barbarism" – "the word of the past might remain alive and something like a new culture be born" (Agamben, 2020).

Thus, analytical psychology, the Frankfurt School, and now Agamben restate the fundamental problem as analyzed by Schiller (1982): how can our age lift itself out of its "deep degradation" and, on the one hand, "emancipate itself from the blind forces of Nature" (forces of which, of course, coronavirus is a manifestation) and, on the other, "return to her simplicity, truth, and fulness" (p. 47)? Schiller described this as "a task for more than *one* century" and in this, at least, he was surely correct.

Notes

1 See Max Weber, "Wissenschaft als Beruf" [1919] (Weber, 1968, p. 594).
2 For an account of how the second chapter of *Dialectic of the Enlightenment*, the famous "excursus" on Homer's *Odyssey*, owes much to Adorno's "productive confrontation" with the neo-Romantic *Kulturkritik* and *Zivilisationskritik* of such German conservative intellectuals as Ludwig Klages (1872–1956) and the poet Rudolf Borchardt (1877–1945), see Vicenzo Martella (2012).
3 For further discussion, see Greisman and Ritzer (1981).
4 Horkheimer (1985). For further discussion, see Schulte-Bockholt (2001) and Schmidt (2007).
5 See Greisman (1976).
6 "Die verwaltete Welt," Hessischer Rundfunk, 19 September 1959; rebroadcast by ORF, Ö1, "Im Gespräch," 14 October 2010.
7 Analogously, shortly after the publication of the *Red Book*, Andrew Samuels observed, "It's not just an archival document, it's a very contemporary document: it says a lot about what's wrong with modern society. This is not just for mystics or for prophetic figures. It's about why living in the kind of society we've got right now drives you crazy – because the inner world, what you've got going on inside you, is not listened to, not wanted on board. We live in a flattened, regulated, controlled society that's also actually out of control, as the economic crisis shows" – and as many global events that have unfolded in the meantime have confirmed (Samuels, 2009).
8 For further discussion, see Bishop (2012).
9 For further discussion, see (Evers, 1987, pp. 186–187).
10 See Adorno's 1974 article on the *Los Angeles Times* astrology column (reproduced as Adorno (2002), pp. 46–171); as well as Greene (2018a, 2018b).
11 The name "Proktophantasmist," constructed out of the Greek *proktos* ("anus") + *phantasma* ("phantom"), is in itself an obvious clue to its satirical function – a point not overlooked even by Rudolf Steiner (1982, p. 53)!

12 On the importance of this dialectic, cf. Jung, 1974, para. 202; and *Transformations and Symbols of the Libido* (1911–1912), where Jung had written: "When some great work is to be accomplished, before which the weak individual recoils, doubtful of his strength, his libido returns to that source – and this is the dangerous moment, in which the decision takes place between annihilations and new life" (Jung, 1991, para. 459).
13 In his *Red Book*, Jung says, "I must catch up with a piece of the Middle Ages – within myself. We have only finished the Middle Ages of – others" (Jung, 2009, p. 330).
14 In *Psychology and Alchemy*, Jung seeks to recuperate not simply medieval alchemy but an older tradition, for at the heart of the second of the two major studies first presented as a lecture at the Eranos Conferences in this volume lies an analysis of the *Liber Platonis quartorum* (Jung, 1968, paras. 357–389).
15 See Jung's lecture of 1941 titled "Paracelsus as a Spiritual Phenomenon" (Jung 1967, paras. 145–238). For a recent attempt to rehabilitate this notion of a purely immanent, non-supernatural form of enlightenment and to apply both to modern art (Paul Cezanne, Mark Rothko, Sol LeWitt, Lee Krasner) and to modern science (the concept of space, the notion of randomness, the shape of the cosmos, and other puzzles of the universe), see Marcolli (2020).
16 At this point, Jung refers in a footnote to the following passage from Gerhard Dorn's *Speculativae philosophiae, gradus septem vel decem continens*: "Whoever wishes to learn the alchemical art, let him not learn the philosophy of Aristotle, but that which teaches the truth . . . for his teaching consists entirely in amphibology, which is the best of all cloaks for lies. When he censured Plato and others for the sake of gaining renown, he could find no more commodious instrument than that which he used for his censure, namely amphibology, attacking his writings on the one hand, defending them by subterfuge on the other, and the reverse; and this kind of sophistry is to be found in all his writings" (*Theatrum chemicum*, vol. 1, Ursel 1602, pp. 255–310 [p. 271]; cited Jung, 1970, para. 425, fn. 224).
17 It would, however, be wrong to see Jung as trying simply to turn back the clock: as he put it in 1911–1912, "*belief should be replaced by understanding,*" for "then we would keep the beauty of the symbol, but still remain free from the depressing results of submission to belief" (Jung, 1991, para. 356).
18 For further discussion, see Pritchard (2002) and Truskolaski (2021).
19 Nevertheless, compare with Jung's defense of incomprehensible jargon in the case of Paracelsus: "There are, however, mitigating circumstances: doctors have always loved using magically incomprehensible jargon for even the most ordinary things. It is part of the medical persona. But it is odd indeed that Paracelsus, who prided himself on teaching and writing in German, should have been the very one to concoct the most intricate neologisms out of Latin, Greek, Italian, Hebrew, and possibly even Arabic" (CW 13 §155).

References

Adorno, T.W. (2002). The Stars Down to Earth: The Los Angeles Times Astrology Column [1974]. In *The Stars Down to Earth and Other Essays on the Irrational in Culture*, ed. S. Crook. London and New York: Routledge. 46–171.

Adorno, T.W., Horkheimer, M. and Kogon, E. (1959). Die verwaltete Welt. Hessischer Rundfunk, broadcast 19 September 1959 (rebroadcast by ORF, Ö1, Im Gespräch, 14 October 2010).
Agamben, G. (2020). *Requiem for the Students*, trans. D. Alan. Available online: https://medium.com/@ddean3000/requiem-for-the-students-giorgio-agamben-866670c11642. Consulted 05.05.2020.
Bishop, P. (2012). *The Archaic: The Past in the Present: A Collection of Papers*. London and New York: Routledge.
Evers, T. (1987). *Mythos und Emanzipation: Eine kritische Annäherung an C.G. Jung*. Hamburg: Junius.
Freud, S. (1961). Civilization and its Discontents [1930]. In *The Future of an Illusion, Civilization and Its Discontents, and Other Works* [*Standard Edition of the Collected Works*, vol. 21], ed. J. Strachey and A. Freud. London: Hogarth Press; Institute of Psycho-Analysis. 57–146.
Greene, Liz. (2018a). *Jung's Studies in Astrology: Prophecy, Magic, and the Qualities of Time*. London and New York: Routledge, 2018.
Greene, Liz. (2018b). *The Astrological World of Jung's "Liber Novus": Daimons, Gods, and the Planetary Journey*. London and New York: Routledge, 2018.
Greisman, H.C. (1976). "Disenchantment of the World": Romanticism, Aesthetics and Sociological Theory. *The British Journal of Sociology*, *27*, 495–507.
Greisman, H.C. and Ritzer, G. (1981). Max Weber, Critical Theory, and the Administered World. *Qualitative Sociology*, *4*(1), Spring, 34–55.
Habermas, J. (1987). The Theory of Communicative Action [1981], trans. T. McCarthy. Vol. 1, *Reason and the Rationalization of Society*. Cambridge: Polity Press.
Horkheimer, M. (1985). On the Sociology of Class Relations [*Zur Soziologie der Klassenverhältnisse*, 1943]. In *Gesammelte Schriften*, ed. A. Schmidt, vol. 12. Frankfurt am Main: Suhrkamp. 75–104.
Horkheimer, M. and Adorno, T.W. (2002). *Dialectic of Enlightenment: Philosophical Fragments*, ed. G. Schmid Noerr, trans. E. Jephcott. Stanford, CA: Stanford UP.
Israel, J. (2001). *Radical Enlightenment: Philosophy and the Making of Modernity, 1650–1750*. Oxford and New York: Oxford UP.
Israel, J. (2006). *Enlightenment Contested: Philosophy, Modernity, and the Emancipation of Man, 1670–1752*. Oxford and New York: Oxford UP.
Israel, J. (2011). *Democratic Enlightenment: Philosophy, Revolution, and Human Rights 1750–1790*. Oxford and New York: Oxford UP.
Jung, C.G. (1954). *The Development of Personality* [*Collected Works, vol. 17*], trans. R.F.C. Hull. London: Routledge & Kegan Paul.
Jung, C.G. (1964). *Civilization in Transition* [*Collected Works, vol. 10*], trans. R.F.C. Hull. London: Routledge & Kegan Paul.
Jung, C.G. (1967). *Alchemical Studies* [*Collected Works, vol. 13*], trans. R.F.C. Hull. London: Routledge & Kegan Paul.
Jung, C.G. (1968). *Psychology and Alchemy* [*Collected Works, vol. 12*], trans. R.F.C. Hull. London: Routledge & Kegan Paul.

Jung, C.G. (1969a). *The Structure and Dynamics of the Psyche* [*Collected Works, vol. 8*], trans. R.F.C. Hull. London: Routledge & Kegan Paul.
Jung, C.G. (1969b). *Psychology and Religion* [*Collected Works, vol. 11*]. London: Routledge & Kegan Paul.
Jung, C.G. (1970). *Mysterium Coniunctionis* [*Collected Works, vol. 14*]. London: Routledge & Kegan Paul.
Jung, C.G. (1974). *Psychological Types* [*Collected Works, vol. 6*], trans. H.G. Baynes and revised R.F.C. Hull. London: Routledge & Kegan Paul.
Jung, C.G. (1991). *Psychology of the Unconscious: A Study of the Transformations and Symbolisms*, trans B.M. Hinkle. London: Routledge.
Jung, C.G. (2009). *The Red Book: Liber Novus*, ed. S. Shamdasani, trans. M. Kyburz, J. Peck, and S. Shamdasani. New York and London: Norton.
Kerényi, K. (1969) Prolegomena. In *Essays on a Science of Mythology*, ed. C.G. Jung and K. Kerényi, trans R.F.C. Hull. New York: Princeton UP. 1–24.
Malinowski, B. (1948). Myth in Primitive Psychology [1926]. In *Magic, Science and Religion and other Essays*. Garden City, NY: Doubleday & Co. 72–123.
Marcolli, M. (2020). *Lumen Naturae: Visions of the Abstract in Art and Mathematics*. Cambridge, MA and London: MIT Press.
Martella, V. (2012). *Dialectics of Cultural Criticism: Adorno's Confrontation with Rudolf Borchardt and Ludwig Klages in the "Odyssey" Chapter of "Dialektik der Aufklärung"*. Ph.D. dissertation, Justus-Liebig-Universität Gießen.
Murray, G. (2002). *Five Stages of Greek Religion [1955]*. Mineola, NY: Dover.
Nakajima, T. (2018). Psychology of the 12th Century Renaissance in Wolfram von Eschenbach's *Parzival*. *Studia Hermetica Journal*, *8*(1) ("Hermetism and the Underworld"), 23–40.
Pritchard, E.A. (2002). *Bilderverbot* Meets Body in Theodor W. Adorno's Inverse Theology. *The Harvard Theological Review*, *95*(3), July, 291–318.
Samuels, A. (2009). [interview on] *Today*, BBC Radio 4, broadcast on 28 October 2009.
Schiller, F. (1982). *On the Aesthetic Education of Man* [1795], ed. and trans. E.M. Wilkinson and L.A. Willoughby. Oxford: Clarendon Press.
Schmidt, J. (2007). The *Eclipse of Reason* and the End of the Frankfurt School in America. *New German Critique*, *34*, 47–76.
Schulte-Bockholt, A. (2001). A Neo-Marxist Explanation of Organized Crime. *Critical Criminology*, *10*, 225–242.
Stein, M. and Arzt, T. (eds). (2017, 2018, 2019). *Jung's Red Book for Our Time. Searching for Soul Under Postmodern Conditions*. Vols. 1, 2, and 3. Asheville, NC: Chiron.
Steiner, R. (1982). *Geisteswissenschaftliche Erläuterungen zu Goethes "Faust", Vol. 2: Das Faust-Problem; Die romantische und klassische Walpurgisnacht*. Dornach: Steiner Verlag.
Truskolaski, S. (2021). *Adorno and the Ban on Images*. London: Bloomsbury Academic.
Weber, M. (1968). Wissenschaft als Beruf [1919]. In *Gesammelte Aufsätze zur Wissenschaftslehre*. Tübingen: Mohr (Siebeck). 582–613.

Chapter 5

Dysrecognition and *Pathos*

Jon Mills

Psychoanalytic observations both inside and outside the clinic suggest that Axel Honneth's (1995, 2012; Fraser & Honneth, 2003) recognition theory relies upon an overly optimistic if not idealistic view of human nature. Although this is an ethical and noble ideal, we must seriously question whether intersubjective recognition "should prove to be a prerequisite of all human sociality" (Honneth, 2012, p. 4). This becomes particularly salient in the case of social collectives that regularly fail to interact through reciprocal recognition even when they become aware of their mutual dependency on each other. For example, people often acquiesce to others for defensive reasons, not because they recognize them as being morally equal. They engage in avoidance or enlist a compromise function to thwart the possibility of the other's aggression being directed toward them. Honneth's optimism "that both sides are compelled to restrict their self-seeking drives as soon as they encounter each other" (p. 15) assumes that ethical self-consciousness and restraint is normative, when this is due to social maturation. From a psychoanalytic point of view, equal recognition of the Other is unrealistic since it is evident that collectives are largely possessed by unconscious complexes, emotional seizures, and attitudinal prejudices that militate against forming such ideal cohesive relations within social harmony.

To explore the confines of Honneth's position, I wish to examine the dark side of recognition, namely, its asymmetrical pathological dynamics. Despite the human need to be acknowledged and understood, we are thrown into an intersubjective ontology that fosters dysrecognition, invalidation, negation of otherness, and a lack of empathy for alterity, especially when attachment pathology and psychic trauma sullies the minds of social collectives.

DOI: 10.4324/9781003215301-5

The Need to be Recognized

We all seek recognition; this is a basic human need.[1] The ego is affirmed by the other, but not at first. There is originally the experience of inequality, whether this be the child's relation to the parent or the bondsman's relation to the lord. Arguably one of the most widely cited sections of the *Phenomenology of Spirit* is Hegel's 1807 discussion of lordship and bondage.[2] In pithy form, spirit or mind (*Geist*) ultimately achieves ethical self-consciousness only by recognizing the other as an equal being. But this is a developmental achievement. In our intersubjective engagement with others, there is a battle for recognition that takes place between subjects. Yet at first, parties in this struggle are unaware that they are looking for recognition, which is unconsciously mediated, the meaning of which is hence initially unclear to those involved. It is only through the process of confronting otherness that we become cognizant of what we truly want. We may observe how this is ontically infused in all spheres of life and plays a key role in our psychological health and social progress. Every human being wants to be recognized by others as an instantiation of human desire. This naturally extends to society. Before society raises itself to the status of improving its cultural practices for the sake of its peoples, including institutionalized ethics, law and order, and distributive justice, it must start with this basic psychic fact. Those who are deprived of recognition fail to thrive, just as infants abandoned to orphanages who are given no nurturance, love, or human touch.

The inequality of recognition first exists when two opposing subjects confront one other. Each wants to be what the other only represents; thus, each is determined to negate the other's independence in order to give one's own self value. This guarantees that the process of recognition is saturated with conflict. Two selves oppose the independence of the other and in so doing assert their independence. Put simply, two mutually confronting selves appear as physical things to each other that act independently and hence freely, which both recognize as being before the other. But freedom is something that must be fought for; it must be achieved or proven. This is why Hegel sees the tussles of recognition as an altercation – a struggle, for it is "a matter of life or death" (Hegel, 1978, § 432).

People are largely seen by their fellows as mere objects – as *things* that exist "out there" in the world, because they are divorced from our emotional and personal lives in order for us to psychologically function. It is only when we contemplate the nature of this otherness that we are confronted with our own normativity: others are and have a self that exists independently from "me." "What is this other?" "What does the other have that I don't have?" "What do I want?" "What do I lack that the other has?" These questions lie on the sunrise of self-consciousness, because we are instantly made aware of the external reality of other human beings who are just like us in essence, although we have separate identities, personalities, and longings. We become aware of our desires through reflection upon (and as projected onto) the other, on the subject that stands before us even though we see this other as an independent (impersonal) object. When we recognize the other as a desirous and intentional being, we are immediately made aware of the subjectivity of the other, one we have an obligation to address. "What does this other want?" This leads us to one of Hegel's most important insights: when we confront otherness, we are entangled in desire and lack, which initiates a skirmish for recognition. Who will be acknowledged in this mutual otherness? Here, subjectivities stand fundamentally opposed to one another.

What is often recognized is not the equality of the other, but rather a scornful inequality, namely, the fact that people often do not care about alterity over their own lives and self-interests, to the point that the Other becomes a dangerous threat to one's safety. Although we may acknowledge that others are independent persons, it does not mean that we "respect others as persons" (Hegel, 1821, § 36). On the contrary, respect is earned. Avoidance, withdrawal, and submissiveness, on the other hand, are defensive modes of self-survival, especially in the face of a powerful opponent. Do our world societies and governments (viz Hegel's Objective Spirit) think about the common universal good for all, or merely their own self-regard and political pressures invested in their own nations and communities? Despite the fact there may be checks and balances designed to help treat citizens fairly, this does not generalize to a universal society of cosmopolitans (namely, citizens of the cosmos) who value all human life equally. Of course, such hypostatization of a so-called collective mind only makes sense as an abstract conception that embodies the spirit of democracy, as imperfect as this may be. But when it comes down to actualizing a universal good, humanity becomes a multiple personality split in its desires, needs, conflicts, demands, and dissatisfactions.

So when Honneth (2012) says that a distributional schema of justice "would have to be replaced by the involvement of all subjects in a given relationship of recognition" (p. 45), he seems to abstract from the reality of human experience. Most people do not readily give up their "egocentric desires for the benefit of the other" (p. 17). Not all people are disposed, let alone capable, of recognizing the other. We may have to contend that, in the end, recognition means tolerance of difference and not merely acceptance of the other, which could still bring about a pragmatic coexistence even if people cannot recognize each other as equals.

Recognition Theory Beyond Hegel

Honneth's turn to Winnicott to bolster critical theory shows many promising redirecting shifts in applied social analysis, but recognition theory also has much to gain by engaging developments in contemporary psychoanalysis since Winnicott's time, including post-object relations paradigms, self psychology, attachment science, intersubjectivity theory, relational psychoanalysis, and mentalization theory (see Mills, this volume, Ch. 13).

The struggle for recognition, as psychoanalysis shows, is present from birth onward – from daycare to death, as each of us is mired in familial, societal, and cultural conflict that saturates our being in the world. The failure to recognize the other and, more insidiously, chronic invalidation and repudiation of different peoples produces and sustains intersubjective and interethnic aggression to the point of murder and war. Here the Hegelian struggle for life and death is a lived reality that affects our conception of social justice and institutionalized forms of recognition. But the point I wish to make here is that dysrecognition may in fact trigger and sustain violence based on an unconscious revolt in reaction to political injustice. Indeed, aggression is not only instinctual, for lack of a better word, hence emanating from biological forces; it is also triggered by relational or interpersonal failures at validation and empathy that are sociologically instituted. When such dysrecognition is performed and sustained by the state, here we may say that a certain unconscious politics is operative on both the individual and collective level of a given society, which can lead to a vicious cycle of perpetration, victimization, and social malaise that always psychologically penetrates those who are marginalized. And this may be intensified as a posttraumatic act that resurrects earlier psychic pain experienced in childhood, especially when invalidation, abuse, and insecure attachments inform the next generation of social pathologies.

Unconscious Prejudice

Much of psychoanalysis is in sympathy with critical theory in its tacit hopes of bettering society, but psychoanalytic observations can be quite pathologizing as well, and for good reason. Here, the two disciplines are critical of the way collectives think and behave. We may speculate that this has to do with, on some level, the way people are raised and taught to think and act in a given cultural milieu, yet we must begin with rudiments. What do people require psychologically in order to thrive? Beyond recognition, I suggest, lie psychic needs for love, validation, and empathy. These are essential for healthy development. When they are lacking, withheld, truncated, or absent, a person, and even whole societies, may develop a traumatic reaction to life. This notion is quite simple in fact, a basic ingredient of the human aspect. When individuals encounter one another, this naturally leads to the mutual desire to be recognized as an individuated, autonomous subject in their own right. People are differentiated and independent, yet each face each other in mutual confrontation. This intersubjective dynamic further entails an implicit perception that each person is opposed to the other as an embodied entity that may do them harm. But this detection does not stop here. In seeing the other as an independent will with needs, desires, intentions, and potentially manipulative, self-serving actions, the other becomes an automatic threat. This triggers a psychological competition (sometimes physically or merely paranoiac confrontation) where one subject will inevitably be bested, while the other takes his or her subservient place in the confrontation. This is a fundamental psychological insight on behavioral dynamics governing human nature that we may all witness in the nursery and on the playground, the foundation for adult politics. This abridged version of explaining how power differentials arise unconsciously when encountering alterity is advanced by psychoanalytic theory in innumerable ways.

One of the major roadblocks that derails a discernable intellectual picture of the need for mutual or collective recognition is in deciphering the anathema of unconscious prejudice that underlies behavioral acts of every person in the world (Mills & Polanowski, 1997). People, societies, and governments do not act rationally, nor should we expect them to. We do not live in a purely adjudicated intellect or logical universe, but rather one derived from the prisms of our base urges, impulses, emotions, and internal conflicts that must undergo a developmental and educational process of exercising self-constraint, affect regulation, behavioral modification, and instructional training in order to achieve psychological and social maturity. The gleanings of reason, truth, virtue, and wisdom are higher-order accomplishments. But this is hardly achieved by everyone. In fact, this level of psychic cultivation is more of an outlier than an actualization for most people. At most we are all striving for the attainment of certain values and ideals. What is more commonplace is that we succumb to our own immediate shortcomings and complexes, moral limitations of character, and attitudinal prejudices that condition how we relate to self, others, and the world.

We must seriously question the prejudicial unconscious forces that drive political states of affairs, from individual and communal choices to international policy, for collective humanity is neither unified in its aims nor prioritizes matters outside of its immediate scope of parochial concerns or regional inclinations. Is the political unconscious a universal phenomenon, namely, is it structurally inscribed in the very ontological fabric of the psyche? With qualifications, all people are predisposed *a priori* to favor certain unconscious attitudes even if they are irrational and ultimately self-destructive. And it is unequivocally taking place on a mass scale across all civilized parts of the world.

What we are witnessing in concrete forms is how the collective psyche is divided based on unconscious politics identified with certain ideologies fortified by cultural relativity and animus toward alterity. Here we should question the capacity of the collective to make rationally informed judgements when wish, self-interest, and insular governmental hegemonies make decisions that affect us all. Yet government is elected by the people in democratic countries, which brings us to question why in recent political times the majority of citizens would vote for leaders – say, in the United Kingdom and America, who are anti-environment, anti-immigration, xenophobic, racist, bigoted, religiously intolerant, misogynistic, anti-gay, and pro-war, just to name a few indecencies. From *Brexit* to the election of US Republican president Donald Trump, humanity should beckon a call to reason. It is no surprise to psychoanalysis that we are witnessing the disintegration of culture, for illogical decisions are unconsciously chosen based on emotional prejudices, which speaks to the greater manifestation of collective social life immersed in its own *pathos*.[3]

A World Without Empathy

Although it is problematic to make mass generalizations, it may not be entirely illegitimate to say that we largely live in a world where there is no proper recognition of the Other as the equiprimordial complementarity of the Self. In other words, the dialectical onto-interconnectedness of identity and difference ensures that self-in-relation to alterity is a mutually implicit dynamic. When we attempt to analyze the human condition extraspectively or scientifically and look into the psyche or soul through an introspective analysis of our interiority, we can discern the universal experiences that all people engage in psychologically, only to recursively fall back into bifurcation that maintains rigid antitheses. The self is experienced and thought *not* to be the other. The *Them* is eclipsed for the *I*, while the *We* becomes occluded.

We may argue that, strictly speaking, humanity is not an identity at all but rather a collection of identities or subjects who largely exist and relate to one another in opposition to mutual difference. Despite the fact that we all maintain shared identifications and values with others throughout our globalized world, not everyone is recognized, nor is this remotely possible given that people are divided based on their desires, conflicts, beliefs, values, identities, and moral principles. Here we should maintain no pretense of a pristine Hegelian sublation (*Aufhebung*) of the subjective individual within objective social consciousness, where the pinnacle of ethics and justice reach their logical zenith in the concrete universals of culture, for this is merely a theoretical abstraction. In fact, much of social reality resists sublation and can indeed regress or withdraw back to early primitive instantiations governed by *pathos*.[4] The absolute unity of the individual within the social as the logical culmination of pure self-consciousness is simply an illusion, although one that may spur along our continual pining for refining social systems of democracy, law, ethics, and justice. Here, reformation and advance is culture's teleological endeavor. Whatever values and ideals societies adopt, they are always mediated through unconscious psychic processes that condition (and taint) the collective (Mills, 2014), even when there are good intentions involved. Although the fantasy of wholeness conceived through Hegel's philosophy of spirit as a self-articulated dynamic complex holism arriving at pure unification of the individual within the collective is a noble ideal, such a grand (if not grandiose) logical synthesis belies the empirical confounds that reflect social reality today marked by division, fracturing, and splitting of peoples, groups, and nations that radically resist unity. The projection of our aggression, hatred, and destructive envy onto a hating Other only ensures mutual conflict and dysrecognition, where some compromises conceivably occur. Despite these limitations and inevitable frictions between individuals and societies, collective identifications among people about ideals and social values do facilitate advances in ethical self-consciousness, which have a concrete impact on social policy and legislative reform that in turn restructure social institutions and the domestic practices of citizens.

One of the reasons for our impasse in achieving collective recognition of all people is a failure to possess, nurture, and demonstrate empathy for others. This failure is intimately tied to a subset of the problem, that is, our inability to foster global identifications with others. Empathy is based on an intersubjective identification with the other as an experiential self just like we are. Each of us stands united in spirit as an egalitarian subject that feels and needs. This basic shared identification with our fellow human beings is what gives empathy its value. But this is never easy to universally expect, let alone institute or institutionalize on a grand scale. It is an awareness that needs to be fostered, the seeds of which begin in early childhood, facilitated by a healthy, emotional holding environment grounded in secure attachments to parents, caregivers, and family members or their surrogates. Through personal experiences of being recognized, validated, shown care and psychological warmth, as well as feeling loved and understood, empathy for others develops as self-realization of the good and the need to embrace it, as does our emotional intelligence in socialization practices. Feeling felt, seeing the pain in others' eyes, and recognizing the experience of the other as a reciprocal self-relation to one's own interior helps to open up an ethical stance we are obliged to extend to the other as a fellow *Thou*. However, this is a form of ethical self-consciousness as felt compassion that not all people are psychologically capable of harboring or showing based upon their own personal plight or tragedies, family upbringing, cultural disenfranchisement, developmental traumas, and so forth. But this does not mean that empathy cannot be awakened or taught. If global societies were to promote empathy as an educational imperative and intrinsic valued commodity as an end in itself institutionalized within a given community or culture – as well as promoting the value of fostering loving emotional attachment to others – the world would be a better place. But when the psyche and society are traumatized, this inevitably trickles down into the very ontological fibers of familial and communal life, where attachment patterns are compromised, and the next generation inherits the collective suffering of the one before it.

Transgenerational Transmission of Trauma

Every persecuted clan, minority, subjugated group of peoples, and those affected by terror, trauma, and diaspora will suffer not only in the generations to come but negatively condition the cultural unconscious complexes of the collective. The Jews, First Nations Native Americans, as well as Sikhs and Shia Muslims, are only a few examples in recent times. When civil disorder, war, and systemic trauma compound matters, such as in the recent migration and refugee crisis that displaced over five million Syrians, existential agony, shared misery, and mental illness are inevitable. Trauma fractures personality and society, where dissociation of the psyche, schizoid phenomena, and soul destruction efface the ability to properly function and lead a normal life, which in turn affects the ability to care for and nurture the young, trust people, develop sympathy and emotional connection to others, and feel safe. When body integrity and physical space are violated, so is the psyche. Others become threatening objects to fear and be wary of. As a result, interpersonal cognitive styles and forms of relationships are altered forever. Phobic, avoidant, and fundamentally paranoiac relations toward life are not uncommon occurrences. The impact on children maims the next generation, which in turn grows up with psychic scars and emotional deficits that are passed on to their children and their future children because basic psychological capacities for intimacy and attachment are compromised in successive generations of parents.

We know from a vast body of research across the social sciences that the psychological and cultural effects of trauma become transgenerationally transmitted through childrearing and socialization practices (O'Loughlin, 2015; O'Loughlin & Charles, 2015). Traumatized individuals within a community of suffering do not relate to their children in normative fashions relatively free of conflict like non-traumatized people do. This in turn affects attachment patterns in the mother-child dyad, neurological arousal levels, cognitive processing, affect regulation, and the ability to meet basic psychological requirements during infancy (see Mills, 2005 for a review). This always impacts on the family unit in the most rudimentary of conditions: parents and their offspring are doomed to be psychically haunted in their own ways, which will be culturally transmitted through subsequent families in future generations by virtue of the fact that such collective trauma is emotionally dominant within the family milieu and society at large. This is inescapable in the most resilient of people: when its aftereffects (*Nachträglichkeit* or *après-coup*) are relived, reconstructed, or memorialized, it leaves an affective aftermath that disfigures the sociosymbolic order.

The trauma of history and its devastating impact on the psyche dismembers the capacity for healthy object relations and the ability to properly trust, love, be perceptually and affectively attuned to the needs of others, and show emotional intimacy, including acceptance, warmth, validation, understanding, and recognition of the unique subjectivity of the other.

Case Illustration

Consider the case of Lily, a Chinese Canadian professional who came to see me for psychological treatment when she was 52 years old following a crisis at work.[5] Her major complaint was an increasingly strained relationship with her boss over a series of complaints about her interpersonal style, friction with co-workers, and difficulty in challenging his authority. Lily was in a high-level Human Resources position as a supervisor for a municipal government sector in a unionized environment. Her main contention was that she was not receiving proper recognition for her work from her boss due to complaints from lower-level staff whom she had to mediate, evaluate, and discipline, as is typical of HR environments. In turn, she received poor annual evaluations from her staff, and the department as a whole, which were shown to her anonymously. She was noted to have a conflictual and confrontational style of communication with almost everyone and was reprimanded by her boss for being difficult, rigid, inflexible, and "defensive." These complaints affected her performance evaluations, promotion opportunities, and salary. Such negative reviews augmented by a lack of recognition of her assigned projects and program developments led to increased frustration, irritability, impatience, and an underlying seething rage.

It soon became apparent that, despite her expertise, advanced education and credentials, and history of success in her position, the municipality was taking active steps to build a constructive dismissal of her employment due to her boss's dislike of her. His dislike was so intense that he stopped speaking to her and reassigned her to report to other superiors who purportedly intimidated, "bullied," and ordered her around without consulting or listening to her input. She was devalued repeatedly by her supervisors to the point that she broke down and cried at a meeting in front of peers due to unrestrained vituperations by a superior. She was forced to file a harassment complaint due to an increasingly hostile work environment and had to seek union representation, which secured her continual employment, but her duties were reassigned, and she lost her supervisory role. As her position at work spiraled into unabating conflict, this had a devastating effect on her self-esteem and morale, where she felt systematically persecuted and victimized, to the point that it precipitated the experiential reliving of her past childhood traumas.

Although Lily was born in Canada, her parents emigrated from mainland China, where they were farmers. At first her father came to find work as a manual laborer in the oil industry in Western Canada, and when he had secured a position and saved enough money, he sent for his wife and elderly parents. Later, the family moved to a small rural community in Northern Canada, where they opened the first Chinese restaurant the town had ever had. Being the only Chinese family to reside there, the business was successful, and they were accepted in the community despite being foreigners. A couple of years later, Lily was born, followed by her brother two years after that.

Lily was repeatedly physically, verbally, and emotionally abused by her mother during her entire childhood. She was never shown love, recognition, or emotional warmth – physical affection or hugs – and was constantly subjected to her mother's verbal tirades, explosive rages, and physical beatings when she did not do exactly what she was supposed to do at the restaurant or in performing domestic tasks. Lily could never anticipate or know when her mother would become erratic: she would spontaneously fly into rages and start beating her with kitchen utensils or her fists and was fond of throwing knives and meat cleavers while in the kitchen. Lily was once taken to the hospital when she was hit in the back of her head with a knife her mother had thrown once it started gushing blood. She was forced to say she had fallen and cut her head. Her brother was also subjected to such lunacy, but to a lesser degree because he was mentally ill from an early age onward, likely exacerbated by his mother's abuse. He had developed schizophrenia and was later institutionalized for his entire adult life: he died in a sanatorium. Lily also suspected that her mother was psychotic, which may in part explain her volatile behavior, but she was functional enough to help run the restaurant. Although Lily survived her childhood, it left an entrenched, traumatized internal structure where she was prone to unpredictable rages, verbal devaluation of others, and unprovoked violence just like her mother. By the time she was an early adolescent, she had gotten involved in drugs, organized a small youth gang who broke into houses to get money, and burned down a lumber yard. After being convicted for arson, she stole her father's car and ran down the local prosecutor while walking on the street. She was sentenced to a youth corrections facility, where she served until she was 18 years of age. She then was homeless, lived on the street, sold drugs, and "did anything to survive." In retrospect, Lily thought this was the only way she could escape her mother's constant abuse.

Remarkably, Lily was "saved" by the Salvation Army, was taken into their physical and spiritual care, educated, and went on to earn a master's degree in one of their religious college affiliate institutions in the United States. She then returned to Canada as a professional adult and entered a successful career until the precipitating events with her boss and co-workers brought on feelings of reliving her childhood abuse. Her conflicts at work started to trigger her chronic, complex unresolved PTSD, which led to unrestrained swearing and devaluation of others, episodes of road rage, and the repeated physical battery of her husband, including even chasing him around the house with a knife – in the kitchen, nonetheless, an apparent identification with the aggressor.

What we may observe in Lily's life and in her family of origin is how various cultural forces of oppression, maltreatment, trauma, and lack of recognition informed the transgenerational transmission of systemic pathology. As is customary in many Asian cultures, brides typically move in with their husbands' parents and extended family. Lily was forced to constantly work in the restaurant from a young age onward, including after school, at night, and on weekends, as did her brother. She remembered her mother constantly fighting with her grandmother, engaging in verbal arguments, and even once witnessed her mother beat her grandmother with a broom. She does not remember anymore fighting between them after that. We may speculate that her mother was looked down upon, rejected, and/or devalued in some manner and was expected to play a subservient and less recognized role by her father's parents, who had demanded respect as elders, having attempted to control or suppress their daughter-in-law. This was a power differential Lily's mother did not observe, especially in a new country where there were no traditional supports nor pressures to conform to Chinese custom.

The family restaurant was on the bottom main floor of a brick building, and the family lived upstairs. Lily recalls that her grandparents both died when she was in middle school, but she said that one of her frequent duties was to bring food to her grandfather's room upstairs, which she always found "scary" because he always remained moot and emotionless, just sitting in a chair looking out the window. It is unclear if he was traumatized, abused, and/or had dementia of some kind, but Lily suspected that her mother had beaten him as well. The transgenerational transmission of cultural trauma is more certain because we know Lily's grandparents and parents had survived the Great Proletariat Cultural Revolution, having been spared from starvation and mass genocide under the Mao regime. During this era, the masses were oppressed by communist ideology by a totalitarian leader, where identification with the collective nation state eclipses the individual personality, not to mention you could be worked to death, murdered at whim, or simply disappear as millions did. Added to this cultural ethos is the stricture that people were not recognized as individual subjects but rather must recognize the communist state and its chairman, its symbolic father. And where pride in social appearance, observance of tradition and ritual, "correctness," and control over emotions is prized, shame is the institutionally sanctioned corollary when one fails to recognize the constraints of custom. Nothing is worse than public humiliation, the ultimate form of dysrecognition.

And what about Lily's father? When he was sick and dying, long after he had moved to a major metropolitan city when her mother died, Lily looked after him in his house when he had developed Alzheimer's. When she repeatedly asked him, "Why didn't you protect me from her? Why did you let her beat me?," all he could say was that he "didn't know" or "couldn't remember." Even on his deathbed, Lily was offered no recognition.

Concluding Postscript

When transgenerational forces of trauma are imposed on the incipient mind, agency is eclipsed by transitory misidentifications in fantasy and reality, leaving a wake of psychic debris that structurally disfigures the self. When one is treated like a thing and not recognized as a proper human being, the subject begins to relate to others as things in a sea of objects where the kernel of the value of reciprocal recognition devolves into intransigent antagonism, strife, fear of alterity, paranoia, sustained aggressivity, and repetition compulsion. When cultural trauma saturates attachment and socialization patterns, we can assuredly predict a future full of human suffering, where psychic and sociological impairment leaves many existential stains. Here we must recognize that the many faces of pathology transfigure our internal natures and scars the social landscape, even when a given individual or society recognizes the collective good in recognizing others.

Axel Honneth's contributions to recognition theory may benefit from revisiting the ontic role of dysrecognition in the psyche and society in a way that poses challenges to a universal vision of intersubjective mutual recognition among world collectives. Although the pursuit of a universal good, ideality, or abstract notion of right may necessarily entail forms of recognition within social institutions and intersubjective practices, there are many psychological and sociological variables that prevent masses from actualizing this utopia, especially when civil societies, not to mention developing countries, are beleaguered by pathological forces that erode mutual respect and empathy for the Other. When overly rational approaches – the morality of reason – are applied to social justice paradigms that do not fully take into account the penumbra of unconscious conflict, emotional prejudice, relational deficits, political ideologies, and psychological incapacities to recognize difference and alterity, then these dynamics present real limitations on what we can credibly expect from social collectives. Until we can convince world populations that mutual recognition is a common good and institutionalize the practical means by which to bring this about, then I am afraid that mutual acknowledgment of difference is the most we can hope for as a preliminary step in redefining our humanistic principles and distributive schemas of justice.

Notes

1 Fredrick Neuhouser (1986) attempts to elucidate the origin of the need for recognition itself by partially claiming that we seek recognition because our own demands for self-certainty are left unsatisfied without the presence and validation of others. This notion is compatible with many psychoanalytic conceptualizations of the development of subjectivity, including attachment theory, object relations theory, self psychology, and interpersonal, intersubjective, and relational perspectives.

2 The problem of alienation and spirit's struggle for recognition has received overwhelming attention in the Hegelian literature. Within this context, there has been an almost exclusive fixation on the master-slave dialectic introduced in the *Phenomenology*. It is interesting to note that Hegel's (1978) treatment of desire and recognition is contrasted differently in the *Encyclopaedia Phenomenology* and the *Berlin Phenomenology* (1981) from that of his Jena period. The most notable difference in his later writings is his scant discussion of self-consciousness in comparison to his original work and that his famous section on "Freedom of Self-Consciousness" has been entirely purged. Hegel's master-slave discussion, or what we may refer to as lord and servant, and more generally the "*relationship* of *mastery* [*Herrschaft*] and *servitude* [*Knechtschaft*]" (Hegel, 1978, § 433, emphasis in original), is given the briefest summation in the *Encyclopaedia*. This is undoubtedly why almost all interpretations of desire and recognition rely exclusively on the Jena *Phenomenology*. It is interesting to note that the terms "master" and "slave" may be translated differently, although most scholars agree that the actual arguments in the two books appear to be essentially compatible. See Mills (2002, pp. 143–149) for an extended discussion.
3 For the ancient Greeks, *pathos* defined the human condition: to be human is to suffer.
4 In *Origins: On the Genesis of Psychic Reality*, I provide my own revisionist amendments to Hegel's dialectical method that take into account the nature of dialectical regression, temporal mediacy, and the ubiquitous nature of contingency that challenges universal pronouncements of an absolute unity of mind (see Mills, 2010, pp. 51–58).
5 She initially entered into weekly psychotherapy spanning many years, which later developed into a five-day-a-week analysis. (All details of the case have been sufficiently disguised to protect the patient's identity.)

References

Fraser, N., & Honneth, A. (2003) *Redistribution or Recognition? A Political-Philosophical Exchange*. Translated by J. Golb, J. Ingram, & C. Wilke. London: Verso.

Hegel, G.W.F. (1817/1827/1830) *Philosophy of Mind. Vol.3 of the Encyclopaedia of the Philosophical Sciences*. Translated by William Wallace & A.V. Miller. Oxford: Clarendon Press.

Hegel, G.W.F. (1967) *Philosophy of Right*. Translated by T.M. Knox. Oxford: Oxford University Press, 1821.

Hegel, G.W.F. (1977) *Phenomenology of Spirit*. Translated by A.V. Miller. Oxford: Oxford University Press, 1807.

Hegel, G.W.F. (1978) *Hegels Philosophie des subjektiven Geistes/Hegel's Philosophy of Subjective Spirit*, Vol.1: Introductions, Vol.2: Anthropology, Vol.3: Phenomenology and Psychology. Edited by M.J. Petry. Dordrecht, Holland: D. Reidel Publishing Company.

Hegel, G.W.F. (1981) *The Berlin Phenomenology*. Edited and translated by M.J. Petry. Dordrecht, Holland: D. Reidel Publishing Co.

Honneth, A. (1995) *The Struggle for Recognition*. Translated by Joel Anderson. London: Polity Press.

Honneth, A. (2012) *The I in We: Studies in the Theory of Recognition*. Cambridge, UK: Polity Press.

Mills, J. (2002) *The Unconscious Abyss: Hegel's Anticipation of Psychoanalysis*. Albany, NY: SUNY Press.

Mills, J. (2005) *Treating Attachment Pathology*. Northvale, NJ: Jason Aronson.

Mills, J. (2010) *Origins: On the Genesis of Psychic Reality*. Montreal: McGill-Queens University Press.

Mills, J. (2014) *Underworlds: Philosophies of the Unconscious from Psychoanalysis to Metaphysics*. London: Routledge.

Mills, J., & Polanowski, J. (1997) *The Ontology of Prejudice*. Amsterdam/New York: Rodopi.

Neuhouser, F. (1986) Deducing Desire and Recognition in the *Phenomenology of Spirit*. *Journal of the History of Philosophy* 24(2): 243–264.

O'Loughlin, M. (ed.) (2015) *The Ethics of Remembering and the Consequences of Forgetting*. Lanham, MD: Rowman & Littlefield.

O'Loughlin, M., & Charles, M. (eds.) (2015) *Fragments of Trauma and the Social Production of Suffering*. Lanham, MD: Rowman & Littlefield.

Chapter 6

Critical Theory and Anti-Semitism
Implications for Politics, Education, and Psychoanalysis

Benjamin B. Strosberg

In the *Dialectic of Enlightenment* (2004), Horkheimer and Adorno articulated a renewed critical project for theory; one meant to contend with a crisis in the social world resulting from contradictions in science and philosophy. They trace this crisis to the instrumentalization of reason, as exemplified by the totalizing social forces that turn the autonomous and reasoning individual against itself (e.g., Stalinism, late capitalism, and Nazi anti-Semitism). The last chapter in the *Dialectic of Enlightenment*, titled "Elements of Anti-Semitism: Limit of Enlightenment," is a psychoanalytic examination of this crisis as it relates to the logic of anti-Semitism. Paradoxically, the irrationalism that permeates modern anti-Semitism is deemed to be consistent with enlightenment reason formulated as the mastery of the unknown through exchangeability, prediction, and control. Ostensible solutions to the problem of anti-Semitism which appeal to that logic (e.g., assimilation, nationalization, reality testing) either fail abjectly or even seem to make the problem worse. Horkheimer and Adorno suggest that anti-Semitism is not merely a matter of psychological prejudice but the collective hate for the negative principle, which resists the totalizing social force of objectification. The negative principle is unbearable within what has become a totalized social order reproducing itself above the heads of individuals. Individual actors need not (and perhaps cannot) be aware of the workings of the social totality as they participate in it. The negative principle is projected onto the Jews who represent, for the anti-Semite, malignant disrupters of total social cohesion. As such, the Jew becomes the unassimilable stranger, akin to the uncanny (Freud, 2001b) or the return of the repressed (Freud, 2001a) haunting the seemingly unified psyche and society as a symptom that challenges the wholeness the individual comes to identify with. Resistance to anti-Semitism, Horkheimer and Adorno insist, must address these social issues.

Horkheimer and Adorno's (2004) approach was unique because it construed anti-Semitism as the limit of Enlightenment rationality and exposes the contradictions and conflicts that define the psychological domain of thought itself. While their reference to "enlightenment" rationality could lead some readers to believe that this formulation of anti-Semitism only refers to modern forms like Nazi anti-Semitism, Horkheimer and Adorno argue throughout the *Dialectic of Enlightenment* that the seeds of Enlightenment thinking are present before the seventeenth- and eighteenth-century European Enlightenment in the ways that humans, even then, made equivalences for the sake of prediction and control (e.g., sacrifices to the gods or the telling of myths). The Enlightenment, which started as a project of liberation and progress, led to the totalization of these processes and thus became regressive and oppressive to the elements of difference and negativity, challenging its harmonious logic. Philosophy and science – remaining faithful to the progress of reason initiated by the Enlightenment – are unable to contend with the contradiction of a "wholly enlightened earth . . . radiant with triumphant calamity" (Horkheimer & Adorno, 2004, p. 1).

In this chapter, I explore how Horkheimer and Adorno (2004) renew the critical aims of philosophy in response to that calamity and the contradictory logic of anti-Semitism. They offer a dialectic of, by, and through reason with the help of what I understand to be the negative moment emphasized in psychoanalysis. Psychoanalytic theory seems to offer the authors a way to think about (and potentially resist) anti-Semitism without recourse to positive formulations of progress that might demand the elimination of conflict and contradiction. I believe that this negative dialectical project remains an ethical way of thinking about oppression today in the fields of critical theory and psychoanalysis. I conclude the chapter with a brief analysis of the continued relevance (and misuses) of this critical psychoanalytic approach – born from the study of anti-Semitism – for politics, education, and clinical work.

The Difficulty in Thinking About Anti-Semitism

Around the globe, anti-Semitic violence is on the rise. Though these worrisome trends have increased dramatically in recent years, anti-Semitism has long been simmering beneath the surface, at times showing itself through fissures in the social fabric, but more often ignored or construed as "family quarrels," as Fanon (2008, p. 87) once put it. It seems that only recently – in light of growing anti-Semitic violence in Europe, the United Kingdom and the United States – that the threat of renewed anti-Semitism has been seriously addressed by the American public. And yet, even now, it is questionable whether anti-Semitism is being recognized for its social-structural tectonics. Anti-Semitism is still often seen as a disguise for or by-product of some other vexing issue (e.g., a response to Israeli violence or pointless nostalgia for a bygone era).

A major obstacle to uprooting anti-Semitism and its violent manifestations is the inherent difficulty in thinking about it clearly. Here are several questions that demonstrate the true extent of this difficulty: are Jews "white"? Is anti-Zionism anti-Semitic? Is Zionism racist? Why has it been so difficult for Jews to assimilate? Is anti-Semitism a social-structural phenomenon (like systemic racism) or merely one more instance of a petty religious or ethnic prejudice? Would anti-Semitic violence really subside if Jews and Palestinians were given a secure homeland and religious freedom? The complexity of the problem is amplified by Horkheimer and Adorno's (2004) assessment of anti-Semitism as the result of collective hatred for an ineradicable negative (and constituting) principal within society. The negative, as a principle, is an important aspect *of* thinking; therefore, anti-Semitism marks the very limits of rational thinking itself.

As one observer noted, anti-Semitism can be broadly defined as

> an irrational belief that by virtue of their faith and/or heredity, Jews pose an actual or potential threat to the safety, security and/or ethical integrity on their non-Jewish neighbors, presumably by seeking (or sustaining) an unfair advantage or attempting to damage or devalue their non-Jewish neighbors behind the scenes, often through (alleged) conspiracies of various kinds. In such cases, the magnitude of the perceived threat varies with the intensity of anti-Semitic sentiments, rather than according to any actual or intrinsic qualities of the people who are feared and despised. Anti-Semitic beliefs and attitudes are then used to justify anti-Semitic practices, ranging from causal disdain (low intensity) to fierce discrimination (high intensity), and from there to occasional episodes of violence that may escalate into genocidal campaigns.
>
> (Burston, 2021, p. 3)

This definition holds true for many forms of anti-Semitism across time. Nevertheless, anti-Semitism is often implicit and hidden from the person who harbors such fears and beliefs. In order to fight anti-Semitism, it is important to start by acknowledging the complexity of the problem, rather than trying to simplify it to make the problem go away, which will only issue in an eventual return of the repressed. Psychoanalysis has provided critical theory with a model for thinking about such problems, where the problems are bound up with the difficulty in thinking, and "think we must."

Anti-Semitism and Psychoanalytic Thinking

The exodus of German-Jewish intellectuals from Germany after the rise of Nazism in 1933 marked a turning point in the academic study of anti-Semitism (Burston, 2014, p. 116). Many of these scholars looked to psychoanalytic theory for their investigations, following in Freud's (2001e, 2001f) footsteps. In some ways, Erich Fromm (1900–1980) also paved the way for these studies with his early work on authoritarianism among blue-collar workers in the Weimar Republic (Fromm, 1984). However, theorists after Fromm suggested that looking to psychology for answers to social questions was a mistake (e.g., Fenichel, 1940) but conceded that a psychology of anti-Semitism could at least illuminate one side of the problem. For example, in his preface to Ernst Simmel's edited volume on psychoanalysis and anti-Semitism (1946), Gordon Allport suggested that anti-Semitism is rooted in the unconscious (Allport, 1946, p. vii). Simmel's (1946) volume included essays from Adorno, Horkheimer, and Fenichel as well as Frenkel-Brunswik and Sanford, with whom Adorno would co-author *Authoritarian Personality* (Adorno et al., 2019).

Adorno et al.'s *Authoritarian Personality* (2019) is an influential empirical and psychological study published in the postwar period uncovering the link between anti-democratic tendencies and anti-Semitic beliefs in the United States. Without trying to explain social phenomena psychologically, as the study has been accused of doing (see Tuffin, 2005, p. 51; Tajfel & Turner, 2004, p. 276; Billig, 1991, p. 126), the researchers tracked social phenomena as they are experienced psychologically. Adorno came to the paradoxical conclusion that psychology is an important domain for the investigation of anti-Semitism even though he rejected the notion of a "psychology of anti-Semitism" (Adorno, 2019, p. lxii). In fact, the *Authoritarian Personality* and Adorno's groundwork with Horkheimer on anti-Semitism can be read as a critique of psychology (formulated as the study of the individual subject) that emphasizes the way the psychological investigation of anti-Semitism undermines the logic of its own subject (i.e., an immanent critique). For instance, Adorno (2019) suggests that the failure of individuation found in the psychoanalytically informed authoritarian study is the disintegration of the concept of a psychological subject:

> This indicates a historical tendency which affects not so much individual psychology than the locus of psychology as such. . . . If the individual, in the sense of an equilibrium between ego, superego, and Id, can no longer be regarded as the characteristic form of today's human beings, psychology may begin to become obsolescent inasmuch as individual actions can no longer be explained adequately in terms of the individual's own psychological household. . . . If the individual can no longer maintain himself by emphasizing his independence and strength, if he can succeed only by giving himself up to collective powers, the classical psychoanalytic interplay of the ego, the superego and the Id is seriously affected, and the old definition of the reality principle through the crystallization of a strong ego does no longer hold true.
>
> (p. lxiii)

For Horkheimer and Adorno (2004), psychoanalysis is not *positively* psychological nor *positively* social but is the investigation of the irreconcilable conflict between the two. It is not enough to formulate social theory without the individual psychological subject, nor is it enough to conceive of that subject as autonomous and individual, nor even is it enough to formulate a social psychology that reconciles the two domains. Rather, they insist that a critical theory must show how the psychological subject undermines itself, and they suggest that psychoanalysis does just that. Here, in this passage from the end of the *Dialectic of Enlightenment* (2004), is another way of formulating this immanent critique:

> In the autonomy and uniqueness of the individual, the resistance to the blind, repressive power of the irrational whole was crystallized. But that resistance was made historically possible only by the blindness and irrationality of the autonomous and unique individual.
>
> (p. 200)

I have, elsewhere, called to this reading of psychoanalysis "negative psychology" to characterize the investigation of how psychology dialectically becomes its opposite, namely, that psychoanalysis shows the contradictory nature of the psychological subject who is not self-identical and who is constituted by the failed aims of wholeness and integration (Strosberg, 2021). Rensman (2017) points out that for Adorno, this dialectical work was implicitly operating within psychoanalysis without detection by Freud, the steadfast Enlightenment thinker (p. 48). Psychoanalysis provides critical theory with the concepts to think contradictions such as "judgement without judging" and "perceiving without a perceiver" in thinking without criticality (i.e., instrumental rationality). Emphasizing these aspects of the psychological subject, "[Horkheimer and Adorno] attempt to show how reason, having regressed to instrumental rationality, has combined in the present era with the domination of nature and social control to form a quasi-mythical compulsion" (Noerr, 2004, p. 232). This compulsion is embodied in anti-Semitism.

Other critics of Adorno et al.'s *Authoritarian Personality* (2019), and Adorno's theory of anti-Semitism more broadly, suggest that its authors focused on right-wing anti-Semitism without addressing the persistence of left-wing anti-Semitism, possibly for political reasons (Burston, 2014, p. 117; see also Burston, 2020, for an extended discussion of Adorno et al. and the problem of left-wing authoritarianism). But this critique misses an important aspect of the study and its theoretical underpinnings. In the study, conservatism and religiosity are found to be highly correlated with authoritarianism by way of anti-Semitism. These characteristics are easily mapped onto right-wing politics owing to the conservatism of right-wing parties. And yet the left *as a ticket* can be just as conservative. There is evidence for this interpretation in the groundwork laid out in the *Dialectic of Enlightenment* (2004). There, anti-Semitism is conceptualized as a structural issue in human reasoning that crisscrosses political allegiances. Anti-Semitism is found in the issue of "ticket mentality itself" on both the left and right (Horkheimer & Adorno, 2004, p. 172). *Ticket mentality*, here, refers to the endorsement of a political party or social platform that always requires overly broad generalizations and approximations. For instance, people vote for the democratic *ticket*, the republican *ticket*, the progressive *ticket*, the fascist *ticket*. "To vote for a ticket," Horkheimer and Adorno (2004) argue, "means to practice adaptation to illusion petrified as reality" (p. 170). And importantly, they are not just referring to electoral voting procedures but are, rather, suggesting that thinking about social issues has, itself, become a process of adopting an ideology or ticket instead of thinking. So-called progressives are no less an enemy of difference if their thinking becomes fixed and conservative as a progressive *ticket*.

Dialectic of Enlightenment Thinking

In the *Dialectic of Enlightenment* (2004), the authors purport to trace the genealogy of the psychological subject ending in the psychoanalysis of anti-Semitism. According to Horkheimer and Adorno's (2004) historical reflections, the human subject fighting for survival seems to have transitioned from animism to the enlightened subject of science and philosophy, intermediated by mimetic ritual practices and early mythical thinking. They insist that the thinking subject is in a crisis of its own making:

> The human being's mastery of itself, on which the self is founded, practically always involves the annihilation of the subject in whose service that mastery is maintained, because the substance which is mastered, suppressed, and disintegrated by self-preservation is nothing other than the living entity, of which the achievements of self-preservation can only be defined as functions – in other words, self-preservation destroys the very thing which is to be preserved.
> (Horkheimer & Adorno, 2004, p. 43)

Modern forms of science and technology, which are designed to control and master nature's forces, mimic the drive toward self-preservation. However, this growing mastery and control of nature's forces has also brought about the growing objectification of humanity and the dominance of instrumental reason over critical reason. This is due to the totalizing processes of sameness, exchangeability, and synthesis on which science and philosophy have been premised. But this is not just a function of science or philosophy as institutions; the drive toward sameness is found to be the very process defining the psychological subject.

Science and philosophy are rooted in the domination of nature. Nature, here, consists in particular differences that resist conceptual generalization *and* that force of sameness that drives humans toward processes of identification. The particularities that are stripped away in order to make things identifiable for the human subject (objectifiable and universally exchangeable) in their *genera* return as the unconscious remainder of (and in) each concept. The generalization, approximation, and abstraction utilized by Enlightenment science and philosophy perform the role that myth once played for civilization in the explanation and prediction of nature. The general concepts of human thought objectify nature through a mediating distance between the concepts used to think with and the things of nature intuited by the senses and identified by the concepts. Myth was already a way to understand nature so as to predict and control its cycles at a distance. Accordingly, Horkheimer and Adorno (2004) claim that "[t]he myths which fell victim to the Enlightenment were themselves its products" (p. 5). Myths were already scientific (as attempts to master nature), and science, which seeks to eradicate myth, is also mythical (e.g., in its totalization, telling of origins, projecting human properties onto nature). Where science becomes mythical, however, the elements of particularity found in the early mimetic forms of human thinking are missing.

What are the particularities found in early forms of mimetic mythical thinking that Horkheimer and Adorno (2004) suggest are missing from mythical modern science? First of all, mimesis can be defined as *direct* representation without the distance provided by general concepts and linguistic signification. Words and concepts refer *to* something at a distance beyond the word or concept itself. The directness of mimesis, on the other hand, is related to the particularity of each representation, much like how proper names refer to a particular person. To preserve themselves, humans learned to mimic their surroundings through direct representation. This was a form of control that was not yet cognitively centralized, though magical ritual was the attempt to harness that power of the mimetic directness between the human and the thing in the natural environment. In other words, the human adapted to the danger of the environment through a form of directness or camouflage such as dressing as an animal, invoking (or not invoking) the name of an animal to make it present or absent, or even ritual sacrifice. This is not an embodiment of a generalized exemplar of *an* animal but a representation of *the* animal. An example of this is the word "bear," which is commonly understood to be a euphemism for the original name for *the* bear, adopted out of fear of the mimetic directness between the name and the thing.

Yet in the move from myth as science to science as myth, the sacrificed laboratory animal becomes the scientific exemplar stripped of its unique qualities and any contact between the animal and what it represents (Horkheimer & Adorno, 2004, p. 7). The particularity of mimetic practices (i.e., magic or cultic ritual) once allowed for the direct representation of *this* sacrificial animal, *this* process. The universal generalizations and approximations of science lead to exactitude but repress particularity. Horkheimer and Adorno (2004) propose that the analysis of this historical process might expose the logic of domination that is in science but also hidden from science. Such exposure, it is wagered, could counteract the effects of that repression.

According to some observers, the style and form by which knowledge and verification are expressed in the *Dialectic of Enlightenment* (2004) transforms its content. For example, D'Arcy (2020) suggests that Horkheimer and Adorno's generalizations about myth, mimesis, and science can be understood as the performance of the same processes that are under investigation. According to D'Arcy the form of presentation in the *Dialectic of Enlightenment* is a performance of mythic narrative akin to the epic of Homer; it tells of myths and their transformations, but is, itself, an epic. Horkheimer and Adorno (2004) retell the mythical origin story of the subject (as Odysseus and as the scientist) but in the form of an epic intimately linked to the particularity of their social moment (i.e., the subject as anti-Semite, fascist subject, concentration camp commandant, etc.). How is the presentation of science as myth different than the way science presents itself? D'Arcy (2020) answers that it is "just what distinguishes epic from myth, a dimension of parody or stylization in the modus operandi of the text," which requires "the ability to recognize and think through the ambiguity of language" (p. 55). The *Dialectic of Enlightenment* explores, performatively, the way that concepts change historically (and ambiguously) into their opposites. The new dialectical project established by the authors is a kind of psychoanalytic philosophy emphasizing the unconscious dimensions of concepts as they are employed. Through false equivalences like that of economic exchange, reason becomes unreason, psychology as the study of the individual thinking subject becomes the study of the failure of individuation, and the drive toward self-preservation becomes indistinguishable from self-destruction.

It is the purpose of this rereading of the *Dialectic of Enlightenment* (2004) to show how the dialectic of Enlightenment thinking, read here as a kind of psychoanalytic thinking and perhaps better concretized in the conception of anti-Semitism explored in the next section, is still helpful in thinking critically beyond the status quo in both critical theory and psychoanalysis.

Anti-Semitism as Case Study of the Dialectic of Enlightenment

In this section, I explore Horkheimer and Adorno's (2004) psychoanalytically informed perspective on anti-Semitism as the limit of Enlightenment rationality, one characterized by the drive toward sameness through the domination of nature and the indirectness of instrumental thinking. This drive toward sameness produces the modern psychological subject while secretly promoting its potential downfall. Manifestations of anti-Semitism stem from the compulsion to destroy the difference (particularity) that persists in defiance of the drive toward sameness. Anti-Semitism has become rooted in the unconscious and marked by the projection of what is both desired and feared onto the social other (a role historically played by the diasporic Jew). Science and philosophy (complicit in the drive toward sameness) become incapable of correcting for the violence perpetrated against otherness. Simultaneously, the loss of that otherness would be the loss of subjectivity, which is established through social conflict with that other. Psychoanalysis, with its emphasis on the negative principle (Freud, 2001d), offers conceptual tools (e.g., the unconscious, the uncanny, projection) for analyzing the contradictory drives and for mounting a defense against anti-Semitism formulated as hate for that same negative principle.

Jewishness as the Negative Principle

The historically Christian and liberal answer to the question of Jewish particularity proposes assimilation into an already existing unity through conversion or secularization, policies aimed at smoothing over differences. But assimilation, as the stripping of particularity, always fails to be completed since assimilation is always a historical process that bestows a new particularity (i.e., the Jewish convert or the secular Jew). Think here of the double bind experienced by European Jewry around the eighteenth century: Jews were persecuted if they did not assimilate, and assimilated Jews were accused of secret allegiances. Even today, almost a quarter of

Americans believe that American Jews are more loyal to Israel than to the United States (ADL, 2020).

Horkheimer and Adorno (2004) assert that "for the fascists the Jews are not a minority but the antirace, the negative principle as such; on their extermination the world's happiness depends" (p. 137). In this modern form of anti-Semitism, Jews play the role of the negative principle necessary for the positivity of self-identification. The Jewish negative principle is the negative within the positive itself, exposing the imposture of the positive. In other words, the Jews come to stand (as the unassimilable strangers) for the failure of social cohesion of the national community while at the same time defining the boundary of that community. The destruction of the Jews, as the destruction of the negative principle, would therefore spell the death of the identity of the ingroup. For the Nazis (and their contemporary counterparts), the negative principle cannot be synthesized by way of assimilation, pushed to the outside through nationhood, nor destroyed, hence the fantasy of total erasure manifested in the "final solution." But it is just that, a fantasy. The Jew merely *represents* this negative principle for the anti-Semite, just as the racial identity of Jews is given *by* the anti-Semite. And so the negative would persist with or without the actual existence of Jews and their particular particularity.

In the anti-Semitic imaginary, the Jew is a malevolent agent, an outsider who ruins the purity of the universal, who refuses to be "absorbed into utility by passing through the cleansing channels of conceptual order" (Horkheimer & Adorno, 2004, p. 147). The particularity that escapes the universalizing force of the conceptual – the unassimilable aspect of Jewish particularity and difference, belonging as much (or more) to the anti-Semite who bestows it – returns like the repressed as "compulsive aversion" (Horkheimer & Adorno, 2004, p. 148). In the failure to assimilate fully, owing to the historical process of assimilation itself, the Jew is positioned as the symptom of social disharmony that returns again and again.

Though shaped by historical processes, these positions are also structural; from this point of view, the ingroup and outgroup could be replaced by other groups. And as uncomfortable as it may be to think about, even the Jew can replace the anti-Semite "as soon as he feels the power of representing the norm" (Horkheimer & Adorno, 2004, p. 140). Anti-Semitism represents merely one form of the unconscious projection of (and defense against) the negative principle *as such*.

Anti-Semitism as the Drive Toward Sameness

The image of the Jewish people harbored by anti-Semites is that of the (sometimes) invisible strangers conspiring against society and ruining the possibility for social harmony with their inherent differences. Anti-Semitism is driven by the wish to impose uniformity and make everyone the same so as to gain social control. Importantly, this control also happens to be the failed striving of the psychological subject. The ego which is tasked with integrating and unifying the psychological subject is also responsible for synthesizing the libidinal drives and mental content to cope with the demands of external reality. The drive toward sameness is found in the logic of identity that defines the ego. The ego unifies experience but is perpetually subverted by an uncanny remainder of disunity coming from its own "eccentric function" being "only what the objective world is for it" (Horkheimer & Adorno, 2004, p. 155). In other words, the ego is constituted by processes like recognition and identification with others. The separate wholeness defining the boundaries of the ego happens to be given by what the ego is not.

Horkheimer and Adorno (2004) show that this process of making everything and everyone the same is not just the project of anti-Semitism or the work of the ego but also the logic of commodification (following Marx) where things (and human beings on the labor market) are stripped of their qualities in order to be exchanged for a universal equivalent. Stripped of their particular qualities, everything serves a social utility within the social totality; this goes for Enlightenment science, which mathematizes qualities; the exchange economy, which relies on equivalences; and the ego, which uses concepts to make the world predictable. The stripping of particular qualities and the drive toward the same is "the primeval-historical entrapment" (Horkheimer & Adorno, 2004, p. 139). Anti-Semitism is the attempt to escape through more of the (Enlightenment) logic of sameness that laid the trap to begin with. These processes amount to the exchange of meaningful qualities of life for the preservation of that life. In other words, anti-Semitism is a self-defeating response to the trappings of the totalized socioeconomic and historical order, which both produces psychological interiority and empties it of meaning.

The destructive consequences of socioeconomic and psychological drive toward sameness are externalized in anti-Semitism. Horkheimer and Adorno explain that "[i]n the image of the Jew which the racial nationalists hold up before the world they express their own essence" (2004, p. 137). The strange and familiar image of the Jew functions as the uncanny, as formulated by Freud (2001b). The uncanny is defined as the process by which the subject experiences a repressed part of itself outside. I take the uncanny to be the horrible return of the repressed – what in the act of ridding is remembered – just as both assimilation and destruction redouble and inscribe the negativity to be eliminated.

Rationality alone cannot combat anti-Semitism because, in its link to power, rationality is inculpated in the logic that brought about anti-Semitism in its current form. But this does not lead (as it might if one stopped here) to an irrationalist solution. *The solution is not merely found in combatting the already existing irrationalities with more rationality but in resisting irrationality in the very process of rationally formulating and justifying solutions.* Any solution to anti-Semitism must grapple with these contradictions. Any irrationality in the rational solution is unjustifiable: think, for example, of the economic arguments against quarantine during the Covid-19 pandemic, or the Israeli lives lost in the fight for Palestinian self-determination, and the suffering of Palestinians in Israel's fight for self-preservation. The difficulty in knowing how to respond to these human tragedies means that more critical thinking is needed, not that we need to stop thinking to start acting irrationally. To do so is to be complicit in the prevailing evil (see Adorno, 2001).

Thinking Anti-Semitism in Terms of Mimesis and Projection

In the *Dialectic of Enlightenment* (2004), the concept of mimesis helps articulate what is repressed for the subject of science and commodity exchange and the way that Jews represent the uncanny terror of facing the repressed, which returns in the other (for the anti-Semite.) The anti-Semite mimics *and* attacks what they fear in themselves (difference, death, otherness, negativity, disorder), swept up in unconscious identification. For instance, Jews have been accused of ritual crimes for centuries, but it is Hitler who becomes a magician acting out the mimetic and deadly ritual with his followers: "all the gesticulations devised by the Fuhrer and his followers are pretexts for giving way to the mimetic temptation without openly violating the reality principle" (Horkheimer & Adorno, 2004, p. 151). In other words, and along the lines of what Freud (2001c) had formulated, the mimetic identification with the destructive leader permits the expression of libidinal and destructive impulses, which had been repressed or projected onto the Jews, without arousing the guilt that would normally accompany them. The temptation of this mimetic process is the promise of social cohesion without sacrificing libidinal gratification. But the promise goes unkept since, in giving way, "[t]he soul, as the possibility of guilt aware of itself, decays" (Horkheimer & Adorno, 2004, p. 164).

Mimesis, formulated as direct representation, is also another way of understanding Freud's death drive (Horkheimer & Adorno, 2004, p. 189), as the drive toward losing oneself in the environment or returning to the directness of natural totality. This is made especially apparent in the link between mimesis and anti-Semitism. "The despoiling of graveyards is not an excess of anti-Semitism," Horkheimer and Adorno (2004) assert. "It is anti-Semitism itself" (p. 150). Similar to the distinction between the death drive and the self-preserving drives in Freud, the sameness of mimesis is distinct from the sameness of synthesis, though both aim, in one way or another, for sameness (e.g., as mastery or as union). Mimesis (like Freud's uncanny) is characterized by a magical proximity to the thing and the potent force of words and thoughts. Synthesis, on the other hand, is indirect and mediated by the uniquely human symbolic system of signification. And yet the drive toward sameness is present in both mimesis and synthesis.

The psychological subject is formed in the gap of indirectness accompanying synthetic operations of the understanding that displaces mimesis. "Bodily adaptation to nature is replaced by 'recognition in a concept,' the subsuming of difference under sameness" (Horkheimer & Adorno, 2004, p. 148). The subject is formed through this displacement and transformation "from reflecting mimesis to controlled reflection" (Horkheimer & Adorno, 2004, p. 148). Reflection is controlled by way of conceptual identification or bringing the object under the organizing force of the subject's concepts by stripping it of its differences. But the mastery of nature afforded by the controlled reflection of the synthetic faculties does not fully root out the uncanny persistence of mimetic directness. Displacement of mimetic reflection preserves the feared thing displaced in the form of a repressed that returns. The symbols (words and images) used to think with have a directness that must continue to be repressed in order to avoid the uncanny terror occurring when, as Freud (2001b) suggests, "a symbol takes over the full functions and significance of the thing it symbolizes" (p. 244). Think, here, of taboo deformations and euphemisms; each instance is a substitution that points the very real directness of words or images and a proximity to something feared that must be kept at bay. The psychic interiority of the psychological subject is opened up through the distance used to defend against over-proximity. In other words, the displacement of mimetic directness – or in psychoanalytic terms repression and projection – opens a space for internality and abstract reasoning. These defenses are so central to the psychological subject that the end of repression would be, according to Adorno (1982), "tantamount to the abolition of his 'psychology'" (p. 136). So the anti-Semite's persecution of the Jews, the longing to fill the gap of indirectness and difference (also a longing for universality and mastery), is the undoing of the psychological subject who, as a subject, is constituted by the very failure to reach its own totalizing and unifying aims.

A critical project cannot aim merely to succeed positively nor to master nature definitively, it must reflect on the mediating projection, the way the perceptions of the surroundings are co-constructed through the concepts projected onto intuitions. Following Kant, human perception is the result of an unconscious synthesis of concepts (understanding) and intuitions (sensibility). In these synthesizing processes of the imagination, the unified subject comes into being as a projection that enables perception. "If mimesis makes itself resemble its surroundings, false projection makes its surroundings resemble itself" (Horkheimer & Adorno, 2004, p. 154). Granted, for Horkheimer and Adorno, there is no escaping the element of projection that is inherent in all acts of perception, what characterizes false projection is the lack of reflection involved. False projection is the default mode of perception, and thus critical reason must actively resist it. For Horkheimer and Adorno (2004), "every percept unconsciously contains conceptual elements, just as every judgement contains unclarified phenomenalistic ones" (pp. 159–160). The illusion of immediacy and presence hides the mediating concepts the subject uses to think with and projects into the surroundings, while at the same time judgement is evacuated of its phenomenalistic content. Critical reason involves the reflection on the one in the other. Without critical reflection on mediation and the historical aspect of concepts used to think with, the concepts can be manipulated without detection, and thus perception made up in part of these concepts can be controlled heteronomously (i.e., by an external authority). Both conceptual certainty and intuitive immediacy must be challenged by the negative and mediated moment of thought in order to resist heteronomy – a heteronomy that fosters anti-Semitism.

Horkheimer and Adorno (2004) are trying to salvage enlightenment autonomy while acknowledging its impurity. "What is at stake," they say, "is not conservation of the past but the fulfillment of past hopes" (Horkheimer & Adorno, 2004, p. xvii). They recognize that for all the paranoid delusions of projection and false immediacy, which Marxists render as false-consciousness, "such blindness is . . . a constitutive element of all judgement, a necessary illusion" (Horkheimer & Adorno, 2004, p. 160). For Horkheimer and Adorno, thinking is an infinite project, and the judicious use of critical reasoning should guide that process. It will perpetually miss its mark, and the ego is even born of this failure. In other words, paranoid projection that can lead to persecution (like anti-Semitism) also gives humanity the power of judgement to fight such persecution and the autonomy and democracy worth fighting for.[1] The ego, despite its illusory properties and destructive inevitabilities, must be salvaged so that reason can persist dialectically beyond its own crisis, especially since the ability to formulate the limits of reason is the work of human morality. "Neither the certainty untroubled by thought, nor the preconceptual unity of perception and object, but only their self-reflective antithesis contains the possibility of reconciliation" (Horkheimer & Adorno, 2004, p. 156). Only the negative and mediated moment in critical thought – reason called to account, by the suffering of the other, for the remainder that insists in its concepts – can reconcile the difficulties in thinking about something as complex as anti-Semitism. It does so by reconciling not in higher synthesis or primordial mimesis but in the critical moment of thought itself, which emphasizes the unconscious side of language as it is used. What could be more psychoanalytic?

Implications of Anti-Semitism as the Limits of Enlightenment

According to the theory described in the previous section, resistance to anti-Semitism in the form of critical reason could lead to "the turning-point of history" (Horkheimer & Adorno, 2004, p. 165). It is a turning point for the whole of history because anti-Semitism is not merely about anti-Jewish prejudice but a wide-reaching social crisis at the limits of enlightenment rationality. The processes of thought that resist anti-Semitism resist all forms of oppression. Critical reason is tasked paradoxically with preventing the violence operative in the marriage of thought and power or reason and force without reverting to unreason. In this formulation, Horkheimer and Adorno (and Adorno, more specifically) have been accused of quietism and conformity stemming from a supposed pessimism and inoperability of such a position (e.g., Whitebook, 2004, p. 79). Adorno (2001) acknowledges the paradox but insists upon its importance as a paradox:

> The situation may well demand . . . that we resist the call of practicality with all our might in order ruthlessly to follow through an idea and its logical implications so as to see where it may lead. I would even say that this ruthlessness, the power of resistance that is inherent in the idea itself and that prevents it from letting itself be directly manipulated for any instrumental purposes whatsoever, this theoretical ruthlessness contains – if you will allow me the paradox – a practical element within itself.
>
> (p. 4)

Hope for a better world lies in the refusal to justify force since such desperate measures obligate us to give up thinking in mid-thought. (Perhaps it is helpful to think of this refusal as a form of nonviolent resistance.) I read this as the negative principle shared by strands of both psychoanalysis and critical theory, with implications for the practice of Freud's three impossible professions, each of which require an impossible choice between social utility and thinking: *politics, education, and psychoanalysis*.

Implications for Politics

Stephan Grigat (2019) uses Horkheimer and Adorno's theory of anti-Semitism to propose political policy and military intervention in the turbulent Middle East. Grigat's work is important in stressing the persistence and social consequences of anti-Semitism and the continued relevance of the Horkheimer and Adorno's critical theory of anti-Semitism for our current historical milieu. Nevertheless, I believe that he falls short of his own moral aspirations. Without careful critical reflection, even the most compelling ethical justification for political action can be complicit in the logic of oppression.

Grigat (2019) grounds his political project on Adorno's (updated) categorical imperative: To think and act "so that Auschwitz will not repeat itself, so that nothing similar will happen" (Adorno, 2004, p. 365). Adorno's imperative is a moral response to mimetic bodily agony when confronted with the other's suffering for which our conceptual understanding is forever inadequate. Grigat (2019) also appeals to a speech given by Adorno on anti-Semitism in the 1960s, where Adorno seems to suggest that in the short-term, "the 'available means of coercion' should be used 'without sentimentality'" (Adorno, 1964, as cited in Grigat, 2019, p. 444). Grigat reads this as a justification (invoking Adorno as the moral authority) for military intervention. Grigat combines this somewhat misleading citation, Horkheimer and Adorno's theory of anti-Semitism, and Adorno's categorical imperative to justify practical and short-term military action against nations led by governments complicit in anti-Semitism. Grigat asserts that the European Union must cut off political relations to all anti-Semitic governments and give unilateral military support to Israel. Grigat is quite correct in his political demand to fight anti-Semitism and anti-Semitic forms of anti-Zionism but undermines the logic on which that demand is based, stopping short of the universal anti-Fascism (which he proposes) by reducing anti-Semitism to anti-Zionism.

Despite Grigat's consideration of Horkheimer and Adorno's theory of anti-Semitism as more than anti-Jewish racism, he claims "[t]he analysis of geopolitical reproduction of antisemtism in the form of *anti-Zionism* is today a central task for a critical theory of antisemitism" (Grigat, 2019, p. 445). With this, Grigat begins to reduce anti-Semitism from hate for the negative principle into something petrified in the territorialized and nationalist struggles in the Middle East:

> Taking Adorno's categorical imperative seriously today means: Giving all possible support to Israel and its armed forces in their defensive struggle against antisemitism in all its forms, while focusing criticism, in both the academic and political spheres, on the anti-Israeli resentment that is encountered.
>
> (Grigat, 2019, p. 457)

In not condemning all hate for the negative principle (be it the image of the Jew or the image of the Palestinian), he recapitulates what he wishes to critique and inadvertently undermines Adorno's categorical imperative.

Grigat (2019) systematically presents the very real anti-Semitic threat from Hamas, Hezbollah, and the Iranian government. And he is rightly pointing to the problem (on the right and the left) of being unable or unwilling to challenge anti-Semitism in all its forms (implicit and explicit). Resisting anti-Semitism and condemning terror, however, should not be conflated with the support for a particular government. Grigat is not wrong: anti-Zionism can be a form of anti-Semitism. But he is also not right. The central task for the critical theory of anti-Semitism is still the development of critical faculties, the resistance to ticket mentality *in toto*, and the categorical opposition to suffering.

A categorical imperative must be followed in all cases to resist oppression wherever it rears its head – Iran, Israel, India, China, United States. More in line with Adorno's critical theory, nationalism itself (Israeli, American, Palestinian), just like ticket thinking (right *and* left), must be challenged. Critical theory cannot turn away from the suffering of any human beings whether they are identified as Israeli or Palestinian. This does not lead to quietism (as is supposed) but to new and nonviolent forms of action. Those who may suggest that this is inoperable on the real world are expressing the abandonment of thought and the abandonment of those who will inevitably be excluded. Grigat can claim that his policy proposal is pragmatic, possible, and even necessary, but he is wrong to claim that it withstands the radical force of Adorno's moral imperative and the *Dialectic of Enlightenment* (2004).

Reason becomes unreason when critical theory is used to endorse and justify violence. This does not mean that people should not defend themselves, but it does lead to more questions about what is meant by "people," "self," and "defense" (see Butler, 2020). Adorno's discussion of a "short-term program," promoted by Grigat (2019), refers to the recourse to authority for the sake of the de-Nazification of Germany. But this authority, Adorno (1964) goes on to explain, is the shock of moral strength. According to Adorno (1964), shock and moral strength go hand in hand (p. 102). Taking Adorno seriously, today, is to stand in solidarity with oppressed people and to recognize the way violence (of thought and action) are unjustly justified. Adorno (2001) wrote that "[f]orce only really becomes evil the moment it misunderstands itself as . . . the sword of God" (p. 174). The immorality of violence is in its rationalization as good. Later in his speech on anti-Semitism, Adorno (1964) claims, quite rightly in my estimation, that "[a]n effective defense against anti-Semitism is inseparable from an effective defense against nationalism in any form. One can't be on the one hand against anti-Semitism, and on the other hand be a militant nationalist" (p. 103). Of course, in the preliminary remarks prefacing his speech, Adorno implores the readers not to take it as authoritative; they should, rather, think critically for themselves.

Implications for Education

Much of Horkheimer and Adorno's Critical Theory points to the position of education as the development of critical thinking, in the struggle against anti-Semitism, authoritarianism, and other forms of heteronomy. Adorno gave lectures and wrote extensively on the central role of this critical education (e.g., Adorno, 1998, 1964). I imagine that the importance of a critical education (stated as such) will not come across to informed readers as particularly extraordinary. A terminological clarification is needed here: where I have just written "education," Adorno refers primarily to the German *Bildung*, which is a concept that contains a cultural specificity missing when translated into English directly as education or even culture, as it is often done. In German, education as pedagogy is referred to as *Erziehung*. Morelock (2017) defines *Bildung*, on the other hand, as "a model state to be achieved by learners through cultivating their own wise intellectual capacities" (p. 67). He goes on to suggest that an adequate definition of *Bildung* must also convey the link between the autonomy of the individual and sociality: the autonomy achieved by *Bildung* is constituted by the ability to contribute socially. So while education is a component of *Bildung*, when reduced to an individualistic or institutional form of education or as a means to an end, the unique cultural characteristics of *Bildung* are missing.

This is precisely what Adorno is concerned with: *Bildung* has been reduced to an instrumental education. Barbarism as the failure of culture is also, first and foremost, the failure of an educational system complicit in the predominance of instrumentalized reasoning and the reproduction of technicians. *Bildung* is a condition of possibility for humanity and the dialectical autonomy necessary for political participation as citizens. Without *Bildung* there is barbarism. Still, Adorno cautions not to mistake his emphasis on *Bildung* for a positive solution in itself. Echoing the dialectical processes developed in the previous section from the *Dialectic of Enlightenment* (2004), Adorno recognizes that *Bildung* is also complicit in "the elimination of the subject in the interest of its own self-preservation" (Adorno, 1959, p. 18). *Bildung* has always also been a way of controlling human drives as a means of achieving social cohesion, and education has become a commodity in the totalized social order instituted by capitalism. Adorno looks to *Bildung* not as a positive utopian image but as an image for dialectical reflection.

The predominance of instrumental reasoning is not so much a consequence of a total lack of education, culture, or *Bildung* but what Horkheimer and Adorno (2004) refer to as a "*Halbbildung*" (i.e., half-education or pseudo-culture). The concept is best articulated in Adorno's essay "*Theorie der Halbildung*" (1972) originally published in 1959 and translated into English under the title "Theory of pseudo-culture" (1993). *Halbbildung* leads to the application of formulas and methods without fostering the self-reflexivity and critical thinking needed to root out unreason in one's own reason. Currently, *Halbbildung* can be witnessed in many facets of contemporary institutional learning and is aggressively present in the growing movement to defund liberal arts programs in the United States (Morelock, 2017). Yet it should be noted that the resuscitation of the liberal arts (like a return to *Bildung* itself) would not constitute a solution. *Bildung* is opposed to *Halbbildung*, but a return to traditional *Bildung* is not the answer. "The measure of the bad new," Adorno (1993) reminds his readers, "is only the bad old" (p. 23). *Bildung* is struck through with contradictions and requires an immanent critique. For instance, the cultural facet of *Bildung* presupposes autonomy but is given heteronomously. The individual can only become autonomous by taking in knowledge from an outside authority. "Thus," Adorno (1993) writes, "the moment [*Bildung*] exists, it already ceases to exist" (p. 24). The solution, then, is not a return to the older form of *Bildung*, nor is it an embrace of a *Halbbildung*, but a critical reflection on the failure of *Bildung*.

In not being able to be corrected directly through pedagogy (i.e., reality testing, transfer of information, teaching methods, etc.), *Halbbildung* functions much like the unconscious. Accordingly, Adorno (1993) offers a somewhat unexpected assertion: "only a deep psychological approach could counteract this tendency in such a way as to prevent its ossification in the early developmental stages and to strengthen critical reflection" (p. 36). This assertion should be qualified with reference to Adorno's reading of psychology: The psychological approach must be a negative psychology – psychoanalysis.

Implications for Psychoanalysis

In Adorno's essay "Education after Auschwitz" (1998) (first published in German as "*Ereihung nach Aucshwitz*" in 1966), he proposes that the dissemination of psychoanalytic theory is an integral feature of this critical education in the wake of Nazi barbarism (p. 191). Adorno recognized that, in conjunction with psychoanalysis, education as pedagogy (*Erzeihung*) is still crucial to developing the capacity for critical reflection on Halbbildung and thus uprooting unreason in the form of instrumentality.

Adorno's reading of psychoanalytic theory focuses on the constitutive tension between the individual and society, the tensions that arise in the meeting of unconscious needs and social prohibitions, as well as the processes involved in learning to learn. Although he insisted on the role of psychoanalysis in critical education, he was reproving of what he saw as the inevitably normalizing aims of clinical practice from which those theories originated. Nevertheless, I believe that Adorno's work (informed by psychoanalytic theory) can, in a neat reciprocity, lend clinicians a model of ethical thinking. Critical education converges with the field of psychoanalysis in terms of the position of authority in clinical work, the location of clinical knowledge, and the development of the subject of that knowing. Gordon Allport (1946) recognized, early on, that anti-Semitism tends to be ego-syntonic and may not be something that can be clinically "cured" person by person (p. vii). Nevertheless, the root cause of anti-Semitism, the false projection and instrumentalization, is potentially present in the subjectivity of all clinical patients. A psychoanalytic practice informed by Adorno's version of psychoanalysis therefore needs to wrestle with the tension between social utility (normalization) and critical thought (the persistence of not knowing). I have found that the work of French psychoanalyst Jacques Lacan (1901–1981) comes closest to such a critical psychoanalysis.

One of the greatest contributions Adorno makes to psychoanalysis – alone and in his work with Horkheimer – is the development of a negative psychology. Thought of as negative psychology, psychoanalysis presents itself as an ally of critical reason, constantly calling the ego's syntheses into quesiton and tracing the perpetual self-undermineing of conscious conceptions, words, and stories. Adorno recognized that the essential aspects of anti-Semitism lie beyond psychology, but he found a back door by which to resist anti-Semitism through the study of the way the psychological subject undermines itself. Ideally, like the processes of critical education and *Bildung*, psychoanalysis is not merely about the content taught by an outside authority but the discovery and fostering of the critical faculties in each individual to resist the untruth, the ability of each individual to see the remainder in their concepts through the recognition of their unconscious processes.

Recently, scholars have been revisiting the intersection of critical theory and psychoanalysis (e.g., Allen, 2020; Allen & Ruti, 2019; Burston, 2020; Butler, 2020; Dews, 1987; Fong, 2016; Honneth, 1995; Mills, 2019; Whitebook, 1996). Allen (2020) suggests that critical theory needs psychoanalysis. I would add that psychoanalysis also needs critical theory. In many ways, Horkheimer and Adorno's (2004) knotty theory of change, of autonomy and of negative dialectical reasoning can be helpful in thinking about what seems impossible in clinical work and what it means to do something that appears impossible.

Conclusion

Horkheimer and Adorno (2004) developed critical theory as a resistance to untruth through a psychoanalytic inquiry into anti-Semitism as the limits of enlightenment reason. They emphasize the negative moment of thought so as to oppose what they call a "false clarity" reinforcing the status quo (Horkheimer & Adorno, 2004, xvii). Clarity can be reasonable and false at the same time since clarity can be grounded in the facts of perception that may be controlled heteronomously by authoritarians, fascists, or a social totality. Without the emphasis on the negative moment of thought, the resistance to anti-Semitism can and has been used by lucid thinkers to justify oppression and militant nationalism, which perpetuate cycles of violence. The drive toward sameness, which manifests as anti-Semitism, is found in the development of the psychological subject, which comes into being through the illusion of false equivalences. Critical reason in the form of immanent critique as developed in the *Dialectic of Enlightenment* can counteract the rational processes usurped by the automatism of the drive toward sameness, which expresses itself as anti-Semitism.

Although Horkheimer and Adorno (2004) borrow and extend a number of psychoanalytic concepts, Adorno was explicitly skeptical of the prospects of a clinical work that could function clinically without simultaneously reinforcing the status quo (Adorno, 2004, p. 273; see also Mariotti, 2009). I disagree with Adorno's rejection of the clinical project; though, he is right to be concerned with its potential normalizing force. I believe that psychoanalysis can and should learn from and extend Horkheimer and Adorno's critical theory in clinical thinking. Psychoanalysis as a clinical project can learn from critical theory to develop negatively psychological processes of treatment that move away from the reliance on narratives of progress and the individualism inherent in the disease model of mental illness and toward change, which is unforeseeable and perhaps even social. This may help psychoanalysis maintain a critical edge in the face of overwhelming pressure – in the current and still very positivistic scientific and philosophical environment – to adapt to the status quo.

There are a number of clinical projects (e.g., phenomenological psychopathology and Lacanian psychoanalysis) that are already pushing against the false clarity and positivism of contemporary mainstream psychology. Lacan's thinking was itself influenced by the *Dialectic of Enlightenment* (Roudinesco, 1997, p. 312), and a number of Horkheimer and Adorno's ethical commitments are already reflected in psychoanalysis influenced by Lacan: an emphasis on the negative movement of thought and the unconscious, attention to the presentation of knowledge, and the relational position of identity and authority (Fink, 1997; Hook, 2017; Lacan, 2006; Laplanche, 1996; Rogers, 2016; Verhaeghe, 2008). Resistance to normative conceptions of health and well-being could lead to the development of new ways of relating to identity and authority, breaking with those that lead to anti-Semitism and other forms of oppression.

Note

1 Horkheimer and Adorno's (2004) adoption of a kind of neo-Kantian epistemology challenges the traditional Marxist notion of "false consciousness" since the intelligibility of the world mediated through the ego's (mostly unconscious) operations always entails elements of projection, oversimplification, and hence some distortion. Similar to their (arguably) heterodox reading of Freud, where getting rid of repression would not leave an unrepressed ego but no ego at all, to get rid of false consciousness would not leave true consciousness but no consciousness at all. Hence, the negative work of critical theory as a form of resistance to untruth.

References

Adorno, T. W. (1964). Zur Bekämpfung des Antisemitismus heute (Fighting anti-Semitism today). *Das Argument, 29*. My translation (Transcript of a speech given November 3, 1962).

Adorno, T. W. (1972). Theorie der Halbbildung. In *Gesammelte Schriften, Band 8: Soziologische Schriften 1* (pp. 93–121). Suhrkamp Verlag (Original work published 1959).
Adorno, T. W. (1982). Freudian theory and the pattern of fascist propaganda. In A. Arato & E. Gephardt (Eds.), *The essential Frankfurt school reader* (pp. 118–137). Continuum (Original work published 1951).
Adorno, T. W. (1993). Theory of pseudo-culture (1959). *Telos, 95*, 15–38. https://doi.org/10.3817/0393095015.
Adorno, T. W. (1998). Education after Auschwitz. In H. Pickford (Trans.), *Critical models: Interventions and Catchwords* (pp. 191–204). New York: Columbia University Press.
Adorno, T. W. (2001). *Problem of moral philosophy* (T. Schröder, Ed. & T. Livingstone, Trans.). Stanford University Press.
Adorno, T. W. (2004). *Negative dialectic* (E. B. Ashton, Trans.). Routledge (Original work published 1967).
Adorno, T. W. (2019). Remarks on *the authoritarian personality*. In T. W. Adorno, E. Frenkel-Brunswik, D. J. Levinson, & R. N. Sanford (Eds.), *The authoritarian personality* (pp. xli–lxvi). Verso.
Adorno, T. W., Frenkel-Brunswik, E., Levinson, D. J., & Sanford, R. N. (2019). *The authoritarian personality*. Verso (Original work published 1950).
Allen, A. (2020). *Critique on the couch: Why critical theory needs psychoanalysis*. Columbia University Press.
Allen, A., & Ruti, M. (2019). *Critical theory between Klein and Lacan: A dialogue*. Bloomsbury.
Allport, G. (1946). Preface. In E. Simmel (Ed.), *Anti-Semitism, a social disease*. International Universities Press.
Anti-Defamation League (ADL). (2020). *Antisemitic attitudes in the U.S.: A guide to ADL's latest poll*. Retrieved March 10, 2021. www.adl.org/news/press-releases/anti-semitic-stereotypes-persist-in-america-survey-shows.
Billig, M. (1991). *Ideology and opinions: Studies in rhetorical psychology*. Sage Publications.
Burston, D. (2014). Anti-Semitism. In T. Teo (Ed.), *Encyclopedia of critical psychology*. Springer.
Burston, D. (2020). *Psychoanalysis, politics and the postmodern university*. Palgrave.
Burston, D. (2021). *Anti-Semitism and analytical psychology: Jung, politics and culture*. Routledge.
Butler, J. (2020). *The force of nonviolence*. Verso.
D'Arcy, M. (2020). Dialectic of enlightenment: Origin stories of western Marxism. In K. Freeman & J Munro (Eds.), *Reading the postwar future: Textual turning points from 1944* (pp. 43–59). Bloomsbury Academic.
Dews, P. (1987). *Logics of disintegration: Post-structuralist thought and the claims of critical theory*. Verso.
Fanon, F. (2008). *Black skin white masks* (C. L. Markmann, Trans.). Pluto Press (Originally published in 1952).

Fenichel, O. (1940). Psychoanalysis of anti-Semitism. *American Imago, 1B*(2), 24–39.

Fink, B. (1997). *A clinical introduction to Lacanian psychoanalysis: Theory and technique*. Harvard University Press.

Fong, B. (2016). *Death and mastery: Psychoanalytic drive theory and the subject of late capitalism*. Columbia University Press.

Freud, S. (2001a). Repression. In *The standard edition of the complete psychological works of Sigmund Freud, volume XVI (1914–1916): On the history of the psychoanalytic movement, papers on metapsychology and other works* (Originally published in 1915).

Freud, S. (2001b). The 'uncanny'. In J. Strachey (Ed. & Trans.), *The standard edition of the complete psychological works of Sigmund Freud, volume XVII (1917–1919): An infantile neurosis and other works* (pp. 217–256). Vintage Books (Original work published 1919).

Freud, S. (2001c). Group psychology and the analysis of the ego. In *The standard edition of the complete psychological works of Sigmund Freud, volume XVIII (1920–1922): Beyond the pleasure principle and other works*, 65–144 (Originally published in 1921).

Freud, S. (2001d). Negation. In *The standard edition of the complete psychological works of Sigmund Freud, volume XIX (1923–1925): The ego and the id and other works* (Originally published in 1925).

Freud, S. (2001e). A comment on anti-Semitism. In J. Strachey (Ed. & Trans.), *The standard edition of the complete psychological works of Sigmund Freud, volume XXIII (1937–1939): Moses and monotheism, an outline of psychoanalysis and other works* (pp. 289–293). Vintage Books (Originally published in 1938).

Freud, S. (2001f). Moses and monotheism. In *The standard edition of the complete psychological works of Sigmund Freud, volume XXIII: Moses and monotheism, an outline of psycho-analysis and other works* (Originally published in 1939).

Fromm, E. (1984). *Working class in Weimar Germany: A psychological and sociological study*. Berg Publishers.

Grigat, S. (2019). The fight against Antisemitism and the Iranian Regime: Challenges and contradictions in the light of Adorno's categorical imperative. In A. Lange, K. Mayerhofer, D. Porat, & L. Schiffman (Eds.), *Volume 1 comprehending and confronting antisemitism* (pp. 441–462). De Gruyter. https://doi.org/10.1515/9783110618594-034.

Honneth, A. (1995). *The struggle for recognition: The moral grammar of social conflicts*. Polity.

Hook, D. (2017). *Six moments in Lacan: Communication and identification*. Routledge.

Horkheimer, M., & Adorno, T. W. (2004). *Dialectic of enlightenment: Philosophical fragments* (G. S. Noerr, Ed. & E. Jephcott, Trans.). Stanford (Original work published 1947).

Lacan, J. (2006). *Écrits: The first complete edition in English* (B. Fink, Ed. & Trans.). W. W. Norton & Co.

Laplanche, J. (1996). Psychoanalysis as anti-hermeneutics (L. Thurston, Trans.). *Radical Philosophy*, *79*, 7–12.

Mariotti, S. (2009). Damaged life as exuberant vitality in America: Adorno, alienation, and the psychic economy. *Telos*, *149*, 169–190. http://doi.org/10.3817/1209149169.

Morelock, J. (2017). Authoritarian populism contra "Bildung": Anti-intellectualism and the neoliberal assault on the Liberal Arts. *Cadernos Cimeac*, *7*(2), 63–81. https://doi.org/10.18554%2Fcimeac.v7i2.2429.

Mills, J. (2019). Contemporary psychoanalysis and critical theory: A new synthesis. *Critical Horizons*, *20*(3), 233–245. DOI: 10.1080/14409917.2019.1616484.

Noerr, G. S. (2004). Editor's afterward, T. W. Adorno & M. Horkheimer, *Dialectic of enlightenment: Philosophical fragments* (G. S. Noerr, Ed. & E. Jephcott, Trans.). Stanford University Press.

Rensman, L. (2017). *Politics of unreason: The Frankfurt School and the origins of modern antisemitism*. SUNY Press.

Rogers, A. (2016). *Incandescent alphabets: Psychosis and the enigma of language*. Routledge.

Roudinesco, E. (1997). *Jacques Lacan* (B. Bray, Trans.). Columbia University Press.

Simmel, E. (Ed.). (1946). *Anti-semitism, a social disease*. International Universities Press.

Strosberg, B. B. (2021). Adorno's negative psychology. *Social and Personality Psychology Compass*, *15*(2). https://doi.org/10.1111/spc3.12578.

Tajfel, H., & Turner, J. C. (2004). The social identity theory of intergroup behavior. In J. T. Jost & J. Sidanius (Eds.), *Political psychology: Key readings* (pp. 276–293). Psychology Press. https://doi.org/10.4324/9780203505984-16.

Tuffin, K. (2005). *Understanding critical social psychology*. Sage. http://doi.org/10.4135/9781446217566.

Verhaeghe, P. (2008). *On being normal and other disorders: A manual for clinical psychodiagnostics*. Other Press.

Whitebook, J. (1996). *Perversion and utopia: A study in psychoanalysis and critical theory*. MIT Press.

Whitebook, J. (2004). The marriage of Marx and Freud: Critical theory and psychoanalysis. In F. Rush (Ed.), *The Cambridge companion to critical theory* (pp. 74–102). Cambridge University Press. https://doi.org/10.1017/CCOL0521816602.

Chapter 7

Critical Theory, Left-Wing Authoritarianism, and Anti-Semitism

Daniel Burston

Authoritarianism: Right and Left

In August of 2021, Thomas Costello and five colleagues at Emory University published a study on left-wing authoritarianism in *The Journal of Personality and Social Psychology*. It was titled "Clarifying the Nature and Structure of Left Wing Authoritarianism" (Costello et al., 2021) and caused quite a stir among social and political psychologists. Why? Because until recently, it was widely assumed among social and political psychologists that left-wingers are essentially anti-authoritarian and that left-wing authoritarianism is rare or nonexistent (Satel, 2021). In the words of Bob Altemeyer, a leading figure in the field of authoritarianism research, left-wing authoritarianism was "the Loch Ness monster of political psychology – an occasional shadow, but no monster" (Altemeyer, 1996, pp. 229)

Costello et al. maintain that Altemeyer and his associates could not find evidence of left-wing authoritarianism (for at least four decades) because they were using inappropriate research tools. Why? Because they had simply administered Altemeyer's celebrated Right Wing Authoritarianism (RWA) scale to self-identified left-wingers, rather than constructing new scales that are specifically designed to detect left-wing authoritarianism.

In an effort to discern the nature and extent of left-wing authoritarianism, Costello et al. abandoned the assumption that left-wing authoritarianism mirrors the tripartite structure of right-wing authoritarianism (i.e., authoritarian aggression, authoritarian submission, conventionalism), as several of their predecessors had done (e.g., Conway et al., 2017). Instead, they resolved to conceptualize left-wing authoritarianism "from the ground up" by a process they called "boot strapping" and, in the process, developed a list of ten "focal constructs" around which to question their respondents (Satel, 2021).

DOI: 10.4324/9781003215301-7

Having constructed new scales and administered them to 7,258 adults, Costello and associates found that there are significant areas of overlap between left- and right-wing authoritarians. These include predilections toward "social uniformity, prejudice towards different others, willingness to wield group authority to coerce behavior, cognitive rigidity, aggression and punitiveness towards perceived enemies, outsized concern for hierarchy, and moral absolutism" (Costello et al., 2020, p. 72).

When asked why left-wing authoritarianism was all but invisible to psychologists till now, Costello et al. traced the problem back to Theodor Adorno's landmark study, *The Authoritarian Personality*, published in 1950, which depicted authoritarianism as a trait shared primarily or exclusively by political conservatives.[1] Costello was not the first person to address this oversight, however. In *The Authoritarian Personality: Continuities in Social Research*, published in 1954 (Christie and Jahoda, 1954), Robert Christie, Marie Jahoda, and Edward Shils took Adorno and associates to task for their left-wing bias. Adorno did not take kindly to these critiques, and as a consequence, sociologists and political scientists who adopted some version of Adorno et al.'s concepts and methods in the decades that followed seldom even admit to the existence of authoritarianism on the Left. Reflecting on this curious state of affairs, Costello et al. noted that

> the possibility that authoritarianism research has a blind spot for LWA is perhaps unsurprising given that *The Authoritarian Personality* was an effort to describe the psychological appeal of fascism, a far-right ideology. But just as psychologists have recently acknowledged the prospect that a systemic overreliance on Western, Educated, Industrialized, Rich, and Democratic (WEIRD) samples has distorted our ability to make generalized claims about human behavior (Gurven, 2018; Henrich et al., 2010), the psychological processes underlying authoritarianism may be challenging to understand when only rightist authoritarians have been studied. As a point of comparison, consider the consequences of using exclusively male samples to develop the diagnostic criteria for a mental disorder. Presumably, this approach would overrepresent symptoms more often found in men and underrepresent those more often found in women. In turn, this bias might lead researchers to conclude that sex differences exist in said disorder (e.g., Yagoda, 2013). A similar process has plausibly occurred in

> political psychology – understanding authoritarianism's manifestations in left- and right-wing populations may be a critical step in clarifying the nature of authoritarianism writ large.
>
> (Costello et al., 2021, p. 3)

Before Adorno et al.

Given Costello's critique of *The Authoritarian Personality*, it bears remembering that Adorno's earliest critic on this score was actually Erich Fromm (1900–1980), who preceded Adorno as the director for social psychological research at the Frankfurt Institute for Social Research from 1927 to 1938 (Jay, 1973; Burston, 1991). With the backing of the institute's director, Max Horkheimer, Fromm had launched a research project on the prevalence of authoritarian attitudes among (skilled and unskilled) blue-collar workers in the private sector, white-collar workers, and civil servants in the Weimar Republic that lasted from 1929 to 1931. To that end, he and his collaborators – Ernst Schactel, Hilde Weiss, and Paul Lazarsfeld – devised a daunting (271 item) questionnaire, which was distributed to 3,300 people, most of whom were working class. Fromm's research convinced him that many nominally Left-leaning workers in the communist and social democratic parties would likely swap their allegiance from left-wing leaders and parties to Hitler and his minions – which they did, of course, and in fairly short order too (Brunner, 1994). A recent illustration of this phenomenon were the thousands of "Bernie bros" who abruptly shifted their allegiance to Donald Trump when they learned that Hillary Clinton had won the Democratic party's nomination.

However, unlike contemporary measures of authoritarianism, which rely on "yes" or "no" answers or else on Likert scales, which purportedly measure the intensity of attitudes and affectivity, Fromm and his collaborators gave their respondents many open-ended questions that they could answer at length, if they so chose, which Fromm and his colleagues interpreted psychoanalytically. Perhaps because of the questionnaire's length, only 1,100 questionnaires were returned. Moreover, because of the worsening political climate, Fromm and his Frankfurt School colleagues soon took flight from Nazi Germany. Fromm left earlier than the rest, in 1933, but it was not until 1937 that he wrote a comprehensive overview of his study in English. To his intense disappointment, Max Horkheimer refused to publish it under the Institute's auspices because it was "too Marxist";

although in truth, Fromm's increasingly outspoken objections to Freudian orthodoxy was another irritant that provoked ill will between Fromm and his erstwhile colleagues. Moreover, and more importantly, from our present standpoint, Fromm insisted that authoritarianism was present in abundance on *both* sides of the political spectrum; an assertion that Horkheimer, Adorno, and their colleagues feared would furnish ammunition for the political Right (Fromm, 1984; Jeffries, 2017).

Now admittedly, a sample size of 1,100 questionnaires, no matter how carefully scrutinized and interpreted, is a slender thread on which to hang such a weighty hypothesis. But the motives that prompted the institute's rejection of Fromm's findings were rather more complicated than that. They hinged just as much on his (evolving) attitudes toward Marx and Freud and their legacies as they did on the actual merits of his study. Realizing this, Fromm left the Institute in 1938 and was replaced by Adorno, who borrowed many features of Fromm's study in his own research design, rendering Fromm's effort, in effect, a pilot study for *The Authoritarian Personality* (Jay, 1973; Burston, 1991; Brunner, 1994) and many studies that followed. Indeed, many of the questions that were featured in his lengthy questionnaire still prove useful when administered to much larger samples than he undertook to analyze. For example, in a recent article titled "Critical Theory, authoritarianism and the politics of lipstick from the Weimar Republic," sociologists Janet Afary and Roger Friedlander documented a study they did in 2011–2012 using many of Fromm's original questions. Their revised and updated questionnaire was distributed online and gleaned nearly 18,000 (male and female) respondents in North Africa and the Middle East (Afary and Friedlander, 2018). Their findings are beyond the scope of this paper, but they demonstrate the robust and continuing relevance of Fromm's early efforts to the study of authoritarianism today.

So the question arises: why isn't Fromm cited among researchers who are currently investigating authoritarianism in the USA? One reason, apart from sample size, is that Fromm's study did not appear in English translation until 1984 (Fromm, 1984; Brunner, 1994). Another is that most current researchers have arbitrarily consigned Fromm's work to the "prescientific phase" of social research (Samelson, 1993). A third reason Fromm's study still languishes in obscurity is that researchers who gravitate to this field of inquiry, like Bob Altemeyer, are predominantly Left-leaning and already so heavily influenced by *The Authoritarian Personality* that they dismiss left-wing authoritarianism as an abstraction, an aberration, or a chimera.

Of course, acknowledging the fact that the research of Adorno, Altemeyer, and others was one-sided, focusing narrowly on right-wing authoritarianism is not to dismiss it out of hand. After all, let's remember that on November 8, 2016, nearly 63 million Americans cast their votes to elect Donald J. Trump president of the United States. As Trump's presidency unfolded, the support of his base remained rock solid, not despite, but apparently *because of* his bigoted, bullying demeanor, his sadism, narcissism, and mind-boggling incompetence evidenced (among other things) in his catastrophic handling of the Covid-19 epidemic. And the fact that 75% of Republican voters *still* believe his brazen lies about Joe Biden and the Democratic Party having stolen the election bodes ill for the future of democracy in this country.[2]

In a recent book titled *Authoritarian Nightmare: Trump and His Followers*, Altemeyer and former White House Counsel John Dean offered us an in-depth study of Trump voters (Dean and Altemeyer, 2021). Their findings demonstrate very high correlations between authoritarianism, on the one hand, and racist, sexist, fundamentalist, and xenophobic attitudes, on the other. Indeed, they say, nothing else predicts the presence of these noxious attitudes in the population at large as surely as an RWA personality profile.

So let's be clear. In the short term, at least, right-wing extremism poses a much graver threat to American democracy, evidenced by the (Trump-led) insurrection on Capitol Hill on January 6, 2021. By contrast, left-wing authoritarianism poses a less immediate but nevertheless significant longer-term threat because it has infiltrated many universities. Indeed, many accomplished scholars and gifted teachers are *already* leaving higher education for other careers because they feel that their universities have been thoroughly captured or compromised by the activist *Zeitgeist* and are utterly beyond redemption. Let us hope they are wrong, because a real, functioning democracy *needs* universities that protect academic freedom and promote viewpoint diversity to remain intact.

Left-Wing Authoritarianism, Dogmatism, and the University

Meanwhile, though their appearance is quite welcome – indeed, long overdue – Costello's left-wing authoritarianism scales, while compelling at first glance, may not be the last word. On the contrary, if past history is any indication, they will probably be subjected to prolonged scrutiny and may require significant modifications and improvements before they are widely adopted. We shall see.

In the interim, the easiest way to differentiate between right and left-wing authoritarians is to attend to the rhetoric their leaders use to galvanize their followers. Right-wing authoritarians typically invoke the "good old days," look to the past for examples of the "good life," and promise to restore or defend traditional class, race, and gender roles and stereotypes. They promise "law and order," appealing to nostalgia, to people's fear of chaos and the loss of status and wealth, and their longing to live in a simpler society (think Donald Trump).

Left-wing ideologues, by contrast, typically tap into people's anger and their yearning for a brighter future, promising justice, equality, and prosperity for all, and especially those who suffered under the old regime, only to renege on these promises with the passage of time (think Mao Zhe Dong). Another convenient rule of thumb – that is, an empirical generalization, true in most cases, if not in all – is that right-wing authoritarians stress the need for religious and/or racial purity as a prerequisite for group membership, while left-wing authoritarians tend to be more inclusive in this respect. More often than not, left-wing authoritarians overlook or ignore racial and religious identity markers but stress the need for ideological purity or (some version of) "political correctness" instead.

That said, ideological differences like these never prevent right- and left-wing authoritarians from behaving in almost identical fashion once they seize power. They stifle, intimidate, and murder their opponents and suppress any hint of principled and democratic opposition through "re-education" in the gulag or forced labor of various kinds. Just consider the careers of left-wing authoritarians like Stalin, Mao Ze Dhong, Robert Mugabe, Hugo Chavez, Nicholas Maduro, and Daniel Ortega.

However, left-wing tyrants like Stalin, Mao, Mugabe et al. all managed to control a governing clique or party that enjoyed popular support at first but behaved in increasingly ruthless and authoritarian ways with the passage of time. By contrast, left-wing authoritarianism has a very different look and feel to it in the USA today. While some left-wingers still fancy themselves as revolutionaries, many prefer to identify as social justice warriors or as anti-racist activists who stand up for the underdog and address collective evils like racism, sexism, homophobia, transphobia, Islamophobia, etc. And while these societal evils certainly need to be addressed, sadly, social justice warriors (SWJs) often coalesce into groups that seek to destroy the reputations and livelihoods of those who disagree with them, in a diffuse, Leftish version of McCarthyism (Hudson and Williams, 2016). How did this trend begin?

In 1950, the same year that Adorno et al. published the authoritarian personality, Fromm described a conversation with a Stalinist who

> exhibits a great capacity to make use of his reason in many areas of thought. When we come to discuss Stalinism with him, however, we are suddenly confronted with a closed system of thought. . . . He will deny certain obvious facts, distort others, or, inasmuch as he agrees with certain facts or statements, he will explain his attitude as logical and consistent. He will at the same time declare that the fascist cult of the leader is one of the most obnoxious features of authoritarianism and claim that the Stalinist cult of the leader is something entirely different, that it is the genuine expression of the people's love for Stalin. When you tell him that is what the Nazis claimed too, he will smile tolerantly about your want of perception or accuse you of being a lackey of capitalism. He will find a thousand and one reasons why Russian nationalism is not nationalism, why authoritarianism is democracy, why slave labor is designed to educate and improve anti-social elements. The arguments which are used to defend or explain the deeds of the Inquisition or those used to explain racial or sexual prejudices are illustrations of the same rationalizing capacity.
>
> (Fromm, 1950, pp. 57–58)

While this description is quite apt, as far as it goes, it does not align well with the contours of contemporary left-wing radicalism. After all, Stalinists were slavishly devoted to or fearfully compliant with the ideas and wishes of one extremely paranoid man who oversaw a brutal reign of terror and demanded strict obedience from Communist parties all over the world. That kind of centralized, hierarchical authority structure is largely absent among most left-wing authoritarians today. And this isn't a new development, either. On the contrary, the radical students of the 1960s organized themselves into a multitude of loose-knit coalitions whose leadership was less centralized, more situational, and whose structure seldom resembled the Soviet model, even faintly.

After the fall of the Berlin Wall in 1989 and the rise of the internet and social media, left-wing authoritarian, like right-wing authoritarianism, became even more diffusely distributed in cyberspace, coalescing around issues that are of national (or international) importance but organizing more horizontally, in grassroots, locally based networks that do not answer to a "central command." Thus, one distinguishing feature of old-fashioned left-wing authoritarianism has all but vanished from the scene.

Another significant shift that has occurred among left-wingers since the 1970s is that many now subscribe to some version of postmodernism, an umbrella term that nowadays covers a multitude of philosophical schools, including structuralism and post structuralism, deconstructionism, Lacanian psychoanalysis, and postmodernism proper. In the early 1980s, Marxist intellectuals like Terry Eagleton and Perry Anderson cautioned that the ascendancy of postmodernism threatened to sever the Left's ties to the needs and perspectives of the working class. And in 1985, Leo Löewnthal, the last surviving member of the Frankfurt School's first generation, voiced serious concerns about the new irrationalism and the sweeping subjectivism fostered by the postmodern trend in philosophy and the social sciences (Lowenthal, 1987, pp. 261–268).

So if centralized authority has vanished and postmodernism is on the rise, what are the most salient features of left-wing authoritarianism today? Several things. One is a pronounced tendency to embrace dogmatic and stereotypical attitudes on issues of gender, race, ethnicity, identity, and politics. Dogmatism refers to the fervent embrace of claims, statements, or beliefs based on premises that are either demonstrably false or are open to reasonable doubt but are nonetheless embraced by large numbers of people. Among those who share these dogmatic beliefs, those who do *not* share them are usually viewed as ethically or intellectually deficient. And among extremely dogmatic authoritarians, people who actually *challenge* their beliefs publicly are deemed to be depraved or dangerous to society and targeted for reprisals of one sort and another. (Dogmatism is commonplace in both religious and political movements, historically.)[3]

Often enough, the beliefs held by dogmatic people are flawed because they are a product of dichotomous (or binary) thinking, which classifies people into one of two simple categories, believers and unbelievers, oppressor and oppressed, perpetrator and victim, colonizer and colonized, White culture and Black culture, good guys and bad guys. Granted, there are instances in which these kinds of categories are useful heuristically. But there are many others where they are not. In cases like these, the tendency to adhere rigidly to these binary classifications is not only profoundly a-historical but masks the real complexity of social and political processes, omitting or suppressing features of reality that don't fit the dogmatists' preferred narrative. People who think in this way are unable to grasp their situation in a comprehensive, nuanced, and realistic fashion and therefore hampered in their ability to change their worlds for the better.[4]

So two invariant features of left-wing authoritarians, namely dogmatism and dichotomous thinking, make them intolerant of difference (or heterodoxy), ambiguity, and complexity. A perfect example of this lamentable trend is the case of Kathleen Stock, formerly Professor of Philosophy at the University of Sussex.

In a book titled *Material Girls: Why Reality Matters to Feminism* (Stock, 2021), Professor Stock asserted that gender roles and identities are socially constructed but that biological sex is real and rooted in our species' evolutionary history. That being so, she said, allowance must be made for sex-based legal rights, as well as gender-based legal rights. Stock never impugned or denied the rights of trans-men and trans-women to alter their bodies, to insist on their preferred pronouns, and to live lives free of discrimination and fear. Nevertheless, her position and pronouncements were parodied, distorted, and quoted out of context by her detractors, and hateful ideas and utterances were knowingly misattributed to her.

As a result, her critics on campus claimed that they did not feel "safe" while she was permitted to teach there. She was accused of violent speech that severely harms trans-people and, like J. K. Rowling, Margaret Atwood, and Martina Navratilova, was vilified as a trans exclusionary radical feminist (TERF). Though the university administration, which was cowering in the shadows, finally came to her defense after several years of steady harassment on campus and online, Stock found the atmosphere at Sussex too toxic to tolerate and resigned after 12 years of teaching.

Now, Professor Stock's case raises several urgent questions. One, of course, is the issue of whether or not what she says is true. But the other, more urgent question (from our present perspective) pertains to the issue of academic freedom; in short, whether or not Professor Stock is entitled to voice her opinions on this subject in a university setting without fear of reprisal and without being subjected to years of slander, harassment, and death threats from an angry mob of students and faculty (in departments other than her own) who were determined to shame, exclude, and ruin her, if possible.[5]

Granted, some statements are so outrageous and offensive that people have a right to protest them vigorously. But since when did asserting the existence of biological sex – something biologists have done for centuries – become "hate speech"? And what on earth could justify the use of death threats as a response to people like Stock? Besides, has anyone in recent memory been vilified, hounded, or dismissed from a university post for defending the opposite position, namely, that sex and gender are *both* socially constructed? No, of course not. Indeed, can you imagine the outrage such a witch hunt would likely provoke in this day and age? But consider, where was the outrage on Kathleen Stock's behalf?

Perhaps one reason Stock was pilloried – both on and off campus – is that her position, and her brand of feminism, is more in keeping with the ideas of feminist philosopher Martha Nussbaum than those of Judith Butler (see e.g., Nussbaum, 1999). Why? Perhaps in some measure because Nussbaum and Stock were both trained in analytic philosophy and tended to clash with queer theory, which is rooted in postmodernism.

If this were an isolated incident, we'd probably be tempted to write it off as an anomaly. Unfortunately, it isn't. It is part of a much bigger and more pervasive assault on academic freedom from left-wing activists bent on hounding heretics out of academe (Hudson and Williams, 2016; Burston, 2020). If left-wing authoritarians continue to vilify those who disagree with them, and if university administrators permit – or in some cases, actually encourage – the dismissal or departure of accomplished scholars and gifted teachers on such flimsy pretexts, academic freedom will eventually perish (Hudson and Williams, 2016; Shullenburger, 2021).

Authoritarianism and Anti-Semitism in the University

Another very common characteristic of left-wing authoritarianism is anti-Semitism, which is often difficult to discern because unlike the Nazis and their predecessors, the newer type of left-wing anti-Semite seldom acknowledges his prejudice against Jews openly. Instead, it is often disguised (or sublimated into) anti-Zionism and vocal support for Islamist organizations (Hirsch, 2018; Randall, 2021). But let's be candid, shall we? There has always been anti-Semitism on the Left. In the nineteenth century, left-wing leaders like Wilhelm Marr, Eugene Dühring, Pierre-Joseph Proudhon, and Mikhail Bakunin openly and repeatedly characterized Jews as an international cabal bent on infiltrating, subverting, and dominating the West through their market machinations and behind-the-scenes chicanery. They made no attempt to disguise or disavow their anti-Semitism, and shared anti-Semitic memes with their right-wing counterparts (Wistrich, 1975). Chief among them, no doubt, was *The Protocols of the Elders of Zion*, a spurious document fabricated by the Czarist police to justify the lethal persecution of Jews in the Russian empire, which claimed precisely the same thing. One of Hitler's favorite books, *The Protocols*, purported to be the proceedings of a meeting of Jewish leaders from all over Europe plotting to infiltrate and take over business, finance, the media, and all branches of government at the turn of the last century and is still widely believed to be an authentic historic document by millions of people around the world (Bronner, 2003).

Adorno et al. discerned and documented very high correlations between the A (for anti-Semitism) scale and the F (for fascism) scale, so we should not be surprised if this correlation holds true for left-wing authoritarians as well. Indeed, we should probably expect it. After all, if experience is any indication, anti-Semitism is closely related to a widespread tendency to endorse and disseminate conspiracy theories. Authoritarian dogmatism and rigidity may stifle rational doubt, but they leave plenty of room for what Erich Fromm called "irrational doubt" (Fromm, 1941; Fromm, 1947). Indeed, an absence of rational doubt creates the ideal conditions for *irrational* doubt to flourish. Why? Because to compensate for their inadequate grasp of reality, and to cover up gaps or inconsistencies in their explanatory models, authoritarians often "fill in the blanks" by creating conspiracy theories to explain (or explain away) anomalies and mysteries that otherwise defy comprehension.[6]

For a recent example of these historic trends, consider the case of David Miller, a former university chair in Political Sociology at the University of Bristol who was fired on October 1, 2021. Miller's critics accused him of fomenting hatred toward the Jewish and Israeli students, by repeatedly describing Israel as "the enemy of world peace," saying that Jews who identified with Israel in any way are all part of a vast conspiracy to promote Islamophobia and anti-Black racism and to undermine academic freedom and freedom of speech (Hirsch, 2021).

Moreover, and even more tellingly, Miller attacked Syrian refugees living in Bristol as dupes of Zionism because of their outspoken opposition to Bashar al-Assad's bloodthirsty, authoritarian regime. Indeed, according to Oz Katerji, a Syrian refugee and journalist, Miller was an active participant in campaigns to *support* Bashar al-Assad and his Russian and Iranian sponsors (Hirsch, 2021) and has since gone on to blame Putin's brutal invasion of Ukraine entirely on NATO, blithely ignoring Putin's extreme ethnonationalism and his appeal to White supremacists. And if that isn't compelling evidence of authoritarian tendencies, what is?

Miller's anti-Semitism is palpably obvious. But instances of subtler, less overt anti-Semitism are becoming distressingly commonplace in academe. For example, at Yale University Law School in September 2021, an equity, diversity, and inclusion (EDI) speaker named Erika Hart gave a talk in which she listed perfectionism, objectivity, a sense of urgency, and "the written word" as examples of "White Supremacy culture." According to Hart, dismantling this oppressive culture would presumably require abolishing prisons, opposing capitalism, and jailing former president Trump (Levine and Byrne, 2021). Well, perhaps. But in so saying, it clearly never dawned on Hart that the law consists entirely of "the written word," that she was addressing Yale's Law School, and that in calling for the abolition of "White Supremacy culture," she was (indirectly) calling for the abolition of the entire legal profession. (And then again, on reflection, how on earth can we possibly jail Donald Trump if we actually abolish prisons?)

The absurdity of Hart's presentation wasn't lost on her audience, and when a law journal editor asked her why her presentation addressed inequities like "fatphobia" and "prettiness privilege" but neglected to mention anti-Semitism, she replied that she had already addressed that issue when she discussed anti-Black racism, because "some Jews are black." The tacit implication of this remark is that anti-Semitism directed against Jews who are *not* Black – that is, a substantial majority in the USA – do not matter. Or perhaps, as one observer speculated, she believed that anti-Semitism is merely a "subset" of anti-Black racism (Levine and Byrne, 2021). In truth, however, anti-Semitism is an ancient and persistent form of ethnic and religious prejudice that predates anti-Black racism by over 1,500 years (Burston, 2021).

For another example of anti-Semitism on campus, consider the case of psychiatrist Robert Albucher and eating disorders specialist Sheila Levine. They each worked closely, and for many years, at Stanford University's Counseling and Psychological Services (CAPS) unit. In 2021, they filed complaints with state and federal authorities through the Louis D. Brandeis Center for Human Rights Under the Law, saying that Stanford University's diversity, equity, and inclusion (DEI) trainings "created and fostered a hostile working environment for Jewish staff," by obliging them to participate in weekly "affinity groups" that were racially segregated – groups in which Jews were repeatedly marginalized and maligned as "powerful and privileged perpetrators who contribute to systemic racism."

In their complaint, Albucher and Levine also stated that egregious instances of anti-Semitic hate crimes on campus were trivialized and dismissed by the DEI facilitators, who simply refused to address them. The first incident involved the hijacking of a Zoom meeting in which the hackers displayed pictures of swastikas, weapons, and used the N-word. When Dr. Levine expressed her horror at the swastika display, she was ostracized and verbally harassed and accused of "possessing the privilege of feeling outraged about racism." In the second incident, swastikas were discovered in Stanford University's Memorial Church, and the seminar leaders refused to address the meaning of the incident and the feelings that they evoked "unless there was time." When they continued to obstruct discussion of this troubling incident, Albucher protested and was effectively hounded out of the group by people using anti-Semitic tropes to vilify him and mock his concerns (Deb, 2021).

Despite the growing number of instances like these, many leftists – including quite a few Jews! – persist in the delusion that anti-Semitism is a uniquely right-wing phenomenon and that collective expressions of support for Islamist organizations intent on destroying Israel are perfectly legitimate. So for example, at a teach-in at UC Berkeley in 2006, Judith Butler (who is Jewish) said,

> Understanding Hamas, Hezbollah as social movements that are progressive, that are on the Left, is extremely important. That does not stop us from being critical of certain dimensions of both movements. It doesn't stop those of us who are interested in non-violent politics from raising the question of there are other options besides violence.
> (Butler, 2006, quoted in Lappin, 2019, p. 12, footnote 17)

Progressive? On the Left? Really? In so saying, Butler willfully ignored the fact that Hamas and Hezbollah are authoritarian political movements that are unabashedly misogynistic, anti-LGBTQ, and anti-democratic.

Granted, her remarks were made before the Arab spring, and one wonders what Butler thinks of Hezbollah today. After all, this Iranian-backed militia fought fiercely to support Assad in the Syrian civil war – a war that claimed the lives of more than 610,000 people and rendered 11 million homeless. The scale and ferocity of Assad and Hezbollah's assault on the Syrian people (and indeed on many Palestinians) completely dwarfs the misdeeds of Israel against her Arab neighbors and citizens. Yet has Butler campaigned to boycott, divest, and sanction Assad and Hezbollah? Not to my knowledge.

Fortunately, not all left-wing philosophers are as blinkered or oblivious on this score. For example, in *Living in The End Times*, Slavoj Žižek notes that

> a disturbing sign of the failure of the radical Left is their uneasiness when it comes to unambiguously condemning anti-Semitism, as if by doing so one would be playing into Zionist hands. There should be no compromise here.
>
> (Žižek, 2011, p. 136)

Žižek then goes on to lament the

> all too easy and uncritical acceptance of anti-American and anti-Western Muslim groups as representing "progressive" forms of struggle, as automatic allies; groups like Hamas and Hezbollah suddenly appear as revolutionary agents, even though their ideology is explicitly anti-modern, rejecting the entire egalitarian legacy of the French Revolution. (Things have gone so far here that some on the contemporary Left even consider an emphasis on atheism as a Western colonial plot.) Against this temptation, we should insist on the unconditional right to conduct a public critical analysis of all religions, Islam included – and the saddest thing is that one should even have to mention this. While many a Leftist would concede this point, he or she would be quick to add that any such critique must be carried out in a respectful way, in order to avoid a patronizing cultural imperialism – which *de facto* means that every real critique is to be abandoned, since a genuine critique of religion will by definition be "disrespectful" of the latter's sacred character and truth claims.
>
> (Žižek, 2011, p. 137)

Žižek believes that the resurgence of anti-Semitism and a fawning and uncritical attitude toward Islamic fundamentalism are symptomatic of the Left's basic impotence and the absence of any meaningful class-struggle in Europe and the United States. Possibly so. But for purposes of this discussion, the more important point is that the right to critique religious dogma is a basic and nonnegotiable dimension of free speech and democratic governance in any society or period of history. To abandon or abridge this basic principle tilts us dramatically toward an authoritarian and/or theocratic mindset. Evidently, this fact did not prevent Michel Foucault from offering his enthusiastic support for the Iranian Revolution of 1978–1979 led by the Ayatollah Khomeni (Afary and Anderson, 2005), who slaughtered, exiled, or silenced many members of his opposition. Ten years later, of course, Ayatollah Khomeini and his followers issued a *fatwa* (or execution order) against Salman Rushdie, author of *The Satanic Verses*, offering millions of dollars in reward for his death. By way of response, fashionable British leftists stopped somewhat short of endorsing the *fatwa* but tacitly sided with Rushdie's would-be assassins by saying that Rushdie had brought this misfortune – which forced him to go into hiding for a decade – on himself by giving offense to the Mullahs (Rushdie, 2012).

At some point during his ten-year confinement, Rushdie reports, it dawned on him that

> something new was happening here: the growth of a new intolerance. It was spreading across the surface of the earth, but nobody wanted to know. A new word had been created to help the blind remain blind: *Islamophobia*. To criticize the militant stridency of this religion in its contemporary incarnation was to be a bigot. A *phobic* person was extreme and irrational in his views, and so the fault lay with such persons and not the belief system that boasted over one billion followers worldwide. One billion believers could not be wrong, therefore the critics must be the ones foaming at the mouth. When, he wanted to know, did it become irrational to dislike religion . . . ? When did reason get redescribed as unreason? When were the fairy stories of the superstitious placed above criticism, beyond satire?
>
> (Rushdie, 2012, pp. 344–345)

In fairness to readers of Muslim heritage, Rushdie obviously overstated his case. There is an important distinction to be made here between Islam and Islamism. The former is a faith, the latter a political movement comprised of groups like Hamas, Hezbollah, al-Quaeda, the Taliban, and ISIS, who are intent on returning humanity to the Middle Ages. Fear of these groups is quite rational; although extreme and irrational fear of Muslims in general is a genuine problem and is especially prevalent on the extreme Right (on both sides of the Atlantic). But Rushdie was partly right too, because the term "Islamophobia" is now frequently invoked to condemn or dismiss any cogent and compelling criticism of Islam's extremist elements, and hurled at almost anyone who raises the question of Muslim anti-Semitism in the context of the endless wrangling over Israel/Palestine.

Zionism and Anti-Zionism

Freud was fond of comparing religion to "a collective obsessional neurosis." For purposes of this discussion, I suggest that we turn that analogy inside out and describe the Left's obsessional anti-Zionism as a new left-wing religion. That being said, it is obviously the case that there are many principled critics of Zionism who are *not* authoritarian. Many, in fact, are – or were – Jewish, for example, Hermann Cohen, Franz Rosenzwieg, Erich Fromm, George Steiner, Tony Judt, and Noam Chomsky. But the fact that some Jews have opposed Zionism historically must not blind us to the fact that many of Zionism's most virulent critics today – like David Miller, who is appealing his dismissal and has many thousands of supporters in the British Labour Party and universities all around the world – are indeed channeling anti-Semitism into their anti-Zionist rhetoric.

To put these remarks in some sort of context, bear in mind that there are currently around 55 majority-Muslim and 22 specifically Arab nation-states in existence today, but only one majority-Jewish state. The human rights abuses that occur in many Arab countries exceed Israel's human rights violations by a considerable margin. So while Israel's misdeeds are indeed abhorrent, without factoring in anti-Semitism, how can we possibly explain the Left's relentless efforts to single out the one and only majority-Jewish state in the Middle East for relentless criticism while minimizing or ignoring the crimes of her adversaries?

Anti-Semitic prejudice was also on display at the *World Conference Against Racism, Xenophobia and Other Forms of Intolerance* (WCAR) in Durban, South Africa, in 2001, when copies of *The Protocols of the Elders of Zion* were openly distributed in the conference hall (Wistrich, 2010, pp. 485–486).⁷ Leaders of the BDS movement played a large role in organizing this conference and often assert that the Zionism was never anything but a racist, colonialist-settler enterprise designed to subjugate people of color. What these same activists seldom, if ever, acknowledge is that their narrative echoes Soviet era anti-Zionist propaganda, which was used to justify a dreadful campaign of anti-Semitic persecution throughout the Soviet empire in the late sixties, seventies, and eighties (Wistrich, 2010, pp. 138–153; Randall, 2021). Despite the repressive campaigns it authorized behind the Iron Curtain – which Martin Luther King Jr. denounced with fervor (Kramer, 2016, chapter 22) – this narrative began to gain currency among African American radicals in the sixties – Malcolm X, Stockley Carmichael, Amiri Baraka, Angela Davis, Jesse Jackson, and others (Fischbach, 2019). And it is this narrative that is in the ascendant now, especially among the young, in part because it has been embraced by many activists in the Black Lives Matter movement (BLM).

That being so, activists nowadays frequently forget that in this same period of time, Israel enjoyed unwavering support from more moderate progressives like Reinhold Niebuhr, Eleanor Roosevelt, Dr. Martin Luther King Jr., Rosa Parks, Bayard Rustin, Robert F. Kennedy, socialist leader Michael Harrington, W.H. Auden and so on. These people steadfastly opposed the (originally Soviet) slogan that "Zionism is racism." Indeed, when UN Resolution 3379 (which condemned Zionism as racist) was passed on November 10, 1975, many of Reverend King's old friends and supporters – including Rosa Parks, Ralph Abernathy, A. Phillip Randolph, Harry Belafonte, and Bayard Rustin – signed a petition for the *Black Americans in Support of Israel* (BASIC) committee and took out a full page ad in *The New York Times* on November 23 to signal their support for Israel (Fischbach, 2020).⁸

These lively controversies within African American and activist communities were chronicled competently by historian Michael Fischbach in two recent books titled *Black Power and Palestine: Transnational Countries of Color* (Fischbach, 2019) and *The Movement and the Middle East: How the Arab-Israeli Conflict Divided the American Left* (Fischbach, 2020). However, one problem with Fischbach's work is that like most of Israel's contemporary critics, he does not acknowledge that the BDS and BLM movements' narratives about Israel confound and/or conflate the categories of "race" and "faith." After all, Zionism created a safe haven for more than 850,000 brown-skinned Mizrahi Jews who fled from persecution in the Middle East and North Africa, over 25,000 black-skinned Ethiopian Jews and many Jews from central Asia – Armenians, Kurds, Tajiks, Afghans – and from India and China as well. As a result, 50% of Israel's present-day population are lineal descendants of Jews from the Middle East and North Africa and are people of color.

That being so, calling Israel an "apartheid state" may be extremely popular in activist circles, but it is also somewhat misleading (Linfield, 2021). If you walk the streets of Haifa or Lod, which have an equal number of Palestinian and Israeli inhabitants, you will not be able to tell the Arabs from the Jews on the basis of skin color or any other physical characteristics. On the contrary, they look remarkably alike, and the only way to tell them apart is by the languages they speak, the clothing they wear, and above all, by the places where they pray. So while anti-racist activists almost invariably compare the situation in Israel and Palestine to apartheid South Africa – and more recently, of course, to Ferguson, MI (Fischbach, 2019; Linfield, 2021) – a closer analogy might be the troubles in Northern Ireland, where differences of faith rather than "race" provoke and sustain hostilities between the two parties.

Moreover, Fischbach's thorough and thoughtful appraisal neglects to consider the attitudes and utterances of the Frankfurt School, which bring much greater nuance and complexity to this discussion. In a masterful book titled *The Frankfurt School, Jewish Lives and Anti-Semitism*, Jack Jacobs chronicles the views of the leading members of the Frankfurt School toward the state of Israel (Jacobs, 2015). It makes for interesting reading, especially in light of today's controversies. So for example, in an article titled "Israel Is Strong Enough to Concede," which appeared in *The Jerusalem Post* in 1972, Herbert Marcuse defended Israel's right to exist, arguing that if the state had materialized before WWII, it could have saved millions of lives. At the same time, he acknowledged the injustices suffered by the Palestinians and conceded that, like all nation states, much of Israel's territory was won by conquest. Nevertheless, he criticized the Occupation and the second-class status accorded to Israeli Arabs, urging Israel to return to the pre-1967 borders, to make peace with Egypt, to help create a viable Palestinian state, and finally to relinquish sovereignty over Jerusalem to the United Nations, making it an international city. In short, he believed that if suitable concessions were made on the Israeli side, a two-state solution was possible, indeed necessary, so that Jews and Arabs could flourish side by side (Marcuse, 1972, reprinted in Kellner, D., 2005, pp. 54–56).

Although it is seldom acknowledged nowadays, Marcuse's opinions in 1972 were almost indistinguishable from those of many Left-leaning Israeli "peaceniks" of that era, the chief difference between them being that he neglected to specify the concessions that adjacent Arab states would have to give to make peace possible, that is, recognizing Israel as a legitimate state, normalizing diplomatic relations, ceasing to harbor or provide support for terrorist groups, etc.

Later, in an interview on March 10, 1977, Marcuse disclosed a little more about his attitude toward Israel. (These remarks appeared in the Winter edition of *L'Chayim*, a Jewish student newspaper at the University of California San Diego.) In this interview, Marcuse took issue with UN resolution 3379, which declared that Zionism is racism, saying in effect that *some* Zionists are indeed racists, but many are not. At the same time, he rightly deplored Israel's arms sales to apartheid South Africa, a policy at odds with the original Zionist ethos.

Nevertheless, in 1977 Marcuse was, if anything, even more emphatic about Israel's right to exist, to defend itself, and to prevent the occurrence of another Holocaust. Once again, he stressed the need for Israelis to make significant concessions for peace, adding now that Arab states must also make significant concessions. Finally, Marcuse acknowledged that anti-Semitism appeared to be in abeyance now but that anti-Semitism and societal tendencies to scapegoat Jews are deep and lingering problems, predicting that the next major crisis of capitalism would provoke another resurgence of anti-Semitism with potentially lethal consequences, as indeed it has (Marcuse, 1977, reprinted in Kellner, D., 2005, pp. 54–56).

By contrast with Marcuse, Leo Lowenthal was somewhat more ambivalent toward Israel. In *An Unmastered Past: The Autobiographical Reflections of Leo Lowenthal*, he recalled that as a young man, he attended the *Freie Judische Lehrhaus* alongside two childhood friends, Erich Fromm and Ernst Simon (Lowenthal, 1987; Jacobs, 2015). While Simon went on to become a deeply committed Zionist and a professor at the Hebrew University of Jerusalem, Fromm dabbled in Zionism briefly, only to repudiate it in 1927, the same year he ceased observing Jewish festivals and dietary laws. Löwenthal's attitude toward Zionism and Israel seems like a compromise between their two positions. He said,

> You know that in my student years in Heidelberg I was a member of the Zionist student organization. But I had joined because I believed strongly in Judaism's messianic mission, its utopian political task. I had hoped that Eretz Israel would be the model for a just society. However, my experience with Zionism followed a path very similar to my later experience with the Communist world movement and the Communist Party. I experienced great disappointment; I felt that the Zionist movement was suffering more and more from what . . . Ernst Simon . . . called the "intoxication with normality." Ideologically, I was not so blinded as to refuse a critical analysis of the settlement policy of the Jewish organizations in Palestine. As I saw it, the Jewish land purchases were an alliance of big Arab landowners and Jewish money at the expense of the Arab peasants and farm workers. I instinctively foresaw that this could lead to bad conflicts, if not catastrophes. . . . This does not mean, I would like to repeat, that I have given up my relation to Jewish motifs or my support of Israel.
>
> (Lowenthal, 1987, p. 114)

Löwenthal's reference to mainstream Zionism's "intoxication with normality" refers to the fact that Jews had lived as dhimmis, or second-class citizens, in Muslim lands for 13 centuries and that the political gains made by European Jewry had recently been wiped out by the resurgence of the genocidal anti-Semitism, which culminated in the Holocaust. Rather than eking out a precarious and marginal existence as second (or third) class citizens in the midst of non-Jewish populations, whose hostility frequently erupted in spasms of collective violence, Zionists of that era wanted Jews to live like a "normal" people and to enjoy "normal" relations with other nations. The early Zionists also believed that cultivation of the land – something forbidden to Jews in most countries for many centuries – is essential to the health and vitality of the Jewish people, fostering a "back to the land" movement and the creation of numerous *kibbutzim* and farming villages, which were the backbone of the early Zionist movement. This is why Jewish philanthropists purchased large tracts of land from the Arab aristocracy.

Clearly, the resulting dispossession and displacement of Arab peasant farmers clashed with Lowenthal's utopian/Messianic hopes of making Israel into the model of a "just society." Nevertheless, he admitted, "I support anything that destroys this anti-Semitic image of the Jew as a weakling, as castrated or effeminate," hinting obliquely that on some level, perhaps, he admired Israel's determination to defend itself against encroaching threats as a sign of newfound resilience in the face of many centuries of bloody persecution and the threats of genocide and annihilation that *still* emanate daily from many of Israel's Arab neighbors and various terrorist organizations.

Given the preceding, one can only surmise that future historians will probably have to choose between two competing narratives about the Middle East conflict. One narrative will present the fledgling state of Israel as a vulnerable and flawed democracy at its inception. But after 1967, as it rose to become a regional superpower, many historians will charge Israel with trampling viciously on the legitimate rights and aspirations of Palestinians under the Occupation, robbing them of their freedom, their dignity, and hope for the future, as well as their homes and livelihoods.

Were Israel's actions always taken without reason or provocation? No, many of their policies and practices were motivated by very practical concerns over the safety and security of its citizens, who were constantly under threat from suicide bombs and terrorist attacks. But other governmental policies and practices that sought to weaken the (already shaky) Palestinian authority and encroached on Palestinians' land and undermined their livelihoods, their freedom of movement, and access to resources were purely punitive, contributing to the humiliation and exclusion of Palestinians from political life, and these have deepened rather than mitigated the mistrust between Palestinians and Israelis, diminishing the chances for peace.

Sadly, however, the Left's dominant narratives today lay *all* the blame for the current state of affairs on Zionism and none on the Palestinian leadership, despite the fact that they are notoriously corrupt and antidemocratic. They also ignore the important fact that the first leader of armed resistance against the (hitherto peaceful) Zionist project was a genocidal anti-Semite, Hajj Amin Al-Husseini, the grand Mufti of Jerusalem (1895–1974), who launched the bloody anti-Jewish riots in Hebron, Jerusalem, Petach Tikvah, and elsewhere in British mandated Palestine in

1920–1921, 1927–1929, and 1936–1939 (Wistrich, 2010, pp. 694–697). The Mufti also helped to orchestrate the Farhud of Baghdad on June 1–2, 1941 – a vicious pogrom that killed 180 Iraqi Jews, maimed many more, orphaned 242 Jewish children, and destroyed more than a thousand Jewish homes and businesses (Wistrich, 2010, p. 677). These horrors were unleashed immediately after the British, who governed Iraq, elevated Jews from their traditional dhimmi status, granting them equal standing with their former Muslim overlords. This destructive killing spree was rationalized on the grounds that Jews were either collaborators of the British (and therefore colonialists) or Zionists.[9] A more likely explanation is that the Mufti's minions were horrified at the prospect of being on an equal footing with Jews.

After his brief sojourn in Baghdad, the Mufti spent most of WWII in Rome and Berlin, where he organized a contingent of Bosnian Muslims to join Hitler's Einsatzgrüppen, murdering some 22,000 Jews in the Balkans. Not content with these murderous deeds, he joined Eichmann and Hitler in planning a genocidal campaign against roughly 75,000 Jews living in Egypt, 500,000 living in Palestine, and another 25,000 living in Syria and Iraq, including those who were *not* Zionists and whose families had lived there for centuries. Had General Montgomery failed to halt and repel General Rommel's tanks at El Alemain on November 4, 1942, that murderous fantasy would have become a horrible reality (Gorenberg, 2021).

After WWII, the Mufti returned to Cairo, where he helped many high-ranking Nazi officers escape justice at the Nuremburg trials by going underground or securing safe passage for them to Argentina. He also saw to it that *The Protocols of the Elders of Zions* was translated into Arabic and many other languages that are spoken in the Muslim world – Turkish, Farsi, Urdu, etc. When the UN declared itself in favor of the creation of Israel in 1947, the Mufti helped to organize an army that was financed, in part, by his good friend Hassan al-Banna, who founded the first Islamist organization, the Muslim Brotherhood, in 1928. The Arab armies were roundly defeated by the Zionist defense forces. So in 1951, when the Mufti learned that King Abdullah of Jordan was making secret peace overtures to Israel, he had him assassinated (Wistrich, 2010).

The Mufti died in 1974, and his passing was mourned by many Arabs, especially Palestinians. So it is both troubling and instructive to note that the Mufti is conspicuous by his absence in Edward Said's book *The Question of Palestine*, a canonical text for anti-Zionists (Said, 1980). Clearly, anti-Zionists like Said prefer to forget or ignore the Mufti or to minimize his importance in Middle Eastern affairs. But the fact remains that the Mufti was a major force in Middle Eastern politics for five decades and still has many admirers among leaders of the Palestinian resistance today. And bear in mind, most Israelis are acutely aware of this history, which the Left seems quite anxious to forget.

With all that said, the real point is this. Right now, civil conversation on all these subjects in North American and British universities is difficult to sustain because both the Zionist and the Palestinian narratives have been carefully curated to highlight the harms that each side inflicted on the other and to minimize or ignore the harms that they inflicted on their adversaries and, indeed, on themselves. This selective inattention breeds a hardening of hearts and an implacable self-righteousness on *both* sides that renders critical historical reflection on the messy, complicated, and ethically ambiguous situation in Israel/Palestine all but impossible anymore. But unless or until the messy complexity of the Arab-Israeli conflict (and the suffering it causes for all concerned) is fully acknowledged by both sides, neither side will trust the other sufficiently to negotiate in good faith, and peace will remain elusive, and anti-Semitism will continue to proliferate in activist circles and university campuses. Similarly, perhaps, unless left-wingers actually acknowledge the presence of authoritarians in their midst and take steps to address and, if need be, distance themselves from them, these trends will continue to bedevil our universities for the foreseeable future.

Notes

1 In "The 'Authoritarian Personality' Reconsidered: The Phantom of Left Fascism," Samir Gandesha rightly points out that Adorno eventually discerned authoritarian tendencies on the German Left but only addressed them belatedly in his private correspondence with Herbert Marcuse (Gandesha, 2019). Adorno's reticence on this score probably contributed to the perception of him as conceiving of authoritarianism as an exclusively right-wing authoritarianism from the 1940s onwards.
2 Three retired generals, Paul Eaton, Antonio Taguba, and Steven Anderson, recently warned that the US Army must start preparing now for the insurrection that is likely to ensue if Trump (and/or the Republican Party) lose the federal election in 2024 (Eaton, P. Taguba, A. & Anderson, S. Dec 16, 2021, "The Military must prepare now for a 2024 insurrection," *Washington Post*).
3 Altemeyer defines *dogmatism* as follows: "Dogmatism is relatively unchangeable, unjustified certainty. It is conviction beyond the reach of

evidence to the contrary. It is, as Rokeach says, closed mindedness." Unfortunately, to the best of my knowledge, Altemeyer did not address the dangers that dogmatism poses to free inquiry in university settings. That said, his DOG (for dogmatism) scale is a vast improvement on Rokeach's initial efforts (Rokeach, 1960).

4   Other cognitive distortions among authoritarians include double standards, double think: treating two irreconcilable ideas or propositions as being true without experiencing cognitive dissonance and major inconsistencies in their worldviews (Altemeyer, 1996, chapter 4; Burston, 2020, chapter 5).
5   Death threats emanating from any quarter, including those that are merely intended to intimidate someone, are inherently authoritarian.
6   That being said, one must remember that authoritarians may have legitimate grievances too. Unfortunately, however, the more authoritarian a person is, the less likely they will be able to identify and address the root causes of their problems in a rational manner.
7   The conference was sponsored by Thabo Mbeki, the second president of post-apartheid South Africa, who is remembered today chiefly for his disbelief in the existence of the AIDS virus and his corrupt financial dealings, which led to his eventual resignation in 2008.
8   It is interesting to note that November 10, 1975, the day that UN resolution 3379 was passed, was also the thirty-seventh anniversary of Kristallnacht, a vicious pogrom in Germany and Austria that foreshadowed the events of the Holocaust. Was this sheer coincidence? Perhaps. But this fact was not lost on the Jewish people.
9   Philip Mendes notes that the eightieth anniversary of the Farhud was greeted by a deafening silence from Arab and pro-Palestinian quarters (Mendes, 2021).

References

Adorno, T. et al. 1950. *The Authoritarian Personality*. New York: W.W. Norton.
Afary, J. & Anderson, K. 2005. *Foucault and the Iranian Revolution: Gender and the Seductions of Islamism*. Chicago: University of Chicago Press.
Afary, J. & Friedland, R. 2018. "Critical Theory, Authoritarianism and the Politics of Lipstick from the Weimar Republic to the Contemporary Middle East". *Critical Research on Religion*. 6 (3), 243–268.
Altemeyer, B. 1996. *The Authoritarian Specter*. Cambridge: Harvard University Press.
Bronner, S. 2003. *A Rumor About the Jews: Anti-Semitism, Conspiracy and the Protocols of the Elders of Zion*. New York: Oxford University Press.
Brunner, J. 1994. "Looking into the Hearts of Workers, or: How Erich Fromm Turned Critical Theory into Empirical Social Research". *Political Psychology*. 15 (4), 631–654.
Burston, D. 1991. *The Legacy of Erich Fromm*. Cambridge: Harvard University Press.
Burston, D. 2020. *Psychoanalysis, Politics and The Postmodern University*. Cham: Palgrave MacMillan.

Burston, D. 2021. *Anti-Semitism and Analytical Psychology: Jung, Politics and Culture*. London: Routledge.

Christie, R. & Jahoda, M., eds. 1954. *The Authoritarian Personality: Continuities in Social Research*. Glencoe, IL: The Free Press.

Conway, L. G. et al. 2017. "Finding the Loch Ness Monster: Left Wing Authoritarianism in the United States". *Political Psychology*. Advance publication online. https://doi.org/10.1111/pops12470.

Costello, T. H., Bowes, S. M. & Lilienfeld, S. O. (2020). "Escape from Freedom: Authoritarianism-Related Traits, Political Ideology, Personality, and Belief in Free Will/Determinism". *Journal of Research in Personality*. 86, 103957.

Costello, T. H. et al. 2021. "Clarifying the Nature and Structure of Left Wing Authoritarianism". *The Journal of Personality and Social Psychology*. Online First Publication, August 12, 2021. http://dx.doi.org/10.1037/pspp0000341.

Dean, J. W. & Altemeyer, B. 2021. *Authoritarian Nightmare: Trump and His Followers*. Brooklyn, NY: Melville Publishing House.

Deb, S. 2021. "CAPS Counsellors Accuse University of Anti-Semitic Practices". *The Stanford Daily*, June 27.

Delgado, R. & Stefancic, J. 2017. *Critical Race Theory: An Introduction*. New York: New York University Press.

Eaton, P., Taguba, A. & Anderson, S. 2021. "The Military Must Prepare Now for a 2024 Insurrection". *Washington Post*.

Fischbach, M. 2019. *Black Power and Palestine: Transnational Countries of Color*. Stanford, CA: Stanford University Press.

Fischbach, M. 2020. *The Movement and the Middle East: How the Arab-Israeli Conflict Divided the American Left*. Stanford, CA: Stanford University Press.

Freud, 1921. *Group Psychology and the Analysis of the Ego*. In S.E. vol. 18. London: Hogarth Press.

Fromm, E. 1941. *Escape From Freedom*. Reprint, Avon Books, New York, 1965.

Fromm, E. 1947. *Man For Himself: An Inquiry into Psychology and Ethics*. Greenwich, CT: Fawcett Premier Books.

Fromm, E. 1950. *Psychoanalysis and Religion*. New Haven: Yale University Press.

Fromm, E. 1984. *The Working Class in Weimar Germany: A Psychological and Sociological Study*. Cambridge: Harvard University Press.

Gandesha, S. 2019. "The 'Authoritarian Personality' Reconsidered: The Phantom of Left Fascism". *The American Journal of Psychoanalysis*. 79, 601–624.

Gorenberg, G. 2021. *War of Shadows: Codebreakers, Spies and the Secret Struggle to Drive the Nazis from the Middle East*. New York: Hachette Book Group.

Gurven, M. D. 2018. "Broadening Horizons: Sample Diversity and Socioecological Theory are Essential to the Future of Psychological Science". *Proceedings of the National Academy of Sciences of the United States of America*. 115 (45), 11420–11427. https://doi.org/10.1073/pnas.1720433115

Henrich, J., Heine, S. J. & Norenzayan, A. 2010. "Most People are Not WEIRD." *Nature*. 466 (7302), 29–29. https://doi.org/10.1038/466029a

Hirsch, D. 2018. *Contemporary Left Anti-Semitism*. London: Routledge.
Hirsch, D. 2021. "The Meaning of David Miller". *Fathom: For a Deeper Understanding of Israel and the Region*, March issue.
Horkheimer, M. 1972. *Critical Theory: Selected Essays*. New York: The Seabury Press.
Hudson, C. & Williams, J., eds. 2016. *Why Academic Freedom Matters: A Response to Current Challenges*. London: Civitas.
Jacobs, J. 2015. *The Frankfurt School, Jewish Lives and Anti-Semitism*. New York: Cambridge University Press.
Jay, M. 1973. *The Dialectical Imagination*. Boston: Beacon Press.
Jeffries, S. 2017. *Grand Hotel Abyss: The Lives of the Frankfurt School*. London: Verso.
Joyce, H. 2021. *Trans: When Ideology Meets Reality*. London: One World.
Kellner, D., ed. 2005. *The Collected Papers of Herbert Marcuse*. Vol. 3, pp. 54–56. London: Routledge.
Kramer, M., 2016. "In the Words of Martin Luther King". Kramer, M. ed., *The War on Error: Israel, Islam and the Middle East*. Brunswick, NJ: Transaction Press.
Lappin, S. 2019. "The Re-Emergence of the Jewish Question". *Fathom: For a Deeper Understanding of Israel and the Region*, May. http://fathomjournal.org/the-re-emergence-of-the-jewish-question/.
Levine, J. & Byrne, K. 2021. "'Offensive' Yale Speaker Claims FBI inflates anti-Semitic Hate Crimes". *The New York Post*, November 6.
Linfield, S. 2021. "Palestine Isn't Ferguson". *The Atlantic*, October 24.
Lowenthal, L. 1987. *An Unmastered Life: The Autobiographical Reflections of Leo Lowenthal*. Berkeley: University of California Press.
Marcuse, H. 1972. "Israel Is Strong Enough to Concede". Reprinted in Kellner, D., ed. 2005. *The Collected Papers of Herbert Marcuse*. Vol. 3, pp. 54–56. London: Routledge.
Marcuse, H. 1977. "Thoughts on Israel, Judaism, etc." Reprinted in Kellner, D., ed. 2005. *The Collected Papers of Herbert Marcuse*. Vol. 3, pp. 54–56. London: Routledge.
Mendes, P. 2021. "The Jibe 'Progressive Except for Palestine' Is a Cynical Political Strategy to Exclude Moderate Progressives from Debates on Resolving the Israeli/Palestinian Conflict". *Fathom: For a Deeper Understanding of Israel and the Region*, November issue.
Nussbaum, M. 1999. "The Professor of Parody". *The New Republic*, February 22.
Randall, D. 2021. *Confronting Anti-Semitism on the Left: Arguments for Socialists*. London: No Pasaran.
Rokeach, M. 1960. *The Open and Closed Mind*. New York: Basic Books.
Rushdie, S. 2012. *Joseph Anton: A Memoir*. New York: Random House.
Said, E. 1980. *The Question of Palestine*. New York: Vintage Books.
Samelson, F. 1993. "The Authoritarian Character from Berlin to Berkeley and Beyond: The Odyssey of a Problem". Stone, W. F., Lederer, G. & Christie, R.

eds., *Strength and Weakness: The Authoritarian Personality Today* (pp. 22–43). New York: Springer Verlag.

Satel, S. 2021. "The Experts Somehow Overlooked the Authoritarianism of the Left". *The Atlantic*, September 25 issue.

Shullenburger, G. 2021. "Why Academic Freedom's Future Looks Bleak". *The Chronicle of Higher Education*, December 8.

Stock, K. 2021. *Material Girls: Why Reality Matters to Feminism*. London: Fleet.

Wistrich, E. 1975. "Socialism and Anti-Semitism in Austria Before 1914". *Jewish Social Studies*. 37 (3/4), Summer–Autumn, 323–332.

Wistrich, R. 2010. *A Lethal Obsession: Anti-Semitism from Antiquity to the Global Jihad*. New York: Random House.

Yagoda, M. 2013. "ADHD is Different for Women". *The Atlantic*. https:// www.theatlantic.com/health/archive/2013/04/adhd-is-different-forwomen/ 381158/

Žižek, S. 2011. *Living in the End Times*. London: Verso.

Chapter 8

The Evolutionary Anthropology of Erich Fromm
The Frankfurt School, Second Nature, and the Existential Crisis of Consciousness[1]

Gary Clark

Introduction

In this chapter I discuss the evolutionary ideas of Erich Fromm. Fromm was unusual among the Frankfurt School thinkers in his extensive engagement with the evolutionary and biological sciences. While his ideas grew out of the same tradition as other members of the school – that is, Hegelian-Marxism – Fromm's originality resides in synthesizing this tradition, with what were at the time of his writing the most recent advances in paleoanthropology and studies of human brain evolution. What is worth noting here is how Fromm integrated the Hegelian concept of *second nature* into his theories of human cognitive evolution.

I also discuss Fromm's writings on psychoanalysis and depth psychology, which formed the other main part of his broad-ranging interdisciplinary conception of human psychology. I explore this aspect of Fromm's thinking in the context of current research in evolutionary and cognitive neuroscience. More specifically, I argue that Fromm's theories of human cognitive evolution, dream life, myth, and the unconscious are congruent with contemporary theories in evolutionary neuroscience that postulate modern forms of secondary consciousness associated with the "ego complex" emerged out of a more archaic primary process brain system.

Erich Fromm, Freud, and the Frankfurt School

Erich Fromm pioneered the use of Freudian thought within the original Frankfurt School during the 1930s and 1940s, offering an astute psychoanalytic analysis of fascism, authoritarian political movements, and the

DOI: 10.4324/9781003215301-8

psychology of social collectivities (Burston 1991; McLaughlin 1996). However, this important role was elided from Frankfurt School "origin myths" due to personality conflicts with other members of the school, career dynamics, funding issues, and other sociological factors associated with scholarly and intellectual network formation (McLaughlin 1998, 1999).

One of the central points of contention that led to the split between Fromm and other members of the Frankfurt School, and his consequent elision from Frankfurt School "origin myths," centered around debates over orthodox Freudianism. While this rift began with Adorno and Horkheimer disagreeing with Fromm over the status of orthodox Freudian theory during the 1930s and 1940s (Durkin 2014, pp. 27–28; McLaughlin 2017, pp. 282–483), it was not until the Fromm-Marcuse debate of the 1950s that the issue came to a head. The debate began in a series of articles in the journal *Dissent* and then entered the broader intellectual and political culture via Marcuse's critique of Fromm in *Eros and Civilisation*, first published in 1955 (Fromm 1955a; Fromm 1956; Marcuse 1955, 1956, 1972, pp. 167–188). It was this presentation of Fromm's thought that contributed to the misunderstanding and simplification of his ideas in both the academy and among the general public – misunderstandings that have been overcome in recent years leading to a reappraisal of Fromm's work (Burston 1991; Durkin 2014; McLaughlin 1998, 1999, 2017)

Marcuse argued that Fromm's revision of orthodox Freudian theory was conformist in nature and conservative politically in that it advocated people adapt to the alienated structures of society as opposed to seeking their overthrow. Consequently, he argued that the revolutionary implications of Freud's theory of the unconscious and sexuality were essentially eliminated from psychoanalysis by Fromm and other Freudian revisionists. But there was also a deeper theoretical dispute at play over the legitimacy of Freud's notion of the death instinct, his hypothesis of the primal horde upon which Oedipal theory was based, as well as the associated concept of libido theory – much of which Fromm deemed questionable. For his part, Marcuse rejected revisionist conceptions of psychoanalysis of the kind developed by Fromm in which it was argued the present environment may cause conflicts not accounted for by the biological model of orthodox Freudianism (Marcuse 1955; McLaughlin 2017, p. 483).

Fromm objected to such characterizations of his ideas. In response to Marcuse, he argued that Freudian theory did not offer a sustained radical critique of contemporary socioeconomic conditions, as he writes in the following:

> Freud made a specific criticism of contemporary society only with regard to one point. He criticizes it for its overstrict sexual morality, which produces neurosis to a greater extent than necessary. This criticism is not at all concerned with the socioeconomic structure of society, but only with its sexual morality.
>
> (Fromm 1955a, p. 344)

Fromm developed his critique of Freudian theory further throughout his career, emphasizing how socioeconomic structures interact with human psychology, producing different forms of character structure in different historical periods. He also emphasized the central role of human consciousness in giving rise to uniquely human existential conditions, as he writes the

> ... central problem of man is not that of his libido; it is that of dichotomies inherent in his existence, his separateness, alienation, suffering, his fear of freedom, his wish for union, his capacity for hate and destruction, his capacity for love and union.
>
> (Fromm 1969, p. 48)

Fromm also argued that Freud's theories were biased by his own patriarchal cultural values and that what he took for a universal Oedipus complex was actually a manifestation of hierarchical and authoritarian patriarchal family structures and values (Fromm 1957, pp. 196–231). Fromm drew on anthropological and archaeological literature in his critique of Freud, highlighting the role of female deities and symbolism in many early civilizations, as well as evidence for matrilineal forms of social organization in contemporary Indigenous cultures (Fromm 1955b, p. 48). One of his most extensive critiques of Freud involved a detailed reading of the Oedipus myth and its articulation in the plays of Sophocles. What Fromm demonstrated is that the plays seem to be more concerned with the authority of the hierarchical patriarchal state and its conflict with earlier matrilineal forms of social organization than with incestuous desire, as Freud had argued

(Fromm 1957, pp. 196–235). It was in such analyses that Fromm demonstrated the explanatory power of socioeconomic critique and the historical contingency of aspects of Freudian theory that had been assumed to be universal aspects of human nature.

Significantly, Neil McLaughlin has argued that since much of contemporary psychoanalysis has moved beyond libido theory, the death instinct, and theories of primal hordes, critical theorists should do the same and engage with new versions of psychoanalysis (McLaughlin 2017, p. 497). He has also argued that Fromm's work is important for critical theory precisely because his effort to combine radical sociology with depth psychology was based on a firm understanding of psychoanalytic theory – while Adorno and Marcuse were dabbling with the Freudian tradition in a highly abstract and speculative matter (McLaughlin 1999, p. 127). McLaughlin also makes the point that much of Fromm's revision of Freudian theory is congruent with contemporary approaches such as "self-psychology, object relations and the interpersonal and relational schools" (McLaughlin 2017, p. 497).

Following McLaughlin's lead in exploring the relevance of Fromm's revision of Freud to contemporary thought, I will analyze his ideas in the context of contemporary evolutionary theory. However, in pursuing such an analysis, I will distinguish Fromm's work from the field of evolutionary psychology (Barkow et al. 1995; Buss 2015). Fromm's approach differs from that of evolutionary psychologists in his attempt to ground psychoanalysis and depth psychology in evolutionary theory. While evolutionary psychologists have not undertaken such a synthesis, some researchers have attempted to develop a reproachment between psychoanalysis, depth psychology, and the evolutionary sciences (Alcaro et al. 2017; Burns 2007; Carhart-Harris and Friston 2010; Carhart-Harris et al. 2014; Clark 2020; Narváez 2014; Panksepp 2004). However, this is an incipient and ill-defined discipline, if it can be defined as such at all. In this chapter I hope to show what a reproachment between psychoanalytic or depth psychological approaches and evolutionary theory would look like, arguing that Fromm's work represents an extensive yet vastly underappreciated synthesis of these different domains of knowledge.

In the following section, I discuss how the Hegelian notion of "second nature" informs Fromm's approach to both socioeconomic critique as well as psychoanalysis. In later sections of this chapter, I will extend these ideas in an analysis of Fromm's evolutionary thought, his conception of human consciousness, debates regarding a universal conception of human nature, and the related issue of cross-cultural affinities in myth, religious symbolism, and conceptions of dream life.

Hegel, Second Nature, and Fromm's Conception of Human Consciousness

It is frequently noted that the philosophical roots of the Frankfurt School can be found in Hegelian Marxist and German idealist thought. For example, Adorno argued that German sociology itself emerged as a speculative science out of Hegelian philosophy and that consequently it ought to embrace its own origin (Moir 2020, p. 56). While acknowledging the importance of Hegelian Marxism and German idealism for critical theory, the differences between Horkheimer, Adorno, Marcuse, Benjamin, and Fromm on a range of important intellectual issues has also been noted (McLaughlin 2017, p. 481). I have already mentioned the differences between Fromm and other members of the Frankfurt School in relation to orthodox Freudian theory, with Fromm offering an anthropologically informed critique of Freud's approach. Throughout his career, Fromm developed and deepened this critique, undertaking an ambitious cross-disciplinary project that drew on numerous disciplines, such as paleoanthropology, archaeology, anthropology, and neuroscience.

While this project makes Fromm unique among the Frankfurt School thinkers, his ideas do nevertheless have affinities with their approach to sociological analysis. Such affinities are most evident in the use of Hegel's concept of *second nature* – a concept developed by other members of the Frankfurt School, yet one which Fromm deploys in unique ways.

Hegel conceived of human consciousness and society in terms of a second nature, which he argued emerged out of a more primal and fundamental first nature. Hegel associates first nature with animal subjectivity, which is comprised of instinct. This form of subjectivity, according to Hegel, differs from human consciousness in that while animals represent external objects in their minds, they do not represent their own subjective states and thoughts as objects of perception. As he writes, an "animal can intuit, but the soul of the animal does not have the soul, or itself, as its object . . . but something external" (Hegel 1991, p. 74). A similar notion is evident in

Fromm's conception of self-consciousness, in which man comes to experience subjectivity in terms of a "split between himself as subject and the world as object" (Fromm 1963, p. 204). This formulation is slightly different to Hegel's but nevertheless alludes to the same phenomenon – that is, being aware of oneself as a subject of experience amounts to having oneself as an object of thought. For Fromm such self-awareness and the associated capacity for conscious and rational discrimination gives rise to the dilemma of choosing certain actions over others – with such capacity for freedom, choice, and rational discrimination being both a blessing and a curse (Fromm 1955b, p. 30).

The capacity to represent subjectivity as an object of thought, is for Hegel, one of the distinguishing features of human consciousness. It is also central to Hegel's political thought and his conception of human society. The development of a second nature, emerging out of a more primary animal or first nature, is what gives rise to habit or custom – or what we would refer to today as culture. As he writes, the general mode of behavior of human beings "appears as custom . . . and the habit of the ethical appears as a second nature which takes the place of the original and purely natural will" (Hegel 1991, p. 195).

While Marx's view of society and history differed from Hegel's in important aspects, it has been argued that Hegel's concept of second nature informs Marx's view of consciousness and history. For example, while Marx does not use the term second nature, his historical perspective of "nature developing into man," his economic analysis, and his concept of "estranged objectification," describe the "spheres of not only objective mind, but also human history, as a second nature in the objective sense intended by Hegel" (Moir 2020, p. 22).

Hegel's concept of second nature is believed to have had significant impact on the thought of Adorno, Horkheimer, Habermas, and Marcuse. While Hegel used the terms habit or custom to describe the liberatory or repressive aspects of a culture or shared societal reality (that is our second nature), the Frankfurt School used the term ideology to refer to the same phenomena. In this sense, the terms second nature and custom were replaced by ideology – but the concepts were very similar, with the Frankfurt School concept of ideology being a more recent application of Hegel's theory of second nature (Moir 2020, p. 20).

The concept of second nature is also central to Fromm's critique of history, culture, and consciousness. Fromm sees the emergence of human consciousness out of a more ancient form of animal consciousness giving rise to a series of psychological dilemmas, crises – and opportunities – which are not found in any other species on Earth. This critique has several dimensions. Firstly, it means that humans have increased capacity for conscious choice in planning their individual and societal goals – a capacity that brings with it its own burdens and responsibilities. Secondly, human psychology for Fromm is characterized by a sense of inner division or dissociation between this more recently evolved second nature and the more ancient aspects of the mind that evolved in earlier periods of our species development – aspects that Fromm associates with the unconscious mind (Fromm 1957, 1992, p. 257). And finally, this unique psychological condition means that humans can develop different forms of social character depending on the cultural environment that they live in and its unique economic and social conditions.

Another important dimension of Fromm's conception of second nature is his distinction between cultural specificity and a universal human nature. In terms of the debate between an essential human nature versus its infinite malleability, Fromm argues that both views are incomplete and that we need to understand both the malleability of human nature in addition to the existence of underlying shared psychic structures shared by all humans and cultures (Fromm 1955b, pp. 21–22). For example, while all humans share a basic psychological substrate in the deep unconscious as a result of our shared evolutionary history, our second nature also means there is significant malleability and plasticity, giving rise to unique variations in both culture and individual character. As he writes when discussing his concept of character:

> It will suffice here to say that character is the relatively permanent system of all noninstinctual strivings through which man relates himself to the human and natural world. One may understand character as the human substitute for the missing animal instincts; it is man's second nature. What all men have in common are their organic drives (even though highly modifiable by experience) and their existential needs. What they do not have in common are the kinds of passions that are dominant in their respective character-rooted passions. The difference in character is largely due to the difference in social conditions (although genetically given dispositions also influence the formation of the character); for this reason one can call character-rooted passions

> a historical category and instincts a natural category. Yet the former are not a purely historical category either, inasmuch as the social influence can only work through the biologically given conditions of human existence.
>
> (Fromm 1992, p. 255)

In the footnote to this passage, Fromm elaborates on the distinction between traits associated with organic drives, and those attributable to character – that is, natural and historical categories. In doing so he references Marx and Engels, connecting his concept of second nature and character formation with a critique of socioeconomic structures:

> This distinction between the two kinds of drives corresponds essentially to the one made by Marx. He spoke of two kinds of human drives and appetites: the *"constant,"* or fixed ones – such as hunger and the sexual drive – which are an integral part of human nature and can be changed only in their form and in the direction they take in various cultures, and the *"relative appetites"* which "owe their origin to certain social structures and certain conditions of production and communication." He spoke of some of these appetites as "inhuman," "depraved," "unnatural," and "imaginary."
>
> (Fromm 1992, p. 255)

We can see here the affinities between Hegel's concept of second nature and Marx's historical perspective of "nature developing into man" noted in the preceding quote. In the following section I expand on these aspects of Fromm's thought in an exploration of his engagement with evolutionary theory and comparative primatology.

Fromm and Evolutionary Psychoanalysis

Fromm is unique among the Frankfurt School thinkers in his ambitious project of grounding Marxism and psychoanalysis in evolutionary theory. While the seeds of this approach are to be found in early work such as *The Sane Society* (1955) it is not until *The Anatomy of Human Destructiveness* (1992 [1973]) that Fromm undertook an extensive reproachment between psychoanalysis, Marxism, and the evolutionary sciences.

The Anatomy of Human Destructiveness was published near the end of his career in 1973. The information available to Fromm when writing *The*

Anatomy of Human Destructiveness was much richer and detailed than that which was available when he was writing in the 1950s. While these earlier works engaged with evolutionary thought, they lacked the extensive and detailed exposition evident in *The Anatomy of Human Destructiveness*. In this later work, he utilized publications by modern researchers in human evolutionary studies such as Adolf Portman, David Pilbeam, the seminal collection edited by Sherwood Washburn, *Social Life of Early Man*, as well as primatological field studies by Adriaan Kortlandt and Jane Goodall on chimpanzees and George Schaller's on mountain gorillas. Many of these researchers laid the foundations for modern evolutionary studies and the role of comparative primatology in reconstructions of the deep human past. The research Fromm undertook to write *The Anatomy of Human Destructiveness* is impressive, and in its broad outlines, the book is congruent with what evolutionary theorists understand today about our origins as a species.

What is unique about the book is how it synthesizes anthropology, the fossil evidence for human evolution, and theories of humankind's primitive or archaic mentality with both psychoanalysis and a deep sociological critique inspired by Hegel and Marx. Evolutionary approaches to human psychology have been extensively developed by evolutionary psychologists (Barkow et al. 1995; Buss 2015; Cosmides and Cosmides 1988). However, this approach tends to neglect the role of socioeconomic structure in the development of individual psychology of the kind developed by Marx – whereas Fromm foregrounds socioeconomic structure.

Further, evolutionary psychology is limited by its reliance on adaptationist models, which presume the existence of a trait in a population is evidence that the trait itself was under selection over evolutionary time, with the further implication that the trait is encoded in the genome. This approach has been criticized by evolutionary biologist Stephen Jay Gould as well as the primatologist Frans De Waal (de Waal 2002; Gould and Vrba 1982). Gould has extended this critique to theories of human brain evolution, arguing that the current uses to which the brain is put may not be the same as those for which it evolved – that is, current utility may be vastly different than evolutionary origin. For example, reading, writing, commerce, and the practices of war make use of the human brain, but that does not mean the human brain evolved to undertake these tasks. That is, the brain of our ancestors has been co-opted or exapted, giving rise to these unique cultural phenomena – phenomena that not did exist among our archaic ancestors when our unique cognitive capacities evolved (Gould 1991).

The notion that the plasticity and malleability of the human brain can perform tasks and result in behaviors and thought processes for which it did not originally evolve provides a useful gloss on Fromm's concept of second nature and the existential dilemmas of human consciousness. For example, there are many human behaviors which do not make sense in terms of evolutionary adaptiveness – for example, suicide as well as familicide are behaviors that prevent a person's genes from being passed on to the next generation and are therefore unlikely to be favored by natural selection. Yet familicide, where men murder their own children and then commit suicide, often after a family separation (Johnson 2005), is a behavioral trait evident in humans that ensures the father's genetic material is not perpetuated into future generations.

A similar conundrum surrounds the issue of suicide, which evolutionary theorists are hard-pressed to explain from a sociobiological perspective, as any trait that leads to suicide would have been selected out of ancestral populations, given that suicide radically reduces reproductive opportunities and therefore reproductive success (de Catanzaro and Lykken 2013). However, Fromm's concept of character formation would make sense of such behaviors. For example, from such a perspective, psychological suffering, depression, violence, and suicide may be considered traits that emerge as a by-product of our unique form of human consciousness and self-awareness. That is, the traits themselves need not have evolved or been under any selective pressure in ancestral populations. In other words, they are exaptations, or evolutionary by-products of cognitive capacities that were selected for.

In fact, in *The Sane Society*, Fromm used the concept of social character to explain the high rates of suicide in prosperous Western nations – which from an orthodox Darwinian perspective seem to be quite inexplicable phenomena. Fromm attributed such high rates to a lack of mental health in those populations – what he called the "pathology of normalcy" or a "socially patterned defect" related to the socioeconomic conditions of consumerist capitalism (Fromm 1955b, pp. 15–28). And these in turn he linked to the more universal problems of human consciousness – the blessing and curse of our psychological uniqueness among the animal kingdom (Fromm 1955b, p. 30). In the following I explore Fromm's engagement with comparative primatology and evolutionary theory and how he uses the insights from these disciplines to expand on his conception of second nature and human character formation.

Fromm's theory of human psychology is based on the differences between humans and other primates. When comparing human and chimpanzee intelligence in *The Anatomy of Human Destructiveness*, Fromm quotes the field primatologist Adriaan Kortlandt:

> All the chimpanzees I observed were cautious, hesitant creatures. This is one of the major impressions one carries away from studying chimpanzees at close range in the wild. Behind their lively, searching eyes one senses a doubting, contemplative personality, always trying to make sense out of a puzzling world. It is as if the certainty of instinct has been replaced in chimpanzees by the uncertainty of intellect – but without the determination and decisiveness that characterize man.
> (Kortlandt in Fromm 1992, p. 135)

Commenting on this passage, Fromm writes that Kortlandt's "observation concerning the uncertainty of chimpanzees . . . is very important for the understanding of the evolution of man's 'second nature,' his character" (Fromm 1992, p. 135). Fromm goes on to attribute the development of our second nature to the evolution of the brain, as he writes:

> The other trend to be found in animal evolution is *the growth of the brain, and particularly of the neocortex*. Here, too, we can plot the evolution as a continuum – at one end, the lowest animals, with the most primitive nervous structure and a relatively small number of neurons; at the other, man, with a larger and more complex brain structure. . . . *Considering these data, man can be defined as the primate that emerged at the point of evolution where instinctive determination had reached a minimum and the development of the brain a maximum*. This combination of minimal instinctive determination and maximal brain development had never occurred before in animal evolution and constitutes, biologically speaking, a completely new phenomenon.
> (Fromm 1992, p. 252).

Fromm also grounded his conception of second nature and our idiosyncratic psychological condition in scientific understanding of the unique developmental or ontogenetic trajectories of human brain growth. As he writes the process of birth, while representing an "important change from intrauterine into extrauterine life," in many respects the "infant after birth is not different from the infant before birth; it . . . cannot feed itself; it is completely dependent on the mother, and would perish without her help" (Fromm 1955b, p. 32). Further on, Fromm elaborates on this idea, stressing the importance of the bond between mother and infant for the early period of development:

> The most elementary of the natural ties is the tie of the child to the mother. The child begins life in the mother's womb, and exists there for a much longer time than is the case with most animals; even after birth, the child remains physically helpless, and completely dependent on the mother; this period of helplessness and dependence again is much more protracted than with any animal. In the first years of life no full separation between child and mother has occurred. The satisfaction of all his physiological needs, of his vital need for warmth and affection depend on her; she has not only given birth to him, but she continues to give life to him.
>
> (Fromm 1955b, p. 43)

What Fromm is alluding to in his comments on "extrauterine life" and a "period helplessness and dependence" is that humans are characterized by extended ontogenetic trajectories where key developmental milestones occur at a later age than in other closely related primates such as bonobos and chimpanzees. It was these observations that led the German zoologist Adolph Portman to develop the notion of secondary altriciality – that is, humans are not fully mature at birth like precocial animals but resemble bird and other mammalian species, which require a significant nesting or nurturing period by the mother before they mature and become independent – which is what Fromm is referring to in the preceding quote about maternal care and extrauterine life.

Portman noted that in contrast to other primates, in which brain growth rates slow down at birth, the rates of neonate brain growth in humans continue throughout the first year of life. This phenomenon means that human newborns are essentially fetuses that are cared for outside the womb – what Portman called the "extrauterine spring" (Portmann 1990, p. 57). Additionally, Portman also noted the different ages in chimpanzees and humans at which growth of the brain dramatically slows down and virtually stops – that is, when the majority of adulthood brain size is achieved. For example, in chimpanzees and early small-brained hominins with comparable brain size to chimpanzees, brain growth slows at approximately 3.5 years, whereas in modern humans, growth continues for an extra three to four years with most of adulthood size not achieved until approximately 6.5–7.0 years (Clark and Henneberg 2015, p. 126; Portmann 1990, pp. 116–111). Additionally, humans have delayed onset of sexual maturity with an extended childhood and adolescent period of growth – for example, while the average age of first birth for chimpanzees is about 11 years (130 months), for humans it is 19 years (232 months) (Clark and Henneberg 2015). This extension of ontogeny is necessary for the development of our unique linguistic and socio-cognitive capacities, and it is one of the central developmental features that distinguish humans from other primates (Bogin 2003; Bogin and Smith 1996; Clark and Henneberg 2017; Locke and Bogin 2006).

This contrast between chimpanzees and humans can be seen in Figure 8.1. For example, it will be noted that after birth and during the first of year life, chimpanzee brain growth tails off, whereas in humans, the fetal rates continue during the first year, with the brain continuing to grow at significant rates for another four to five years after this. What is also worth noting is the decreased capacity of human infants to grasp hold of the mother when compared to chimpanzee infants, which results from both our different hand morphology as well as the vertical vector of upright, bipedal posture. It is this different nursing strategy that is believed to underpin both the intensification of maternal care in the hominin lineage – what Fromm called a protracted period of helplessness and dependency – as well as the evolution of our unique social psychology and intellectual abilities (Clark and Henneberg 2015; Falk 2004, 2009, 2016).

Significantly, in *The Anatomy of Human Destructiveness*, among a number of other researchers, Fromm acknowledges Portman as one of the sources he used in developing his theory (Fromm 1992, p. 149). Such influence seems to be evident in his discussion of the continuity between intrauterine and extrauterine life quoted above. Given such influence, it is no surprise that Fromm writes the following when discussing his conception of human brain evolution: "Not only is [man's] brain not fully developed at birth, but the state of disequilibrium in which he finds himself leaves him as an open-ended process to which there is no final solution" (Fromm 1992, p. 285).

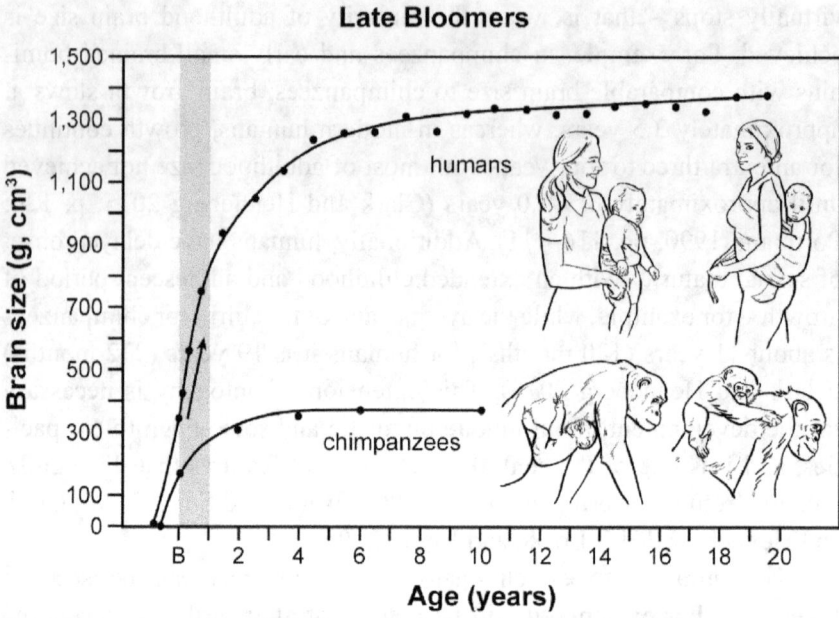

Figure 8.1 This figure illustrates the different developmental trajectories of chimpanzee and human brain growth. See text for details.

From: (Falk 2016). With permission from the author.

As already noted, Fromm uses his theory of human brain evolution and the emergence of our second nature when distinguishing between traits and behaviors that are evident in different cultures as opposed to those shared by the entire species of *Homo sapiens*. Later I will explore this distinction in a discussion of myth and religious symbolism, which, as in Jung's concept of archetypes and the collective unconscious (Jung 2014), Fromm sees as the expression of a shared universal human nature underlying the myriad manifestations of cultural specificity. Such a shared nature underlies Fromm's principle of universalism and his conception of the basic unity of the human race that informs his radical humanism (Durkin 2014, p. 43). In developing this aspect of his thought in an evolutionary context, Fromm draws an analogy between anatomy, brain function, and psychology:

> The main argument in favor of the assumption of the existence of a human nature is that we can define the essence of *Homo sapiens* in morphological, anatomical, physiological, and neurological terms. In

fact we give an exact and generally accepted definition of the species man by data referring to posture, formation of the brain, the teeth, diet, and many other factors by which we clearly differentiate him from the most developed nonhuman primates. Surely we must assume, unless we regress to a view that considers body and mind as separate realms, that the species man must be definable mentally as well as physically.

(Fromm 1992, p. 248)

Yet his conception of brain evolution also takes account of how our unique cognitive capacities may give rise to variation in behavior with the emergence of self-awareness and moral choice – which, as noted previously, he associates with the concept of second nature. As Fromm writes:

Man is guided by his intellect to make right choices. But we know also how weak and unreliable this instrument is. It is easily influenced by man's desires and passions and surrenders to their influence. Man's brain is insufficient not only as a substitute for the weakened instincts, but it complicates the task of living tremendously. By this I do not refer to instrumental intelligence, the use of thought as an instrument for the manipulation of objects in order to satisfy one's needs; after all, man shares this with animals, especially with the primates. I refer to that aspect in which man's thinking has acquired an entirely new quality, that of self-awareness. Man is the only animal who not only knows objects but who knows that he knows.

(Fromm 1992, p. 253)

Here Fromm is making a similar point to that noted previously in the discussion of Hegel's concept of second nature, which gives rise to the capacity to differentiate and think of oneself as a thinking subject distinct from objects in the world. This capacity to self-objectify or to have thoughts about thought processes – that is, to know that we know – is referred to by cognitive scientists as metacognition (Lou et al. 2017; Qiu et al. 2018). Significantly, this capacity is thought to be associated with the default mode network, which comprises unique components of human neural architecture not evident in our closest living relative, such as the chimpanzee (Rilling et al. 2007). This network is also involved in uniquely human abilities, such as language and conceptual processing (Rilling et al. 2007), theory of mind (Mars et al. 2012), and mental time travel – that is, the ability to create internal representations of situations in the past and future and to imaginatively project ourselves into those situations (Ostby et al. 2012).

It is also worth noting that the default mode network is believed to be associated with secondary consciousness and the self-reflective capacities of the human ego complex studied by Freud and Jung – capacities that are believed to develop out of primary process affective brain systems (Carhart-Harris and Friston 2010; Carhart-Harris et al. 2014). Secondary consciousness and the associated default mode network are also implicated in various forms of psychopathology (Geumsook et al. 2010; Whitfield-Gabrieli and Ford 2012; Carhart-Harris et al. 2013), which seem to be associated with overly rigid or inflexible thinking (Carhart-Harris and Friston 2019) and overactive internal rumination (Zhou et al. 2020).

When thinking about the relationship between ontogeny (individual development) and phylogeny (evolution of the species), it is worth noting that primary consciousness is believed to be more ontogenetically and phylogenetically primitive than secondary consciousness. In other words, in both individual development as well as over evolutionary time, subcortical primary processes are superseded by upper brain cortical processes associated with secondary consciousness (Hobson 2014, p. 109). Additionally, it is during the adolescent period of growth that we see maturation of the default mode network and a transition from primary to secondary consciousness – that is, from subcortical to more cortical control of behavior (Fair et al. 2008; Jones 2013). Significantly, it is also during the period of adolescent maturation that we see the onset of many forms of psychopathology (Jones 2013).

What I want to emphasize is that the transition from primary to secondary consciousness seems to be associated with the evolution of our unique developmental trajectories and that the extension of brain ontogeny during infancy, childhood, and adolescence is a crucial aspect of our cognitive uniqueness. The further point I wish to make is that such extension most likely underpins the aspects of human self-awareness that were of major concern to Fromm. This argument is made by Jonathan Burns in his book *The Descent of Madness: The Evolutionary Origins of Psychosis and the Social Brain*. Burns attributes our species' unique vulnerability for psychopathology to the extension of brain growth trajectories over evolutionary time that I have outlined in the previous section. What is worth noting is Burns's view that Fromm was correct in his analysis of the needs of the "social brain" and the role of "moral aloneness" and "alienation" in the genesis of psychopathology – at both the individual and cultural level (Burns 2007, pp. 72–74). It is hoped that the grounding of Fromm's work in contemporary studies of human brain evolution of the kind developed in the previous section and in the work of Burns can be taken up and developed by other Fromm scholars and Frankfurt School theorists.

With this model forming the background of the discussion, I now want to turn to Fromm's writings on religion and the underlying experiential phenomena that he argued underpin different religious traditions. This will lead to a consideration of the dissociation from the deeper ground of being, that is, the unconscious, that Fromm believed characterized the cultures of modernity. I will analyze this dissociation in terms of the model discussed previously while also outlining how Fromm advocated integrating the archaic ground of consciousness with our modern empirical and rationalist scientific mindset.

Psychological Anthropology and the Forgotten Language

In his discussion of religious modes of consciousness, Fromm advocates the development of an "empirical psychological anthropology" (Fromm 1969, p. 48). Fromm's conception of such an approach to religion was an extension of the ideas discussed previously regarding the "dichotomies" inherent in man's existence, "his separateness, alienation, suffering, his fear of freedom, his wish for union, his capacity for hate and destruction, his capacity for love and union" (Fromm 1969, p. 48). For Fromm, dealing with these aspects of existence were the central concern of the world's religions. In the following, I explore Fromm's writings on religion, dream, and myth, all of which (he argues) are manifestations of unconscious psychological processes – aspects of human experience that have been largely abdicated by the culture of rationalist modernity.

Numerous researchers have argued that archetypal "unitive" religious experiences involving "ego dissolution" and a sense of "oceanic boundlessness," the acute psychedelic state and dream life, all represent a phase transition from secondary to primary consciousness (Carhart-Harris and Friston 2019, pp. 317 and 336; Hobson 2002; Kettner et al. 2019, p. 4).

Significantly, such a phase transition is believed to represent a regression from ego consciousness to a more primitive mode of consciousness of the kind that both Freud and Jung referred to as the unconscious (Carhart-Harris and Friston 2019; Carhart-Harris et al. 2014). It has also been argued that such a transition, and the associated unitive experience, is what underpins the archetypal and cross-cultural religious experience studied by Jung (Carhart-Harris et al. 2014; Clark 2021).

Significantly, the experience of nondual awareness that characterizes Asian meditation and contemplative practices, where the rigid distinction between subject and object is collapsed, seems to be associated with alterations in the default mode network and a shift from egocentric to allocentric spatial processing (Josipovic 2013). In developing his concept of a universal substrate of experience underlying cultural diversity, Fromm has argued that overcoming the confines of the ego is the ultimate aim of all the "great humanistic religions" – that is, "overcoming the limitations of an egotistical self, achieving love, objectivity, and humility." He singles out the contemplative practices of Buddhism in this context (Fromm 1960, p. 18) but nevertheless argues that a similar impulse is to be found in other traditions that emphasize "giving up the wish to hold onto the 'ego' [and] leaving the prison of one's selfishness and separateness" (Fromm 1969, p. 48). Fromm developed these ideas further in a number of books dealing with psychanalysis, Zen Buddhism, and various other religious traditions (Fromm 1950, 1960, 1969).

Fromm argued that modern humans have become dissociated from the deeper ground of being that finds expression in religious experience, dream, and myth – in part due to the overemphasis on rationality associated with the Western Enlightenment (Fromm 1957, p. 8). However, he does not believe a regression to unconscious processes solves the dilemmas of modernity. As he argues, while unity is sought through religious experience, it is "not the regressive unity found by going back to the preindividual, preconscious harmony" but unity on a new level, which can only be arrived at "after man has experienced his separateness." This new unity represents for Fromm the "full development of man's reason, leading to a stage in which reason no longer separates man from his immediate, intuitive grasp of reality" (Fromm 1960, pp. 40–41).

This is an important aspect of Fromm's work that speaks to contemporary debates regarding the Western Enlightenment and European modernity.

For example, in recent decades, Enlightenment rationality and the culture of modernity has been predominantly analyzed in negative terms – and for good reason, too, given its association with colonialism, marginalization of the mentally ill, sexism, ecological devastation, dualistic separation between humanity and nature, as well as growing rates of mental and societal ill health (Clark 2003, p. 43; Foucault 2013; Merchant 2019; Paradies 2020; Plumwood 1993, 2005). Fromm was cognizant of these devastating aspects of modernity, and he provided a penetrating analysis of their cultural, psychological, and underlying socioeconomic causes. However, his approach possessed significant dialectical nuance generally lacking in the works cited previously.

Fundamentally, Fromm did not want to abandon the Enlightenment project, nor the promises of rationality and science. As an alternative to a regressive abandonment of rationality, modernity, and empirical investigation – important developments of our species' unique cognitive capacities – Fromm argued for an ethic in which rationality and consciousness are integrated with the deeper aspects of human nature – that is, our "experiential core ... buried in our unconscious" (Fromm 1992, p. 256). In the terms of the model outlined in this chapter, such a state of unity requires the integration of primary process affective states associated with subcortical brain systems, with our more recently evolved secondary process cortical systems.

Throughout his work, Fromm argued that much of the existential distress suffered by modern humans results from being dissociated from our shared "experiential core," which he argued is present in people "of all cultures" (Fromm 1992, p. 256). While modern humans have become dissociated from this experiential domain and have consequenlty forgotten this unique symbolic language, it still exists in myth and dream (Fromm 1957). In this sense, dream and myth are expressions of the shared experiential substarte underlying individual and cultural diversity. Dream and myth are also considered to be the keys by which modern humans can unlock this lost experiential domain – that is, the forgotten langauge of unconscious symbolism (Fromm 1957).

Fromm also argues that we can use myth and dream to decipher the nature of prehistroic religion and the experiential substrate out of which the world religions developed. Citing archaeological evidence of ritual in 500,000-year-old deposits associated with Peking Man (that is, *Homo erectus*), Fromm suggests one of the means we may be able to understand humankind's primitive or archaic mentality is through analyzing our own mind – that is, the unconscious and more specifically its manifestations in dream life (Fromm 1992, p. 256).

This approach is similar to that developed by the archaeologist David Lewis Williams, who, in his reconstruction of humankind's "ancient mind," has noted parallels between dream life and altered states of consciousness – states of consciousness evident both in contemporary shamanic practices as well as depictions in Paleolithic cave art. Lewis Williams's theory is similar to the one developed in this chapter – that is, given shared neurological structures amongst all members of *Homo sapiens*, we would expect affinities between the various manifestations of religious consciousness in different cultures (Lewis-Williams 2004, p. 130; Lewis-Williams and Challis 2011, pp. 80 and 199).

Significantly, shamanic trance has been associated with reduced activity in left hemisphere default mode forms of self-consciousness, as well as a shift to the evolutionarily older right-hemisphere-dominant mode of awareness that is believed to have characterized the early stages of hominin evolution (Flor-Henry et al. 2017). It is important to note that a similar reduction in activity in the default mode network was noted in the discussion of the alterations of brain architecture that seem to correlate with the archetypal religious experience – of which shamanic trance may be a variant (Winkelman 2010).

Given the skepticism regarding a universal human essence in postmodern theory and the social sciences and the antithetical position coming from the evolutionary and biological sciences, which asserts cross-cultural universals (Barkow et al. 1995; Carroll 1995), Fromm's navigation of a middle path between these two views holds significant promise. Durkin has suggested the importance of Fromm's "universalism" and "radical humanism" in countering the relativism of postmodernism and post-structuralism. In this chapter I have sought to extend and deepen that approach by situating Fromm's work in the context of the evolutionary sciences. More specifically, we may consider archaic primary process brain systems as the neurobiological substrate that gives rise to cross-cultural affinities in myth and religious symbolism. Additionally, we may attribute the various manifestations of cultural and individual specificity to the evolution of our more recently evolved form of secondary consciousness – or what Fromm referred to as character-based traits associated with our second nature.

Fromm was unique among the Frankfurt School thinkers in his extensive engagement with the evolutionary sciences. However, his ideas do possess significant affinities with other members of the school in his deployment of the Hegelian concept of a second nature. In synthesizing this concept with an anthropologically informed critique of Freudian theory, Fromm was able to develop a sociologically nuanced conception of depth psychology that highlighted the role of socioeconomic factors in the development of both individual and cultural psychopathology. Additionally, such pathologies may be considered as emergent properties of our species' unique cognitive capacities.

In this essay I have analyzed such capacities in the context of contemporary evolutionary and cognitive neuroscience, highlighting how such research can both inform and enrich our understanding of Fromm's ideas. More specifically, the model outlined here not only illuminates Fromm's concepts of character formation and second nature, but they also deepen our understanding of his conception of the unconscious and the emergence of self-conscious awareness during human evolution. This model suggests an evolutionary transition from an archaic form of affect-based primary consciousness to the meta-cognitive capacities associated with secondary consciousness, the default mode network, and the human ego complex.

I have also suggested how this model can illuminate Fromm's notion of integrating our modern rationalist and empirical mindset with our more ancient primary process brain system. Elsewhere I have applied this model to Jungian psychology, arguing that it can be used to illuminate Jung's concept of individuation – that is, the integration of consciousness and the ego complex with our ancient primary process brain systems, or what Jung referred to as the collective unconscious (Clark 2017, 2020, 2021). Additionally, in both Fromm and Jung, we have a rich source of ideas on how contemporary humans can integrate their modern empirical and rationalist mindset with the more archaic ground of being – that is, the universal substrate of consciousness that underlies the diversity of human cultures.

Such an approach also provides a way of humanity moving forward into a new stage in the development and evolution of human consciousness. As opposed to a rejection of humanism, modern rationalism, and the hard-won achievements of science as being ethnocentric and inherently oppressive, such an approach seeks to integrate these achievements with the modes of being that were often negated by such rationalist epistemologies and ontologies. Such modes of being are evident in humanity's various religious traditions, in Indigenous cultures, and in the religious practices believed to characterize the hunter-gatherer ancestors of contemporary humans. And they are also, Fromm suggested, evident in the unconscious processes manifest in the dream life of modern humans, processes that provide a key to unlock the forgotten language of unconscious symbolism and its unique affect-based cognitive mode. As we move into the future, such individuation becomes imperative at both the individual and collective level, as humanity seeks to integrate its modern dissociated psychosocial orientation with the archaic ground of being – that is, integrate our first and second natures. Or to use the terminology of evolutionary neuroscience, the integration of our subcortical primary processes systems with upper brain cortical processes associated with secondary consciousness, the default mode network, and the human ego complex.

Note

1 Throughout this essay I will be using the gendered term "man" for humanity or the human species. Fromm used this term throughout his writing, and while acknowledging its sexist overtones in English, he argued that the equivalent word in German – that is, *Mensch* – is a sexless term used to describe the human species. When the term "man" is used, I therefore hope the reader will interpret this as a biological definition – that is, describing the human species, in contrast to other species such as chimpanzees or earlier species in the hominin lineage that may have been ancestral to *Homo sapiens* (for further discussion, see Durkin 2014, p. 15).

References

Alcaro, Antonio, Stefano Carta, and Jaak Panksepp. 2017 The Affective Core of the Self: A Neuro-Archetypical Perspective on the Foundations of Human (and Animal) Subjectivity. *Frontiers in Psychology* 8:1424–1424.

Barkow, J. H., L. Cosmides, and J. Tooby. 1995 *The Adapted Mind: Evolutionary Psychology and the Generation of Culture*. Oxford: Oxford University Press.

Bogin, B. 2003 The Human Pattern of Growth and Development in Paleontological Perspective. In *Patterns of Growth and Development in the Genus Homo*. A. J. Nelson, G. E. Krovitz, and J. L. Thompson, eds. Pp. 15–44. Cambridge Studies in Biological and Evolutionary Anthropology. Cambridge: Cambridge University Press.

Bogin, B., and B. H. Smith. 1996 Evolution of the Human Life Cycle. *American Journal of Human Biology* 8(6):703–716.

Burns, J. 2007 *The Descent of Madness: Evolutionary Origins of Psychosis and the Social Brain*. London: Taylor & Francis.

Burston, D. 1991 *The Legacy of Erich Fromm*. Cambridge, MA: Harvard University Press.

Buss, D. 2015 *Evolutionary Psychology: The New Science of the Mind*. London: Taylor & Francis.

Carhart-Harris, R. L., and K. J. Friston. 2010 The Default-Mode, Ego-Functions and Free-Energy: A Neurobiological Account of Freudian Ideas. *Brain* 133(4):1265–1283.

Carhart-Harris, R. L., and K. J. Friston. 2019 REBUS and the Anarchic Brain: Toward a Unified Model of the Brain Action of Psychedelics. *Pharmacological Reviews* 71(3):316.

Carhart-Harris, R. L., et al. 2013 Functional Connectivity Measures after Psilocybin Inform a Novel Hypothesis of Early Psychosis. *Schizophrenia Bulletin* 39(6):1343–1351. DOI: 10.1093/schbul/sbs117. Epub 2012 Oct 8. PMID: 23044373; PMCID: PMC3796071.

Carhart-Harris, R. L., et al. 2014 The Entropic Brain: A Theory of Conscious States Informed by Neuroimaging Research with Psychedelic Drugs. *Frontiers in Human Neuroscience* 8.

Carroll, J. 1995 *Evolution and Literary Theory*. Columbia, Missouri: University of Missouri Press.

Clark, G. 2003 History and Ecology: The Poetry of Les Murray and Gary Snyder. *Interdisciplinary Studies in Literature and Environment* 10(1):27–53.

Clark, G. 2017 The Dionysian Primate: The Default Mode Network, Psychopathology and the Psychedelic Brain. *Entheogenesis Australis Psychedelic Symposium 2017, Victoria Australia* 2017a:25–27. Entheogenesis Australis.

Clark, G. 2020 Integrating the Archaic and the Modern: The Red Book, Visual Cognitive Modalities and the Neuroscience of Altered States of Consciousness. In *Jung's Red Book for Our Time: Searching for Soul under Postmodern Conditions*. M. Stein, T. Arzt, ed. Asheville: Chiron Publications.

Clark, G. 2021 Carl Jung and the Psychedelic Brain: An Evolutionary Model of Analytical Psychology Informed by Psychedelic Neuroscience. *International Journal of Jungian Studies*:1–30.

Clark, G., and M. Henneberg. 2015 The Life History of Ardipithecus Ramidus: A Heterochronic Model of Sexual and Social Maturation. *Anthropological Review* 78(2).

Clark, G., and M. Henneberg. 2017 Ardipithecus Ramidus and the Evolution of Language and Singing: An Early Origin for Hominin Vocal Capability. *HOMO – Journal of Comparative Human Biology* 68(2):101–121.

Cosmides, J. T., and L. Cosmides. 1988 *The Evolution of War and Its Cognitive Foundations Institute for Evolutionary Studies Technical Report*. Presented at the Evolution and Human Behavior Meetings, Ann Arbor, MI. https://www.cep.ucsb.edu/papers/EvolutionofWar.pdf

de Catanzaro, D., and D. T. Lykken. 2013 *Suicide and Self-Damaging Behavior: A Sociobiological Perspective.* Amsterdam, Netherlands: Elsevier Science.

de Waal, Frans B. M. 2002 Evolutionary Psychology: The Wheat and the Chaff. *Current Directions in Psychological Science* 11(6):187–191.

Durkin, K. 2014 *The Radical Humanism of Erich Fromm.* London: Palgrave Macmillan US.

Fair, D. A., et al. 2008 The Maturing Architecture of the Brain's Default Network. *Proceedings of the National Academy of Sciences* 105(10):4028–4032.

Falk, D. 2004 Prelinguistic Evolution in Early Hominins: Whence Motherese? *Behavioral and Brain Sciences* 27(4):491–503; discussion 503–583.

Falk, D. 2009 *Finding Our Tongues: Mothers, Infants and the Origins of Language.* New York: Basic Books.

Falk, D. 2016 Evolution of Brain and Culture: The Neurological and Cognitive Journey from Australopithecus to Albert Einstein. *Journal of Anthropological Sciences* 94:99–111.

Flor-Henry, Pierre, et al. 2017 Brain Changes During a Shamanic Trance: Altered Modes of Consciousness, Hemispheric Laterality, and Systemic Psychobiology. *Cogent Psychology* 4(1):1313522.

Foucault, M. 2013 *History of Madness.* London: Taylor & Francis.

Fromm, E. 1950 *Psychoanalysis and Religion.* New Haven, CT: Yale University Press.

Fromm, E. 1955a The Human Implications of "Instinctivistic" Radicalism: A Reply to Herbert Marcuse. *Dissent* 2(4):342–349.

Fromm, E. 1955b *The Sane Society.* New York: Rinehart.

Fromm, E. 1956 A Counter-Rebuttal. *Dissent* 3(1):81–83.

Fromm, E. 1957 *The Forgotten Language: An Introduction to the Understanding of Dreams, Fairy Tales, and Myths.* New York: Grove Press.

Fromm, E. 1960 *Zen Buddhism and Psychoanalysis.* Sydney: Allen & Unwin.

Fromm, E. 1963 *The Dogma of Christ.* New York: Henry Holt and Company.

Fromm, E. 1969 *You Shall be as Gods: A Radical Interpretation of the Old Testament and Its Tradition.* Robbinsdale, MI: Fawcett Premier.

Fromm, E. 1992 [1973] *The Anatomy of Human Destructiveness.* New York: Henry Holt and Company.

Geumsook, S., et al. 2010 Altered Resting-state Connectivity in Subjects at Ultra-high Risk for Psychosis: An fMRI Study. *Behavioral and Brain Functions* 6(1):58.

Gould, Stephen Jay. 1991 Exaptation: A Crucial Tool for an Evolutionary Psychology. *Journal of Social Issues* 47(3):43–65.

Gould, Stephen Jay, and Elisabeth S. Vrba. 1982 Exaptation-A Missing Term in the Science of Form. *Paleobiology* 8(1):4–15.

Hegel, G. W. F. 1991 *Hegel: Elements of the Philosophy of Right.* Cambridge: Cambridge University Press.

Hobson, A. 2002 *The Dream Drugstore: Chemically Altered States of Consciousness.* Cambridge, MA: MIT Press.

Hobson, A. 2014 *Psychodynamic Neurology: Dreams, Consciousness, and Virtual Reality*. London: Taylor & Francis.
Johnson, C. H. 2005 *Come with Daddy: Child Murder-Suicide After Family Breakdown*. Perth: University of Western Australia Press.
Jones, P. B. 2013 Adult Mental Health Disorders and Their Age at Onset. *The British Journal of Psychiatry* 202(s54):s5–s10.
Josipovic, Zoran. 2013 Neural Correlates of Nondual Awareness in Meditation. *Annals of the New York Academy of Sciences* 1307(1):9–18.
Jung, C. G. 2014 *Collected Works of C. G. Jung, Volume 9 (Part 1): Archetypes and the Collective Unconscious*. R. F. C. Hull, transl. Princeton: Princeton University Press.
Kettner, Hannes, et al. 2019 From Egoism to Ecoism: Psychedelics Increase Nature Relatedness in a State-Mediated and Context-Dependent Manner. *International Journal of Environmental Research and Public Health* 16(24):5147.
Lewis-Williams, D. 2004 *The Mind in the Cave: Consciousness and the Origins of Art*. London: Thames & Hudson.
Lewis-Williams, D., and S. Challis. 2011 *Deciphering Ancient Minds: The Mystery of San Bushman Rock Art*. London: Thames & Hudson.
Locke, John L., and Barry Bogin. 2006 Language and Life History: A New Perspective on the Development and Evolution of Human Language. *Behavioral and Brain Sciences* 29(03).
Lou, H. C., J. P. Changeux, and A. Rosenstand. 2017 Towards a Cognitive Neuroscience of Self-Awareness. *Neuroscience & Biobehavioral Reviews* 83:765–773.
Marcuse, H. 1955 The Social Implications of Freudian Revisionism. *Dissent* 2(3).
Marcuse, H. 1956 A Reply to Erich Fromm. *Dissent* 3:79–81.
Marcuse, H. 1972 *Eros and Civilization: A Philosophical Inquiry into Freud*. Great Britain: Abacus.
Mars, Rogier B., et al. 2012 On the Relationship Between the "Default Mode Network" and the "Social Brain". *Frontiers in Human Neuroscience* 6:189–189.
McLaughlin, Neil. 1996 Nazism, Nationalism, and the Sociology of Emotions: Escape from Freedom Revisited. *Sociological Theory* 14(3):241–261.
McLaughlin, Neil. 1998 How to Become a Forgotten Intellectual: Intellectual Movements and the Rise and Fall of Erich Fromm. *Sociological Forum* 13(2):215–246.
McLaughlin, Neil. 1999 Origin Myths in the Social Sciences: Fromm, the Frankfurt School and the Emergence of Critical Theory. *The Canadian Journal of Sociology/Cahiers canadiens de sociologie* 24(1):109–139.
McLaughlin, Neil. 2017 The Fromm – Marcuse Debate and the Future of Critical Theory. In *The Palgrave Handbook of Critical Theory*. M. J. Thompson, ed. Pp. 481–501. New York: Palgrave Macmillan US.
Merchant, C. 2019 *The Death of Nature*. New York: HarperOne.
Moir, Cat. 2020 Second Nature and the Critique of Ideology in Hegel and the Frankfurt School. In *Hegel and the Frankfurt School*. P. Giladi, ed. Pp. 115–139. New York: Routledge.

Narváez, D. 2014 *Neurobiology and the Development of Human Morality: Evolution, Culture, and Wisdom.* New York: W. W. Norton.

Ostby, Y., et al. 2012 Mental Time Travel and Default-Mode Network Functional Connectivity in the Developing Brain. *Proceedings of the National Academy of Sciences* 109(42):16800–16804.

Panksepp, J. 2004 *Affective Neuroscience: The Foundations of Human and Animal Emotions.* Oxford: Oxford University Press.

Paradies, Yin. 2020 Unsettling Truths: Modernity, (De-)coloniality and Indigenous Futures. *Postcolonial Studies* 23(4):438–456.

Plumwood, V. 1993 *Feminism and the Mastery of Nature.* London: Routledge.

Plumwood, V. 2005 *Environmental Culture: The Ecological Crisis of Reason.* London: Taylor & Francis.

Portmann, A. 1990 *A Zoologist Looks at Humankind.* New York: Columbia University Press.

Qiu, Lirong, et al. 2018 The Neural System of Metacognition Accompanying Decision-Making in the Prefrontal Cortex. *PLoS Biology* 16(4):e2004037–e2004037.

Rilling, J. K., et al. 2007 A Comparison of Resting-State Brain Activity in Humans and Chimpanzees. *Proceedings of the National Academy of Sciences* 104(43):17146–17151.

Whitfield-Gabrieli, Susan, and Judith M. Ford. 2012 Default Mode Network Activity and Connectivity in Psychopathology. *Annual Review of Clinical Psychology* 8(1):49–76.

Winkelman, M. 2010 *Shamanism: A Biopsychosocial Paradigm of Consciousness and Healing.* Westport, CT: Praeger.

Zhou, Hui-Xia, et al. 2020 Rumination and the Default Mode Network: Meta-Analysis of Brain Imaging Studies and Implications for Depression. *NeuroImage* 206:116287.

Chapter 9

Colonizing the American Psyche

Virtue and the Problem of Consumer Capitalism

John R. White

Introduction

Large swaths of news media in the United States routinely underline supposedly strong oppositions between the two major political parties and between so-called "conservatives" and so-called "liberals." But what is perhaps psychologically more interesting is what the mainstreams of each of these points of view assume to be beyond question: an economic structure and social system designed around consumer capitalism. If there is any one social force in the United States and any one collective psychological factor that is properly speaking "esoteric," that is to say, "hidden in plain sight," it is the meaning, nature, and problem of consumer capitalism. Political rhetoric aside, consumer capitalism is not only seen but more importantly *experienced* to be simply "the way things are," the unquestioned and unquestionable form of social life in general in America. Indeed, any attempt even to question the legitimacy and potential range of consumer capitalism in the US at the national level or any attempt to insist on, for example, non-market values informing the marketplace are routinely met with cries of undermining liberty, of totalitarianism, of communism, and of any number of other poorly considered and generally inaccurate epithets.

For the psychoanalytic practitioner generally and the Jungian practitioner in particular, the fact that consumer capitalism has such a hold on the American collective invites consideration of its nature as a psychological force. Economic sociologists have pointed out for generations that the basic components of capitalism in any of its forms are historically contingent and thus are a far cry from "the way things necessarily are." Thus, the fact that, to the contrary, these components are experienced as essentially the nature of things already suggests a number of psychologically important questions, among them: why do Americans take consumer capitalism simply to be the nature of things? Is there something of what Jung calls a "cultural complex" around consumer capitalism and, if so, how do we characterize it, why does it exist, and how did it get so potent? How can a force of such magnitude for the American mind at the same time be so "hidden in plain sight," as if it is beyond critical questioning?

These sorts of questions go well beyond a chapter-length study and consequently will only be touched on throughout. I will instead focus my attention on psychological points that I think must be worked through prior to a fuller response to the preceding questions. I will, first, consider consumer capitalism as a psychological problem for individuals and, with the help of traditional critical theory, elucidate some of the ways in which collective assumptions and some unfortunate but in part intentionally produced psychological habits seem to merge to form the collective complex around consumer capitalism in the US, having a substantial impact on individual psychology. Second, I will turn to describing some of the mechanisms by which individual Americans get psychologically infected with this complex and what I take to be some of the consequences of this situation in the clinical setting. Finally, I will turn to the largely unmined concept of virtue from ancient philosophy, a notion I think can benefit psychoanalytic practitioners working with patients suffering under the influence of this cultural complex.

Psychology of Prejudice

The Frankfurt School, especially in its first generation, produced a substantial body of philosophy and social science very relevant to the current psychological and psychoanalytic problem of consumer capitalism. The research of many of the members of the school was frequently in dialogue with the work of Sigmund Freud, including some of its most well-known members. In philosophy, for example, Herbert Marcuse's work became something like a household name among Left-leaning academics in the sixties, including *Eros and Civilization*, which was billed as a study of Freud. In psychology, Eric Fromm is without doubt the most famous within the Frankfurt circle and his work is consistently in dialogue with Freud. Thus, the psychoanalytic aspect of critical theory is by no means accidental to it.

However, one of the more valuable concepts one might draw from the Frankfurt School for analyzing the psychology of consumer capitalism derives from their study of anti-Semitism. The experience of the Frankfurt circle, once they moved to New York City, included at least one important surprise: through the years in New York, these researchers found that there was more overt anti-Semitism in the US than in the Germany they had left behind in the thirties. It was in many ways a different sort of anti-Semitism from the contemporary German variety, to be sure: it didn't necessarily result in anything like widespread political ideology around the Jews, or death camps, or expose itself, say, through explicit scapegoating of Jews concerning national problems. But this form of anti-Semitism was also more widespread and far less informed by history, culture, or other at least partially rational sources than the version of anti-Semitism prevalent in Germany. Consequently, this sort of anti-Semitism was not such that it could be either rationally substantiated or rationally refuted because it wasn't born of rational or, in other words, conscious grounds at all. This anti-Semitism was both communicated and held subconsciously: it was both assumed and propagated via uninformed, affectively charged stereotypes, subliminally communicated, without even purportedly rational sources.

Now it is this latter point that is crucial for our understanding of consumer capitalism, namely, that powerful psychological forces are communicated from the collective, often without even a modicum of conscious rationality, and that such communications can be potent forces within the individual human psyche. This point is of course not news for anyone who knows Carl Jung's thought or who practices in a Jungian way. And yet, though Jung clearly saw that the collective and individual psychology are interconnected, that the psyche is a sensorium not only for individual unconscious processes but also for collective unconscious processes, Jung did not develop much by way of illuminating the psychic mechanisms – to use an old Freudian metaphor – by which this communication occurs.[1]

In contrast to Jung, one of the things that the Frankfurt School analysis of anti-Semitism does is attempt to understand the individual psychic process whereby one receives, for example, such subliminal or subconscious messaging. While this issue runs throughout the work of the Frankfurt School from the late thirties onward, its most detailed study is the various works of the *Studies in Prejudice,* and especially in the work known as *The Authoritarian Personality*, at the time a cutting-edge work of advanced social science. The title *Authoritarian Personality* might give one the impression that the work is about the psychology of people we call "authoritarians" like, say, Benito Mussolini, but the study is not so much about authoritarians as about the people who support and in various ways identify with authoritarians and authoritarian societal structures. After all, authoritarian figures are often not the biggest problem in authoritarian settings; rather, the vast numbers of people who either explicitly support the authoritarian or those who look the other way and offer implicit support are in many ways the bigger problem. The concept of the "authoritarian personality" thus concerns those who explicitly or implicitly cooperate in authoritarian systems and how such people are controlled subconsciously, including by affectively charged stereotypes communicating something more potent than mere "information": they communicate an implicit system of values and behaviors that subliminally implicate how one is to function properly within a social system. These messages are conscious enough to influence behavior yet unconscious enough that they are difficult to recognize or therefore criticize (Adorno et al., 1969; Wiggershaus, 1995).

Let me summarize in an extremely schematic way some of the conclusions that might be drawn from *The Authoritarian Personality* and some of the related documents by the Frankfurt School. According to their analysis, the dominant American personality type is particularly susceptible to subconscious suggestion. This implies that when something is communicated to Americans of this dominant type, the communication tends to be taken as innocent until proven guilty, providing it conforms with currently held and largely bourgeois values and views. This is so, in part, because Americans are neither taught nor do they typically use much by way of critical thinking – critical thinking not only about what someone else says but also about one's own reactions and impulses, for example, about what we nowadays call "implicit biases." This lack of critical thinking produces, we might say, a tendency to assume that all knowledge claims are equal, and so, in the end, I can simply follow my own preferences, my own prejudices. Consistent with this, Americans of this personality type tend to tell stories – both to themselves and to others – attempting to make these often irrational and contradictory ideas appear coherent and reasonable rather than questioning the preferred narrative. Thus, people of this dominant type are often resistant to new information or new interpretations that might challenge their chosen narrative about the meaning of things. Furthermore, of particular importance for our purposes, this dominant American personality type displays what the Frankfurt scholars call a "weak ego," meaning that it is highly susceptible to subliminal messaging and is therefore easily manipulated via imaginative and emotional life. Consequently, there is a specific and intense impressionability in many Americans, one that is largely unconscious and therefore difficult to combat (Adorno et al., 1969; Wiggershaus, 1995).

Relevance for Consumer Capitalism

There is reason to think that the US of the last dozen or so years is worse in these respects than it was in the thirties and forties, when *The Authoritarian Personality* was being researched and written, due in part to the vast network of images used on social media and the specific power those images have on the subconscious mind. The analysis of *The Authoritarian Personality* was intended not only as a diagnosis but also as a warning that, since Americans are highly susceptible to subliminal messaging, they are open targets for any authoritarian who knows how to manipulate the subconscious messaging system and use it to rise to power and retain it. That message either didn't get through or was not heeded in political circles, yet the message was probably not lost on the advertising industry, the central engine of consumer capitalism.

For consumer capitalism is not just an economic system but precisely a system of suggestion through subliminal messaging, primarily via advertising. It is, as Daniel Bell (2001) aptly puts it, a "technology of desire," a system that manipulates desires in a way to obtain profit and certainly without concern for the potentially negative effects on the psychology of the consumer. In other words, advertising is not just one industry among many but is the crucial psychological key to consumer capitalism. Just as the Frankfurt circle argued that anti-Semitism spreads in America largely due to the typical American personality type and the affectively charged images and stereotypes it uncritically accepts, similarly virtually anything that can be communicated subliminally in the language of the unconscious – affect and image – can be used in a parallel way to dominate a personality of this type, at least through repeated use.

It is difficult to overestimate the importance of this point for mental health professionals who work psychoanalytically. First, this description suggests that many of our patients, at least insofar as they fit the profile described by the Frankfurt School, may be substantially under the psychological hegemony of consumer capitalism through subconscious means. On one level, that is no surprise, and it has been known since the ancient world that the ruling order must use symbols and images to dominate what we nowadays term the "subconscious mind," to win loyalty, devotion, and so forth. Yet the current usage of images is not quite as neutral as that ancient usage, in part because of the delivery system: images are delivered to the mind directly and constantly through electronic means and can, especially in an age where many of us are working electronically, have much greater impact due, if nothing else, to greater repetition. But this poses a very important problem for those of us who work psychoanalytically because image contents of the unconscious mind are therefore often not neutral productions of an autonomous psyche and not only regarding content but also form. For example, being invaded electronically by advertising is not just about products but about identity: it not only sells products but says, through the endless repetition, "you consist in being a consumer" – and perhaps consist in nothing else. It is probably no accident that, for example, American elections are treated in our news networks as a combination of sports commentary and beauty pageant, talking either about strategy or appearance and virtually never about policy. The message is that you are a consumer of the process and not, by implication, a citizen, so you are only to care about the strategy or the appearance, not issues of political significance or of potential importance to you as a citizen. This is just one way in which issues of psychological identity and, at least implicitly, self-esteem are in fact closely associated with these sets of problems.

Furthermore, our work as psychoanalysts in part depends on the capacity of our patient to produce images. But when images are habitually *given* rather than spontaneously *produced*, mustn't that at least affect how we understand the images? While it might seem on the surface that it doesn't much matter if the associated image is a spontaneous dream or a character from a preferred television show, that may not be true. In the final analysis, media and advertisers are primarily image producers and image deliverers, and if nothing else, the consistent spiritual diet of such images is likely to make our imagination passive with respect to images given and undermine our spontaneous capacity to produce our own images. Since it becomes more and more difficult to differentiate which of the imaginative products of our patients arise from them and which are primarily passively received from the collective, we might at least wonder if our image-based consumer society is producing essentially collective imaginations rather than genuinely individual imaginations, something which must at least inhibit psychological process to the extent that individuation is the goal – in principle producing "mass personalities" rather than genuine individuals.

We can perhaps begin to see how the psychic mechanism described by the Frankfurt School works equally well for advertising. Ludwig von Mises (2014), one of the great theoreticians of capitalism, says that the experience of *unease* is the basis of human action (at least the "action" of *homo economicus*): it is unease of some sort that incentivizes one to change one's life in some way. If we take Mises's idea to be basically on the mark, then we can understand how advertising works: (1) produce unease in the potential consumer through imaging and (2) offer an image of a proposed solution to the unease that will drive the potential consumer to economic action. The primary tool for this, as we know from the Frankfurt School, is to use affect and image – the language of the unconscious mind, often couched in stereotypes – to produce unease about not being among those who are "successful," "happy," or "fulfilled" and to propose some product that will alleviate that situation.

If this analysis is on target, it suggests that, for consumer capitalism, *producing emotional and psychological unease is the point*. It is in fact generally most beneficial for the system to produce an experience of unease where none is already present since unease will tend to produce actions conducive to new consumption, at least if the appropriate sort of economic action is implicit in the messaging. Indeed, if one can produce unease around existentially significant issues, all the better, since the latter as a rule never go away and will likely produce a consumer who returns again and again. Also, as a corollary to this point, having disordered and unmanaged desires are more conducive to consumer capitalism than having ordered desires: a person who has a basically ordered life, who knows what he or she wants from life and lives according to that ideal and thus excludes consumption not conducive to this ideal, is less likely to be a consistent consumer than one who is unclear, unsure, and more subject to unease around desires: the more indiscriminate the desire, the more likely one will purchase something to reduce the unease.

Consequently, the "sweet spot" of advertising links up existentially important longings and anxieties, such as concerns around safety, security, family, aging, income, success, developmental issues, death, and the like, with some real or imaginary unease pointing to some product purportedly resolving that unease. This is the sweet spot because existential desires and anxieties refer to questions of ultimate meaning and thus never go away. Constantly evoking existential desires and anxieties and linking them to products, if done well, is therefore an excellent way to guarantee a consistent market. Unfortunately, it is also an excellent way to cause emotional and psychological disturbances at a mass level.

This process is achieved in a largely subrational way, that is, in a way neither fully conscious nor therefore fully mediated by reason and freedom – just the way the Frankfurt School suggested that anti-Semitism spreads. Indeed, it must be done in a subrational way, since the goal is to persuade people to do what is inherently irrational, namely, attempt to solve existential concerns and anxieties in nonexistential ways. At a rational level, buying that new model of Jeep that the commercial images with that successful looking 40-year-old dude and his 28-year-old blond passenger in tow will not resolve, say, one's midlife crisis, concerns over aging, or existential death anxiety. Yet the images, music, and other accompanying effects suggest it can do just that, and that is typically how the unease is produced: a stereotyped picture of who the consumer "ought" to be, producing unease that one is not that, and then a message that one becomes that stereotype if one purchases the advertised product. The process typically occurs more through emotionally charged images rather than verbal messaging, assuring the process remains subrational.

Put schematically:

1. Human beings are by nature beings of desire, including existentially significant anxieties and longings.
2. Through affect and image (such as stereotypes) working subconsciously and subliminally, indiscriminate unease and desire is both produced and transformed into a definite and determinate desire for a commodity, by linking it in a subrational and subvolitional way via advertising, that is, by means of subconscious association.

3. Among the consequences of this, (a) existential desire and anxiety are mitigated for a time through diversion but always return precisely because they are existential and thus always active to some extent, to the benefit of the market; (b) life becomes emotionally unfulfilling because consumption is an attempt at an irrational solution to existential desires and anxiety and cannot ameliorate them.
4. We become defined – and define ourselves – through our consumption. The soul is colonized by consumer capitalist practice through habitual transformation of existentially significant desires into acts of consumption.
5. The process must be repeated and instilled, lest the irrationality of trying to satisfy existential concerns in a nonexistential way be discerned. In other words, consumer capitalism first and foremost must peddle consumer capitalism.

Consumer Capitalism in the Consulting Room

What Sort of Person?

There was a common trope among ancient philosophers, both Greek and Roman, regarding the analysis of social structures. They would ask, what sort of person does a political and social system produce? Plato, for example, in his most famous work, *The Republic*, analyzes the political structure of the city by comparing it to an equivalent structure of the soul. As Plato puts it, through the words of Socrates, "the city," or in other words, society, "is the soul written in large letters" (Plato, 1992). Plato proceeds to analyze different kinds of souls and their places in the city. This question suggests, then, that we expect any social system to produce a certain sort of psyche or person, and we might further say that the quality of psyche or person typically produced by the system tells us a good deal about the social system that tends to produce it. This is true because human beings by nature adapt to the social systems of which they are a part and will tend to adapt therefore not only to what is positive within the system but also to its pathology.

Given what I have described and to some extent illustrated in the previous section, what do we have a right to expect in our consulting rooms? What sort of psyche, as it were, can we expect a society like that which I have described to produce? For one, we would expect that, to the extent that people live amidst and according to a society organized around consumer capitalism, they will tend to experience unmanaged and often seemingly unmanageable and largely unconscious instincts and desires, precisely because the system attempts not to *resolve* legitimate unease but to *produce* unease, preferably unease about existentially significant desires, since these will tend to evoke the purchase of commodities long term.

At the same time, we would expect many patients, including some of the same ones, to be totally unsure what their own desires in fact are. We would expect at least some to feel like their desires are planted in them, so to speak, from without, and others not to know because they can't discern which are planted and which are not. These doubts have, as one consequence, a general inertia around pursuing any ambitious goal because of general ambivalence around desires.

We would also expect that those living in a society organized around consumer capitalism to seek existential solace in excessive consumption, that is, to attempt to manage existential anxieties and dissatisfied existential longings by consuming material commodities and yet also to find such consumption only a brief diversion and ultimately dissatisfying. The amount of consumer debt Americans typically live with may be one indication of this characteristic.

Furthermore, we would expect to hear metaphors from the unconscious around issues of abundance and scarcity. The reason for this is that life within the ethos of consumer capitalism tends to be assessed according to *quantity* (how many consumer goods, how much money, etc.) rather than *quality* (goods and money serving a higher and more worthwhile life).

Two Characteristic Impacts

Permit me to illustrate some of these points with two characteristic types of clinical situation. I will call them (1) the puritan-hedonist situation and (2) the *ressentiment* situation.

Puritan-Hedonist Situation

Puritanism is still a potent force in the US, but that fact is not always recognized because it frequently emerges in the form of an enantiodromia. There frequently are in our patients, in other words, either puritanical and repressive attitudes toward pleasures associated with the body, nature, and affects or else a kind of anti-puritanical excessive hedonist pursuit of those same pleasures, and often an oscillation between them. Yet though pleasure is thematic in each case, pleasure tends to be conceived as a mere physical response to external stimuli.

But neither of these views, I would suggest, is a healthy way of relating to pleasure. The reason for this is that genuine pleasures are, as a rule, not ends in themselves but are meant to lead to an experience of expanding life (Scheler, 1973; White, 2012; White, forthcoming a). Another way of putting this is that pleasure values are at the service of vital values or, in other words, values whose purpose is making us feel more alive, healthier, more expansive. Neither repressive puritanism nor anti-puritanical hedonism are examples of relating to pleasure in a way that is expansive to feelings and values of life. While it is part of the older analytic traditions always to think the puritanical-repressive type of person needs to be healed through abreaction, the hedonistic type of patient needs it just as much, since neither is experiencing pleasure for the sake of expanding life (White, forthcoming a).

Yet these attitudes, at least in their current forms, seem to arise at least in some measure from the unease produced by consumer capitalism. After all, if one does in fact feel more alive due to pleasure, that is an experience of a qualitatively higher value than pleasure per se, and the residual satisfaction from it usually implies that one does not currently need more pleasure, quantitatively speaking – not a situation conducive to the aims of consumer capitalism, which must consistently produce unease so that one seeks a greater quantity of stimuli. Otherwise put, the consumerist ethos aims to produce psyches susceptible to needing ongoing stimuli, not to those capable of experiencing higher values.

Needless to say, this is a difficult situation within the consulting room. For one, some patients don't quite believe there is an option outside puritanical repression, on the one hand, and hedonistic excess, on the other, and thus live amidst oscillating frustrations. Further, unless one can relate to the higher principle of life beyond the pleasures, the pleasures themselves tend not to have lasting positive impacts, since the pleasures pass even as life remains (Scheler, 1973). Hence, the development of stances and attitudes conducive to experiencing higher, vital feelings based on pleasure states are often never achieved or are at least quite difficult to achieve due to the ingrained habits born of consumer capitalism.

The Ressentiment *Situation*

Philosopher Friedrich Nietzsche and, later, phenomenologist Max Scheler, developed the concept of *ressentiment*. Both wrote in German and used the French term because the German did not seem to express sufficiently what they were after. Clinically speaking, much of what we characteristically term "anger" and more often "rage" is in many cases better described as *ressentiment*.

What is *ressentiment*? It consists in intense feelings of resentment, which have become disengaged from the original experiences which produced them and which therefore become an ingrained, consistent attitude without a single, definite object. Rather than being motivated by objects, it "seeks" its objects for the satisfaction of affective release, primarily to vent itself on. I often refer clinically to *ressentiment* as a kind of psychological pus or infection that tends to permeate conscious life and often makes a person generally cynical, susceptible to extreme frustrations often around apparently small things, and leads a person to denigrate values in others in order to make themselves feel less inferior. While I can't develop this point here, I will say that the most potent effect that *ressentiment* has on a person is that it distorts the feeling function to the point that the latter *inverts the experience of values*, that is, it makes a person experience what they know to be higher values as if they are lower and what they know to be lower values as if they are higher (Nietzsche, 2009; Scheler, 1998).

Ressentiment occurs when a person experiences him- or herself as entirely impotent concerning some existentially significant hope or desire, in the face of what is experienced as a more powerful force inhibiting it. Anger, rage, unforgiving resentment thus arise, especially when there is no outlet for such powerful emotions. Typically, feelings like envy, thirst for revenge, and vindictiveness also accompanying *ressentiment* (Scheler, 1998). *Ressentiment* is, though it has rarely been considered clinically, I believe, a very powerful force in human psychology, but especially when the collective social structure is organized around consumer capitalism. Why so?

The primary reason is that the promise of consumer capitalism, buttressed by media and the advertising industry, is far different from most people's experience of it. For one, as we have seen, the advertising industry uses existential anxieties and desires to advertise its typically petty products, products that couldn't possibly satisfy existential needs.

Consequently, deep dissatisfaction, overwhelming frustration, and a feeling of impotence to get what one needs among consumers (and therefore patients) is the natural outcome. Furthermore, even structural features of capitalism that go beyond its consumer function make it difficult not to feel dissatisfied. For example, the message one receives as a laborer is that one just needs to "work hard" and one can somehow make it within the consumer economy. Yet it is intrinsic to industrial capitalism, as already Adam Smith pointed out in the eighteenth century, that there is an inherent downward pressure on the wages due to the commodification of labor (Smith, 1999). Thus, many patients experience not only *ressentiment* around consumption but also around labor, because working hard often does not seem enough to succeed: ironically, commodification of higher management favors increases in their salaries while commodification of labor works to decrease theirs. Once again, the promise is one thing, the reality quite another, making a substantial part of the population highly susceptible to *ressentiment*. Notice too the importance of the abundance-scarcity images mentioned previously in this situation because *ressentiment* is always, to some extent, based on a feeling of inner scarcity: if the promise is unlimited abundance if I work hard, but though I work hard, there seems to be nothing I can do to obtain that abundance, I feel inner scarcity and impotence as well as something of a human failure, due to lack. The entire system is likely to produce narcissistic wounding throughout the population.

As a whole, patients are often in deep confusion about what they really want, about whether they can get what they want, and why they aren't getting at least what they think they want amidst social structures organized around consumer capitalism. They are often left with intense *ressentiment* but – just as one expects with *ressentiment* – not sure who or what to blame for it. Not infrequently, they turn it on themselves and end up with a deep self-loathing for what is in most respects not entirely their fault. Furthermore, they often can get no respite from these feelings because they can't break out of the puritan-hedonist situation I outlined in the previous section and experience at least some higher values of life beyond the petty pleasures of pure stimulus-response.

Going back, if we ask, what sort of psyche or person does this system produce? We find that it is often the sort of person who has difficulty around pleasure and satisfaction, a person deeply insecure about the nature and value of his or her own desires, and a person deeply confused about existential meaning, at least in part because they have been sold a bill of goods about the level of happiness consumer capitalism can deliver, and they can't figure out why they have not succeeded in getting it.

Virtue and Individuation

Having made a case for some of the problems associated with consumer capitalism, is there any hope for healing? Let me note from the outset that my concern here is not to pose some social alternative to consumer capitalism: that is for professionals in other areas from the psychoanalyst. You will note that my concerns and criticisms here have not touched so much on the system itself as on the consequences of the system for the individual psyche, something that I believe a mental health professional has some expertise in, though he may not, for example, have expertise in social system transformations. With that in mind, my question concerns not the system but rather whether there is hope for individual people, for example, patients in a clinical setting, within the current social climate.

Healing Consumers

One possible source for aiding the individual patient can be drawn from ancient philosophy and especially ancient philosophical ethics. It might seem surprising that I turn to ethics, but it is important to understand that "ethics" in the modern period is usually understood in a quite externalist fashion, as if it is about external actions and behavior, and in fact contemporary ethics often avoids as much as it can concerning genuine psychology (MacIntyre, 1984). In contrast, ancient ethics virtually *was* a psychology – even if not only that – because it understood ethical life to be about the cultivation of the soul or psyche. Thus, when a person is ethically developed, on this ancient model, it is because that person has cultivated what in common speech we might simply call "good habits" or what the ancients called "virtue."

The nature of habit is broached to some extent in Jungian literature but primarily in terms of typology, for example, whether one is introverted or extraverted, or for example a thinker or feeler, suggesting here that the issue of habit pertains solely to questions about psychological types, or in other words, the basic modes of psychic adaptation. The ancient philosophers, in contrast, were concerned with habit not primarily in terms of the dominant form of adaptation (typology) but rather in terms of whether one cultivated the soul and, in particular, cultivated *desires*. For the ancient philosophers, one aimed to cultivate desires in conformity with what was called in Greek *nous*, that is, the higher part of the soul ordered by the divine, parallel to what Jungians would call "the Self" (White, forthcoming b). This responsiveness to the Self led to one ordering and habituating one's instincts and desires in a way at least coherent with and preferably expressive of one's response to the Self. Notice that this is less about orientations of adaptation than developing habits conducive to whatever appears to be the better aspirations of the person, though it is also true that the development of virtue impacts and generally improves adaptation.

The traditional language for this sort of habit is "virtue." In our time, the concept of virtue has been somewhat subverted – when it is mentioned at all – as for example in the contemporary notion of "virtue signaling." Whatever the value of that latter notion in its own context, it unfortunately links virtue with moralism and dogmatism, something quite inimical to the original understanding of virtue. The ancient concept of virtue was not moralistic at all because it was not about any external constraining of behavior; it was rather about cultivating desires in such a way that, over time, one actually *wants* to do what was best and right and in one's own best interests (Aristotle, 2014). Just as the term "cultivation" suggests, one is not trying to repress desires but rather orient and habituate them toward positive ends and do so oneself and from one's own responsiveness to the Self, not by external constraint. The assumption here, which I believe can be verified by each of us phenomenologically, is that instinctual desires, as a rule, tend to be indiscriminate in their ends and are rarely good guides as to how best to fulfill themselves in a way consistent with one's life narrative – a factor advertising plays on. The same desire for food, drink, sex, or sleep, for example, sometimes leads to ends conducive to one's life goals and other times leads one away from them. Thus, something else must, as it were, be added to instinctual impulses and desires to render them more useful to our life goals.

This additional something is virtue. Virtue then is a developed habit orienting desires, instincts, and impulses in such a way that they serve our life projects, presumably in part determined by our responsiveness to the Self. I hope it is clear already at this point that virtue is not repressive because it does not seek to limit desires per se but to order and channel desires toward some vision of what counts as both good and beneficial. Indeed, one might expect a virtuous person to feel desire more intensely than the non-virtuous person because the narrower channel, so to speak, intensifies the momentum. Virtues are neither puritanical nor prudish, therefore, because they assume that desires are basically good but are generally in need of cultivation and habit to make them such that they typically work in the direction of a positive and determinate end.

The varied definitions of virtue among the ancient philosophers are interesting for our purposes because they rarely amount to proper philosophical definitions at all. Rather, the definitions often amount to saying something like, "Look at a virtuous man and do what he does," the ancient concept of virtue incidentally always being defined exclusively through the male of our species, a definite prejudice by contemporary standards. The conclusion to be drawn from these definitions for our purposes is that though virtue is often difficult to define, one knows it when one sees it. I might not be able to define that specific quality of courage my patient has when she faces her psychological shadow, but I know that it is courage.

A further consequence of this sort of definition is that it suggests virtue is not merely habitual behavior. If it were just a description of behavior, there's no clear reason why we couldn't define it, since behavior is observable. The point is that virtue is a disposition of the personality that expresses itself in behavior but is not itself merely a system of behavior. The same observable behavior can arise from quite different motivations and inner attitudes, but the virtuous person as a rule evinces a certain quality of personality different from the person who lacks it. We can, for example, recognize the difference between a generous act that might be performed by anyone and a truly generous *person*, the latter possessing a certain personality quality that also assures us that, in most cases, that person will act generously because in some sense "that's who he or she is."

Virtue and Consumer Capitalism

While I don't want to underestimate the difficulty of developing positive psychological habits and while I quite admit that it is usually a bit of trial for any of us to do so, since it seems our nature both deeply desires individuation and psychological development but also often recoils from doing things that consistently move us in that direction, hopefully even this brief sketch intimates something of why I think virtue includes one key to dealing with the negative impacts of consumer capitalism on the psyche.

Most of the ancient philosophers assumed the psyche is teleological, that it has a purposefulness internal to it that seeks its own development, something which Jung also assumed and which Jung directly drew from the ancient sources. The ancients also assumed we are beings of desire and that our desires tend to be indiscriminate but can be cultivated in a way that is consistent with our life narrative (MacIntyre, 1984). Indeed, the ancient philosophers, especially of the Platonic and Aristotelian variety, thought that this cultivation was not only about action but also about ends. In other words, they thought I could, for example, train myself not only to act in certain ways but to learn to *want* ends that I might not want at first. This was indeed one of their practical assumptions about virtue, namely, that if I don't want what is in my interest, virtue will tend to change *the experience itself* so that I begin to want what I at first did not want.

Needless to say, this vision of the soul is largely in contrast and even in contradiction to the model of consumer capitalism. On the consumerist model, desires are not only indiscriminate but it is to the advantage of the system that they remain so. Further, insofar as the desire has a definite form, it is to be molded primarily by external and subliminally communicated forces, that is, subject to outer control, rather than functioning based on internal and autonomous agency. Consequently, both desire insofar as it is indiscriminate and desire insofar as it is habituated are formed for the benefit of the system via subconscious control. Furthermore, existential anxieties are neither mitigated nor resolved but rather provoked through unease and heightened frustration, without any clear way to manage that frustration.

In contrast, the ancient model of virtue assumes desires should be molded primarily by an internal and conscious vision of what makes a life worth living and cultivated in those terms, in terms of a narrative of life's meaning. Further, rather than bringing an inner sense of scarcity, the development of virtue tends to bring a sense of inner fullness, in sharp contrast to the emptiness of the heart consumer capitalism banks on, so that one will purchase what cannot satisfy. This ancient model of virtue also hits directly on my two examples of the puritan-hedonist situation and the *ressentiment* situation, since among the classical virtues are what were traditionally called the "cardinal virtues," temperance, prudence, justice, and fortitude, which, with a little reflection, we can see to be sharply opposed to the psychological conditions of each of those situations. The virtue of temperance, for example, concerns cultivating a sense for pleasure that is at the service of life, in contrast to the puritan-hedonist problem. The virtue of justice, which assumes a commitment to an order of goods and values conducive to everyone's well-being, tends to counteract the conditions that produce *ressentiment*, as does the general feeling of inner abundance and agency that virtue evokes.

Conclusion

This description of virtue is by no means a panacea for every psychological problem associated with consumer capitalism. Furthermore, until one can help one's patients to be liberated enough from the hegemony of the consumerist ethos over their souls, it can be ineffective even to suggest notions of virtue, because their experience will tend to be the opposite that this model suggests. If one's patients live always amidst the disturbance and frustration of consumerism, they may not be able to believe or understand that desire can be cultivated and cultivated in a way that it doesn't have to be responsive to the subliminal images with which the patient is inundated. Thus, talking about virtue will not yet be of much help in this situation.

However, if one has patients who are free enough of the consumerist ethos that they can reflect on their own desires, on what are the genuine objects of those desires, on which desires are theirs and which not, talking a bit about virtue and the idea that desire can be cultivated and intensified toward one's genuine life aspirations can be a great help. This is particularly so in the stage of analysis Freud calls the "working through" of insight. How often one hears from one's patients: "Now I understand . . . but what do I do with that knowledge?" One possible response is the development of virtue, that is, the developing of habits conducive to the confirmation and intensification of desire by purposely thinking, feeling, and acting on them, in short, by living them.

While virtue is not a major theme in the psychoanalytic tradition, it has lurked there at times, and fine thinkers like Erik Erikson have even used the notion explicitly (Erikson, 1981). Still, a full-blown development of what I am suggesting here would require a larger articulation of how one would describe, discuss, and aid a patient in the development of virtue than I have given. In my clinical experience, one can successfully communicate and encourage virtue in patients once they understand that you do not mean something moralistic and repressive but rather a cultivation and directing of desire habitually toward goods conducive to their life narrative. Virtue can, in other words, be both a useful clinical concept and a partial buttress against the impact of consumer capitalism on the soul.

Nonetheless, the development of virtue or of any helpful psychological habits that aid in the resistance to consumer capitalism will always be difficult in a context in which consumer capitalism is accepted uncritically and fostered as the only possible solution to social and economic problems. Such habits will also be difficult to develop if we cannot cultivate a capacity to say "no" to capitalist excess and cannot recognize the level of subconscious control to which we are subject and work out ways to aid patients in clinical settings who are suffering under this consumerist hegemony. Recognizing some of the social structures and subconscious mechanisms I have described comprise at least a first step for those of us working analytically in settings dominated by consumer capitalism, but also a fuller solution can only be crafted based on ideas similar to the ancient concept of virtue.

Note

1   Jung's general lack of interest in so-called "psychological mechanisms" is suggested in many ways, for example, through his overly broad use of the concept of "projection," which covers virtually any and all psychic and experiential distortions, including ones that had already been differentiated from projection sufficiently by Freud and his followers.

References

Adorno, T. W., Frenkel-Brunswik, E., Aron, B., Levinson, M. H., & Morrow, W. (1969). *The authoritarian personality*. New York: Norton.
Aristotle. (2014). *Nichomachean ethics*. Ed. C. D. C. Reeve. Indianapolis: Hackett.
Bell, D. (2001). *The cultural contradictions of capitalism*. New York: Basic Books.
Erikson, E. H. (1981). *Insight and responsibility: Lectures on the ethical implications of psychanalytic insight*. New York: Norton & Company.
MacIntyre, A. (1984). *After virtue*. Notre Dame: University of Notre Dame Press.
Mises, L. V. (2014). *Human action: A treatise on economics*. Ed. B. B. Greaves. Indianapolis, IN: Liberty Fund, Incorporated.

Nietzsche, F. W. (2009). *On the genealogy of morality: A polemic.* Trans. M. Clarke & A. Swensen. Indianapolis, IN: Hackett Pub. Co.

Plato. (1992). *The republic.* Trans. G. M. A. Grube. Ed. C. D. C. Reeve. Indianapolis: Hackett.

Scheler, M. (1973). *Formalism in ethics and non-formal ethics of values: A new attempt toward the foundation of an ethical personalism.* Trans. and ed. M. S. Frings & R. L. Funk. Evanston, IL: Northwestern University Press.

———. (1998). *Ressentiment.* Trans. and ed. M. S. Frings. Milwaukee, Wis: Marquette University Press.

Smith, A. (1999). *The wealth of nations.* Ed. A. S. Skinner. London: Penguin.

White, J. (2012). Person and environment. Vital sympathy and the roots of environmental ethics. In M. Sanders and J. Wisniewski (Eds.), *Ethics and phenomenology.* Lanham: Lexington Books.

———. (Forthcoming a). *On the psyche of psychoanalysis: Max Scheler's contribution to psychoanalytic clinical theory and practice.*

———. (Forthcoming b). *The Jungian analyst in between life and death. Clinical ethics in the age of pandemic.*

Wiggershaus, R. (1995). *The Frankfurt school: Its history, theories and political significance.* Trans. M. Robertson. Cambridge: Polity Press.

Chapter 10

No Sex Without Coffee: The One Nature and Its Superstructures
Elements of Freudian Materialism

Robert Pfaller

A "Natural Science". And No Psychoanalytic Theory of Culture?

Sigmund Freud's characterization of psychoanalysis as a "natural science"[1] seems at first glance to diminish the prospect of a psychoanalytic approach to the questions of culture. However, this attribution does not so much imply a restriction of its subject matter nor a rejection of normative judgment: after all, even scientific medicine itself, with concepts such as "pathology," "cure," "favorable outcome," "benign manifestation," "appropriateness of intervention" – not to mention the broader questions of medical ethics, such as regarding the legitimacy of euthanasia etc. – presupposes a normative basis for its clinical actions. And so all clinical disciplines must constantly ask themselves a question of cultural theory – namely, from where they derive their norms and whether they are not merely following certain currently prevailing interests.[2] Just as much, every clinical discipline, at least since Molière, has to ask itself the question whether one should perhaps start with what patients perceive as a suffering at an imagination underlying the sensation – and thus at a culturally produced symptom. Every natural-scientific clinic is obviously forced as such to a determination of its own limit, and in order to make this determination, it has to cross this limit a little bit in the direction of cultural theory.

A Norm for Science: Do Not Conceive of More Than One Nature!

However, Freud's claim of a scientific character for psychoanalysis can also be understood in a completely different way – namely, as a philosophical partisanship. Then it was not a description of psychoanalysis but rather a *prescription* for it. As a prescription or demand, it would mean that the goal must be "to establish psychology on a similar basis as any other natural science, e.g., physics."[3] This would be a precise counterpart to the philosopher Benedict de Spinoza's demand that the laws of human affects be investigated in exactly the same way as, say, those of circles or triangles and precisely not in the same way as those who had written about them up to that point. For according to Spinoza:

> Most writers on the emotions and on human conduct seem to be treating rather of matters outside nature than of natural phenomena following nature's general laws. They appear to conceive of man to be situated in nature as a kingdom within a kingdom: for they believe that he disturbs rather than follows nature's order, that he has absolute control over his actions, and that he is determined solely by himself.[4]

To demand a natural scientific approach for psychoanalysis and psychology in this context would therefore mean to presuppose that the human psyche is also a part of nature and that it is subject to the same laws as all other parts. The basic thesis of philosophical materialism is that there is only one nature. Or as Spinoza puts it: "nature is always the same, and everywhere one and the same in her efficacy and power of action."[5]

This view also underlies Freud's remark according to which "spirit and soul [are] objects of scientific research in exactly the same way as any things foreign to man."[6] This presupposition means for Freud's enterprise to distrust all descriptions in which the psychic facts are traced back to two sources that are different in nature. For example, Freud replaces the common term "conscience," which refers to a dualism, with the term "super-ego," which derives from the conception of a single nature: accordingly, the superego is an "advocate of the id."[7] The energy of denial and punishment of the ego is exactly the same that would otherwise have put the ego in tension from the id through drive excitations. Only in this way can Freud explain the first paradox of the super-ego – namely, why the super-ego punishes even more severely when drive excitations are denied than when they are fulfilled. For a dualistic conception, on the other hand, which considers conscience to be a "masterpiece of creation" or an element of "divine origin"[8] of a nature quite different from all the "earthly" things it prohibits, this injustice, this sadism, must remain a mystery. And while the common opinion considers the conscience to be the good in man, Freud recognizes in the need for punishment exercised by the super-ego the "worst enemy of therapeutic effort."⁹

Good Drives, Evil Culture?

This materialistic monism also characterizes Freud's conception of culture. Freud therefore also distrusts all views that, in contrast to the previously described constellation between supposedly earthly drives and heavenly conscience, understand precisely the supposed drive nature of man as something good and worthy of protection, and culture, on the other hand, which acts in a "standardizing," deforming and restricting manner, as something harmful and dispensable.¹⁰ In this respect, Freud does indeed recognize decisive differences between different cultures and also between the different lived norms that prevail "at ground level and on the first floor"¹¹ among different classes within one and the same culture. Certain cultures and certain classes cultivate such a high degree of drive renunciation that they produce neuroses. Such cultures, however, Freud calls "cultures," under quotation marks – as, for example, in the title of his essay "'Civilized' Sexual Morality and Modern Nervous Illness." For such pathogenic "cultures" not only damage individuals and their drive claims, rather, they also damage something about the culture itself. Freud writes,

> The assumption is obvious that under the rule of a cultural sexual morality health and vitality of the individuals can be exposed to impairments and that finally this damage of the individuals by the sacrifices imposed on them reaches such a high degree that on this detour also the cultural final goal would be endangered.¹²

For culture has the claim to promote the happiness of the individuals (this concept of culture is represented by the late Freud as well as by the early Freud¹³). But if it makes them ill instead, it does not deserve the name of culture. After all, culture is there for people – and not vice versa people for culture, so that no human sacrifice for it would seem too high. Freudian cultural criticism is also downright monistic. It does not criticize culture in the name of the drives that are supposedly untouched by it but rather in the name of culture itself.

At the same time, however, Freud doubts whether the restriction of the drives actually comes from culture alone. One of Freud's most interesting and daring thoughts is the concept of an "organic repression" that precedes all cultural sexual repression and is merely "superstructured" by it.[14] Already in the *Three Essays* Freud had, after all, shown how the apparently joyous anarchy of infantile partial drives is subjected to restriction and hierarchization in the establishment of genital primacy.[15] It is nothing extraneous to the drives; rather, it is drives that first oppose the drives. This insight explains the pessimistic assessment, characteristic not only of the mature Freud, "that something in the nature of the sexual drive itself is not favorable to the achievement of full satisfaction."[16]

The Concept of "Superstructure"

Incidentally, Freud develops here probably the most precise concept that the all too often misunderstood and abused philosophical concept of "superstructure" has ever received.[17] Something at the "base" (in the psychoanalytic case: at the sexual drives) itself opposes the base and demands superstructure. Thus, the base, in order to be base, needs a superstructure. And not only that: it is also a requirement of the base to make this superstructure appear as something alien to it, independent of it. Nothing has such tangible and down-to-earth, interest-led, materialistic reasons as idealism, which declares culture to be something heavenly, disinterested (the real "miracle," i.e., the real cultural achievement in need of explanation, is rather philosophical materialism).[18] One can illustrate this sophisticated relationship with the situation, familiar at least from movies, where two people, say, after a dinner together, are faced with the question of whether to spend the night together. Significantly, and as obvious and mutual as this desire may be, it requires a covering (however transparent): one must ask something like, "Would you like to come in for a coffee?" It is the sexual desire itself that confronts itself here and demands its superstructure. Its direct pursuit, on the other hand, would be its ruin.

For this reason, philosopher Louis Althusser drew on Freud to free Marxist philosophy both from its stubborn mechanistic variant (which conceived of culture only as a mere, fully derivable reflex of the economic basis without any life of its own) and from its Hegelian variant, which saw in all phenomena of a society the same, openly apparent "contradiction" that must of itself necessarily lead to a higher stage of development. In a series of programmatic texts, Althusser called for replacing the Hegelian concept of contradiction with the Freudian concept of "overdetermination."[19] In this way, by the way, Althusser succeeded in providing Marxist theory, on the one hand, with a conception of the "relative autonomy" of the parts of the social whole and, on the other hand, with a conception of the unpredictable, contingent, "aleatory" character of history (and of the necessity of this contingency).

This leads to a new overall picture: now it is no longer a simple base that acts on an equally simple superstructure – about as one billiard ball bumps the next one; rather, first of all, the base is no longer something simple. There is, so to speak, a "base 1" (Althusser calls it the "determinant in the last instance"), which gives its stage directions in secret, behind the scenes, and determines which role its representative on stage, the "base 2," is to take – whether it is to play the leading role (as a "dominant" in Althusser's sense) or a supporting role. Accordingly, one is dealing with the influence of a whole on its parts, and a representative of this whole appears as one of its parts among others. The causality that then appears is therefore never an undisguised one, which would take place without "metonymic" shifts (from the whole to the part), overdeterminations, or superstructurings. That is why Althusser writes, "From the first moment to the last, the lonely hour of the 'last instance' never comes."[20] Thus, it is never to be observed how a first ball bumps another, second one; rather, that whole is to be reconstructed, which, so to speak, necessitates several balls at the same time and their "overdetermined" interplay – just the same way as a sex desire requires an invitation to coffee.

The Necessary Indeterminacy of Basic Concepts

This results in the peculiarity that in psychoanalysis, as in Marxist theory, precisely those central concepts that are supposed to serve as explanations of phenomena exhibit a necessary indeterminacy: "economy" or "relations of production" cannot be shown or sharply defined as determinants in the last instance any more than "sexuality," for example. For psychoanalysis, Alenka Zupančič has recently astutely pointed out this elusiveness of the psychoanalytic concept of sexuality and this "ontological" impossibility of precisely determining sexuality. This, however, does not arise from an error at the level of concepts, but is, as Zupančič points out, indicative of the relations at the level of things themselves, a symptom of an "ontological" distortion or curvature in the structure of the world.[21]

Insofar as these consequences arise from the materialist assumption of a single nature, they coincide once again with a Freudian comment on natural science. From today's point of view, perhaps somewhat surprisingly, Freud states once that only the humanities are capable of precise definitions of their basic concepts, whereas the natural sciences have to accept a necessary indeterminacy in this respect:

> I have repeatedly heard the disdainful remark that one can think nothing of a science whose supreme concepts are as fuzzy as those of libido and drive in psychoanalysis. But this reproach is based on a complete misunderstanding of the facts. Clear basic concepts and sharply outlined definitions are only possible in the humanities, as far as these want to grasp an area of facts in the framework of an intellectual system formation. In the natural sciences, to which psychology belongs, such clarity of the generic terms is superfluous, even impossible. . . . Yes, even physics would have missed its whole development if it had to wait until its concepts of substance, force, gravitation and others reached the desirable clarity and precision. The basic ideas or supreme concepts of the scientific disciplines are always left undefined at first.[22]

This necessary indeterminacy concerns, as we can now add, in particular also the concept of "nature" within the Freudian conception of "natural science."

Clinical Symptoms: Distorted Images of Great Social Productions

Precisely from the philosophical monism of Freud's concept of nature arises the consequence that psychoanalysis cannot limit itself to the realm of the clinic. This already follows from Freud's thesis that the impulse to all cultural achievements consists of sublimated sexual energy,[23] as well as vice versa from the fact that, as is well-known, Freud assigned the "moral and aesthetic tendencies in the ego the drive to repression."[24]

Whoever conducts psychoanalysis starting from the assumption of a single nature must therefore be interested in the totality of the prevailing libidinal drives in each case; there can therefore be no sufficient clinical research without taking cultural theory into account, and vice versa. Freud exemplifies this relationship of mutual dependence in his text "Obsessive

Actions and Religious Practices,"²⁵ where he first explains some seemingly incomprehensible features of obsessional neurosis with the aid of certain features of religious ceremonial; then, however, the explicative relationship is suddenly reversed in the text, and Freud is able to solve some of the puzzles of cultural history on the basis of the already known "miniaturization tendency" of obsessional neurosis and its underlying dynamics – above all, the conspicuous aggression tendency of some religions against parts of their own ritual stock.

If it is true that one nature incessantly fabricates cultural superstructures wherever it stands in opposition to itself, then it must be assumed that the stock of symptoms of a particular culture (or of one of its epochs) can only be examined in relation to its stock of superstructures. In this sense, Freud famously remarks that the neuroses show striking correspondences with certain cultural formations, indeed that they can be downright conceived as "distorted images of the great social productions."

> One could dare to say that a hysteria is a distortion of an art creation, an obsessive neurosis a distortion of a religion, a paranoid delusion a distortion of a philosophical system.²⁶

Thus, according to Freud, every clinical symptom has a "normal model" in culture. Every pathology thus also owes its specific shape to the relationship to the culture of its time, without which it cannot be understood.

However, some of Freud's remarks here possibly point to a rather complex relationship between symptom and cultural normal model. For first of all, it could be that a certain condition of culture spares individuals from symptom formation or at least makes it largely invisible. Freud introduced the excellent term of "crooked cure" [*Schiefheilung*] for this connection between culture and clinic.²⁷

A culture obsessed with rituals could make any individual obsessional neurosis disappear. Where, for example, there are many religious people or operators of "positive cults,"²⁸ perhaps almost no obsessional neurotics would be found.

Accordingly, we would have to assume a complementary relationship, a fundamental non-simultaneity of symptom and "normal model" [*Normalvorbild*]. For example, in the taboo societies studied by Freud, obsessional neurotics were hardly to be found; whereas in Vienna around 1900, morality was predominantly based on the principle of guilt, but at most in remnants on the moral shyness or shame that constituted the moral system of the taboo societies.[29] The "*Resemblances Between the Mental Lives of Savages and Neurotics*," named in the subtitle of Freud's essay *Totem and Taboo*, would thus in reality be differences, which are founded in the fact that one culture has a normal model for this form of defense, while the other can only locate it in the realm of pathology. Freud remarks the same thing with regard to the decline of religiosity in modern societies:

> Even those who do not regret the disappearance of religious illusions in the cultural world of today will concede that they offered those bound by them the strongest protection against the danger of neurosis as long as they themselves were still in force.[30]

This complementarity and non-simultaneity of cultural normal model and clinical "distorted image" would be based on the circumstance, repeatedly considered by Freud, that what appears as ego-dystonic striving on the scale of the individual can become the ego-syntonic ideal on the level of the collective: "What belonged to the deepest in the individual soul life becomes the highest of the human soul in the sense of our evaluations through the ideal formation."[31] The "private vices" would thus be public virtues, as depicted in Bernard de Mandeville's famous *Fable of the Bees*, as soon as they were collectivized.[32] And privatization of what was once collectively appreciated led, conversely, to individual rejection and repression.

The "Normal Model": Avoider or Causer of Neurotic Misery?

This finding, however, is in a peculiar contradiction to the circumstance stated by Freud that an overly ambitious ideal formation in the form of a "cultural" sexual morality drives individuals into neurosis. Is the "normal model", for example of a religion with its rituals as well as its sexual moral prohibitions, now the avoider or the causer of the neurotic disease?

Here Freud has left psychoanalytic clinic and cultural theory, a truly not-too-small nut to crack. One could perhaps formulate the resulting research question as follows: when does cultural idealization succeed in "sublimating" individual strivings that would otherwise have to lead to neurosis? And conversely, when does this very ideal formation become the cause of repression and neurosis, without opening up a socially respected way out for the neurotic forms of defense in a ritual activity? Or to put it in Freud's own drastic words borrowed from the proverb: under which cultural conditions does the "young whore" (just like all her counterparts of the other sex) have a chance to become an "old fuddy-duddy,"[33] and under which ones must she become a neurotic?

Possibly Freud's text "Obsessive Actions and Religious Practices" provides a hint here. In it, Freud shows how compulsive acts are finally replaced by prohibitions (abulia) in the course of an increasing miniaturization. Larger compulsive acts had to be given up, when the presence of the repressed in the defensive act itself became too obvious. And this development from "positive" to "negative cults" regularly also characterizes, as Freud states, the history of the great religions.[34] In the prohibition, however, finally too little breakthrough could be contained, in order to still make possible for the individuals the way out into the "crooked cure."

How Culture Assigns the Drives Their Place in the Psychic Apparatus

This opens the perspective on a second relationship between pathology and culture considered by Freud. For the "collectivization" of a symptom does not always seem to mean its elevation to a respected, ego-syntonic ideal, even according to its own collective standard. As a consequence, the spreading to the social standard cannot produce a crooked cure.

This can already be recognized by the elementary features of the taboo societies, whose moral principles appear to the members of these cultures as ego-dystonic, not justifiable, and "nonsensical." In the transgression of the taboo laws, the individuals are rightly innocent before their own eyes, but they see themselves forced to judge the matter with the view of a "dumber," naive observer, who judges only according to the appearance.[35] On the other hand (in contrast to Freud's own misleading comparison[36]), Kant's categorical imperative as the supreme commandment of reason represents, if not an I-syntonic, then at any rate a reason-syntonic principle par excellence: the ego may perhaps still be caught in "pathological" inclinations (in Kant's sense) such as pity or sympathy, but its reason will have to see its necessary ideal in the generality of the moral law.

Let us draw the following preliminary conclusion: the conflictual drive base produces cultural superstructures that have a specific effect on this base. In particular, the cultural superstructure determines where within the psychic apparatus certain drive components can be located – in the id, the ego, or the super-ego. For example, sexuality can be localized in the id as an annoying vice, or as an occasionally prescribed[37] "folly" (in the sense of Erasmus of Rotterdam); it can be reckoned, as by the hippies, for example, as an ego-conforming, joyful, and socially beneficial, peace-loving practice on the level of the ego; or it can even migrate, for example in the form of the ancient "marital duties," into the department of the super-ego. Depending on the case, this makes certain forms of defense either necessary or superfluous. Individuals may come into conflict with certain of their aspirations, or they may feel in harmony with them. And the conflicts, like the harmonies, can change their location and frontline within the psychic apparatus.

The "New Pathologies" – and Culture's Contribution

This seems particularly important in view of the fact that at the present time a number of "new pathologies" pose a considerable challenge to psychoanalysis: depression, addictions, certain fears, panics, anorexia, feelings of emptiness, self-injuries, low desire syndromes, etc., in many cases represent new forms of suffering, mostly covered only by descriptive notions, in which, at least at first glance, there seems to be a conspicuous absence of any secondary process as well as any transference.[38] They seem to block the access to the unconscious. Opponents of psychoanalysis therefore already sometimes speak of a "disappearance of the unconscious" and would perhaps also like to see psychoanalysis itself disappear with it.

However, if one remembers Freud's cultural-theoretical-clinical monism, the situation is clearly different. One will probably not be able to adequately describe the currently widespread pathologies without looking at the changes in the cultural superstructures. Already in 1998, Alain Ehrenberg had very well described some of these changes in his book *The Exhausted Self*.[39] Whereas until a few decades ago there was a restrictive sexual morality in which individuals wanted some things but were not allowed to do everything, today, according to Ehrenberg, it is almost the other way around: a permissive sexual morality allows people to do many things, but they find themselves more and more unable to want them.

Instead of a crisis of repressing frowned-upon desires, there is now a crisis of wanting; its typical symptom is depression.

Psychoanalytic theory will do well to recall its best cornerstones for analyzing this situation. Obviously, due to culture, some of the psychic drives have now changed their place within the topic; as a consequence, they leave individuals even more perplexed than the classical pathogenic "cultural" sexual morality. Only through a precise examination of the changed cultural superstructures will it be possible to find the key to understanding these new pathologies, seemingly free of conflict and yet so fraught with suffering.

It may be possible to add some descriptive as well as explanatory features to the picture drawn by Ehrenberg. The culture of postmodernism that has prevailed in rich Western capitalist societies since the 1980s has brought about some changes that have not been without effect on the topical organization of the psyche of its members. On the one hand, this culture is relatively permissive, but on the other hand, it is so only because everything universal and all norms are repugnant to it. Universalistic principles, ethical ideals, unwritten institutions of sociability and politeness, ideas of beauty as well as gender roles appear to postmodernism as "normative" and only hinder the supposed development of individuals and identity-political groups. The Freudian idea that ideals are also sources of pleasure, since, as Freud notes, there is always "a sensation of triumph" "when something in the ego coincides with the ego ideal,"[40] is alien to this culture. The only ideal of postmodernism, one might say, is for the self to be its own ideal – in keeping with the pop-culture-dominating imperative to "Be yourself!" (or as Ehrenberg puts it, "être soi").

On the one hand, this means that individuals largely lose the incentive of higher ideals; they cannot acknowledge anything greater than themselves, and perhaps in brief moments feel at one with the role provided for them by the ideal. On the other hand, however, the lack of such higher (or considered higher) cultural values means that certain practices can no longer represent excesses appreciated or even "commanded" by culture;[41] they can no longer be given higher value. Without an upper floor, nothing can be sublimated from the lower floor.[42]

This seems consistent with the variant considered by Freud, wherein the spread of a practice no longer leads to its elevation. Thus, cultural conformity no longer rewards individuals with "crooked cure"; rather, it is precisely their unrestrained compliance with the prevailing cultural forms that apparently leads them into a kind of "crooked disease." [*Schieferkrankung*].

People who might not have become neurotic before now become so by following the imperatives of a culture of postmodernity, which suggests to them the rejection of all saving ideals. Committed to their own ego, many today find themselves as perplexed by the ego-dystonic social dimensions of sexuality as they are by the claims of their own desires. And unable to follow sociable precepts such as the little "rites of interruption" – by which people can procure for themselves the "Sacred in everyday life"[43] well described by Michel Leiris (for example, by talking about something other than work during a coffee break) – individuals form new forms of illness. The social imperatives of postmodern culture are paradoxically imperatives of asociality because of their hostility to everything universal.[44] Sociability is to be banned from public space because of its "normative," ego-dystonic character; the social utopia of postmodernism is therefore a completely aseptic public space in which no one touches anyone else. As a grotesque prolongation and parody of these postmodern tendencies appear the emergency measures imposed at the moment of writing this text to ward off the Corona virus, in which so-called "social distancing" is proclaimed as the highest virtue of social behavior.

And while earlier generations rebelled against the prevailing norms in the name of supposedly better norms, we are currently experiencing perhaps the first generation in living memory that is not rebelling against its parents' generation.[45] Whereas in the past the protest of the young, which was at least partially recognized as socially useful and innovative, had its clinical distorted image in the "neurotic protest" of the hysterics, today the normal social model of far-reaching protestlessness may itself be the accommodation, if not the cause, of what in postmodern times would have to be called "neurotic affirmation."

These cursory remarks can admittedly not claim to provide the detailed investigation of the phenomena. They are only meant to show that we are currently not dealing with a disappearance of the unconscious but only with a culturally conditioned rearrangement of the corresponding forces – and that psychoanalysis, due to its materialistic monism, which always takes into account the total stock of symptom and culture formations, is perhaps even the only theory that possesses the necessary tools for diagnosis and improvement. If the new pathologies currently seem to confront the clinic with massive puzzles, perhaps it is psychoanalytic theory that will one day be able to reply (in the words of Villiers de l'Isle-Adam), "This sphinx has found its Oedipus!"

Notes

1 Siehe dazu z. B. Sigmund Freud (1924 1925d): *An Autobiographical Study*, in *Gesammelte Werke*, Bd. XIV. Frankfurt a.M. 1999, S. 31–96, hier S. 84; *SE*, 20: 7–70; here: 57. Sigmund Freud (1940a 1938): *An Outline of Psychoanalysis*, in *Gesammelte Werke*, Bd. XVII, *Studienausgabe* (hereafter *S.*) 63–123, hier *S.* 81; *Standard Edition* (hereafter *SE*), 23: 139–207; here: 159. Cf. Christfried Tögel: »›Eine grobe Ungerechtigkeit‹: Psychoanalyse keine Naturwissenschaft? Zu Freuds Verständnis von Theorie und Empirie«, www.freud-biographik.de/Toegel%2020EINE%20GROBE%20 UNGERECHTIGKEIT%BB%20PSYCHOANALYSE%20KEINE%20 NATURWISSENSCHAFT.pdf (accessed 19.3.2020).
2 Siehe zu diesen Fragen André Michels, Susanne Gottlob & Bernard Schwaiger (Hg.): *Norm, Normalität, Gesetz*. Wien/Berlin 2012. In the preface, the editors pointedly note, "Thus psychoanalysis faces the double reproach of wanting to adapt the individual to the standards (norms) of society, but not satisfying those of the natural sciences" (my translation, ibid., p. 9).
3 Freud 1940a [1938], *An Outline of Psychoanalysis*, S. 81. *SE*, 23: 159.
4 Spinoza, Benedict de: On the Improvement of the Understanding. *The Ethics. Correspondence*. Trans. from the Latin, with an Introduction by R. H. M. Elwes. New York: Dover, 1955: 128.
5 Spinoza, ibid.: 129.
6 Sigmund Freud (1933a). *New Introductory Lectures on Psycho-Analysis*, in *Studienausgabe*, Bd. I. Frankfurt a.M. 1989, S. 448–608, hier: *S.* 586; *SE*, 22: 1–182; here: 158.
7 Sigmund Freud (1923b). *The Ego and the Id*, in *Studienausgabe*, Bd. III. Frankfurt a.M. 1989, S. 273–330, hier: *S.* 303; vgl. auch S. 319.; *SE*, 19: 1–66; here: 36; cf. also 52.
8 A conception that may feel encouraged by Immanuel Kant's comparison of the conscience with the starry sky; cf. Freud (1933a). *New Introductory Lectures on Psycho-Analysis*, in *Studienausgabe*, Bd. I. Frankfurt a.M. 1989, pp. 448–608, here: p. 500; *SE*, 22: 1–182; here: 61.
9 Sigmund Freud (1933a). *New Introductory Lectures on Psycho-Analysis*, S. 541; *SE*, 22: 1–182; here: 109.
10 This kind of cultural criticism is typical not only for Jean-Jacques Rousseau's view, which is usually used as the key instance of this, but also, for example, by the ancient Cynics, who, as is well-known, declared the sense of shame to be an expendable, easily dismissible, merely culturally persuaded conceit. See for this Diogenes Laertius: *Leben und Meinungen berühmter Philosophen*, Hamburg 1990, S. 328ff.

11 For this reference to the title of a play by Johann Nestroy, see Sigmund Freud (1916–17): *Introductory Lectures on Psycho-Analysis*, Bd. I. Frankfurt a.M. 1989, S. 33–446, hier: *S.* 345. *SE*, 15: 1–239 and *SE*, 16 241–463; here: 352.
12 Sigmund Freud (1908d). "Civilized" sexual morality and modern nervous illness, in *Studienausgabe*, Bd. IX. Frankfurt a.M. 1989, *S.* 9–32, hier: *S.* 13. *SE*, 9: 177–204, here: 181.
13 Siehe dazu Sigmund Freud (1930a). *Civilization and its Discontents*, in *Studienausgabe*, Bd. IX. Frankfurt a.M. 1993, S. 191–270, hier: *S.* 217; *SE*, 21: 57–145; here: 85.
14 Siehe dazu Sigmund Freud (1905d): *Three Essays on the Theory of Sexuality*, in *Studienausgabe*, Bd. V. Frankfurt a.M. 1989, *S.* 37–146, hier *S.* 85; *SE*, 7:123–243, here: 178. Cf. Freud (1930a), *S.* 229; *SE*, 21: 57–145; here: 98. For Freud's use of the notion of "superstructure" see for example Freud (1916–17): *Introductory Lectures on Psycho-Analysis*, in *Studienausgabe*, Bd. I. Frankfurt a.M. 1989, pp. 33–446, here: p. 377; *SE*, 15: 1–239 and *SE*, 16 241–463; here: 389; Sigmund Freud (1923b). *The Ego and the Id*, in *Studienausgabe*, Bd. III. Frankfurt a.M. 1989, pp. 273–330, here: p. 304; *SE*, 19: 37.
15 Siehe Freud (1905d). *Three Essays on the Theory of Sexuality*, S. 62–85; *SE*, 7:123–243, here: 152–178.
16 Freud (1930a). *Civilization and Its Discontents*, S. 208; *SE*, 21: 57–145; here: 76.
17 See for this, Philippe de Lara: Superstructure, in Georges Labica (Hg.): *Dictionnaire critique du marxisme*. Paris 1982: 846–851.
18 This paradox has been well acknowledged by Epicurus, who states, "Someone who insists that everything happens by necessity cannot object when someone else says that not everything does. For they say that thing too thanks to necessity" (Epicurus, Fragment 40 from Usener's 1887 *Epicurea*).
19 See for this Louis Althusser: "Contradiction and Overdetermination," www.marxists.org/reference/archive/althusser/1962/overdetermination.htm (accessed: 2022–01–31) and "On Marx and Freud," trans. by Warren Montag, in: *Rethinking Marxism*, Vol. 4, No. 1 (Spring, 1991), pp. 17–30, www.tandfonline.com/doi/abs/10.1080/08935699108657950?journalCode=rrmx20 (accessed: 2022–01–31).
20 Louis Althusser: "Contradiction and Overdetermination," www.marxists.org/reference/archive/althusser/1962/overdetermination.htm (accessed: 2022–01–31)
21 Siehe Alenka Zupančič: *What Is Sex?* Cambridge and London: MIT Press, 2017.
22 Freud (1925d [1924]). *An Autobiographical Study*, S. 84f.; *SE*, 20: 7–70; here: 57.
23 Siehe Freud (1908d). "'Civilized' Sexual Morality and Modern Nervous Illness," *S.* 18; *SE*, 9: 177–204; here: 187.
24 Freud (1923b). *The Ego and the Id*, S. 303; *SE*, 19: 1–66; here: 36.
25 Sigmund Freud (1907b). Zwangshandlungen und Religionsübungen, in *Studienausgabe*, Bd. VII. Frankfurt a.M. 1989, *S.* 11–21; *SE*, 9: 115–127.
26 Sigmund Freud (1912–13). *Totem und Tabu*, in *Studienausgabe*, Bd. IX. Frankfurt a.M. 1993, *S.* 287–444, hier: *S.* 363; *SE*, 13: 13–161; here: 73.

27 Sigmund Freud (1921c). *Group Psychology and the Analysis of the Ego*, in *Studienausgabe*, Bd. IX. Frankfurt a.M. 1993, S. 61–134, hier S. 132; *SE*, 18: 65–143; here: 141.
28 For the distinction between "positive" and "negative" cults, see Emile Durkheim: *The Elementary Forms of the Religious Life*, 2nd ed. London: Allen and Unwin, 1976.
29 On the distinction between shame and guilt cultures, which is also extremely relevant for psychoanalytic theory, see Ruth Benedict: *The Chrysanthemum and the Sword. und Schwert. Patterns of Japanese Culture,* London et al.: Routledge and Kegan Paul, 1977; cf. Richard Sennett: *The Fall of Public Man*. New York: Knopf, 1977.
30 Freud (1921c). *Group Psychology and the Analysis of the Ego, S.* 132; *SE*, 18: 65–143; here: 119.
31 Freud (1923b). *The Ego and the Id, S.* 303; *SE*, 19: 1–145; here: 36.
32 Bernard [de] Mandeville: *The Fable of the Bees. Private Vices, Public Benefits*. Norderstedt: Hansebooks, 2018.
33 Siehe Freud (1905d). *Three Essays on the Theory of Sexuality*, S. 140; *SE*, 7: 123–243; here: 238.
34 As we might add from today's perspective, this dynamic also shapes everyday culture: positive cults such as greeting, complimenting, offering cigarettes, etc. are increasingly replaced by negative cults and prohibitions.
35 I have devoted a more detailed analysis to this motif in Robert Pfaller: *On the Pleasure Principle in Culture. Illusions Without Owners*. London and New York: Verso, 2014, chapter 9.
36 Siehe Freud (1912–13). *Totem and Taboo*, S. 292; *SE*, 13: 7–161; here: 14.
37 In this respect, I have tried to show that from the "lower" instances of the psychic system emanate not only drive claims but also social imperatives, together with a corresponding observation. That is why I suggested to speak of a "sub-ego." See Robert Pfaller: The Sub-Ego. Description of an Inferior Observing Agency, *Problemi*, 3(3), 2019: 143–156.
38 See for this Karl Stockreiter: *Die neuen Formens des Symptoms. Vom allmählichen Verschwinden des Unbewussten*. Unpubl. Manuscript, 2020.
39 Alain Ehrenberg: *La Fatigue d'être soi – dépression et société*. Paris: Odile Jacob, 1998.
40 Freud (1921c). Group Psychology and the Analysis of the Ego, *S.* 122; *SE*, 18: 65–143; here 131.
41 Siehe zu dieser Formulierung Freud (1921c). *Group Psychology and the Analysis of the Ego, S.* 122; *SE*, 18: 65–143; here: 131.
42 For clarification, it should be added here that the "commandments" to excess come not only from the super-ego but especially in certain forms of sociability or generosity from the "sub-ego." On birthdays, it is simply "proper" to toast the celebrant with champagne. The individual alcoholism can probably be "healed" and spared by such a commanded transgression to a certain extent. These are mild, foolish imperatives, which have the advantage over the "higher," more I-syntonic imperatives that they do not lend themselves to expansion into fanatical convictions. The advantage of the imperatives of the lower ego is that (like the principles of magic and taboo) they never had to be

believed. No one has to be convinced himself that drinking champagne on his birthday helps, and yet somehow it seems to help.
43 Michel Leiris: The Sacred in Everyday Life, https://opencuny.org/religionandthesacred21/files/2015/10/The-Sacred-in-Every-day-life-Michel-Leiris.pdf (accessed: 2022–02–02).
44 See for this, for example, Andreas Reckwitz: *Die Gesellschaft der Singularitäten. Zum Strukturwandel der Moderne*. Berlin: Suhrkamp, 2017.
45 For example, "Fridays for Future" is a thoroughly parent-friendly and highly parent-supported protest.

Chapter 11

Shrinking Vistas
Critical Theory, Psychoanalysis, and the Postmodern Mire

Kurt Jacobsen

Martin Jay's *The Dialectical Imagination* introduced a generation – indeed several generations – of scholars to the Frankfurt School and its ambitious integration of psychoanalysis into a reinvigorated, freewheeling, nondogmatic Marxist analysis of society.[1] A psychoanalytically astute historical accounting of the family and of childhood promised to provide the "crucial link between Freud and Marx," Loewenberg noted, "between the micro-individual and macro-social economic scenes, in each epoch."[2] And there is obviously no reason why accounts should cease at childhood.

This radical scholarly vision was also an expansive one, which plumbed the complex psychic interior of humankind in a multitude of circumstances and cultures. The reason why dialectical reason does not disintegrate in these adventurous applications is because the project is firmly moored in historical materialism. The world, and our comprehension of it, does not flail about on a jellied platform of treacherously inadequate words. The unconscious was not only not "structured like a language," as Lacanians insist, it was a potentially liberatory force, to the degree it can be flushed out, detected, and integrated into consciousness.

Sartre, Fromm, and Reich were among those who attempted to meld Marx and Freud, with varying degrees of success. Those quests were all rooted, or strived to be rooted, in a materialist substrate, very unlike an influx of postmodernists enamored of Lacan, Lyotard, Derrida, Deleuze, and less problematic, Žižek. The Frankfurt critical theorists were all mindful of the dynamic class conflict within which they conducted their oft-derided "mandarin" inquiries. For a dramatically peripatetic band scrabbling through a Great Depression, two world wars, and a hair-trigger Cold War, this was not very hard to do.

The musty teleological expectations of party line Marxists were woefully inadequate and even counterproductive in spotting the system's

DOI: 10.4324/9781003215301-11

snares and figuring out what was really at play. A capitalist crisis by itself, no matter how dire, simply did not augur a new utopian dawn. People operated not only by what they encountered in what has come to be called "bare life" but also by what they have been accustomed or conditioned to see and expect. Analysts and activists had to account fully for subjective factors without at the same time exaggerating their importance.

Since the 1970s, aspiring avatars within psychoanalysis mounted a challenge to the conceptual framework (and Enlightenment values ambivalently underpinning it) that propelled the critical theorists and their far-flung and disparate successors. What remains for critical theorists if they succumb to postmodernist critiques whose word-centric acid dissolves the emancipatory project that motivated the Frankfurt School, for all its multilayered cultural critiques? Is all the critical theory–inspired work since Jay's book appeared now a superseded or spent force? Is the ultimate lesson of Lacan that the otherwise admirable "ruthless criticism of everything existing" can devour critical theory itself? Do we heed, and enlist in, the Lacanian turn which unravels any basis for a Marxist-psychoanalytic critique in the first place? Why? Because after Lacan, the pathetic porous "subject" is so hamstrung and befuddled by an unacknowledged "lust for error" that he/she/they are trapped forever in a maze of detours and dead ends supposedly inherent in language. Terminally and gratuitously sicklie'd o'er by the pale cast of thought. Who and what does this Lacanian strain of "ruthless criticism" serve anyway, and is it as ruthless as it pretends to be when addressing its own origins and motives?[3]

In what follows, I reflect on the animating purposes of the Frankfurt School, the occasional parallels with Lacan, and the exceedingly strange but entirely understandable displacement of one critical approach by the other in much of academe today. The critical theorists opened many intellectual doors, but sadly, one doorway led some enthusiasts to a Swiftian plane of tragicomic logorrhea, of word-centric neurosis, and of game-theory fancies replete with geometric exigencies, parabolas, and Borromean knots signifying nothing much.[4]

Critical Theory Rebooted

The thrill of discovering Frankfurt School critical theorists in the seventies was that they pried open a stilted universe of inquiry. Many scholars who were newly attracted to critical theory literature were not and never would be Marxists in any party or ideological sense. But they saw in its profoundly subversive formulations a powerful critique of a consensual liberal paradigm consisting of narrow positivism, naive statistics, and formal theory. To penetrate beneath the level of appearances, one needed to understand external politico-economic forces in history and the ways in which various actors in different class locations process the events they are engaged in and thereby decide how to act together or against each other. Psychohistory of the Eriksonian stripe was another exciting route to the pursuit of the same comprehensive (which Sartre called "totalizing") goals, though sanitarily shorn of any Bolshevik taint.[5] By contrast, political psychology was, and still is, largely a psychologistic evasion of, rather than an illuminating complement to, rigorous political and economic analysis. Another boost for critical theory was that Marx's *Economic and Philosophical Manuscripts* came to circulate widely around the same time, casting the hitherto stern and off-putting Marx in a far different and utopian-philosophical light.

The supreme problem for the Frankfurt school, given what they witnessed in a Nazifying Europe, was that economic conditions alone did not shape or predict political outcomes. Economic determinism was finally *kaput* (except perhaps in the pages of the *Wall Street Journal* and the *Financial Times*). There were also cultural and psychological factors internal to collectivities and to individuals that mediated how they reacted to their plights. The touchstone of critical theory, wherever else it wandered, was man's self-emancipating activity in the historical process, in class struggles we are all engaged in whether we realize it or not, for which psychoanalysis seemed to offer a set of keys that promised to unlock the darkest and most distant obstructions.

Max Horkheimer summarized critical theory's bold, bristling approach as contending "that the fact that subjective interest in the unfolding of society as a whole changes continuously in history is not regarded as a sign of error, but as an inherent factor of knowledge," and indeed that to

> realize an explicit interest in a future rational society the prerequisite is that the individual abandon the mere recording of facts, that is, mere calculation; that he learn to look behind the facts; that he distinguish the essential from the superficial without minimizing the importance of either; that he formulates conceptions that are not simple classifications of the given, and that he continually orient all his experience to

definite goals without falsifying them: in short, that he learn to think dialectically.⁶

For Marcuse, critical theory subsumed "ontological tension between the essence and appearance, between 'is' and 'ought,' which become historical tensions, and the 'inner negativity' of the object world becomes understood as the work of the historical subject – man in his struggle with nature and society." The couch-bound adjustment-oriented solipsism of the classic and (sometimes unjustly) lampooned Park Avenue or Hampstead shrink was summarily ditched here.

> Reason becomes historical reason. It contradicts the established order of men and things on behalf of existing societal forces that reveal the irrational character of the order – for "rational" is a mode of thought and action which is geared to reduce ignorance, destruction, brutality, and oppression.⁷

The intrinsically subversive goals for the here and now could not be clearer.

For all the accusations of patrician pessimism lodged against them, critical theorists clung to a stubbornly optimistic creed; without which, after all, there was little point to their endeavors.⁸ Theodor Adorno's controversial co-authored inquiry into the roots and causes of the authoritarian personality was the most famous of these expeditions.⁹ All the adapted psychoanalytic conceptual tools would prove useful for taking on the complacent pluralists and behavioralists who essentially claimed – with a good deal of justice at the time – that in postwar industrial societies, conscious class conflict (below the top rungs, which went unmentioned except for rebels like C. Wright Mills)¹⁰ pretty much gave way to the muting and dissipating influences of ethnicity, creed, locality, culture, gender relations, and so on.¹¹ The latter factors had to be encompassed in any persuasive and useful social analysis.

The Frankfurt project spearheaded by Horkheimer, Marcuse, and Adorno never lost sight of their emancipatory goal, so that the scholars they influenced could discard the more downbeat political implications of Freud and other psychoanalytic practitioners whilst highlighting the revolutionary content and potential they espied. Marcuse arguably brought this tendency to a head with the publication of *Eros and Civilization* in 1956 with its landmark critical conceptual markers, such as "surplus repression."

The Frankfurt critiques of what went hideously awry in the Soviet Union gave nothing away in ferocity and venom to standard conservative critics,[12] though we now know that just as you don't have to be German to be a Nazi, you don't have to have been a Soviet citizen to be a party-liner credulously absorbing what apparatchiks on MSNBC or Fox News choose to spew. And on a similar note, Fromm's survey research in the 1930s revealed that much of the German working class, including left-wingers, and not just the communists, were alarmingly authoritarian in their family lives and in their expectations of whichever force installed a new order.[13] These alarming discoveries reputedly stirred preparations to exit Germany more swiftly than the Frankfurt scholars otherwise might have done – a rare case of researchers being saved by their findings.

Herbert Marcuse published both *Eros and Civilization* and *One Dimensional Man*, including in the latter a widely ridiculed but now more resonant plea for a "pacified technology." Both volumes became classic meta-critiques of modern capitalist cunning and dissimulation. Capitalism adapted grudgingly but swiftly to the tacit social contract with Labor, forged in the 1930s, by securing its ideological hold via consumer culture (with some groups obviously excluded or slighted) and reinforced a cult of managerialism against any hint of worker control and participatory democracy. Marcuse showed how the system's use of "repressive desublimation" seduced a newly expanded middle class into its thrall or at least into passive acquiescence. Marcuse made sparkling sense of what a young generation were encountering in the Vietnam and post-Watergate era. (Fromm too, as a distant sort of Frankfurt alumnus, authored many fascinating and more accessibly written books on topics such as the sources of human destructiveness in a land of paradoxical plenty.)[14] What was gravely underestimated then was the sheer tenuousness of the gains that the middle class – achieved in the fleeting "golden age," 1945–1973.[15] The fact that the (more or less) evenly split gains between capital and labor were liable to be eroded at the first opportunity was not widely appreciated or feared.[16] Meanwhile, critical theorists bemoaned the lack of appropriate "preconditions" for revolutionary change in this brief era of middle-class prosperity.

Critical theorists were excoriated for obsessing about the cultural realm, toward which circumstances and the lack of overt class conflict originally propelled them. The allegedly ethereal sages were too detached from, or not alert enough to, what transpired on the shop floors and the service industry offices in management-labor battles. While it's difficult to find anything more acerbic and satisfying than Marcuse's essay on William Calley and My Lai, there really wasn't much work that tackled the kind of subjects that preoccupied contributors to the *New Left Review* or *Monthly Review*. The saving grace was that critical theory relentlessly attacked the pretensions of positivism, of value-neutrality, of brute empiricism (as did C. W. Mills and others), and measured everything in terms of contributions to anticipated emancipatory outcomes. Ironically, in the most vulgar of Marxist terms, recent conditions might be "ripening" in the US via a corporate donor-controlled legislature, oligarchs bailed out whilst 11 million people lost their homes and, to add salt in the wounds, paid taxes to shore up the fortunes of the sociopathic swindlers whose machinations caused their downfall. The result? Still no national health care system, the steady offshoring of skilled jobs, and steadily declining chances to attain even a pallid version of the American Dream and the ominous enveloping of all these trends by a climate emergency.

The critical theorists actually never lost sight of the economic base during their patrician forays into the innards of the interrelated superstructure. Progress in their heyday seemed stalled, after all, because too many people were amenable, consciously or otherwise, to integrating resignedly or rancorously into the seemingly stable system. Even as "golden age" conditions frayed, sputtered and reversed, the grip of a subtle system of domination on consciousness remained strong. What needs to be done now is to identify, expose and counter these conscious, subconscious, and unconscious influences despite their appearances – when they do appear – as perfectly natural, inevitable as or immutable laws of nature.

"For Marx, man's senses only bring him into contact with appearances; the essence of anything, the major relations of which it is composed, can only be learned through lengthy investigation and study," Ollman noted. Here, controlled experiments (where possible), reductionism, imaginative reconstruction of broken links, and the like make use of the results of immediate perception to uncover the "hidden substratum."[17] Few intellectual tasks are more exhilarating than stripping a false layer of maya, of illusion, of lies, or of deadening habit to get at an underlying truth, or telling aspect of it. But one nagging question that postmodern philosophers, raised for all of us is how far does one reasonably go in such escapades? Doesn't ruthless *mean* ruthless and "must not be afraid of its own conclusions"?[18]

Freud Refurbished

Freud himself is customarily regarded as a forbiddingly conservative curmudgeon, but his record mostly indicates otherwise.[19] He worked with a wide circle, including many socialist psychoanalysts.[20] His advocacy of free clinics for the non-bourgeois and his looking grimly upon the Soviet experience is a shared view with many left-wing critics unconnected and indeed antagonistic to the CP. And then there was Freud's general decency. What the Frankfurt scholars did with Freud, his followers, and any number of apostates was to adopt their tools to purposes of political analysis (far less so, to agitation) without apologies and with some remarkable speculative extensions.

No theoretical sally surpassed Marcuse's simple yet seditious concept of "surplus repression." This radical notion upended every conventional economics textbook, every tiresome establishment nostrum, and all the assiduously cultivated cynicism that induced us to succumbing to the status quo. The implacable world of scarcity no longer objectively confined us; it was other quite identifiable forces that did the job and impeded human liberation and satisfaction. Certainly, adequate means were technologically available – though their concomitant environmental costs were ill understood – so that the entire rationale for civilization to meanly dole out dribs and drabs to the toiling masses evaporated into thin air. The socio-economic system had no excuse except inertia and crude self-interest to continue as it did, a message that was deeply unwelcome in the upper tiers. Just as psychoanalytically inflected critical theory proved itself most revealing in investigating the generation of consent, let us call it, in affluent mass consumer conditions, the familiar mechanisms of capitalist exploitation kicked into gear again, albeit in streamlined neoliberal guises. Still, the Frankfurt critiques remained relevant to any analysis of the "totality" of exploitative activity. The critical theorists never relinquished the tight bond between coruscating critique and emancipatory aims.

The Lacanian Striptease

Enter Jacques Lacan. The Lacanian perspective is hardly unprecedented in its ardent attentiveness to language and its relation to the psychic field. R. D. Laing, Lacan's younger contemporary, argued that "the choice of syntax and vocabulary is a political act that defines and circumscribes the manner in which 'Facts' are to be experienced. Indeed, in sense it goes further and even creates the facts that are studied."[21] Laing was quick to admit he was operating along the same grooves as many existential and phenomenological analysts, who in turn had their own forerunners to cite. So the clarion call sounded before Lacan, though the earlier concerns were not so dire that they cast the knower who uncovers this "fact" about facts as perforce surrendering to perpetual doubt or chasing one's own tail, which is what the dogged and allegedly universal pursuit of the *objet petit a*, for example, amounts to.

Instead, Laing noted,

> The "data" (given) of research are not so much given as taken out of a constantly elusive matrix of happenings. The quantitatively interchangeable grist that goes into the mills of reliability studies and rating scales is the expression of a processing we do on reality, not the expression of the processes of reality,[22]

Which is a rather useful alert that helps us to grasp the contours of ideological or intellectual systems that we cannot help but inhabit. Laing was untroubled by "turtles all the way down" ontological implications, because any such plummet presumably would crash head-on into the formative (as well as distortive) effects of tangible interest-laden institutions. We still manage, however imperfectly, to operate, critique, reconstruct, and love in rational purposive ways, whatever the sway of hitherto unconscious forces.

So Lacan asserted that the unconscious is structured like a language (which one?) and furnished us with plenty of gnomic maxims, such as "Speech is the murder of the thing" and that the "Real is what does not depend on my idea of it" (which is close to Erik Erikson's likewise coy definition of reality as that which we cannot do anything about).[23] To many jaded onlookers, everything interesting or comprehensible in Lacan's *oeuvre* is paralleled, or close enough, to what a horde of predecessor analysts already detected or averred. Lacan also ingratiatingly told youngsters that most of their teachers are stupid, a sentiment that resonated deeply with the French students and associates in the "moment of madness" spring of 1968.[24] Across the Atlantic Ocean, some US students, at any rate, came to understand the acute legacy of the McCarthy years in curbing, if not wiping out, social critique among most of their university teachers, who were intimidated rather than just stupid.[25] Still, who can cavil when Lacan stipulates "an urgent task to isolate, in concepts that are being deadened by routine use, the meaning we recover when we re-examine their history and reflect on their subjective foundations," or urges us to question master narratives?[26]

Nothing sabotages clarity, let alone the Frankfurt School's goal of emancipation, more swiftly than the diktat that words "cannot completely convey exactly what we want them to mean."[27] Who says, and more to the point, perhaps, so what? It's rather like being informed one has no free will, which, if one is badgered or beguiled into accepting this proposition, circularly proves it to be true. One countermove is embracing the trusty Alfred E. Neumann motto "What – me worry?" because the ballyhooed "best" is patently the enemy of the good here inasmuch the Lacanian take is obstructive to the aspirations for social justice. A fair but abstract philosophical question otherwise gets elevated, suffocatingly, to a supreme presupposition so that we behold the cartoon centipede, asked which foot it puts forward first, tumbling to the dirt in a froth of indecision and angst.

The symbolic order, like ecclesiastical original sin, condemns us to exile from the paradise of totally knowing ourselves due to the slipperiness of the incorrigibly paltry words we wield. Yet we willy-nilly participate in a shared order where meanings are liable to alter in the passage along the mysterious circuits between ourselves and delivery to others. There is "meaning in the unconscious but the meaning cannot enter the chain of language without suffering a fundamental loss so therefore it escapes description."[28] Lacan insisted on the "materiality of language that transforms an organic given to a symbolic creation" even though the words will always fail us because, among other impedimenta, they are suffused with narcissism, which is a contention that might well be regarded as a humbling or cautionary point but instead is treated as a fundamentally discrediting one.[29]

But with that said, did Freud ever promise, let alone require, *total* knowledge of ourselves in order to be comfortable within our skins or societies? Still, we must ruthlessly criticize everything, mustn't we? Peel all those pesky cloudy membranes deftly away until something (or nothing) emerges.

The first step in this process can be a giddy and addictive moment. Penetrating appearances is surely what Marxist analysis portends, moving, for example, beyond legal appearances of free equal exchange to the grubby extortive tricks underlying it. Exposing power and its hidden operations is both heady and hazardous, as we see in what the US security state does today in its vendetta against Julian Assange and in its bipartisan maltreatment of whistleblowers. Reforming an establishment, let alone toppling it, cannot happen so long as their narratives go unchallenged. So if one peel is bracing and several are elating, then why not go all the way to unconscious depths? The core is posited by Lacan as a realm addled by fantasy elements (as many psychoanalysts would agree) and by treacherous language itself, so that like Gertrude Stein's Oakland childhood home, there is no "there" there – or maybe something even worse. All these presuppositions queasily smack of a late night college dorm bull session in which some wag proves by a *faux* logical device that God or morality or you yourself do not exist.

Lacan's "mirror stage," which heralds our tentative formation of ourselves, was richly anticipated by George Herbert Mead's symbolic-interactionism and by neo-Freudian Henry Stack Sullivan's emphasis on the role of "reflected appraisals" and later by the relativist manifesto by Berger and Luckman, who five decades or so ago presaged the infiltration of the academic citadel by Lacanians.[30] My own field, political science, tolerates Lacanians (while disdaining non-Lacanian psychoanalysis in general), who, like too many quantitative colleagues, are incapable of understanding, let alone appointing or promoting anyone who is not one of their own.[31] For Lacanians, Sigmund Freud, his followers, and his apostates were uniformly misguided deviants who had to be discarded, like booster rockets, to make way for the culminating revelatory wisdom of Lacan. For academics, Lacan offered a temptingly abstruse word game, requiring a form of hermetic knowledge, and was applicable to numerous topics where scholars could parse their quarries as arbitrarily as they pleased and posed no real threat to reigning authorities inside or outside the campus.

For all the hearty denunciations of critical theorists as effete mandarins (especially during Adorno's ordeal during the student tumult in 1968), they were models of wicked subversion compared to Lacanians. According to Lacan, we all are in vain pursuit of the *objet petit a*, which is a sating of an insatiable or unsatisfiable instinct – and it is an instinct, not a temporary obsession – and there is no learning from it. Empty signifiers are not easily distinguishable from whatever their antonyms are. If there is any insight that Lacanians provide that does not already exists in the wide

Freudian multiverse, one is hard put to find it – and ironically that quest amounts to another *objet petit a* if one wishes to engage in this rewarding but, by definition, superfluous hunt.

What Lacanians promote is not class consciousness or critical theory but a seductive stoicism for the well-nourished and well-lettered. Marcus Aurelius, not Marx, seems to be their guiding light. The war is within, and we know it because a French sage conjured a recondite framework, all-encompassing in its verbal fetters, positing unconscious processes that pervade and disfigure every aspect of human experience. The world ironically shrivels into a Satanic place, filled with booby traps and deceits – especially self-deceits – and there is no exit, except presumably an "authentic" Lacanian analysis. Most Lacanians dare not disturb the universe outside the consulting room, but go J. Alfred Prufrock one better by making a virtue of it. Of course, in such a placid, flaccid universe, Lacanians are the arbiters of unreason. Much like the Straussians or scientologists, bearers of light, the Lacanians affirm one another as truly "cleared" entities and loftily pity the rest of us.

Recognition of the inner drives at play within us is not a path to a liberation, as it is with Freudians, but rather a conceited concession to an immovable yet made-up reality. Exactly how does this philosophical stance aid anyone in subordinate tiers in a world of class struggle? The general materialist analysis of our plight is that the upper class and its minions are capturing all added wealth, winning a class war they insist does not even exist. What is there in Lacanianism that induces one to side with the oppressed or the workers rather than, say, in a Panglossian way that all is for the best in the best of all possible worlds that we can reasonably expect? The Freudians and their intellectual offspring went through more than a century of turmoil over the same heated questions, but few shrinks pretended, or got away with pretending, that politics and economic interests were not involved or important.

The stoic view stems from the proposition that "so much of our disappointment and rage, after all, stem from the clash between our misperceptions of things and the reality of things." All very well. The way one behaves one-on-one with a cop (at, say, a traffic stop) or pays taxes is likely to be different than the way one views and experiences the police in the wider society or the skewed systemic way in which taxes are allocated and collected. This is a long game we are involved in, which is very different than resignedly saying that is the way things are or, with the late conservative don Michael Oakeshott, that this is the best of all possible worlds, and everything in it is a necessary evil.

The critical theorists were preoccupied with the problem that, regardless of a flurry of *objet petit a*s, the vagaries of *jouissance* and unreliable signifiers, the overarching economic system (and the powerful if monomaniacal actors running it) have duly converted and subordinated their own self-serving symbolic-interactionist systems into instrumental interpretations that dominate almost everyone.[32] The rapture of the positivist forms of science are no different in their diversionary capacity than the insidious gnawing away at the basis for any genuine knowing inherent in Lacan, yielding a philosophy utterly aligned with neoliberal designs to convert everything into a commodity or else thin air so long as it keeps the surplus value seeking machinery in motion.

As Habermas noted with respect to scientists, what is required here is "self-reflection which would show that the subject of the process of inquiry forms itself on the foundation of on intersubjectivity that as such extends beyond the transcendental framework or instrumental action" in the case of positivists and, in the case of Lacanians, of morbidly insular frameworks.[33] Lacan posed a self-sabotaging core, which, if consented to, functions as a deterrent for reasoned action. The upshot is what the critical theorists would term quietist, for all the contrarily intriguing and passionate sallies of a Žižek. The theoretical arbitrariness is disturbing. So is their ritualistic cramming of all material and other models into Lacanian categories so that they are digested in just the way Lacanians desire. The scarcely disguised contempt with which many Lacanians treat anyone they deem not privy, fit, or capable of embracing their creed is not an endearing trait either.

All priesthoods are alike. Why choose – (and it is a choice) – to view the unconscious inherently as if it were a perpetual saboteur? Another valid enough choice is the soaring one surrealists proposed, very much in the spirit of the critical theorists:[34]

> Surrealist activity escapes from rhetoric; it endeavors to extend human experience, to interpret it outside the limits and framework of a narrow rationalism. . . . Rapt hope in the future, interpretation of the marvelous as a sign of the beyond . . . concern to lift all prohibitions to

attain the "life of presence, nothing but presence" hope of changing the world by liberating desire – such are the motifs which lead Breton to condemn the writers who speak of asceticism or dualism and to cherish those who promise the reconciliation of man with the world and with himself. . . . Revolution is for Breton only one of man's tasks – a task that derives its sense only in the ought of its end, which must be thought or felt independently of means to attain it.

Conclusion: The Pale Cast of Thought

One can find exceptions to this portrait of the Lacanian enterprise. Žižek is one, and so are Ian Parker, Adrian Johnston, and Robert Pfaller. But it is instructive to note that Žižek and Parker committed themselves to historical materialist studies before they began to dally with Lacan. For the critical theorists, dialectical reason evolved from the commendable side of an Enlightenment, an Enlightenment that was also tainted by dangerous and domineering technological impulses. A largely 1960s generation was attracted to Jay's *The Dialectical Imagination* and the scholars he introduced because it promised a vibrant and expansive approach to the wider pressing social problems they wanted to solve or at least alleviate.

When Lacanians write glibly that "powerful State interests use the trick of repetition, to increase their status while trying to alleviate anxiety about their not having any basis for authority other than manipulation of images and signs to repeat their claims and insist on their privileges," one detects a cramped kind of language game, a deliberate and premeditated one, and not the lack-fixated Lacanian formulation.[35] Have the writers ever heard tell of the modern state's monopoly on legitimate violence and willingness to deploy it whenever necessary to buttress its "mastery over the void"?[36] How does this Weberian nugget come into play? Humans are reduced by Lacan to what can be faultily represented, a far cry from the libidinal creature in classical psychoanalysis who, apart from being at the outset divinely selfish, was unruly and freedom-seeking too. Revolutionary material, one might call it. Lacan departs from rather than returns to Freud, as Daniel Burston catalogues.[37]

Horkheimer held that "rational knowledge does not controvert the tested findings of science; unlike empiricist philosophy, however, it refuses to terminate with them."[38] The Frankfurt School excoriated the purveyors of "subjective reason," wherein the subject, who carelessly or artfully examines his ends and presuppositions, becomes the criterion of truth, and in this respect, Lacan and his followers seem devout perpetrators. The critical theorists fretted that science implicitly collaborates with the prevailing distribution of power, while Lacan disarms them even of trust in language for self-defense. Chomsky noted that science "should be encouraged (though fallacious argument and investigation of silly questions should not), but it is not an absolute value," and if the implications of research are regressive or inane, then why pursue it?[39] Bruno Bettelheim, well outside radical camps, nonetheless championed Freud's humanistic thrust, demonstrated the beauty and clarity of Freud's use of language, which was treated as an instrument for clarifying thought and feelings, not disarraying them.[40] Bettelheim may be wrong and Lacan right, but we possess no decisive and indisputable means by which to determine the verdict. So where shall we place our bets? The critical theory goal of the enrichment and emancipation of humanity may be wildly idealistic. Even so, it seems preferable to an arcane Lacanian doctrine as attractive, engrossing, and frivolous as any Milton Bradley board game of yore. Marx in his 1843 letter advocating ruthless criticism also noted that "reason has always existed, only not always in reasonable form."

Notes

1 Martin Jay, *The Dialectical Imagination; A History of the Frankfurt School and the Institute for Social Research 1923–1950* (New York: Little, Brown and Company, 1973). The literature on the Frankfurt critical theorists since has been vast. I leave it to other essayists to fill out the bibliography, for fear of annoying repetition.
2 Peter Loewenberg, *Decoding the Past: The Psychohistorical Approach* (New York: Alfred A. Knopf, 1983), p. 33.
3 One should acknowledge that Lacanians, according to one savant, come in at least three adversarial breeds: "none of whom is very willing to compromise: anti-Lacanian psychoanalysts wanting to protect disciplinary orthodoxy against the infiltration of purportedly metaphysical forces; external (non-psychoanalytical agencies) perceive the Lacanian ideology as the pinnacle of an inherently abusive scheme and Lacanian psychoanalysts themselves pitting one interpretation of the master's narrative against the other." Danny Nobus, "Knowledge in Failure: On the Crises of Legitimacy within Lacanian Psychoanalysis," in Ann Casement (ed.), *Who Owns Psychoanalysis?* (London: Karnac, 2004), p. 204. None of the adversarial aspects seem to me to matter regarding inclusion as subjects of this essay.

4 See, for example, Philip Mirowski, *Machine Dreams: Economics Becomes a Cyborg Science* (New York: Cambridge University Press, 2002).
5 Kurt Jacobsen, "The Devil His Due: Psychohistory and Psychosocial Studies," *Psychoanalysis, Culture and Society*, 26 (September 2021), pp. 304–322 as well as Kurt Jacobsen, "Paradigmatic Saboteurs: Eriksonian Psychohistory and its Vicissitudes," *Journal of Psychosocial Studies*, 13, 2 (June 2020), pp. 165–178.
6 Max Horkheimer, *Critical Theory: Selected Essays* (New York: Herder & Herder, 1972), pp. 162, 181.
7 Herbert Marcuse, *One Dimensional Man* (New York: Beacon Press, 1964), pp. 11, 118.
8 See Stuart Jeffries, *Grand Hotel Abyss: The Lives of the Frankfurt School* (London: Verso, 2016).
9 Theodor Adorno, Else Frenkel-Brunswick, Daniel J. Levinson, and R. Nevitt Sanford (eds.), *The Authoritarian Personality* (New York: Harper, 1950) Also see Robert Altemeyer, *Right-Wing Authoritarianism* (Winnipeg: Manitoba University Press, 1981). A considerable literature has arisen just on differences between these two books.
10 C. Wright Mills, *The Power Elite* (New York: Oxford University Press, 1956).
11 Ralf Dahrendorf, *Class and Class Conflict in Industrial Society* (Stanford: Stanford University Press, 1959).
12 On the degrading of dialectical thinking in the USSR, see Herbert Marcuse, *Soviet Marxism* (New York: Vintage Press, 1961), pp. 121, 122. Also on Soviet ideology as a "triumph of subjective reason," as a logical formalism abjectly obedient to a totalitarian status quo, see Max Horkheimer and Theodor Adorno, *Dialectic of Enlightenment* (New York: Herder & Herder, 1972), pp. 26–27.
13 E. Fromm, *The Working Class in Weimar Germany: A Psychological and Sociological Study* (Cambridge: Harvard University Press, 1984). Also see Gotz Aly, *Hitler's Beneficiaries: How the Nazis Bought the German People* (London: Verso, 2016).
14 E. Fromm, *The Anatomy of Human Destructiveness* (New York: Holt, Rinehart and Winston, 1972).
15 Stephen Marglin and Juliet B. Schor, *The Golden Age of Capitalism* (New York: Oxford University Press, 1992).
16 The customary cite here, recognizing the rollback of workers' shares of income and wealth since the 1970s, is Thomas Piketty's *Capital in The 21st Century*, most of all because its sensational sales signaled that the phenomenon no longer could be ignored in polite circles.
17 Bertell Ollman, *Alienation: Marx's Concept of Man in Capitalist Society* (Cambridge: Cambridge University Press, 1971), p. 89.
18 Karl Marx, Letter to Arnold Ruge (September 1843). Robert Tucker, "The Marx-Engels Reader," https://genius.com/Robert-c-tucker-the-marx-engels-reader-chapter-14-for-a-ruthless-criticism-of-everything-existing-annotated.
19 See Kurt Jacobsen, *Freud's Foes: Psychoanalysis, Science and Resistance* (Lanham: Rowman & Littlefield, 2009), Chapter 1.
20 See Russell Jacoby, *The Repression of Psychoanalysis: Otto Fenichel and The Political Freudians* (Chicago: University of Chicago, 1986); Elizabeth Danto,

Freud's Free Clinics: Psychoanalysis and Social Justice (New York: Columbia University Press, 2007); Lynne Layton, Nancy Caro Hollander, and Susan Gutwill, eds. *Psychoanalysis, Class and Politics: Encounters in The Clinical Setting* (London: Routledge, 2006); Joanna Ryan, *Class and Psychoanalysis* (London: Routledge, 2017); and Daniel Jose Gaztambide, *A People's History of Psychoanalysis* (Lanham: Lexington Books, 2021).

21 R. D. Laing, *The Politics of Experience* (New York: Ballantine, 1968), p. 62.
22 Ibid.
23 Charles Sanders Peirce, whom both French postmodernists and critical theorists disdained, put his case this way: "There are real things, whose characters are entirely independent of our opinions about them, those realities affect our senses by regular laws" and "any man, if he has sufficient experience and reason enough about it, will be led to the true, one conclusion." *Peirce's Essential Writings*, edited by Edward C. Moore (New York: Beacon Press, 1973), p. 133. See Jurgen Habermas's critique of Peirce as offering "an evolutionary substitute for lost instinctual mechanisms." *Habermas, Knowledge and Human Interest* (New York: Beacon Press, 1971), p. 134.
24 Nobus, "Knowledge in Failure," p. 209; Sherry Turkle, *Psychoanalytic Politics: Jacque Lacan and Freud's French Revolution* (London: Free Associations Books, 1992, 2nd ed), Chapter 1. Also see, for a wider critical survey of the "hermeneutics of suspicion," Peter Dews, *Logics of Disintegration* (London: Verso, 1987).
25 For a trenchant view of Lacan as recklessly revising rather than returning to Freud, see Daniel Burston, *Psychoanalysis, Politics and the Postmodern University* (New York: Palgrave, 2020). "For example, Lacan described the ego as a particular kind of object in the subject's field of experience, whereas Freud insisted – repeatedly, both early and latter – that the ego's operations are for the most part entirely unconscious, a fact that Lacan (and Lacanians generally) glibly ignore." p. 49.
26 Jacques Lacan, *Ecrits* (New York: Norton, 2002).
27 Charlotte Epstein, "Who Speaks? Discourse, the Subject and the Study of Identity in International Relations," *European Journal of International Relations*, 17, 2 (2010), p. 336.
28 Alexandre Leupin, *Lacan & the Human Sciences* (Omaha: University of Nebraska, 1991), p. 3.
29 Ibid., p. 2.
30 Thomas Berger and Peter Luckmann, *The Social Construction of Reality* (New York: Doubleday, 1967).
31 On this group quirk see Kurt Jacobsen, "Perestroika dans la Science Politique Americain," *L'Economie Politique*, 26, 2 (Winter 2004–2005), pp. 95–105.
32 Habermas, *Knowledge and Human Interests*, pp. 134–135.
33 Ibid., p. 139.
34 Ferdinand Alquie, *The Philosophy of Surrealism* (New York: Barnes and Noble, 1972), p. 42.
35 Willy Apollon and Richard Feldstein (eds), *Lacan, Politics, Aesthetics* (Binghamton: SUNY Press, 1996), p. xiii.
36 Ibid.

37 Burston, *Psychoanalysis, Politics and the Postmodern University*, p. 51 onward.
38 Max Horkheimer, *Critical Theory: Selected Essays* (New York: Seabury Press, 1972), p. 211
39 Noam Chomsky, "Psychology and Ideology," in *For Reasons of State* (New York: Vintage 1973), p. 360.
40 Bettelheim rued any rendition of psychoanalysis perceived and consumed "as a purely intellectual system," Bruno Bettelheim, *Freud and Man's Soul* (New York: Vintage, 1983), pp. 6–7.

Chapter 12

Mapping the White Unconscious

Critical Race Theory, Whiteness Studies, and Psychoanalysis

Daniel Burston

Introduction

Nowadays, phrases like "critical race theory," "anti-racism," and "wokeness" are used interchangeably in daily conversation, both by advocates and critics of these movements. This usage may or may not be welcome or warranted, but it is certainly a sign of the times. After all, all these movements were brought into being by the stubborn persistence of racism in American life. Since the murder of George Floyd in May of 2020, critical race theory and its offspring, whiteness studies, have gained ground in academia, in medicine, the mental health professions, and the business and entertainment worlds. Because they now have a substantial impact on classroom instruction in our universities, and increasingly influence contemporary psychoanalytic discourse, they are immediately relevant to the concerns of critical theorists, who have been (more or less) continuously engaged in an intimate and ongoing dialogue with psychoanalysis ever since Max Horkheimer recruited Erich Fromm to the Frankfurt Institute for Social Research in 1927.

Of course, the circumstances in which the (mostly Jewish) founders of the Frankfurt School found themselves were different from those confronting contemporary American anti-racists activists today. The Nazis' stated mission was to achieve world domination for the "Aryan race" and to obliterate the chief obstacle to their plans, namely, "world Jewry." To achieve their goals, the Nazis had to nullify the progress made over two hundred years of gradual de-ghettoization when, in the wake of emancipation, Jewish intellectuals and artists played an increasingly active role in German art and letters or became prominent scientists, doctors, lawyers, etc. After centuries of isolation and bloody persecution, German Jews were accepted

DOI: 10.4324/9781003215301-12

grudgingly into the mainstream, only to have the gains they made over two centuries completely overturned by the rise of fascism (Elon, 2003).

As is well-known, the early history of the Frankfurt School is inseparable from this historical context. In effect, Horkheimer and his colleagues all watched as the legacy of German Enlightenment and the promise of equality crumbled and vanished into thin air (Elon, 2003). And this was merely a prelude to the genocide to come! As a result, the first generation of Frankfurt School theorists were preoccupied with understanding and exposing the roots of anti-Semitism but had comparatively little to say about anti-Black racism in the USA (and elsewhere) during the 1920s, 1930s, 1940s, and 1950s. This oversight was understandable, however, because while the myth of "White Supremacy" was central to the Nazis' program of world domination, anti-Semitism was *always* its central focus. By contrast, anti-Black racism was almost an afterthought. an ever-present and taken-for-granted feature of Nazi ideology, but never its primary target.[1]

That state of affairs shifted somewhat during the 1960s, when two Frankfurt School alumni who chose to remain in the USA rather than return to Germany welcomed and embraced the civil rights movement. Erich Fromm's socialist-humanist approach to social activism drew on the prophets for inspiration and had a great deal in common with the nonviolent struggle for civil rights embraced by Dr. Martin Luther King Jr. (McLaughlin, 2021, Chapter 4). By contrast, Herbert Marcuse had a good deal more sympathy for the Black power movement and the Black Panthers, evidenced, among other things, in his mentorship of Angela Davis (Jeffries, 2016, pp. 319–322). Sadly, however, neither of these theorists developed systematic or expansive theories to account for or to redress anti-Black racism, and the Frankfurt School's neglect of this issue left a gaping lacuna for other theorists to fill in the course of time.

Given the circumstances in which critical theory arose, the fact that some critical race theory practitioners claim a sense of kinship or continuity between critical theory and critical race theory calls for careful reflection. And here, I confess, I advise caution. Why? First, because the term "critical theory" is used too broadly nowadays to include thinkers as disparate as Antonio Gramsci and Jacques Derrida, both quite famous, but neither of whom were connected to the Frankfurt School for Social Research. Another reason to be cautious in drawing comparisons between critical theory and critical race theory is that the latter is deeply influenced by postmodernism, while critical theorists like Leo Lowenthal and Jürgen Habermas were sharply critical of postmodernism (Lowenthal, 1987; Jeffries, 2016).

Finally, on a more personal note, my latest book, titled *Anti-Semitism and Analytical Psychology: Jung, Politics and Culture* (Burston, 2021), takes an unsparing look at C.G. Jung's invidious comparisons between the "Aryan unconscious" and the "Jewish unconscious." As I pondered Jung's harmful declarations on this score, it became quite evident to me that anyone who ventures to speculate about the "collective unconscious" of another "race" or racialized group is in danger of succumbing to and/or perpetuating stereotypes and caricatures that can be harmful, while remaining blissfully unaware that they are doing so (see e.g., Burston, 2021, Chapter 3). So while critical race theory got off to a promising start in relation to psychoanalysis, I am deeply dismayed by the remarks of some contemporary psychoanalysts who speculate about the "White mind" or the "White unconscious," who veer sharply into dangerous territory.

Critical Race Theory and Psychoanalysis

Critical race theory emerged from a body of scholarship in the legal profession launched by the late Derrick Bell, the first African American to get tenure teaching law at Harvard in 1971. In the 1980s, Bell and his associates called attention to the prevalence and persistence of racism in America and to the steady erosion of the gains made by the Civil Rights movement because of adverse decisions by the Supreme Court. As a cumulative result of these decisions, and the market machinations of powerful business elites, said Bell, the dream of racial equality remains elusive because structural racism and profound economic disparities still blight the lives of African Americans, Indigenous people, and other minorities of color.

In the 1990s, critical race theory began to influence and penetrate other fields, including education, political science, sociology, philosophy, and more recently, health care, public health, and theology as well. It also spawned a new academic field, whiteness studies (Delgado and Stefancic, 2017, pp. 85–92). As Delgado and Stefancic point out,

> For several centuries, at least, social scientists have been studying communities of color, discoursing learnedly about their histories,

cultures, problems and future prospects. Now a new generation of scholars has put whiteness under the lens and examined the construction of the white race. If, as most contemporary thinkers believe, race is not objective or biologically significant but constructed by social sentiment and power struggle, how did the white race in America come to exist, that is, how did it come to define itself?

(Delgado and Stefancic, 2017, p. 85)

Given its expanding spheres of influence inside and outside the university, it was only a matter of time before critical race theory and whiteness studies began to influence the mental health professions – psychoanalysis, psychology, psychiatry, and social work. This is a relatively recent development, so it is worth noting that one of the founders of critical race theory, Charles Lawrence III, employed psychoanalytic concepts quite skillfully in a landmark paper titled "The Id, the Ego and Equal Protection: Reckoning with Unconscious Racism" in the *Stanford Law Review* in 1987 (Lawrence, 1987). Lawrence made the point that racism is normal in our society, not an aberration or the exception, nor even a product of overt psychopathology. And to that end, he addressed the defense mechanisms – like displacement, reversal, repression, denial, projection – by means of which the majority of citizens who are "well adjusted" to a racist society remain smugly oblivious to their own racist attitudes and behavior and perpetuate it without a trace of self-awareness or remorse. He also demonstrated how Supreme Court decisions sometimes reflect an unconscious racist bias shared by the dominant (white) majority in diverse ways, becoming, in effect, an instrument of white supremacy, a critique that seems especially relevant given the composition of the Supreme Court today and the battle over Steven Breyer's future replacement on the bench.

To drive his point home, Lawrence described American racism as both a crime and a disease, which, strange as it may sound, was both a brave and eloquent indictment and an unfortunate choice of words. Calling racism a crime is a potent figure of speech but is not a statement of fact. On the contrary, racism is obviously *not* a crime – at least in purely legal terms – when the law actively permits or encourages its presence and persistence in the body politic. Neither is it an infectious illness or degenerative disorder that threatens the well-being of the racist person. These are analogies or metaphors at best. Lawrence might have been wiser to follow Erich Fromm's usage and call racism a "socially patterned defect" (Fromm,

1941), or even a "pathology of normalcy" (Fromm, 1955) – something akin to a deficiency disease, except what is lacking in people so afflicted are not vital nutrients or sunlight but a lively conscience and a keen critical faculty, faculties which have been stunted or atrophied under the pressure of social forces (Burston, 1991).

In 2008, Professor Lawrence published another article that dwelt on what he termed the "collective unconscious" of white society and acknowledged that his earlier claim that everyone is racist – regardless of their skin color – was designed to diminish the defensiveness of his white colleagues in the legal profession, an effort to mitigate or sidestep their resistance to his argument. His honesty on this score is commendable, but sadly, these remarks may also have set the stage for some worrisome developments today, when psychoanalysts now purport to elucidate "the White unconscious," borrowing tropes from critical race theory and Whiteness studies and applying them in a heavy-handed and polemical fashion. In the process, they end up trying to rewrite history and disseminating banal stereotypes and harmful generalizations about white-skinned people, which obscure our common humanity and deepen the tensions and divisions between white and non-white-skinned communities through a new brand of racial essentialism, one which bears an uncanny resemblance to the racial stereotypes they claim to deplore, almost as if they were their inverted mirror image.

Aruna Khilanani: Guilt, Rage, and "White Psychopathy"

Let us start with Dr. Aruna Khilanani, a board-certified forensic psychiatrist and psychoanalyst who delivered a talk titled "The Psychopathic Problem of the White Mind" for Grand Rounds at Yale University's Child Study Center on April 6, 2021. Her virtual talk was open to the public and was well received, although it was only made available to students and faculty who had Yale ID, accompanied by a "trigger warning" that her talk contained profanity and violent imagery. Dr. Khilanani's talk was surreptitiously recorded by a member of the audience and "leaked" to journalist Katie Herzog, who published some of her remarks and interviewed her for Bari Weiss's substack, titled *Common Sense* on June 4, 2021.

Before getting to the substance of her remarks, a bit of context is in order here. In her interview with Katie Herzog, Dr. Khilanani disclosed that she trained in medicine and psychiatry at Columbia, Cornell, and New York University. Before studying medicine, however, Dr. Khilanani earned an MA at the University of Chicago, where she majored in English literature and critical theory. Her studies at the University of Chicago appealed to her, she says, because she was already interested in "the unconscious" and in other (unspecified) "different ways of thinking." However, when asked what she meant by "the unconscious," she told Katie Herzog the following:

> Critical theory is about how you are positioned in the world. Ever since I was a little kid, since I've interacted with people who are white, and especially white women, I would notice that things were really off. So what I've done by going through psychoanalytic training, which is all about getting in touch with the unconscious, is literally work backwards. I'm like, "OK, I've noticed that white people tend to put me in certain roles. White women will experience me this way, white men will experience me this way." I'm going to use psychoanalysis to work backwards and treat all of this as a projection to see what I can learn about their mind.

Two things are striking about this response to Herzog's question: first, the lack of clarity and specificity, and second, a tendency to conflate critical theory and psychoanalysis. (Yes, the histories of psychoanalysis and critical theory are intricately intertwined, but at the end of the day, they are *not* the same thing.) Moreover, when asked about the nature of the unconscious, she answered elliptically and promptly lapsed into autobiographical reflection. Indeed, as the interview unfolded, Dr. Khilanani never defined or attempted to describe more fully what she means by "the unconscious," beyond the observation that it has something to do with how people "organize" their anxiety. Worse yet, in this same interview, Dr. Khilanani asserted that the unconscious "is different for everybody," an assertion that flatly contradicts her essentialist perspective on "the White mind" and white guilt, which we address further in the next section.

Nevertheless, her remarks here do illumine her motives for undergoing psychoanalysis. By her own admission, she embarked on psychoanalytic training primarily to understand how *other* people – specifically, white people – act, think, and feel as they do toward *her*. A desire for deeper self-knowledge and/or acquiring the knowledge and skill to remedy unnecessary suffering in others – the usual motives that prompt people to enter analysis – are not even mentioned in passing here.

With these thoughts in mind, let's turn to the actual substance of her remarks. Here are some things Dr. Khilanani said on April 6, 2021:

> This is the cost of talking to white people at all. The cost of your own life, as they suck you dry. There are no good apples out there. White people make my blood boil.
>
> (Time stamp: 6:45)

> I had fantasies of unloading a revolver into the head of any white person that got in my way, burying their body, and wiping my bloody hands as I walked away relatively guiltless with a bounce in my step. Like I did the world a fucking favor.
>
> (Time stamp: 7:17)

> White people are out of their minds and they have been for a long time.
>
> (Time stamp: 17:06)

> We are now in a psychological predicament, because white people feel that we are bullying them when we bring up race. They feel that we should be thanking them for all that they have done for us. They are confused, and so are we. We keep forgetting that directly talking about race is a waste of our breath. We are asking a demented, violent predator who thinks that they are a saint or a superhero, to accept responsibility. It ain't gonna happen. They have five holes in their brain. It's like banging your head against a brick wall. It's just like sort of not a good idea.
>
> (Time stamp 17:13)

Now in fairness, before she unleashed this torrent of abuse, Dr. Khilanani informed her audience:

> I want you to observe your thoughts and feelings as I talk. I said, there's a difference between a thought, a fantasy, and an action. Now, my reflection on my own rage was actually that I was feeling impotent. So that's where I was going with that. And kind of normalizing

feelings of hatred. This is stuff that exists and I need to dive deep within myself to reflect on how it is that I got here. So there is a reality here, like did I actually cut white people out of my life? Absolutely.

The cumulative impression one gets from these remarks is that Dr. Khilanani never intended to deliver a well-researched, well-thought-out presentation but decided well in advance of her talk to simply unleash her anger and contempt for white people, declaring that there is no point in talking to them (although, by her own admission, that is precisely what she was doing at the time). Apart from the catharsis she evidently hoped to achieve by expressing her rage and disappointment so forcefully, the purpose of Dr. Khilanani's talk, as she herself admits, was to *normalize feelings of hatred*. And this too poses a problem. To "normalize" something is to make it more prevalent or more commonly accepted than it was previously. But normalizing hatred is precisely the opposite of what civil rights leaders like Dr. Martin Luther King and Desmond Tutu sought to do. Indeed, they counselled their followers to confront their oppressors with dignity and resolve and to speak truth to power but *not* to hate their oppressors, even as they challenged their bizarre racial prejudices and sought justice and equality for themselves and their children. After all, hatred is a toxic emotion that fosters an atmosphere of fear and mistrust, which in turn obstructs cooperation and collaboration among individuals and groups.

So though many Americans will doubtless defend Dr. Khilanani's (First Amendment) right to "normalize feelings of hatred," if she so chooses, this tactic sounds and feels much more like political theater than it does like a searching and scholarly analysis. This becomes apparent in her disclaimer to Katie Herzog:

> So when I was saying that talking to white people is useless, I'm not actually really saying it's useless because if I really thought it was useless I wouldn't devote time to doing this. I'm talking about an experience that I have, that people of color have, of futility when coming up against a psychological defense. So it's an experience of futility.

So there we have it. Rather than engaging her audience in searching reflection on the sense of futility people of color often feel when attempting to discuss race matters with white folks, Dr. Khilanani *performed* it in front of a live audience, believing this approach would have more impact. Did it? Who knows. Either way, this still begs the question whether "the normalization of hatred" and the denigration and dismissal of the vast majority of white-skinned people in the name of theory (or indeed, of anything else) really advances the cause of social justice for people of color or whether the kind of racial essentialism that Dr. Khilanani promotes threatens to derail or disfigure that project in the long run. Here are some examples of her racial essentialism. In conversation with Katie Herzog, Dr. Khilanani said the following:

> People of color, myself included, suffer from being positioned in the world, psychologically, and the stuff that goes with it: violence, this, that. Now, white people suffer from problems of their own mind. They suffer with trust, they suffer with intimacy, they suffer with closeness, shame, guilt, anxiety. They suffer with their minds. Don't get me wrong, people of color are also neurotic and have their own stuff and ups and downs. But there is a fundamental issue I think that is very unique to white suffering and I think that's their own mind.

Sadly, this way of framing the issue sidesteps the fact that experiences of trauma and loss, abuse, and neglect have a similar impact on our psyches regardless of the color of our skin and that poor whites are also "positioned" in a way that exposes them to a far greater risk of suffering from ill health, violence, incarceration, suicide, substance abuse (and so on) than their more affluent white counterparts and that with the rise of neoliberalism, impoverished and marginalized white folk comprise an increasingly large percentage of the overall (white) population. Moreover, and more importantly, on reflection, it averts attention from the fact that many people of color also struggle with issues of intimacy, loss, guilt, shame and anxiety, and with unresolved (and often unconscious) inner conflicts concerning their parents, siblings, and families of origin, whether they seek treatment or not. Yet Dr. Khilanani insists that the suffering of white people is merely "of their own mind" and "unique," and when asked why, she replied,

> It's going to be hard for me to give you a one sentence soundbite on this but I would say, a high level of guilt. I've never seen anything like this before. Other than in white people not eating bread, an incredible

level of shame. Feeling really exposed all the time. A lot of perfectionistic tendencies. Not letting themselves move forward. Experiencing themselves as passive a lot.

When pressed to elaborate, Dr. Khilanani continued, saying,

> White people have an intense level of guilt. I have never seen a level of guilt that I see among white people. I mean, white people don't eat bread. Think about that. There have been wars all over the world over grains and bread and only here, white people are depriving themselves. Think about that shit.

Furthermore, she adds,

> Everyone has this gluten allergy and you're like, what the fuck is a gluten allergy? That's a psychosomatic symptom. If you actually talk to a GI doctor, they're going to say, "Well, there's Celiac and there's everything else" with a wink, and you know what the "everything else" is. It's all the guilty gluten people.

And by way of further explanation, she says,

> I don't deny that people may get symptoms, but how is it that all these people suddenly now, after all the violence has occurred, are not eating bread. It's like the weirdest fucking thing.

And finally, she said, "The bread is about guilt and needing to keep them in a state of deprivation and stay guilty." When asked by Katie Herzog whether she thinks that white people actually *should* feel guilty, Dr. Khilanani replied, "No, I think guilt is the most useless emotion on the planet. What function does it serve? It's not helpful."

So in Dr. Khilanani's learned opinion, any and all sensitivity or aversion to gluten that falls short of Celiac disease in severity, that is, is not actually life threatening, *must* be psychosomatic in origin, despite the fact that many accomplished medical doctors and researchers disagree clearly with her appraisal. She ignores the fact that many non-white people also suffer from gluten sensitivity and deems avoidance of gluten – and more specifically, of bread – to be rooted in lingering guilt feelings associated with colonialism and the lies that were promulgated and designed to support it but provides not a single shred of evidence – beyond her clinical intuition – that this is in fact the case. She then adds that guilt is "the most useless emotion on the planet" that "serves no useful purpose."

This last remark is illuminating because it stands in stark contrast with Freud's ideas about human development and with mainstream psychiatric opinion. Indeed, by the end of their sophomore year, every psychology major has learned that one of the hallmarks of psychopathy is precisely the *absence* of real guilt or remorse over a person's past misdeeds. So on the one hand, Dr. Khilanani claims that white people are psychopaths. On the other, she claims that they are riddled with guilt and psychosomatic disorders. Clearly, something is amiss here. You cannot maintain both these positions simultaneously without lapsing into double think or complete incoherence. These reflections also serve as a reminder that in Freud's estimation, guilt is emphatically *not* a useless emotion; that in optimal circumstances, that is, when one's guilt feelings are not excessive or irrational, but proportionate to our actual deeds or phantasies, its presence serves to curb antisocial behavior and preserve a measure of decency and civility in human affairs.

The preceding reflections also prompt a question *not* raised by Katie Herzog in her interview with Dr. Khilanani, namely, whether white people, thus construed, are qualified to treat patients and/or train psychoanalysts who are not white-skinned. Based on Dr. Khilanani's remarks, one would assume that the vast majority of white clinicians are at once so guilt-ridden and so oblivious to their own collective "psychopathy" that they are unsuitable as therapists for non-whites. This suspicion is buttressed by Dr. Khilanani's remarks on white people's political leanings. For example, she scorns liberals and claims that conservatives are psychologically healthier because

> they are more in touch with their anger and negative feelings. They can articulate it. They can say it, they're not covering it up or like "Oh my god, I'm amazing, I love all people." There's not all this liberal fluff of goodness. Conservatives can go there. They can say things that are uncomfortable that I think liberals would shirk at or move away from or deny.

She continues,

> I would feel more comfortable hanging out with Anne Coulter than a lot of liberals because she's unlikely to do anything. She's in contact

with her anger and her hatred, and I think that needs to be worked through, don't get me wrong, for the country to heal, but she's actually in contact with those feelings that a lot of people can't say out loud and that's a safer space. Now do I agree with her? No. But liberals have no access to that at all. The thought is forbidden.

Evidently, then, Dr. Khilanani regards liberal sentiments as inauthentic or superficial and deeply divorced from the repressed rage that all white folks presumably feel because their privilege is being threatened by communities of color. Liberals, by this account, espouse good intentions at the conscious level but lack the inner honesty – and by implication, the courage and self-awareness – to admit to themselves that they are riddled with fear and resentment. So we may ask ourselves, would people like these make good psychoanalysts? Not bloody likely. And yet the vast majority of psychoanalytically oriented clinicians currently in practice are white and would probably identify as "liberal" or left of center if asked. So one wonders, if this view of racial and political polarities prevails in the analytic profession, will it dictate that white psychoanalysts and psychotherapists must be screened for suitability (in light of some as yet unspecified criteria) before being permitted to treat or train non-white people in future? (More on this point later.)

In any case, the essentialist binary that Dr. Khilanani constructs and the fact that she would feel more comfortable in Anne Coulter's company than in the presence of "a lot of liberals" hints at a chilling subtext. Perhaps her preference is not merely because Coulter is (allegedly) more honest, authentic, or "healthy" than her liberal counterparts but because Coulter's politics are profoundly illiberal (or anti-liberal), and on some level, Dr. Khilanani shares Coulter's contempt for liberal values, an attitude increasingly prevalent among critical race theorists (Pyle, 1999), the American Left (Applebaum, 2021), and in university settings generally (Delgado and Stefancic, 2017; Boghossian, 2021). One can only imagine how she feels toward Black liberals, both in and outside the psychoanalytic profession!

Donald Moss: Parasitic Whiteness and the Emotional Plague

We'll return to Dr. Khilanani presently. Meanwhile, let's examine another recent publication that follows along similar lines. Approximately one month after Dr. Khilanani's talk, Dr. Donald Moss published an article titled "On Having Whiteness" in the May issue of the *Journal of the American Psychoanalytic Association (JAPA)*. The article caused a considerable stir both in and outside of psychoanalytic circles (Moss, 2021). Much of the controversy surrounded the circumstances of its publication since the paper was perceived by many readers as a hoax designed to discredit psychoanalysis, although its author was (and is) a respected psychoanalyst, who taught for many years at the New York Psychoanalytic Institute and the San Francisco Center for Psychoanalysis.

But before addressing Dr. Moss's substantive claims, I must start by acknowledging his good intentions. While I strongly disagree with his position, I don't doubt that he meant well when his paper was first conceived. When you consider the crushing weight of the injustices and indignities heaped on African Americans and people of color every day, a trend that spans four centuries in the United States, you can only recoil in horror. You urgently want to say or do something to shake white-skinned people out of their complacency and indifference and motivate them to take action in the name of justice and human decency. Or if you've gradually lost hope on this score, as Moss sometimes seems to have done, you may wish to lament that fact loudly and publicly, in the faint hope of gaining a better hearing that way.

On his professional web page, Dr. Moss says that he has been analyzing and addressing "structures of hatred" against racial minorities and the LGBTQ+ communities since the 1980s, a very commendable thing. Psychoanalysis must engage such issues as the psychological damage experienced by victims of prejudice and persecution is very real. Thankfully, the analytic profession's responsiveness on this score is reflected in the growing number of LGBTQ+ people in positions of authority in psychoanalytic training institutes (Woods, 2020).

Unfortunately, however, African Americans still comprise a vanishingly small percentage of analysts today – merely .007% (Woods, 2020). In response to this disturbing state of affairs, The New York University Postdoctoral Program in Psychotherapy and Psychoanalysis formed a Committee on Ethnicity, Race, Class, Culture, and Language, chaired by Dr. Alexandra Woods. Like Dr. Khilanani and Dr. Moss, Dr. Woods is deeply dismayed by "systemic Whiteness" and the role it presumably plays in maintaining psychoanalysis as a "White Citadel." But it is one thing to be horrified and prodded into action in response to hardships suffered by communities of color and quite another to argue that one's skin color makes one deeply disposed to act in contemptible and antisocial ways, which is where Moss's argument finally ends up.

In his abstract, Dr. Moss says that Whiteness is

> a condition one first acquires and then has – a malignant, parasitic-like condition to which "white" people have a particular susceptibility. The condition is foundational, generating characteristic ways of being in one's body, in one's mind, and in one's world. Parasitic Whiteness renders its hosts' appetites voracious, insatiable, and perverse. These deformed appetites particularly target nonwhite peoples. Once established, these appetites are nearly impossible to eliminate. Effective treatment consists of a combination of psychic and social historical interventions. Such interventions can reasonably aim only to reshape Whiteness's infiltrated appetites – to reduce their intensities, redistribute their aims, and occasionally turn those aims toward the work of reparation.
>
> (p. 356)

Dr. Moss goes on to explain that the term "Whiteness" is capitalized to denote "Parasitic Whiteness," which he defines as (1) a way of being, (2) a mode of identity, and (3) a way of knowing and sorting the objects constituting one's human surround, a condition that, he claims, should not be confused with being phenotypically white-skinned. Nevertheless, he insists that people who *are* white-skinned are uniquely susceptible to acquiring it, and that once acquired, it is nearly impossible to treat. From that point onward, he says, mitigation and harm reduction are the most effective treatment options. Moss then goes on to say that

> Parasitic Whiteness infiltrates our drives early on. The infiltrated drive binds id-ego-superego into a singular entity, empowered to dismiss and override all forms of resistance. The drive apparatus of Whiteness divides the object world into two distinct zones. In one, the Whiteness infiltrated drive works in familiar ways – inhibited, checked, distorted, transformed – susceptible, that is, to standard neurotic deformations. In the other, however, none of this holds true. There the liberated drive goes rogue, unchecked and unlimited, inhibited by neither the protests of its objects nor the counterforces of its internal structures.
>
> (pp. 356–357)

So Donald Moss declares that Parasitic Whiteness "infiltrates" our "drive apparatus," collapsing the various psychic agencies (id, ego, super-ego) into a single entity bent on domination. But how is a psychic collapse this catastrophic possible, absent a florid psychosis? He doesn't say. Nevertheless, according to Moss, this process begins when the infant first experiences stranger anxiety and starts to become cognizant of her caregivers' group boundaries, or definitions of "us" and "them" – that is, those who belong to the caregivers' trusted reference group and those who do not. In theory, at least, this way of framing things allows for the possibility that if a white-skinned infant's caregivers embrace people of color among their kin and friendship groups, the infant will be spared the "infiltration of the drives" that drives them to become "unchecked, unlimited, inhibited by neither the protests of its objects nor the counterforces of its external structures." But more often than not, says Dr. Moss, the result is a sadistic mode of relatedness toward people who are not white.

> Holding these objects in place, inflicting pain on them – this sadism becomes the exquisite and economical solution to any apparent conflict between wanting and hating. Parasitic Whiteness further demeans its nonwhite bodies and beings by way of a naturalizing system of naming and classification. Once it has mapped and transformed its nonwhite objects into such a fixed taxonomical category, the rogue sexuality of Parasitic Whiteness can expand its aim. It permanently maps them as external/away, and from there, wherever that is, these objects are available for limitless use – limitless labor, of limitless kind.
>
> (p. 357)

Stripped of excess verbiage, Dr. Moss is saying, in effect, that white-skinned people are extremely susceptible to acquiring a sadistic and exploitative mode of relatedness toward non-whites that leads them to control and enslave them. Once acquired, this rigid and internalized "taxonomy" is basically locked in and insusceptible to external influences that might take their development in a pro-social direction.

There are several problems with this argument. The first and most obvious is that many white-skinned people who were raised in overtly racist environments have become abolitionists, civil rights supporters, and anti-racist activists. Even so, Moss does not desire to understand or explain the psychological processes that prompt many white-skinned people to repudiate the "taxonomy" that is presumably hardwired into their psyches shortly after birth and to oppose the horrors and injustices it brings about, though he doubtlessly counts himself among their number.

Another problem with this argument is that it directly contradicts Sigmund Freud's views on human nature. In Chapter 5 of *Civilization and Its Discontents* (1930), Freud wrote that

> people are not gentle beings in need of love, who at most can defend themselves if attacked. Rather they must also recognize among their drive impulses a powerful tendency to aggression. Their neighbor, consequently, is not merely a potential helper or sexual object for them. Rather, they are also tempted to gratify their aggression on him, to exploit without compensation his capacity for work, to use him sexually without his consent, to seize his possessions, to humiliate him, to cause him pain, to torture and to kill him. *Homo homini lupus.* Who, after all the experiences of life and history, will have the courage to dispute this observation?
>
> (p. 85)

Now, whether you agree with Freud or not, the fact remains that he described the desire to dominate and exploit our fellow human beings as a generic human attribute. In other words, said Freud, the willingness or propensity to injure, exploit, and humiliate other human beings, which Dr. Moss deems to be chiefly front-loaded into the psyche of white infants is, in truth, innate and universal and resides within all of us. If so, it is not merely the product of the newborn infant's "positioning" in the social and cultural nexus, or of a rigid, internalized (and socially constructed) "taxonomy" that gives license to white-skinned people to dominate, exploit, and humiliate non-white people.

While you may not share Freud's grim assessment of human nature, there is plenty of evidence to back it up. Just consider the history of slavery, which was practiced all over the world long before European and Anglo-American imperialism began to shape the contours of global politics. Please consider – were the Sumerian Kings or the Egyptian Pharaohs, who enslaved many dark-skinned people, white? Were the Akkadians, Hittites, Chaldeans, Assyrians, Babylonians, Phoenicians, or Persians white? Were the Tartars, Turks, Huns, and Mongols white? Were the agrarian empires of India, China, Korea, Japan, and Southeast Asia, where untold millions were enslaved for centuries before European imperialism set foot in Asia, governed by white-skinned people? Were the Incas, Aztecs, Mayans, Toltecs, Olmecs, etc., white? Were the Muslim conquerors who controlled North Africa, the Middle East, and large swathes of Central Asia white?

Obviously not. But why rely solely on Freud's testimony? In *Transformations in Slavery*, historian Paul E. Lovejoy noted that

> slavery has been an important phenomenon throughout history. It has been found in many places, from classical antiquity to modern times. Africa has been intimately connected with this history, both as a major source of slaves and as one of the principle areas where slavery was common. Indeed, in Africa, slavery lasted well into the 20th century- notably longer than in the Americas. Such antiquity and persistence require explanation, both to understand the historical development of slavery in Africa in its own right and to evaluate the relative importance of the slave trade to this development.
>
> (Lovejoy, 2012, p. 1)

In a preface to the third edition of his book, Lovejoy acknowledged that one of his aims in undertaking his research was "to confront the reality that there was slavery in the history of Africa, at a time when some romantic visionaries and hopeful nationalists wanted to deny the clear facts (p. xxiii)." Moss doesn't deny the facts outright, however. He just ignores and sidesteps them completely.

So let's be candid, shall we? For all its shortcomings, Freud's grim appraisal of human nature has a lot of evidence to support it. By contrast, Donald Moss's theory of Parasitic Whiteness has none – or none to speak of, apart from his own autobiographical reflections and two meager case histories. Instead, Moss offers up florid conjectures couched in metaphors of "parasitism," "mapping," and "verticality" but entirely divorced from the actual history and practice of slavery before and outside of the European and Anglo-American orbits, where domination, exploitation, and humiliation were widely practiced by non-whites against other communities of color.

Besides, on reflection, to insist that white-skinned people are uniquely susceptible to these "perversions" and drive "deformations," as Moss calls them, appears to imply that human nature is basically good, but that white-skinned people are more heavily endowed with sadistic and antisocial traits than non-whites because of their acquired "taxonomy," a kind of second nature that can seldom, if ever, be remedied. In some ways, Moss's claims about Parasitic Whiteness are reminiscent of what Wilhelm Reich called "the emotional plague" (Reich, 1976), a deep and pervasive deformation of the psyche, which its victims and carriers are utterly unconscious of. Both these ideas lean heavily on the metaphor of disease. The difference here is that Parasitic Whiteness is deemed to be primarily an affliction of white-skinned people, while the emotional plague, as Reich conceived it, is present in every form of racism and does not discriminate on the basis of skin color.

So far, we've noted two basic problems with Moss's argument. First, he cannot explain how many white-skinned people (himself included) escape their early conditioning and become abolitionists, vigorous champions of equal rights, or anti-racist activists of one sort or another. Second, his portrayal of white-skinned people as being uniquely susceptible to acquiring the sadistic, exploitative, and dehumanizing mode of relatedness he calls "Parasitic Whiteness" is dramatically at odds with the facts of human history and lacks any real evidence to back it up. Of course, generous souls may insist that we honor the lived experience of the victims of racism, many of whom may honestly believe that white-skinned people are innately more prone to sadism and exploitation than non-whites. After all, they have suffered much, and quite apart from the harms inflicted on their ancestors, the mechanisms that *still* reinforce structural inequality today are numerous and take the form of exclusionary or predatory lending and housing practices, voter suppression, water and food insecurity, drug abuse and the "war on drugs," overcrowded schools and prisons, gang life, police brutality and mass incarceration, the "school-to-prison pipeline," and so on.

Mindful of these egregious wrongs, activists and their allies often *privilege* the testimony and beliefs of the victims of contemporary racism, prompted by a deeply felt sense of solidarity with the oppressed. But this course of action is a decision, a choice – *our* choice – and is not a guarantee of validity or veracity by any means. As a result, people who "center the voices" of oppressed minorities today but who ignore or dismiss the historical record on sadism and slavery run the risk of fostering a subtle kind of anti-white racism, one which deems sadism and exploitation to be far more prevalent among white-skinned people than among non-white populations.

Finally, Dr. Moss's contention that Parasitic Whiteness is almost impossible to "treat" evinces a very pessimistic attitude toward the future of race relations and a kind of moral masochism that prompts people to wallow in endless self-recriminations while harboring the delusion that this attitude constitutes evidence that they are morally superior to other white-skinned people who don't share their perspective. Though it may not be apparent at first, moral masochism of this complexion is really a gift to the radical Right and to right-wing pundits, politicians, and "influencers" all around the world.

Dr. Moss concludes his essay with the following reflections. He writes,

> To turn Whiteness into an object for thought one must first look for a point of stillness. This point actually does not exist. After all, Whiteness, in its mature form, generates a volatile totality from which there is no clear exit, no clear escape. To pursue that exit, to hope for even temporary escape . . . depends, I think, on a kind of conceptual mobility, a willingness to use metaphors and similes for only as long as they serve, and then to move on. For me, here, the most important of those metaphors have been "parasite," "mapping," and "verticality." Each seemed to me both stable and elastic, capable of simultaneously supporting thought and providing a jumping-off point whenever that support felt exhausted. And, of course, psychoanalysis provides something other than similes and metaphors. It provides a reliable theoretical/technical structure, one we can count on, one that, in spite of its limitations, will hold up – has held up – as we all try to achieve the requisite conceptual, emotional, and personal nimbleness to grapple with the Whiteness that, whoever we are, infiltrates our interior and exterior surround.
>
> (p. 370)

Moss encourages readers "to use metaphors and similes for only as long as they serve, and move on." That tacit implication of this methodological maxim is that when your preferred metaphors are no longer serviceable, you may adopt another one, or perhaps jump back and forth among your chosen metaphors to make your case. He never acknowledges the fact that metaphors and similes do not always illuminate. They can also seduce, mislead, and obfuscate. And though he does not say so in so many words, of course, one can't escape the impression that this nimble rhetorical strategy of juggling metaphors spares him the requirement of providing solid, tangible evidence for his claims. (Is it merely my imagination, or is this odd behavior for a psychoanalyst?)

Conclusion

Needless to say, psychoanalysts must never turn a blind eye to the mind-boggling injustices that afflict communities of color in the USA, especially in the case of patients or trainees who are placed in their care or under their supervision. Nor can they support the dominant narratives that perpetuate these injustices. But neither can they abdicate their responsibility to critique statements or positions that are a-historical, lack substance, or are riddled with contradictions and glaring omissions. If they do so, they are liable to indulge in sweeping and untenable generalizations that may mask a deeper despair about achieving genuine equality and understanding among whites and communities of color.

Sadly, the fact that Dr. Khilanani's talk at Yale University and Dr. Moss's article occurred merely a month apart indicates that critical race theory and whiteness studies have penetrated the halls of academia and made inroads into the psychoanalytic and psychiatric worlds as well. Unfortunately, given our diminishing attention spans, our growing appetite for sound bites and slogans, and our collective anguish over the long-standing injustices faced by non-white citizens in the USA, the pernicious nonsense Dr. Khilanani spouted will probably have a strong appeal to many readers on both sides of the Atlantic. Indeed, to many of them, it probably seems far more "authentic" or "real" than genuine scholarship.

Furthermore, it is ironic, indeed astonishing, that some psychoanalysts (like Donald Moss) espouse a kind of racial essentialism embodied in reductive binary categories to explain extremely complex social realities. The stark, Manichean simplicity of binaries like these afford people a false sense of moral clarity, multiple opportunities for virtue signaling, and a sense of pride for being on what they imagine is "the right side of history." But clinical experience demonstrates that simple binaries often belie much that lies beneath the surface, and psychoanalysis was designed to wrestle with ambiguity, contradictions, and complexity in the individual psyche and society at large.

These reflections, in turn, prompt other awkward questions, questions that are currently unanswerable but warrant careful and painstaking reflection going forward. Will ideas like these continue to make inroads (or gain converts) in the psychoanalytic world? The answer, I believe, is yes. But if so, as time elapses, will psychoanalysts discard their former discipline and school-specific criteria for credentialing practitioners as competent to treat or train people of color, and will they attempt to articulate brand-new criteria along these lines? And if so, who will decide what these new criteria are and how to measure compliance with them? And how will compliance with these guidelines be enforced?

I do not know the answers to these questions. Nor does anyone else at present, I suspect. We must wait and see. Meanwhile, looking to the future, Dr. Alexandra Woods strongly recommends that psychoanalytic organizations and institutes provide additional (and carefully focused) scholarships and mentoring for promising candidates from communities of color from the beginning of their undergraduate careers onward. She also recommends that courses focusing on culture, race, and class always be included in the institute's core curriculum and that all the courses offered at psychoanalytic include a "socio-psychoanalytic lens."

From a pedagogical standpoint, these are *excellent* ideas that merit swift adoption and, in fact, are long overdue. But she also recommends that analytic institutes drop the requirement of holding a PhD and make analytic training available to social workers with an MA degree. The potential benefits to this approach are fairly obvious. Doing so would boost enrollments considerably, help rectify past injustices and the current (mostly financial) impediments to psychoanalytic training for people of color. It may also make psychoanalytic theory and practice more relevant to the other mental health professions in the process. But what of the potential drawbacks, the unintended consequences of lowering standards for scholarship among aspiring analysts? This idea requires further reflection and study.

So Dr. Woods's recommendations for transforming psychoanalytic institutes merit serious discussion. But even so, the question remains: are phenotypically white-skinned people uniquely or overwhelmingly prone to psychopathy, sadism, and a desire to enslave others? The answer to this question is an emphatic no because the vast preponderance of historical evidence suggests otherwise and because – to the best of my knowledge – no one has yet offered a remotely plausible scientific explanation *why* this might be the case. (Nor will they, in all likelihood.)

Another question: are Dr. Khilanani's and Dr. Moss's utterances and ideas on this score actually representative of critical race theory and whiteness studies, or do they represent a departure from them? I don't know, but I suspect that the answer is still moot. Personally, I would very much *like* to believe that Khilanani's and Moss's racializing attitudes toward white-skinned people are not shared by the mainstream in activist communities. But even if they are merely fringe or minority views, talks and texts like these still pose a potential danger to our collective well-being. Why? Because highly credentialed academics and clinicians now speak and theorize openly in this manner in Ivy League settings, and in the process – without intending to, perhaps – furnish right-wing media with "weapons of mass distraction" to divert attention from far more pressing problems like income inequality and climate change, problems that bedevil – and may soon destroy – our body politic and our entire planet.

Note

1   That being said, Adorno's appraisal of jazz, a (largely) African American musical genre, was riddled with ethnocentrism and racist tropes (Jeffries, 2016, pp. 186–189), driving a formidable wedge, as it were, between himself and many members of the African American community. In *Mein Kampf*, Hitler railed against "the Jews" (i.e., Benny Goodman) for bringing Negro musicians to the Rhineland, and the Nazi party followed suit by condemning jazz for encouraging "race mixing." And on reflection, that is precisely what swing music did, bringing white and black artists (and their respective audiences) together in public spaces to share their love of music. That being so, one might have expected Adorno to approach jazz more sympathetically. But as Stuart Jeffries notes, Adorno's appraisal was based almost entirely on the performance of (mostly white) European jazz ensembles in Weimar, and he studiously avoided live jazz performances when he lived in Los Angeles. Adorno's unwillingness to engage with live jazz during his American sojourn casts doubt on his attitude and intentions. At best, it conveys a smug, Eurocentric contempt for all things American. At worst, his characterization of jazz as "sadomasochistic" and his (decidedly weird) invocation of notions like the castration complex and premature ejaculation to explain jazz syncopation and the instrumental styles smacks of racist prejudice.

References

Applebaum, A. 2021. "The New Puritans." *The Atlantic*, October.
Burston, D. 1991. *The Legacy of Erich Fromm*. Cambridge, MA: Harvard University Press.

Burston, D. 2021. *Anti-Semitism and Analytical Psychology: Jung, Politics and Culture*. London: Routledge.

Delgado, R. & Stefancic, J. 2017. *Critical Race Theory: An Introduction*. New York: New York University Press.

Elon, A. 2003. *The Pity of It All: A Portrait of the German-Jewish Epoch, 1743–1933*. London: Picador.

Freud, S. 1930. *Civilization and Its Discontents*, edited by T. Dufresne, translated by Gregory Richter. Toronto: Broadview Press, 2016.

Fromm, E. 1941. *Escape From Freedom*. New York: Avon Books, 1965.

Fromm, E. 1955. *The Sane Society*. London: Routledge Kegan Paul, 1963.

Herzog, K. 2021. "Interview with Dr. Aruna Khilanani." *bariweiss.substack.com*, June 4.

Jeffries, S. 2016. *Grand Hotel Abyss: The Lives of the Frankfurt School*. London: Verso.

Lawrence, C. 1987. "The Id, the Ego and Equal Protection: Reckoning with Unconscious Racism." *Stanford Law Review*, 39, pp. 317–388.

Lawrence, C. 2008. "Unconscious Racism Revisited: Reflections on the Impact and Origins of 'The Id, the Ego and Equal Protection.'" *Georgetown University Law Center*. https://scholarship.law.georgetown.edu/facpub/339.

Lovejoy, P. 2012. *Transformations in Slavery*. Cambridge: Cambridge University Press.

Lowenthal, L. 1987. *An Unmastered Past: The Autobiographical Reflections of Leo Lowenthal*, edited by Martin Jay. Berkeley: University of California Press.

McLaughlin, N. 2021. *Erich Fromm and Global Public Sociology*. Bristol: University of Bristol Press.

Moss, D. 2021. "On Having Whiteness." *Journal of the American Psychoanalytic Association*, 69/2, pp. 355–371.

Pyle, J. 1999. "Race, Equality and the Rule of Law: Critical Race Theory's Attack on the Promises of Liberalism." *The Boston Law Review*, 6. http://lawdigitalcommons.bc.edu/bclr/vol40/iss3/6.

Reich, W. 1976. *People in Trouble*. New York: Farrar Straus & Giroux.

Woods, A. 2020. "The Work Before Us: Whiteness and the Psychoanalytic Institute." *Psychoanalysis, Culture and Society*, 25/2, pp. 230–249.

Chapter 13

Critical Theory and Contemporary Psychoanalysis

Jon Mills

Axel Honneth's recent turn to psychoanalysis to bolster critical theory has promising potential to augment interdisciplinary studies on a critical theory of society. Setting aside disputes on theoretical incompatibilities between the two disciplines, such as those that revolve around rival conceptions of the nature of human aggression that challenge the ubiquity of prosocial behavior, the role of the negative, the question of a morality of reason (*Vernunftmoral*), and the rejection of an innate principle of destruction attributed to a death drive (*Todestrieb*), Honneth seeks to "make a critical theory of society dependent upon psychoanalysis (in the broadest sense of the term)."[1] It is important for the discipline of critical theory to understand that there are many forms of contemporary psychoanalytic thought that are already in simpatico with their overall project. In this chapter, I hope to show that modes of compatibility already exist, and that by engaging contemporary psychoanalytic perspectives, critical theory may further prosper.

Honneth's desire to supplement a moral psychology guided by psychoanalytic insights can only advance the field. Here he embraces an essential tenet of the primacy of unconscious processes operative in all individuals and on every conceivable strata of social collectives:

> At a very fundamental level, we should expect that within the social world, there will be affects and motives that are inaccessible to consciousness. In order to be able to take account of the opaque, unconscious motives expressed in anxiety, longings for attachment, desires for togetherness and fantasies of submission, we need a psychological theory of the subject, a theory of socialization that takes sufficient account of the genesis of unconscious affects in our individual

biographies. I do not yet see any other theory better suited to this demand than some version of psychoanalysis.²

He continues to ask, What of the many varieties of psychoanalysis best serve this purpose? He stipulates that the most suitable theory must take into account the "socialization milieu of society as a whole,"³ and this would be the best candidate to adopt. He concludes that "object relations theory" best fits this criterion.

But psychoanalysis has come a long way since Freud and the early object relations theorists came onto the scene. In fact, we can say that all of psychoanalytic theory has been subsumed in new paradigms that have built on these foundational ideas, the details of which I will outline in what follows. Honneth favors Winnicott's work, yet there have been many notable contributions in psychoanalysis since his time that have paved the way for new developments and redirections in clinical and applied theory as well as cultural critique. In fact, it could be argued that critical theory is behind the times, notwithstanding Winnicott's timeless influence. It is understandable why objects relations, which is really about people relations, is an attractive supplement to critical theory because it shows that Self-in-relation-to-Society involves ontologically inseparable processes. Individual development transpires within a relational and psycho-socio-symbolic order that is given as part of our facticity or thrownness into an intersubjective matrix of socialization and the structuralizations of culture. But contemporary psychoanalytic paradigms offer many more nuanced approaches to conceiving personal and social development than those present in Winnicott's pioneering work, and critical theory may find these equally attractive, compelling, and compatible with its overall project.

Although Honneth suggests that object relations theory "might represent a danger to Critical Theory, robbing it of the psychoanalytical impulse of negativity,"[4] this is hardly the case. In reality, object relations perspectives are not in conflict with classical psychoanalysis given that Freud advanced both the object relations and ego psychology movements, only that it is a matter of *emphasis* in any psychoanalytic paragon on human nature and social relations to highlight certain psychological dynamics over others. One does not have to emphasize an either/or scenario or bifurcation between society and the individual and ask us to choose which model or causal force is more correct or operative as we can plainly see a confluence of psychoanalytic observations at play in all aspects of social reality, personality formation, and subjective analysis both inside and outside of the consulting room with palpable empirical correlates. Whether we claim human aggression and destruction is the result of endogenous propensities or the internalization of the negative affective effects of socialization, it really becomes an irrelevant quibble.

What matters is how negativity manifests and corrodes harmonious social relations that both critical theory and psychoanalysis are concerned about ameliorating. Although I believe Honneth's tendency to jettison drive theory[5] is misguided based upon the empirical fact that we are embodied and have internally derived desires, conflicts, and pulsions to contend with, this does not mean that we should not explore points of connection and consilience where both psychoanalysis and critical theory become intimate partners in attempting to better society. It is here that Honneth has rejuvenated the notion of recognition as integral to understanding the social dynamics of intersubjectivity and hence recasts an ethical vision for humanity. It is within this context that I hope to introduce contemporary psychoanalytic paradigms that move beyond classical models yet complement redirecting shifts in emphasis that both psychoanalysis and critical theory attempt to accomplish.

From Classical Theory to Object Relations

Despite the fact that recognition theory was arguably introduced by Hegel, the notion of recognition and intersubjectivity have become popular concepts in psychoanalysis originating from early object relations theorists onward. The object relations movement was paved by Freud when he introduced the notion that the aim (*Zeil*) of a drive (*Trieb*) is to seek satisfaction through an object (*Objekt*), which Freud mainly considered to be other people and their functions.[6] Although an object is the "most variable" of all instinctual activity, that is, unconsciously motivated, he ultimately privileges human connection and our need for relatedness with others in order to fulfill our desires, which brings us satisfaction. In fact, the social dimension to Freud's classical theory is made most explicit when he discusses the need for "primary relatedness" through the process of "identification," which is "the earliest expression of an emotional tie with another person."[7] An emotional connection is an important ingredient of identification because we simply don't identify with just anyone, as attachment research affirms. There is a selective aspect to identification, and we can see it operating quite unpretentiously during childhood when a child takes his or her parents as an ideal and wants to possess them and/or be like them, often displayed through bonds of affection and play. Freud goes on to say that it is "a very important form of attachment to someone else, probably the very first, and not the same thing as the choice of an object."[8] And Freud specifically concedes that for each gender, the mother becomes the original and most important model of identification,[9] which is "established unalterably for a whole lifetime as the first and strongest love-object and as the prototype of all later love-relations – for both sexes."[10] Here Freud clearly states that "love has its origin in attachment"[11] beginning with the appropriation of the mother's body. From these passages, Freud is clearly describing an intrapsychic process of incorporating the attributes and qualities of another subject (in German, *Person*) encountered through ongoing intersubjective, relational exchange.

Although there may be a categorical distinction between interpersonal relations (i.e., based in selectivity, affectivity, qualitative engagement, and so forth as modes of relatedness) and intersubjectivity (i.e., based in mutual recognition, but embracing abstractly rational and normatively universal, collectively binding, socio-symbolic-institutional structures), here Freud is setting the stage for a shift from drive theory to interpersonal and social psychology the object relations movement picked up. This is particularly the case for Winnicott, which Honneth largely relies on for his sources on Freud, who must form his own synthesis by subsuming drive theory into his new ideas, which at the time were controversial within conservative psychoanalytic circles.

The emotional processes of identification, internalization, and love as primary relatedness are all part of attachment processes that are relational in nature, as well as the specific acquisition of values and moral agency that accompany the development of the superego (*Über-Ich*) or conscience based upon the internalized interpersonal patterns of relatedness that come from familial and cultural life. Freud is quite clear when he attributes super-ego development to relational factors:

> Throughout later life it represents the influence of a person's childhood, of the care and education given him by his parents and of his dependence on them – a childhood which is prolonged so greatly in human beings by a family life in common. And in all this it is not only the personal qualities of these parents that is making itself felt,

but also everything that had a determining effect on them themselves, the tastes and standards of the social class in which they lived and the innate dispositions and traditions of the race from which they sprang.[12]

In this pithy yet condensed paragraph, Freud perspicaciously captures the essence of character as an internalized identification with the parents' personal qualities, aesthetics, preferences and prejudices, group loyalties, and revered values that are socially constituted. Here Freud is emphasizing the nature of relationships within family life and how the peculiar aspects of certain personality traits and characteristics from one's parents are internalized within the subject, which were in turn historically instilled in one's parents from their own familial and cultural upbringing – what today we may refer to as the transgenerational transmission of family heritage. From this standpoint, psychic life cannot be bifurcated from familial life that resides within a community of others, and communal life cannot be understood unless it takes into account patterns of relatedness based on the types and qualities of relationships that historically constitute society.[13] All these ontic – hence relational – preconditions are necessary for psychic maturation in general.

Precursors to Contemporary Psychoanalytic Theory

Philosophy remains largely unaware of the developments in postclassical schools of psychoanalysis since the time of Freud. The British object relations movement gained prominence in the United Kingdom after Freud's death and may be attributed to the pioneering works of Melanie Klein, D. W. Winnicott, and W.R.D. Fairbairn, while during the same time period, but quite independently, attachment theory was introduced by John Bowlby. Ego psychology mainly dominated medicalized American training after this period championed by Anna Freud, Harry Guntrip, and Heinz Hartmann among others; however, Harry Stack Sullivan initiated the American Interpersonal tradition, which further led to the development of self psychology originated by Heinz Kohut.[14] Since this time, contemporary movements have recapitulated a return to the object relations, interpersonal, and self psychological schools, which puts more emphasis on intersubjectivity, attachment, and relationality.[15]

As a forerunner to contemporary relational and intersubjectivity theory, object relations perspectives introduced a paradigm shift from the intrapsychic to the interpersonal, from the life of endogenous motives within to how the external environment, primarily caregivers, impacts on psychological development. Social philosophy remains largely ignorant of these postclassical developments within the psychoanalytic domain, and this fact matters because postclassical movements have turned to the interpersonal in ways that throw light on socialization, a key concern of critical theory. Updating our understanding of the formation of the self and the role of the family and psychosocial matrices is of salient relevance to the Frankfurt School for one of its innovations in materialist theory was to insist on the irreducibility of the individual and the importance of the family in society.

It was Donald Winnicott who primarily initiated this shift in emphasis in the field by introducing important concepts such as the "transitional object," the "holding environment," and the "good-enough mother"; although other analysts such as Ian Suttie, Sándor Ferenczi, W. R. D. Fairbairn, Michael Balint, and Harry Stack Sullivan, to name a notable few, also emphasized the primacy of object-relationships that departed from classical theory. And let us not forget that Erich Fromm was the only clinical psychoanalyst identified with the Frankfurt School who emphasized the social dimension of interpersonal relations in culture. Object relations theorists generally agree that the loving, caring, affectionate, emotionally available, and empathically attuned responsiveness from the mother (or her surrogate) during child-rearing shapes a secure personality, facilitates healthy self-development and social adaptation, and is the precursor to developing mature adult relations marked by the capacity for productivity, psychological stability, compassion for others, and emotional intimacy, among other personal qualities and prosocial attributes. Those who are deprived of or suffer from these early optimal experiences grow up with more challenges in living, coping, and flourishing, if not a crippled capacity for being.

Winnicott reminds us that transitional phenomena and the role of fantasy helps all people establish a psychological basis for reality. For Winnicott, transitional phenomena refer to the infant's attempt to differentiate self from (m)other inherent in the separation-individuation process, develop a sense of self and personal identity distinct from what is "not-me," and acquire personal autonomy through fantasy about objects (both illusory and symbolic) as a way of relating to the world separate from one's parents while at the same time developing a real relationship with them. When we refer to transitional objects or processes, popular analogues are a child's pacifier, soft objects (like a blanket), toys, or stuffed animals that are used to provide emotional comfort during times of separation or to substitute for the mother during her absence, but they can be any object or concept that serves as psychic organizers, which allows the subject to transition into developing a psychic space of individuation, independence, and personal control mediated through fantasy. These are cultivated psychic capacities, hence developmental accomplishments that allow a child to create an internal life and recognize objects that are not identical with the self. Objects come to represent a state of transition from the symbiotic (fantasized) merger with the mother to a differentiated matrix of being separate and existing outside of the child's own existence and relation to its mother. These phenomena may be said to transpire within all individuals beginning in infancy and forms the basis of imagination, thought, and creativity. In Winnicott's words:

> Transitional objects and transitional phenomena belong to the realm of illusion which is at the basis of initiation of experience. This early stage in development is made possible by the mother's special capacity for making adaptation to the needs of her infant, thus allowing the infant the illusion that what the infant creates *really exists*.[16]

Here, illusion becomes the cornerstone for the *beginning* of experience; hence, it provides a mediatory psychic function within an intermediary space. This "intermediate area of experience" is a border concept and provides the transitionary rubric necessary for fantasy construction. In other words, illusion intervenes in its apprehension and encounter with the real. Furthermore, the relation between reality and fantasy is blurred at this stage of infantile development, where each is collapsed into an isomorphism of the other.

Transitional objects and phenomena are psychically constructed (hence imagined) as a means to secure attachment, sustain maternal comfort and affectional bonds during absences, self-soothe, and ward off depressive anxiety and negative emotional events that besiege the nascent psyche, as well as channel destructive fantasies. Extending the notion of transitional phenomena as transmutational internal objects that perform a particular self-regulatory function, Heinz Kohut introduced the notion of a "selfobject,"[17] which is an aspect of an object incorporated into the self, usually another person or a part or property of another person, but it can also be an inanimate object or abstract idea that carries a particular quality and performs a certain internal task of maintaining psychic continuity and cohesion of the self. To be more precise, it is the *function* that constitutes the selfobject and not the person for it is the *experiences* evoked by such objects that allow us to analyze their internal presence and affects. For Kohut, selfobject experiences become the building blocks of psychic reality and serve to mirror the intrinsic worth and integrity of the subject as well as validate and strengthen self-structure. Functional objects and their representations become the evoking-sustaining-responding matrix that maintains self-organization, facilitates healing in the disruption-restoration process, and contributes to the undoing of self-injury incurred by the experiential subject when it undergoes depletion, fragmentation, or emptiness. Winnicott's framework can be expanded to accommodate Kohut's conceptual scheme of the selfobject. It is here that Honneth's reliance on Winnicott becomes ripe for a Kohutian revision.

In psychological terms, selfobject representations are derivative of unconscious motivations, conflicts, values, and narcissistic longings the internalized selfobject contributes to psychic economy, which serves to maintain and restore the self from internal rupture. Selfobjects preserve specific transferences as intrapsychic relations to internalized images that evoke and facilitate an enduring state of self-cohesion, even though self-structure is always in flux and undergoes permutations. One of the most important selfobject function is that of *mirroring*, where the sense of acceptance, recognition, and appreciation is conceived as a confirming and validating aspect of the self, as well as *idealizing* functions, where inner resonance states evoke perfection and ideality and conserve a sense of goodness through identification with the infallible idealized selfobject, qualities that are lacking in the subject yet vicariously fulfilled through such idealization, twinship, or merger fantasies with the revered other or their representations. Both transitional phenomena and selfobject experiences place great importance on the maternal "facilitative" environment or, more specifically, on the attachment system between child and mother, which is the locus of the developmental capacity for mutual recognition.

Attachment Theory and Relationality

One of the most celebrated findings in contemporary psychological research is the centrality of attachment in human development.[18] Attachment is a universal biosocial instinct influenced by the contingencies of the maternal environment comprising innate motivations to procure safety via proximity to selected love objects during early childhood, most often one's parents or their surrogates. Object attachment is a unique and special form of affectional bond to a select few identified caregivers and is characterized as a process of emotional connection based upon affective ties, relational longings, and primary identifications with love objects. Attachment processes are normative in every human culture; are highly influential on neurological development and the regulatory system, right hemisphere brain lateralization, affect regulation; and the development of personality, adjustment, and psychopathology.[19]

Attachment patterns become organized at the representational and behavioral levels. Representational models or schemas of self and others are constructed and serve to facilitate internal cohesion of the self, judge the accessibility and willingness of figures to provide functions of protection, warmth, and care, and to guide future appraisals and goal-directed behavior. Beginning in infancy, we develop such internal working models of self and others that are both positive and negative in content and form. Healthy representations are equated with feelings of lovability and security in the child, while dysfunctional representations proliferate when the attachment figure is perceived negatively, which leads to various defensive exclusions or strategies that allow the child to cope with negativity, intrusiveness, and incongruity that jeopardizes one's psychological sense of safety. Within all these psychoanalytic schools, it becomes easy to appreciate how early interactional patterns by parents, family members, and caregivers condition relationality and the development of the self, social adaptation and maladjustment, and how the transitional subject comes to view society and the world at large.

Psyche and Socialization

With the introduction of the British school of psychoanalysis, the bridge from unconscious fantasy to the external presence of others, drive theory to primary relatedness, and the self within society, the subject-object split was closed. As with Freud's qualification that individual psychic processes can never stand apart from social psychology and the cultural environs that impact on both personal subjectivity and the objective conditions that interpolate society, so too many critical theorists turned to psychoanalytic paradigms to bolster social philosophy. For Marcuse, psychological categories are political categories and are inseparable from the broader sociological forces that shape civilization. As he tells us, "psychological problems turn into political problems: private disorder reflects more directly than before the disorder of the whole, and the cure of the personal disorder depends more directly than before on the cure of the general disorder,"[20] namely, sick society. Marcuse is very clear in his insistence that the individual is determined by "the societal forces which define the psyche."[21] Yet at the same time, psychology becomes the foundation of sociology and the cultural dynamics and institutional organizations that in turn inform the psychological.

If you begin with the premise that all human beings are psychological creatures and that all inner experience is psychologically mediated, then by natural extension, this would apply to the notion of the social and specifically the politics of desire instantiated within any community. And if you start with the premise that the psychological is shaped by the social, then the same argument applies. Groups are psychologically informed and inform others right down to a single subject, whether this applies to our families, cohorts, communities, the provincial or nation state, and so forth. From Jung to Heidegger and Lacan, we are thrown into a collective psychic matrix and socio-symbolic order that informs our being in the world. Here the individual develops within the social, and the social within the individual.

Although this may seem patently circular, causal questions are always tricky and subject to paradox and undecidability in providing an unequivocal explanans. That is why it may prove useful to view these dichotomous categories as comprising a dialectical structure where neither can be discussed in isolation nor are ontologically separate from one other, for each are mutually implicative in any discourse we posit about human beings. This is why I prefer to bracket such antinomies and view the self in relation to itself and others within worldhood as being *overdetermined* in causal influence and import. One does not have to bifurcate the arrangements of society from naturalized psychology to see how their dynamic processes and co-occurrence pressurize and inform one other within a systemic unit. We can surely observe how certain structures and political policies within societies lead to more problems in living and suffering in individuals and how natural psychological processes such as desire, envy, greed, rage, entitlement, aggression, and so on are intensified and play out through pathological enactments when societies undergo material deprivation, economic austerity, tragedy, trauma, war, political oppression, and so on. When social institutions, capitalistic enterprise, and the populace do not acknowledge or recognize disenfranchised subgroups and the extreme hardships they face due to race, socioeconomic, and educational disparities that privileged classes do not face, social fabrics begin to fray in tatters.

Psychoanalytic Recognition Theory

As I have mentioned elsewhere,[22] contemporary recognition theory has much to gain by engaging psychoanalytic recognition theory. The notions of recognition and intersubjectivity form a central position in contemporary psychoanalytic discourse,[23] particularly amongst object relations, self psychology, interpersonal, and relational traditions,[24] not to mention its primacy in the consulting room.[25] In her annexation of Hegel, Jessica Benjamin has advocated for moving beyond the doer and done-to binary to advocating for a tertiary moral comportment of recognition the analyst is obliged to adopt in treatment,[26] while Marilyn Nissim-Sabat argues that dysrecognition should be viewed as neither victimization nor survival.[27] Although there are many nuanced theories of intersubjectivity in psychoanalysis that have emphasized various characteristics over others,[28] which I have critiqued at length,[29] the details of which do not concern us here, there is typically a privileging of the respective subjectivities that form the analytic dyad as a reciprocal relational unit, even if such relations are asymmetrical. Whether in society or the clinic, psychoanalysis is sensitive to power differentials and their unconscious relations that give rise to modes of entrenched opposition, need for control, resistance to others' demands, pathological accommodation, subjugation, and transferential enactments that thwart mutual recognition. This is why, in part, the ethical turn in psychoanalysis is enjoying a resurgence of consciousness raising and social activism that echoes the earlier days of critical theory.[30]

Given that Honneth finds Stern to be an extension (if not a corrective) of Winnicott, the nuances post-object relations perspectives have to offer are worth noting in future efforts at initiating dialogue and generating a simpatico – if not synthesis – with critical theory. From drive to ego, object, self, relationality, and intersubjectivity – all transpiring within intrapsychic, interpersonal, familial, and communal organizations within our social and cultural ontology, psychoanalysis has moved a long way from postclassical models while subsuming these theoretical developments within new traditions of thought. Because the nuances are so vast, they are beyond the scope of this immediate project. But with any theoretical developments, suffice it to say that it becomes a matter of *emphasis*. While we may focus on these redirecting categorical shifts in theory (clinical, social, applied) or on the microdynamics of specific forms, contexts, contents, and functions, such as in attachment processes, affectivity, empathic attunement, mentalization, mirroring, relational vulnerability, shame, the intersubjective system that comprises the mutual negotiation and co-construction of the analytic dyad, hence the interpersonal field that entwines two subjects in their relational engagement, and so on, we can readily see that contemporary psychoanalytic thought has something to offer critical theory.

Psychoanalysis from classical theory to attachment and objects relations perspectives, the interpersonal and self psychology schools, and new directions in the emphasis on egalitarianism within relationality as a mutual intersubjective exchange all capitalize on the primacy of a *recognizing principle* where acknowledgment, validation, empathy, emotional attunement, and genuinely relating to another subject as a human being is coveted. This view is further informed by the developmental, behavioral, and cognitive neurosciences that recognize how psychological processes are advanced in individuals and societies when such parameters are observed, which carries tangible benefits to citizens who advance their own child-rearing practices, social institutions, and culture. In the end, people grow up to be happier, better adjusted, more productive, capable of nurturing the psychological needs of their children, and contribute to society as a whole.

Concluding Postscript

Psychoanalysis teaches us that whatever values and ideals societies adopt, they are always mediated through unconscious psychic processes[31] that condition the collective in both positive and negative ways and in terms of relations of recognition and patterns of social justice. Contemporary critical theory may benefit from engaging postclassical and current trends in psychoanalytic thought that have direct bearing on the ways we conceive of and observe how individuals operate within social collectives. Implications for critical theory need to reflect upon how the psychosocial matrix of self and society both facilitate and hinder optimal social arrangements and fabrics of justice as it takes up the question of normativity. The tensions between normative development, individual identity formation, social reproduction, concepts of justice, legal and political equality, economic redistribution, social ethics and democracy, institutionalized relations of recognition, moral reason, and the pursuit of human freedom all have overlapping and interdependent ontic manifestations.

Critical theory cannot negate the reality of social pathology but rather engage its origins, appearances, conflictual dynamics, mitigating circumstances, and unintended consequences of the prevailing conditions of socialization on their own terms with the hope that an applied psychoanalytic expatiation on social phenomenology can expand the depth and breadth of human relations and open up a permissible space for interdisciplinary discussion. Engaging the more nuanced perspectives of contemporary psychoanalysis has the potential to sharpen critical theory as a discipline and unlock new possibilities toward collaboration, synthesis, and unification, an agenda we must leave for future research.

Notes

1 Honneth (2012), p. 195.
2 Honneth (2012), pp. 195–196.
3 Honneth (2012), p. 195.
4 Honneth (2012), pp. 198–199.
5 See Honneth (2012), p. 200.
6 Freud (1915), p. 122.
7 Freud (1921), p. 105. Later Freud (1932–1933) reiterates this point more clearly: "Identification (*Identifizierung*) . . . [is] the assimilation of one ego [*Ich*] to another one, as a result of which the first ego behaves like the second in certain respects, imitates it and in a sense takes it up into itself" (p. 63).
8 Freud (1932–1933), p. 63.
9 Freud (1931), p. 225.
10 Freud (1940), p. 188.
11 Ibid.
12 Freud (1940), p. 209.
13 Freud (1921) fully appreciated the *social phenomena* involved in psychic development, and he specifically tells us so: "Rarely and under certain exceptional conditions is individual psychology in a position to disregard the relations of this individual to others. In the individual's mental life someone else

is invariably involved, as a model, as an object, as a helper, as an opponent; and so from the very first individual psychology ... is at the same time social psychology as well" (p. 69). Within this same context, Freud emphasizes "the relations of an individual to his parents," as well as siblings, friends, love interests, and even his doctor – namely, the psychoanalyst: "in fact all the relations which have hitherto been the chief subject of psycho-analytic research – may claim to be considered as social phenomena" (p. 69).

14 See Bacal and Newman (1990) for a review.
15 See my critique in *Conundrums: A Critique of Contemporary Psychoanalysis* (Mills, 2012).
16 Winnicott (1971), p. 14.
17 Kohut (1971) first makes reference to "self-objects" as "objects which are themselves experienced as part of the self" (p. xiv).
18 Inspired by the pioneering work of John Bowlby and Mary Ainsworth, there has been a spate of research in infant observation, child development, cognitive and social psychology, evolutionary biology, neuroscience, psychopathology, clinical assessment, psychotherapy, and ethnology that support attachment theory as a viable explanatory model of human development. Contemporary researchers such as Mary Main, Judith Solomon, Carol George, Erik Hesse, Peter Fonagy, Mary Target, Karlen Lyons-Ruth, Beatrice Beebe, Alan Shore, and Arietta Slade are just a few notable academics and clinicians who have made substantial contributions in this area (see Mills, 2005b, and Cassidy & Shaver, 1999, for an overview).
19 Although Honneth relies largely on Daniel Stern, whom he takes to provide compelling evidence for an extension and correction of Winnicott on attachment, all contemporary attachment theory is premised on developmental science and the outgrowth and extensions of the seminal work of John Bowlby (1969, 1988), Winnicott's contemporary. Bowlby's classical model of attachment rests on the interrelatedness of three main constructs: (1) activation of the attachment behavioral system, (2) the role of self and object representations, and (3) strategies at defensive exclusion. For the field of developmental psychology, the attachment system is an evolutionarily informed process that motivates and regulates internal goal-directed behaviors and intentions aimed to promote and procure proximity to love objects for the purpose of protection from encroaching threats that may disrupt desired levels of security. A variety of internal and external conditions may affect the system, including perceived alterations in the environment as well as the dispositions and behaviors of attachment figures, which leads to a dynamic tension between the mother's and infant's individual needs. Low activation levels are correlated with positive internal states and feelings of safety, while high activation levels are mobilized during the presence of intense negative affect, anxiety, alarm, fear, or dread. When the attachment figure is perceived as being unavailable or inconsistent, apprehension, anger, and sadness are typical accompanying emotional reactions.
20 Marcuse (1955), p. 21.
21 Ibid.
22 See Mills (2019).

23 See Benjamin (1988); Mills (2002); Stolorow and Atwood (1992).
24 See Bacal and Newman (1990); Mitchell (2002).
25 Mills (2005b); Stolorow et al. (1987).
26 Benjamin (2004).
27 Nissim-Sabat (2009).
28 Cf. Aron (1996); Lacan (1977); Orange et al. (1997); Renik (1993).
29 See Mills (2005a, 2012).
30 Goodman and Severson (2016); Kiehl et al. (2016); Orange (2016).
31 Although the different schools of psychoanalytic thought offer their own nuanced theoretical frameworks, one universal belief is that there are unconscious processes operating within the psyche that stand in relation to social organizations that reinforce them. See Mills (2014) for a comprehensive overview of the philosophies of the unconscious in Hegel, Freud, Jung, Lacan, Heidegger, Sartre, Winnicott, and Whitehead.

References

Aron, L. (1996). *A Meeting of Minds*. Hillsdale, NJ: The Analytic Press.
Bacal, H.A. & Newman, K.M. (1990). *Theories of Object Relations: Bridges to Self Psychology*. New York: Columbia University Press.
Benjamin, J. (1988). *The Bonds of Love*. New York: Pantheon Books.
———. (2004). Beyond Doer and Done To: An Intersubjective View of Thirdness. *Psychoanalytic Quarterly*, LXXIII (1), 5–46.
Bowlby, J. (1969). *Attachment and Loss: Vol. 1. Attachment*. New York: Basic Books, 1982.
———. (1988). *A Secure Base*. New York: Basic Books.
Cassidy, J. & Shaver, P.R. (Eds.) (1999). *Handbook of Attachment: Theory, Research, and Clinical Applications*. New York: Guilford.
Freud, S. (1966–95 [1886–1940]). *The Standard Edition of the Complete Psychological Works of Sigmund Freud*, 24 vols. Trans. and gen. ed. James Strachey, in collaboration with Anna Freud, assisted by Alix Strachey and Alan Tyson. London: Hogarth Press. Hereafter as Standard Edition.
———. (1915). *Instincts and Their Vicissitudes. Standard Edition*, Vol. 14., pp. 117–140. London: Hogarth Press.
———. (1921). *Group Psychology and the Analysis of the Ego. Standard Edition*, Vol. 18. London: Hogarth Press.
———. (1931). *Female Sexuality. Standard Edition*, Vol. 21, pp. 225–243. London: Hogarth Press.
———. (1932–1933). *New Introductory Lectures on Psycho-Analysis. Standard Edition*, Vol. 22. London: Hogarth Press.
———. (1940). *An Outline of Psycho-Analysis. Standard Edition*, Vol. 23, [1938], pp. 144–207. London: Hogarth Press.
Goodman, D.M. & Severson, E.R. (Eds.) (2016). *The Ethical Turn*. London: Routledge.

Honneth, A. (2012). *The I in We: Studies in the Theory of Recognition.* Cambridge, UK: Polity Press.

Kiehl, E., Saban, M. & Samuels, A. (Eds.) (2016). *Analysis and Activism.* London: Routledge.

Kohut, H. (1971). *The Analysis of the Self.* Madison, CN: International Universities Press.

Lacan, J. (1977). *Écrits: A Selection,* trans. A. Sheridan. New York: Norton.

Marcuse, H. (1955). *Eros and Civilization.* London: Penguin Press, 1970.

Mills, J. (2002). *The Unconscious Abyss: Hegel's Anticipation of Psychoanalysis.* Albany, NY: SUNY Press.

———. (Ed.) (2005a). *Relational and Intersubjective Perspectives in Psychoanalysis: A Critique.* Northvale, NJ: Jason Aronson.

———. (2005b). *Treating Attachment Pathology.* Latham, MD: Aronson/Rowman & Littlefield.

———. (2012). *Conundrums: A Critique of Contemporary Psychoanalysis.* New York: Routledge.

———. (2014). *Underworlds: Philosophies of the Unconscious from Psychoanalysis to Metaphysics.* London: Routledge.

———. (2019). Dysrecognition and Social Pathology: New Directions in Critical Theory. *Psychoanalysis, Culture & Society,* 1, 1–16.

Mitchell, S.A. (2002). *Relationality: From Attachment to Intersubjectivity.* Hillsdale, NJ: Analytic Press.

Nissim-Sabat, M. (2009). *Neither Victim Nor Survivor: Thinking Toward a New Humanity.* Lanham, MD: Lexington Books.

Orange, D.M. (2016). *Nourishing the Inner Life of Clinicians and Humanitarians.* London: Routledge.

Orange, D.M., Atwood, G. & Stolorow, R.D. (1997). *Working Intersubjectively: Contextualism in Psychoanalytic Practice.* Hillsdale, NJ: The Analytic Press.

Renik, O. (1993). Analytic Interaction: Conceptualizing Technique in Light of the Analyst's Irreducible Subjectivity. *Psychoanalytic Quarterly,* LXII, 553–571.

Stolorow, R.D. & Atwood, G. (1992). *Contexts of Being: The Intersubjective Foundations of Psychological Life.* Hillsdale, NJ: The Analytic Press.

Stolorow, R.D., Brandchaft, B. & Atwood, G. (1987). *Psychoanalytic Treatment: An Intersubjective Approach.* Hillsdale, NJ: The Analytic Press.

Winnicott, D.W. (1971). *Playing and Reality.* London: Routledge.

Index

Page numbers in *italics* indicate figures.

Abernathy, Ralph 174
Abraham, Karl 91n6
academic freedom 162, 166–167
Adorno, Theodor: aesthetic theory and 5, 21; anti-Hegelianism and 5; on authoritarianism 159–161, 164, 168, 180n1; on *Bildung* 150–151; categorical imperative and 148–149; on collective regression xviii, 82–85; constitutive subjectivity and 18; critical reasoning and 150, 152; critical theory and 2–3, 12, 153; critique of instrumental reason 99; *Die verwaltete Welt* broadcast 97–98; "Education after Auschwitz" 152; on elitist cultural industry 10; enlightenment and 4; exact fantasy and 14; on failure of individuation 135; on fascist propaganda 83–85; Frankfurt School and 160–161; Freudian theory and xx, 87, 188; Fromm critique of 160; on German sociology 189; Habermas critique of 99; on institutional evil 97; materialism and 2–3; Nazism and xvii, 3, 82; negative psychology and 152–153; neo-Romantics and 111n2; non-reified forms of synthesis and 5; on progress and regression xvii–xviii, 82–84, 96; psychoanalysis and 2–3, 12, 152–153; racist appraisal of jazz and 285n1; second nature concept and 190; "*Theorie der Halbildung*" 151; totally administered society and 9, 20, 97; *see also Authoritarian Personality, The* (Adorno et al.); *Dialectic of Enlightenment, The* (Horkheimer and Adorno)

advertising 215–218
Afary, Janet 161
African American activists 174, 265
African American psychoanalysts 275–276, 284
Agamben, Giorgio 110–111
aggression: authoritarianism and 158–159; dysrecognition and 118; Freud on 44, 51–54, 56–58; human nature and 118, 122, 279–280, 287; ontogeny and 27; phylogeny and 27; religion and 237; sublimation and 52, 57–60; *Todestrieb* (death drive) and 26–27, 29–30, 39, 45, 47, 52, 54, 57
Ainsworth, Mary 300n18
Albucher, Robert 169–170
Allen, A. 153
Allport, Gordon 134, 152
al-Qaeda 173
Altemeyer, Bob 158, 161–162, 180n3
Althusser, Louis 40–41, 48, 234–235
American Interpersonal tradition 291
Amidon, K. S. 91n7
analytical psychology: critical theory and 101, 109; emancipatory goals of 111; Enlightenment and 96, 107, 109; Jung and 95, 101–102, 105–106, 110; reality of the psyche and 110; unconscious possession and war in 106
Ananke (necessity) 3, 6, 8–9
Anatomy of Human Destructiveness, The (Fromm) 192–193, 195, 197
Anderson, Perry xvii, 165
Anderson, Steven 180n2

anti-Semitism: in academe 168–171, 180; anti-democratic tendencies and 134, 170; critical reasoning and 145–147, 150; defined 133–134; ego-syntonic 152; false projection and 145–146, 152; fascism and 47, 141, 168; Frankfurt School and 213, 218, 265; Horkheimer and Adorno on 82, 97, 131–133, 135–138, 140–150, 153–154; imposition of uniformity and 142–143, 153; instrumental reasoning and 131, 151–152; irrationalism and 131–133, 135, 140, 143; justification for military intervention 147–148, 150, 153; left-wing authoritarianism and xiv, 136, 167–173, 180; as limits of enlightenment reason 146–147, 153; mimesis and 143–145; Muslim 170–173; Nazism and 132, 134, 141, 264–265, 285n1; negative principle and 131–133, 140–141, 147–149, 153; political policy and xiv, 147–150; psychoanalysis and 82, 134–135, 137–138, 140, 142, 152–154; right-wing authoritarianism and xiv, 136; as ticket mentality 136–137, 149; unconscious and 134, 140–141; in the United States xiv, 133–134, 141, 213; violence and 132–133; *see also* anti-Zionism

Anti-Semitism and Analytical Psychology (Burston) 266

anti-Zionism: African American activists and 174; anti-Semitism and 133, 148–149, 173–174, 178–179; Arab countries and 178–180; Fromm and 173, 176; left-wing authoritarianism and 167–169, 173–174, 178–180; Soviet era 174

Arab countries: anti-Jewish riots in 179; anti-Zionism and 178–180; competing narratives on 180; concessions for Israel/Palestine and 176; human rights violations 171, 173, 178–180

archetypal theory 96, 106, 109

Aristotle 18, 49, 108

Assad, Bashar al- xxi, 169, 171

Assange, Julian 256

Atropos (the ineluctable) 3, 6

attachment theory: cultural trauma and 128; emergence of 291; emotional health and 119, 122–123, 289–290;

human development and 295, 300n18, 300n19; identification and 289; object relations theory and 295; recognition and 115, 118; relationality and 295; representational models and 295; subjectivity and 128n1; transitional phenomena and 293–294

Atwood, Margaret 166

Auden, W. H. 174

authoritarianism: Adorno on 159–161, 164, 168, 180n1; aggression and 158–159; anti-Semitism and 136, 167–169; cyberspace and 165; death threats and 166, 181n5; dichotomous thinking and 165–166, 181n4; dogmatism and 165–166, 180n3; fascism and xx, 159; Fromm on 134, 160–161, 164; irrational doubt and 168, 181n6; political conservatives and 159; psychological processes and 159–160; subconscious messaging and 215; support for 214; *see also* left-wing authoritarianism; right-wing authoritarianism

Authoritarian Nightmare (Dean and Altemeyer) 162

Authoritarian Personality, The (Adorno et al.): on anti-Semitism 134–136; critical theory and 250; critique of 2, 136, 160; left-wing authoritarianism and xx, 164; political conservatism and 159, 161; on support for authoritarian figures 214–215

Authoritarian Personality, The (Christie and Jahoda) 159

Bakunin, Mikhail 167
Balint, Michael 77, 292
Banna, Hassan al- 179
Bannon, Steve xxi
Baraka, Amiri 174
barbarism: collective regression to xviii, 84, 101; Enlightenment self-destruction and 3, 5; as failure of culture 150; Holocaust and xviii; Nazism and 152; post-scarcity society as prevention for 9; spiritual 104; technological 110–111
Beckett, Samuel 21
Beebe, Beatrice 300n18
Belafonte, Harry 174
Bell, Daniel 215
Bell, Derrick 266

Benjamin, Jessica 19, 297
Benjamin, Walter 3
Berlin Phenomenology (Hegel) 129n2
Bernfeld, Siegfried 1
Bettelheim, Bruno 260
Biden, Joe 162
Bildung 150–151, 153
biogenetic recapitulation: death instinct and 76, 79–81; evolutionary progress and 71–74, 80–81; Frankfurt School and 67, 81; Freud on 66–67, 74–83, 89–90; Haeckel on 67–74; historico-material critique and 89–90; involution and 74–79, 82–83, 91n6
Bishop, Paul xx
Black, Hannah xxi
Black Americans in Support of Israel (BASIC) 174
Black Lives Matter movement (BLM) 174
Black Panthers 265
Black Power and Palestine (Fischbach) 174
Black power movement 265
Bolshevik Revolution (October 1917) 26, 55, 59
Bolshevism: Freud critique of 26–41, 43–47, 53–56; socialism and 59; Stalinism and 28–29, 34; *see also* Marxism
Bowlby, John 291, 300n18, 300n19
Bowler, P. 91n4
Boycott, Divestment, Sanctions (BDS) movement 174
brain: affect and 22; archaic primary process 193, 201, 204–205; authoritarianism and 159, 181n4; default mode network 199–200, 204, 206; ego complex and 185, 200, 206; evolution and 185, 193–201; human growth and 196–198, *198*, 199–200; malleability of 193–194; metacognition and 199; primates and 196–197, *198*; second nature concept and 195, 199; transgenerational transmission of trauma and 123–124
Breivik, Anders xv
Breyer, Steven 267
Brickman, C. 91n4
Brunner, José 47
Burns, Jonathan 200–201
Burston, Daniel xx, 91n3, 259, 262n25, 266
Butler, Judith 167, 170–171

cancel culture xxii
Capital (Marx) 35
Capital in The 21st Century (Piketty) 261n16
capitalism: competition and 57–61; dissatisfaction and 223; Labor and 251; performance principle and 7; personifications/bearers of 60–61; postmodernism and 241; principle of exchange and 3; proletarian perspective and 38; Protestantism and 33; socioeconomic critique and 194; stock market crash of 1929 xvii; sublimations of aggression in 57–61; super-ego and 32–33; surplus repression and 7; totally administered society and 97; *see also* consumer capitalism
Carlson, E. T. 91n4
Carmichael, Stockley 174
Castoriadis, Cornelius 20, 22
Chamberlain, J. E. 91n4
Chomsky, Noam 173, 260
Christie, Robert 159
civil society xiii–xx, 128
Clark, Gary xx
Clinton, Hillary 160
Cohen, Hermann 173
collective unconscious 198, 205, 213, 268
commodification 142, 223
communism xvi, 10, 27–28; *see also* Marxism
Communist Manifesto 58
Condorcet, Nicholas de xv
consciousness: altered states of 204; domination of unconscious 22; false 13, 40; Freud on descent of 78; Fromm on 190–191; Jung on evolving 106; philosophy of 18–19; primary 200–201, 205; primitive 202; rationality and 203; repression and 15; secondary 185, 200–201, 204–205; second nature concept and 190–191, 194; subjectivity and 190; trauma and 78; *see also* unconscious
conspiracy theories 168
consumer capitalism: advertising in 215–218, 222; American collective and 211–214, 220; cultural complex around 212; healing consumers 224–226; images and 216–217; impact on the psyche 219, 221, 223–224, 227; Lacan on 30, 33; production of unease and

217–218, 220; psychological problem of 211–224; puritan-hedonist situation 220–221, 223, 227; *ressentiment* situation 222–223, 227; socioeconomic critique and 194, 211; subconscious messaging and 215–219, 228–229; virtue concept and 212, 226–229
Contribution to the Critique of Political Economy, A (Marx) 41
Costello, Thomas 158–160, 162
Coughlin, Charles xiv
Coulter, Anne 274–275
Covid-19 95, 110–111, 143
critical education 150, 152–153
critical race theory: anti-Black racism and 266–268; anti-racism and 264; critical theory and 264–266; emergence of 266–267; liberal values and 275; postmodernism and 266; psychoanalysis and 266–268, 283–284; racial essentialism and 283, 285; *see also* whiteness studies
critical theory: analytical psychology and 101, 109; critical race theory and 264–266; critique of positivism 154, 249, 252; culture and 251–252; far-right rhetoric and xv; Frankfurt School and 248–252, 260, 260n1; Freud and xix, 12; Fromm and xx, 188; German idealism and 189; Hegelian Marxism and 189; historical dialectics of Marx and 105; Marxism and 249; negative principle and 147; object relations theory and 288; psychoanalysis and xx, 19, 135, 153–154, 188, 212, 287–288, 298–299; radicalization of 3; resistance to untruth and 154n1; as response to Marxism xvii–xix; totally administered society and 97; unreason and 149
crypto-revisionism 91n3
cults 237, 239, 245n28, 245n34
cultural Marxism xv, xxii
culture: commandments of 241, 245n42; critical theory and 251–252; disintegration of 120–121, 150; drives and 239–241; Freud on 233–234, 236–239; happiness and 233; modernity and 201, 203; pathology and 237–243; positive/negative cults and 237, 239, 245n28, 245n34; postmodernism and 241–242; protestlessness and 242, 246n45; pseudo-culture and 151; psychoanalytic approach to 231, 236–243; religious consciousness in 204, 206; restriction of the drives and 233–234, 243n10; second nature concept and 190–191; shame versus guilt 237–238, 245n28; subsumption to economics 98; super-ego and 31, 33–34; superstructure concept and 237, 240–241; symptom formation and 237
culture industry 9, 82, 97–98

D'Arcy, M. 139
Darwin, Charles 69–70
Davis, Angela 174, 265
Dean, John W. 162
death drive (*Todestrieb*): aggression and 26–27, 29–30, 39, 45, 47, 52–54, 57; emergence of theory of 70; Eros and 45–47, 49, 53; human nature and 30, 46–47; industrial domination and 89; mimesis and 144; pleasure principle and 89
default mode network 199–200, 202, 204, 206
Delgado, R. 266
Dell, Stanley M. 101
democracy: capitalist control of 251; collective and 117, 121; Enlightenment thought and 107, 146; Habermas defense of 11; Israel and 178; need for universities in xxii, 162; right-wing extremist threat to xx–xxi, 162
depth psychology 185, 188, 205
Der Amerikamüde (Kürnberger) 97
Derrida, Jacques 265
Descent of Madness, The (Burns) 200
Dialectical Imagination, The (Jay) 247, 259
dialectical materialism xvi–xvii, 89
Dialectic of Enlightenment, The (Horkheimer and Adorno): on anti-Semitism 82, 97, 131–138, 140–150, 153–154; concept of mimesis in 138–139, 143–144; critical theory and 3, 12, 95; critique of the Enlightenment 107; on the culture industry 98; enlightenment versus myth and 95–98, 110; false projection and 145–146, 152; on Homer's *Odyssey* 4, 99, 111n2; on instrumentalization of reason 131, 151–152; on myth 138–139; neo-Kantian epistemology and 154n1; notion of primordial nature 98–99; on progress and regression 82, 84; on self-destruction of enlightenment 82, 96; totally administered society and 5, 21, 97

Die Stimme des Innern (Jung) 101–102
Die verwaltete Welt broadcast 97–98
diversity, equity, and inclusion (DEI) xxii, 169–170
dogmatism 165–166, 180n3
domination of nature 3–5, 136–137, 139–140, 144
Dorn, Gerhard 112n16
dreams: altered states of consciousness and 204; childhood regression and 76; Freud on 76, 78, 88; Fromm on 185, 189, 201–204, 206; fulfillment of wishes and 78, 88; human dissociation from 202–203; psychoanalysis and 76; trauma and 78; unconscious and 206
Dühring, Eugene 167
Durkin, Kieran 68, 204
dysrecognition 115, 118, 127–128, 297

Eagleton, Terry 165
Eaton, Paul 180n2
Economic and Philosophical Manuscripts (Marx) 249
"Education after Auschwitz" (Adorno) 152
Ego and the Id, The (Freud) 33
ego psychology 288, 291
Ehrenberg, Alain 240–241
Einstein, Albert 30
empathy 115, 122–123, 128
Encyclopaedia Phenomenology (Hegel) 129n2
"End of Utopia, The" (Marcuse) 9
Engels, Friedrich 31–32, 43, 192
Enlightenment: Adorno and Horkheimer critique of 107; anti-Semitism and 132, 140, 146–147; critical theory and xviii, 3; critique of ideologies 39–40; dialectic of 3–5, 139–140; escape from mythic fate and sacrifice 4; evolutionary optimism and 81; forms of 107; historicity of 107; Jung's skepticism on 102–107; limits of rationality and 146–147, 153; logic of sameness and 142; Marxism and xvi, xix; myth versus 95–98; non-supernatural 112n15; opposition to tyranny 98; radical and non-radical 107; rationality and 202–203; religion-science differences and 39–40; self-destruction of 82, 96; technophilia and xvii
Epicurus 244n18
equity, diversity, and inclusion (EDI) 169
Erikson, Erik 228, 254

evolution: anthropology and 185, 188–189, 192–199; consciousness and 78; Freud's metapsychology and 67; Fromm on 185, 188–189; human cognitive 185, 193–201; involution and 74–82, 91n6; phylogeny and 68; progressive 69–74; psychoanalysis and 192–193; reason and 13; recapitulationism and 66, 68–76, 80–81; secondary consciousness and 204–205; second nature concept and 185, 188–189, 195–196
evolutionary psychology 69, 72, 188, 193
Exhausted Self, The (Ehrenberg) 240

Fable of the Bees (Mandeville) 238
Fairbairn, W. R. D. 291–292
familicide 194
Fanon, Frantz 133
Farhud of Baghdad 179, 181n9
far-left *see* left-wing authoritarianism
Farrakhan, Louis xiv
far-right *see* right-wing authoritarianism
fascism: anti-Semitism and 47, 141, 148, 168, 265; authoritarianism and xx, 159; European rise of 2, 81; group formation and primal horde 84–85; Left and xx–xxi, 180n1; propaganda and 83–85; regression and 96; ticket mentality and 136; totally administered society and 97
Faust (Goethe) 103, 105
Federn, Paul 1
Ferenczi, Sándor 77, 292
Fischbach, Michael 174–175
Fliess, Wilhelm 78
Floyd, George 264
Fonagy, Peter 300n18
Ford, Henry xiv
Foucault, Michel 172
Frankfurt Institute for Social Research xvii, xviii, xx, 1, 81
Frankfurt Psychoanalytic Institute 1
Frankfurt School: anti-Black racism and 265; anti-Jungian outlook 96, 98; critical theory and 248–252, 260, 260n1; cultural influence of 109; emancipatory goals of 250, 252–253, 255; Freudian thought and 185–186, 253; Fromm and xx, 83, 160–161, 185–186, 264; ideology concept and 190; integration of critical theory and psychoanalysis 19; materialism and 11; notion of primordial nature 98; as outsiders 12; philosophical roots of 189; psychoanalysis and 1, 3;

psychology of consumer capitalism and 212–213; recapitulationism and 66–67, 74, 81, 83, 90; rise of Nazism and 265; study of anti-Semitism 213, 218, 265; on subconscious messaging 213–216; Zionism and 175–176

Frankfurt School, Jewish Lives and Anti-Semitism, The (Jacobs) 175

Freud (Rieff) 47

Freud, Anna 1, 291

Freud, Sigmund: on biology as destiny 17, 90; critical theory and xix, 12; critique of Marxism 26–41, 43–47, 53–61; on culture 233–234, 236–239; dictatorship of reason and 23; Habermas and 11–18; on helplessness of humans 49–52; historical materialism and 30–32, 34–36, 39, 42–43; Hobbes and 47–48; on human nature 27, 29, 44, 46–47, 49–52, 56; link to Marx 247; loss of daughter 70, 78; Marxist critique of 8; notion of maturity 21–22; patriarchal cultural values and 187; philosophy of history 81, 84, 86; on psychoanalysis as natural science 36, 43, 231–232, 236; on religion 35, 173, 238; on social phenomena in psychic development 299n13; somatic and 14; on the uncanny 143–145; use of language 260; on *Weltanschauungen* 34–36, 39, 41, 44; *see also* Freudian theory; psychoanalysis

Freud, Sigmund. *Beyond the Pleasure Principle*: biogenetic recapitulation and 68, 79–80; Eros's life drives and 45; Eros-versus-*Todestrieb* in 49; involution and 77; on regression 79; *Todestrieb* (death drive) and 26, 76

Freud, Sigmund. *Civilization and Its Discontents*: on aggression 44, 279–280; on Bolshevism 26–30, 54; on cultural super-ego 31, 33; Eros-versus-*Todestrieb* in 45–47; on evolution and involution 75; on progress xviii; on unconquerable nature 99

Freud, Sigmund. *New Introductory Lectures on Psycho-Analysis*: on aggression 44, 52; on Bolshevism 30, 35, 54; on cultural super-ego 31, 33, 43; Eros-versus-*Todestrieb* in 47; synthesis of Marxism and psychoanalysis 41

Freud, Sigmund. *Works: Ego and the Id, The* 33; *Future of an Illusion, The* 8, 50; *Group Psychology and the Analysis of the Ego* 83, 91n9; *Inhibitions, Symptoms and Anxiety* 49–50; *Interpretation of Dreams, The* 76; *Moses and Monotheism* 91n8; "Obsessive Actions and Religious Practices" 239; *Project for a Scientific Psychology* 49–50; "Question of a *Weltanschauung, The*" 30, 35, 41, 44, 54, 56; *Three Essays on the Theory of Sexuality* 74, 77, 234; *Totem and Taboo* 48, 66, 77, 80, 82–83, 238

Freudian theory: on aggression 44, 52–54, 56–58; on archaic inheritance 67–68, 80, 87–88; on biogenetic recapitulation 66–68, 74–86, 89–90; crypto-revisionist reading of 68, 91n3; death drive (*Todestrieb*) 26–27, 29–30, 39, 45–47, 49, 52–54, 57, 70, 144; on degeneration 91n6; on descent of consciousness 78; drives and 26, 44–47, 52; on Eros 45–47, 50–53; on evolution and involution 74–82, 91n6; Frankfurt School and 1, 185–186, 253; Fromm revision of orthodox 161, 186–189, 212; group formation and primal horde 83–85, 91n8, 91n9; on identification 289–291, 299n7; Lacan revision of 262n25; Marcuse critique of 6–9, 47–48, 79, 85–88, 90, 212; normal model and 237–239; object relations and 188, 288–290; on the Oedipus complex 91n1, 187–188; pleasure principle and 6, 9, 52; primary narcissism and 20; on progress and regression xviii, 67–68, 79–82, 87; reality principle and 3–4, 6, 8–9, 87–88; reverse recapitulationism and 74–81, 86, 89; super-ego and 31–34, 43, 232–233, 290–291; superstructure concept and 234–235; theory of perversion 89; on the unconscious 14–16, 22, 33, 83, 86, 202, 262n25

Friedlander, Roger 161

Fromm, Erich: Adorno and Horkheimer disagreement with 186; *Anatomy of Human Destructiveness, The* 192–193, 195, 197; anti-Zionism and 173, 176; approach to religion 201–204; on authoritarianism 134, 160–161, 164, 251; character formation and 191–192, 194–196, 199, 205; civil rights movement and 265; critical theory and xx, 188; critique of Adorno 160; evolutionary anthropology and 185, 188–189, 192–201, 205–206; Frankfurt

School and xvii, 83, 160–161, 185–186, 264; on human brain evolution 197–199; on interpersonal relations 292; on irrational doubt 168; Marcuse critique of 66, 68, 86, 186–187; on modernity 201–203; on mother-infant bond 196–197; psychoanalysis and 1, 188; psychological anthropology and 201–204; on racism 267–268; rejection of Freudian drives 90n1; rejection of Oedipus complex 67, 90n1; revision of Freudian orthodoxy 161, 186–189, 212; *Sane Society, The* 192, 194; second nature concept and 185, 189–192, 194–196, 199, 205–206; self-consciousness and 190–191, 194; on social brain 201; socioeconomic critique and 187–189, 191–194; *Studies in Authority and the Family* 2; on the unconscious 185, 191, 198, 201–206; universality principle and 198, 204
Future of an Illusion, The (Freud) 50

Gabay, Alfred J. 107
Galloway, George xxi
Gandesha, Samir xxi, 180n1
Generelle Morphologie der Organismen (Haeckel) 70–71
George, Carol 300n18
Germany: anti-Semitism and 213; *Aufklrung* in 107; authoritarianism and 180n1, 251; *Bildung* in 150; democracy and 11; flight of scholars from 134, 160, 265; idealist thought in 189; Jewish intellectuals in 264–265; Kristallnacht pogrom 181n8; rise of Nazism in 102, 134, 160; *see also* Nazism
Goethe, Johann Wolfgang von 103–105
Goodall, Jane 193
Gordon, Peter 2
Gould, Stephen Jay 91n2, 193
Gramsci, Antonio 27, 41, 43, 265
Grand Hotel Abyss (Jeffries) xx
Grigat, Stephan 147–149
Guntrip, Harry 291

Habermas, Jürgen: critical theory and 12–14; critique of Adorno and Horkheimer 99; critique of postmodernism 266; defense of democracy 11; exact fantasy and 14; on false consciousness 13; on human nature 11; ideal speech situations and 17–18; impact of Freud on 11–18; Kantianism and 11; *Knowledge and Human Interests* 12, 17; on language 13–18; on necessary and surplus repression 13–16; on Nietzsche 13; psychoanalysis and 12–13; second nature concept and 190; on systematically distorted communication 17; *Theory of Communicative Action* 99; transcendental quest and 18; unconscious and 14–16; word- and thing-representations and 14–17; working-class theory and 12
Haeckel, Ernst: biogenetic recapitulationism and 67–73; *Generelle Morphologie der Organismen* 70–71; physicalist materialism and 81, 91n7; progressive evolutionary psychology and 69, 71–74, 80–81; *Wonders of Life, The* 72
Haeckel's Law 69, 71, 74, 76, 89
Halbbildung 151
Hall, G. Stanley 81
Hamas 149, 170–171, 173
Harrington, Michael 174
Hart, Erika 169
Hartmann, Heinz 291
Hegel, Georg W. F.: *Berlin Phenomenology* 129n2; dialectical regression and 129n4; *Encyclopaedia Phenomenology* 129n2; holism and 121; ontological disclosures and 49; *Phenomenology of Spirit* 116, 129n2; recognition theory and 19, 116–117, 129n2; second nature concept and 185, 188–190, 192, 199, 205
Heidegger, Martin xix, 99
Herzog, Katie 268–269, 271–274
Hesse, Erik 300n18
Hessischer Rundfunk 97
Hezbollah 149, 170–171, 173
historical materialism: competition and 57–58; economistic vulgarizations of 43; Freud and 30–32, 34–36, 42–43; Marxism and xvi, xx, 30–32, 34–36, 39–40, 42–43; postmodernist dismissal of xix; proletarian class consciousness and 38; social development and 35–36; super-ego theory and 34, 42–43
Hitler, Adolf 143, 160, 168, 179, 285n1
Hobbes, Thomas 26, 47–48
Homer 99, 111n2, 139
Honneth, Axel: on attachment 300n19; critical theory and xx, 19–20, 118, 287; on Habermas 18; pro-social forces and 19–20; psychoanalysis and 19–20;

recognition theory and 115, 118, 128, 289; relational psychoanalysis and 19–20; resistance to drive theory 289–290; Winnicott and 118, 288, 290, 294, 297

Horkheimer, Max: anti-Hegelianism and 5; on class difference and organized criminality 97; on collective regression xviii, 82; critical reasoning and 150; critical theory and 2–3, 12, 153, 249–250; critique of instrumental reason 99; *Die verwaltete Welt* broadcast 97–98; on elitist cultural industry 10; enlightenment and 4; Fromm and 160; Habermas critique of 99; on Haeckel's physicalist materialism 81, 91n7; Institute for Social Research and xvii–xviii, 1; Marx-Freud synthesis and xvii; materialism and 2–3, 81; Nazism and xvii, 3, 82, 265; on progress and regression 82–83, 96; psychoanalysis and 3, 12; on rational knowledge 259; second nature concept and 190; on student activism xxiii; *Studies in Authority and the Family* 2; totally administered society and 9, 20; *see also Dialectic of Enlightenment, The* (Horkheimer and Adorno)

Hull, R. F. C. 101

human development: attachment theory and 295, 300n18, 300n19; brain growth and 195–198, *198*, 199–200; language and 15, 199; primary narcissism and 8; primary/secondary consciousness and 200; psychic needs for love and empathy in 119; psychopathology and 200–201, 274; repression and 15; transitional phenomena and 20, 292–293

human nature: aggression and 118, 122, 279–280, 287; behavioral dynamics in 119; Freud on 27, 29, 44, 46–47, 49–52, 56; Habermas on 11; helplessness (*Hilflosigkeit*) and 49–52; malleability of 191, 194; Marx on 27; need for love and 119; pleasure principle and 56; recognition and 115–119; social relations and 288–289; sublimation and 51–52; *Todestrieb* (death drive) and 30, 46–47

Hussein, Saddam xxi
Husseini, Amin al- 178–180

identification 289–291, 299n7
intersubjectivity 18, 118, 258, 289–292, 297–298

ISIS 173
Islamism 173
Islamist organizations 167, 170–172
Islamophobia 163, 168, 172–173
Israel: anti-Jewish riots in 178–179; anti-Semitism and 141, 143, 148, 178; anti-Zionism and 168, 178; BDS and BLM narratives on 174; competing narratives on 178, 180; human rights violations 171, 173, 175, 180; Islamist targeting of 170; Jewish people of color in 174–175; military support for 148; support for Zionism and 174; two-state solution and 175–176; UN Resolution 3379 and 174, 176, 181n8

Israel, Jonathan 107

Jackson, Jesse 174
Jacobs, Jack 175
Jacobsen, Kurt xx
Jacoby, Russell 26, 37
Jahoda, Marie 159
James, William 105
Jay, Martin 247, 259
Jeffries, Stuart xx, 285n1
Jews: anti-Semitism and xiv, 131–134, 140, 142–145, 176; anti-Zionism and 173; assimilation and 140–141; far-left rhetoric on xiv; genocidal campaigns against 177–179; Holocaust and xviii, 176–177, 181n8; negative principle and 131, 140–141; people of color 174–175; whiteness and xiv, 133
Johnston, Adrian xx, 259
Judt, Tony 173
Jung, Carl G.: alchemy and 105–109, 112n14, 112n16; analytical psychology and 95, 101–102, 105–106, 110; "Analytical Psychology und Weltanschauung" 99, 101; archetypal theory and 96, 106, 109, 112n17, 198; on consumer capitalism 212; *Die Stimme des Innern* 101–102; on the Enlightenment 102–107; evolving consciousness and 106; Frankfurt School rejection of 96, 98; on Goethe 103–105; on incomprehensible jargon 109, 112n19; individuation concept and 205; on instrumental reason 101; on language 109; *lumen naturae* and 107–108; *Mysterium coniunctionis* 100, 107; "Paracelsus as a Spiritual Phenomenon" 112n15; on the persistence of Judeo-Christianity

103–104; persistence of the archaic and 101; on psychological mechanisms 213, 229n1; *Psychological Types* 99, 102; *Psychology and Alchemy* 112n14; "Psychotherapists or the Clergy" 100; on race and collective unconscious 266; on reality of the psyche 101, 213; *Red Book, The* 95, 109, 111n7, 112n13; regression of libido and 104, 112n12; on scientific attitude 105; *Transformations and Symbols of the Libido* 112n12; on unconquerable nature 99–102; on the unconscious 99–100, 104, 202

Kant, Immanuel 5, 33, 145, 239, 243n8
Katerji, Oz 169
Kennedy, Robert F. 174
Khilanani, Aruna 268–276, 283, 285
Khomeni, Ayatollah 172
King, Martin Luther, Jr. 174, 265, 271
Klages, Ludwig 111n2
Klein, Melanie 291
Knowledge and Human Interests (Habermas) 12, 17
Kogon, Eugen 97–98
Kohut, Heinz 291, 294, 300n17
Korsch, Karl 43
Kortlandt, Adriaan 193, 195
Kürnberger, Ferdinand 97

Lacan, Jacques: critical psychoanalysis and 152; critical theory and 248, 260n3; critique of Hobbes 48; on the ego 262n25; on Freud and the natural sciences 13, 36; on the Imaginary 40; impact of *Dialectic of Enlightenment* 154; on language 253–260; Marxism and 29–30; negative thought and 154; postmodernism and 165; revision of Freudian orthodoxy 262n25; *Seminar VI (Desire and Its Interpretation)* 30; stoicism and xx, 257–258; subjectivity and 260; super-ego and 33; on the unconscious 247, 254–258; utopian transformation of society and 30
Laing, R. D. 253–254
language: Habermas on 13–18; human development and 15, 199; Jung on power-words in 109; Lacan on unconscious as 247, 253–257; materiality of 255; unconscious symbolism and 203, 206
Laplanche, Jean 17
Lawrence, Charles, III 267–268

Lazarsfeld, Paul 160
left-wing authoritarianism: academic freedom and 166–167; Adorno on 161, 180n1; anti-Semitism and xiv, 136, 167–173, 180; anti-Zionism and 167–169, 173–174, 178–180; behavior of 163; dichotomous thinking and 165–166; dogmatism and 165–166; higher education and xxi–xxii, 166–169; horizontal organizing of 165; ideological purity and 163; overlap with right-wing 159–160; postmodernism and 165; research in 158–163; rhetoric and 163; social justice and 163–164; universities and 162
Lehner, Ulrich L. 107
Leiris, Michel 242
Lenin, Vladimir I. xvi, xxiii, 55
Letters on the Aesthetic Education of Humankind (Schiller) 101–103
Levine, Sheila 169–170
Levi-Strauss, Claude xviii
Lewis Williams, David 204
LGBTQ+ people 276
Lily (case study) 124–127, 129n5
Living in The End Times (Žižek) 171
Loewald, Hans 20, 22
Loewenberg, Peter 247
Lovejoy, Paul E. 280
Löwenthal, Leo 165, 176–178, 266
Lukács, Georg 43
lumen naturae 107–108
Luria, A. R. 32
Luxemburg, Rosa xxiii
Lyons-Ruth, Karlen 300n18

MacDonald, Kevin xv
Main, Mary 300n18
Malinowski, Bronisław 96
Mandeville, Bernard de 238
Marcuse, Herbert: Adorno and xxi; biogenetic recapitulation and 68, 79, 87; civil rights movement and 265; critical theory and 250; critique of Fromm 66, 68, 86, 186–187; de-biologized use of reverse recapitulation and 85–87, 89–90; defense of sexual perversions 89; embrace of countercultural movements 10; "End of Utopia, The" 9; Freudian theory and xx, 6–9, 48, 86, 188; impact of social forces and 296; on Israel 175–176; on necessary and surplus repression 7–9, 13, 37, 253; "Obsolescence of the Freudian Concept

of Man, The" 9; *One Dimensional Man* 251; on progress and regression 88; psychoanalysis and 12; reappraisal of the death drive 68; second nature concept and 190; *Studies in Authority and the Family* 2; theory of perverse sexuality and 8; totally administered society and 9–10, 20; utopian transformation of society and 6–9; on William Calley and My Lai 252

Marcuse, Herbert. *Eros and Civilization*: biogenetic recapitulation and 87–90; critique of capitalism in 251; critique of Freud 6, 9, 47–48, 79, 85–88, 90, 212, 250; critique of Fromm 66, 68, 86, 186; nonrepressive civilization and 6, 87; recapitulationism and 67, 83; on struggle between pleasure and reality principles 87–88

Marr, Wilhelm 167

Martella, Vicenzo 111n2

Marx, Karl: *Capital* 35; on consciousness 190; *Contribution to the Critique of Political Economy, A* 41; *Economic and Philosophical Manuscripts* 249; Enlightenment thought and xvi, xix; on historical materialism xvi, xviii, 35–36, 43; historical perspective and 190, 192; human beings as *zoon politikon* 49; on human nature 27; link to Freud 247; technophilia and xvii; theory of ideology and 41

Marxism: abolition of private property and 28–29; aggression and 44; class societies and 38; counter to Freud critique of 31–41, 43–47, 53–61; critical theory and xv, 249; critique of Freud 8; critique of religion 39–40; dialectical materialism and xvi–xvii; domination of nature and 4; epistemology and 36–38; false consciousness and 40, 146, 154n1; Freud comparison to religion 34–36, 38–41; historical materialism and xvi, 30–32, 34–36, 39–40, 42–43; lack of subjective dimension 1–2; necessary and surplus labor in 6–7; non-neutrality and 38; overdetermination concept and 234–235; psychoanalysis and 2, 26–28, 32–33, 41–42, 57, 60–61, 247–248; revolutionary vanguardism and xvi–xvii; theory of ideology and 39–41

Material Girls (Stock) 166

materialism 2–3, 11; *see also* historical materialism

Mbeki, Thabo 181n7

McCarthy, Thomas 12

McLaughlin, Neil 188

Mein Kampf (Hitler) 285n1

Mendes, Philip 181n9

metacognition 199

Mikhailovsky, Nikolay 35

Miller, David 168–169, 173

Mills, C. Wright 250, 252

Mills, Jon xx, 129n4, 301n31

Milošević, Slobodan xxi

mimesis 138–139, 143–145

mirroring 294

modernity 21, 35, 77, 84, 201–203

Morelock, J. 150

Moss, Donald 275–283, 285

Movement and the Middle East, The (Fischbach) 174

Muslim Brotherhood 179

Mysterium coniunctionis (Jung) 100, 107

myth: archetypal dimensions of 96; enlightenment versus 95–98; human dissociation from 203; religious symbolism and 198, 203; science and 138–139; understanding of nature and 138–139

Nakajima, Tatsuhiro 108–109

natural science: causal-explanatory concepts and 15; Haeckel and 71, 91n7; objectivity and 37; psychoanalysis as 36, 43, 231–232, 236, 243n2

nature: domination of 3–4, 136–137, 139–140, 144; human objectification of 138; myth and 138–139

Navratilova, Martina 166

Nazism: Adorno and Horkheimer on xvii, 3, 82; anti-Black racism and 265, 285n1; anti-Semitism and 132, 134, 141, 264–265, 285n1; barbarism and 152; Heidegger and xix; Holocaust and 76, 177, 179; regression and 82; White supremacy and 265; *see also* Germany

necessary repression 6–9, 13–15

Neuhouser, Fredrick 128n1

Neumann, Alfred E. 255

neutrality 37–38

Niebuhr, Reinhold 174

Nietzsche, Friedrich xix, 13, 222

Nissim-Sabat, Marilyn 297

Nussbaum, Martha 167

Oakeshott, Michael 258
objectivity 37–38, 169, 202
object relations theory: attachment theory and 295; critical theory and 288; Freud on 288–290; Fromm's revision of Freudian theory and 188; identification and 289–290; impact of trauma on 124; interpersonal relationships and 292; psychoanalysis and 288–289, 291; self-objects and 294, 300n17; subjectivity and 128n1
"Obsolescence of the Freudian Concept of Man, The" (Marcuse) 9
Odyssey (Homer) 99, 111n2
Oedipus myth 187
Ollman, Bertell 252
One Dimensional Man (Marcuse) 251
"On Having Whiteness" (Moss) 276
ontogeny: aggression and 27; biogenetic recapitulation and 66; defined 68; phylogeny and 66–67, 71–72, 79, 89, 200; primary consciousness and 200; trauma and 79
Ontogeny and Phylogeny (Gould) 91n2
Orban, Victor xiv
Origin of Species (Darwin) 69
Origins (Mills) 129n4
Other: archetypal theory and 106; lack of empathy towards 115, 122–123, 128; prejudicial forces and 122; recognition and 115, 117–118, 121; as threat to safety 117, 122–123, 140
overdetermination concept 234–235

Palestine 173, 175–176, 178–180
Paracelsus 107, 112n19
"Paracelsus as a Spiritual Phenomenon" (Jung) 112n15
Parasitic Whiteness 277–282
Parker, Ian 259
Parks, Rosa 174
pathos 120–121, 129n3
Peirce, Charles Sanders 262n23
performance principle 7, 9
Peterson, Jordan xv
Pfaller, Robert xx, 259
Phenomenology of Spirit (Hegel) 116, 129n2
philosophical materialism 234
philosophy of history 3–4, 81, 84, 86
phylogeny: aggression and 27; biogenetic recapitulation and 66, 77, 79; defined 68; evolutionary progress and 71–73; individual psychology and 89; ontogeny and 66–67, 71–72, 79, 89, 200; primary consciousness and 200
Pick, D. 91n4
Piketty, Thomas 261n16
Pilbeam, David 193
Pittenger, Frank xx
Plato 219
pleasure principle: death drive and 76, 89; Freud and 6, 9, 52; human nature and 56; perverse sexuality and 8; reality principle and 9, 88; repression and 88; struggle with reality principle 88; sublimation and 52
pleasures 221, 223, 241
Portman, Adolf 193, 196–197
positivism 154, 249, 252
postmodernism: asociality imperatives and 242; critical race theory and 266; critical theory and xv, 248; dismissal of Enlightenment thought xix; hostility to universality 241–242; left-wing authoritarianism and 165; permissive culture and 241–242; queer theory and 167; relativism and 204; rise of xviii–xix
post-structuralism xix
Pragmatism (James) 105
prejudice: anti-Black racism and 168–169; emotional 120, 128; psychology of 131, 212–215; unconscious 119–122, 128; *see also* anti-Semitism; racism
primary consciousness 200–201, 204–205
Proktophantasmist 103, 111n11
Protestantism 33
Protocols of the Elders of Zion, The 168, 173, 179
Proudhon, Pierre-Joseph 167
psyche: advanced/archaic strata of 22; collective decision-making and 120; drives and 239–240, 245n37; dysrecognition and 128; emotional plague and 281; Freud on 45, 51, 53; impact of consumer capitalism on 219, 221, 223–224, 227; impact of trauma on 122–124; Jung on 100–102, 106, 110; pro- and anti-social forces in 19; socialization and 295–297; social phenomena and 291, 299n13; soma and 16

psychoanalysis: African American analysts and 275–276, 284; anti-Lacanian 260n3; anti-Semitism and 134–135, 137–138, 140, 142, 152–154; contemporary movements in 291–292; critical race theory and 266–268, 283–284; critical reasoning and 152; critical theory and xx, 13, 19, 135, 153–154, 188, 212, 287–288, 298–299; critique of religion 39–40; culture and 231, 236–243; deification of Freud and 36, 38; dreamwork and 76; evolutionary theory and 192–193; Frankfurt School and 1, 3; Horkheimer and Adorno on 135–136; indeterminacy in 235–236; individual psychological subject and 135–136; LGBTQ+ people in 276; libidinal drives and 236; linguistic turn and 13–17; Marxism and 2, 26–28, 32–33, 41–42, 57, 60–61, 247–248; as natural science 36, 231–232, 236; negative principle and 140–141, 147, 152–153; new pathologies and 240; non-neutrality and 39; norms of 231, 243n2; object relations theory and 288–289, 291; pathologizing and 118; power differentials and 119; pro-social forces and 19; psychodynamic forces and 14–15; racism and 276, 283; recognition theory and 297–298; relational 19–20; sexuality and 235; sublimation and 51–52; theory of perverse sexuality and 8; transitional phenomena and 20; unconscious and 298, 301n31; virtue concept and 228–229; whiteness studies and 267–284
Psychological Types (Jung) 102
Psychology and Alchemy (Jung) 112n14
"Psychopathic Problem of the White Mind, The" (Khilanani) 268
psychopathology 200–201, 274, 295
puritan-hedonist situation 220–221, 223, 227
Putin, Vladimir xiii, xx–xxi, 169

"Question of a *Weltanschauung*, The" (Freud) 30, 35, 41, 44, 54, 56
Question of Palestine, The (Said) 179

racial essentialism 268, 272, 275, 283, 285
racism: anti-Semitism and 168–169; anti-white 281; civil rights movement and 265; critical race theory and 266–268; experiences of 281; Frankfurt School and 265; Fromm on 267–268; Nazism and 265, 285n1; psychoanalysis and 276, 283; racial essentialism and 268, 272; in the United States 264–265, 276, 283
Randolph, A. Phillip 174
Reagan, Ronald 10
reality principle 3, 6, 8–9, 87–88
recapitulationism: colonialist notions of racial superiority and 77, 87, 89, 91n4; degeneration and 69, 74–77, 91n4; evolutionary progress and 66, 69–76, 80; Frankfurt School and 66–67, 74, 81, 83, 90; Freud's reverse 74–86; Haeckel on 69, 71–74; metapsychological 68, 83, 90; social critique and 66; *see also* biogenetic recapitulation
recognition: collective society and 127; cultural trauma and 127–128; dysrecognition and 115, 118, 127–128, 297; empathy and 122–123; Hegel and 19, 116–117, 129n2, 289; Honneth and 115, 118, 128, 289; inequality of 116–117; intersubjectivity and 289–290, 297; Lily (case study) 124–127; master-slave dialectic and 116, 129n2; need for 115–118, 128n1; Other and 115, 117–118, 121; psychoanalysis and 297–298; self-consciousness and 115–117, 129n2; unconscious prejudice and 119–120
Red Book, The (Jung) 95, 109, 111n7, 112n13
Reich, Wilhelm 2, 281
relational psychoanalysis 19–20
religion: aggression and 237; anti-Zionism as 173; cults and 237, 239, 245n28; cultural affinities and 204; egotistical self and 202; Freud on 35, 173, 238; Freud on Marxism as 34–36, 38–41; Fromm approach to 201–204; fundamentalism and 11; psychological anthropology and 201–202; public critique of 171–172; symbolism and 198
Rensman, L. 136
Republic, The (Plato) 219
ressentiment 222–223, 227–228
revolutionary vanguardism xvi–xvii
Ricoeur, Paul 8, 14
Rieff, Philip 47–49
right-wing authoritarianism: anti-Semitism and xiv, 136; behavior of 163; critical theory rhetoric and xv; extremist threat

to democracy xiv, 162; fascism and 159; horizontal organizing of 165; overlap with left-wing 159; populism and xiii, xx; pseudo-conservatism and xxiii; religious/racial purity and 163; research in 159–162; rhetoric and 163; threat of xiii–xiv, xv, xxi, xxiii, 162; tripartite structure of 158
Right Wing Authoritarianism (RWA) scale 158, 162
Rokeach, M. 181n3
Roosevelt, Eleanor 174
Rosenzweig, Franz 173
Rousseau, Jean-Jacques 48, 243n10
Rowling, J. K. 166
Roy, Jean 48
Rückert, Friedrich 80
Rufo, Christopher xv
Rushdie, Salman 172–173
Russell, E. S. 71
Rustin, Bayard 174

Sachs, Hans 1
Said, Edward 179
Sallust 96
Samuels, Andrew 111n7
Sane Society, The (Fromm) 192, 194
Sassoulitch, Vera 35
Satanic Verses, The (Rushdie) 172
Schactel, Ernst 160
Schaller, George 193
Scheler, Max 222
Schiller, Friedrich 101–103, 111
Schmidt, Conrad 31
Schoenberg, Arnold 21
Schorske, Carl 81
secondary altriciality 196
secondary consciousness 185, 200–201, 204–205
second nature: brain development and 195, 199; character formation and 191–192, 194–195, 199, 205; evolutionary thought and 185, 188–189; Hegelian concept of 185, 188, 190, 192, 199, 205; human consciousness and 190–191, 194; psychoanalysis and 188
Self: division of 16; ego-integration and 5; integration of 21, 23; interaction and 19–20; mirroring and 294; Other and 121; responsiveness to 225; self-objects and 294, 300n17; transgenerational transmission of trauma and 127; virtue and 225

self-consciousness: ethical 122; Fromm on 190; Hegel on 129n2; recognition and 115–117, 129n2; second nature concept and 190–191; shamanic trance and 204; social relations and 121–122
self-objects 294, 300n17
self psychology 291
Seminar VI (Desire and Its Interpretation) (Lacan) 30
sexuality: cultural superstructure for 240; indeterminacy in 235; perverse 8, 89; postmodernism and 241; social dimensions of 242; unconscious and 186
Shils, Edward 159
Shore, Alan 300n18
Shultz, Dana xxi
Simmel, Ernst 134
Simon, Ernst 176–177
Sketch for a Historical Picture of the Progress of the Human Mind (Condorcet) xv
Slade, Arietta 300n18
slavery 279–280
Smith, Adam 223
socialist/communist societies 53, 57, 59
social justice warriors (SWJs) 163–164
Social Life of Early Man (Washburn) 193
social psychology: critical theory and 135; group formation and 84; human development and 197, 300n18; individualism and 296, 300n13; object relations theory and 290; psychoanalysis and 135; working class and xvii
social relations 288–291, 298, 300n13
society: anti-Semitism and 132–133; disintegration of culture and 9, 120; emancipation of 9, 21, 87; exploitation in 7, 13–14; lack of empathy and 115, 122–123, 128; Marxism and 30–32, 36, 38, 40, 57; mass consumerism and 9; mutual difference and 121–122; mutual recognition and 116–118, 121, 128; quantum of toil in 6–7; recapitulationary parallelism and 90; relationships and 291–292, 300n13; threat of aggression to 52, 57; totally administered 9, 95–97, 111n7; trauma and 115, 122–124, 127; unconscious prejudice and 119–122; utopian transformation of 7–9, 12
Socrates 219
Solomon, Judith 300n18
Sorkin, David 107
Soros, George xiv

South Africa 173, 175–176
Soviet Union: anti-Zionism and 174; degrading of dialectical thinking in 261n12; Frankfurt School critique of 251; Freud critique of xviii, 26–28, 35, 54; Lacan on revolution in 30; Leninism and 29
Spinoza, Benedict de 232
Stalin, Joseph xvi, 28, 163–164
Stalinism 28, 34, 164
Stefancic, J. 266
Steiner, George 173
Steiner, Rudolf 111n11
Stern, Daniel 297, 300n19
Sternhell, Zeev 107
Stock, Kathleen 166–167
Strachey, James 56
Strosberg, Benjamin B. xx
Studies in Authority and the Family (Horkheimer) 2
Studies in Prejudice 213
subconscious messaging: advertising and 215–218; American susceptibility to 215–216, 228–229; consumer capitalism and 213–219, 228–229; images and 216–217; production of unease and 217–218; psychic mechanisms for 213–214, 217, 229
subjectivity: animal instinct and 189; anti-Semitism and 152; constitutive 18; loss of otherness and 140; Marxism and 1; non-reified forms of 5; recognition theory and 124, 128n1; self-consciousness and 117, 190; social relations and 296; transcendental 18
sublimation 51–52, 57–60
suicide 73, 194
Sullivan, Harry Stack 291–292
Sulloway, F. 91n6
super-ego: children and 31; cultural 31, 33–34; drive excitations and 232–233, 240; Freudian 31–34; historical materialism and 34, 42–43; imperatives of 245n42; relational factors in 290–291
superstructure concept 234–235, 237, 240–241
surplus repression 6–9, 13–15
Suttie, Ian 292

taboo societies 237–239
Taguba, Antonio 180n2
Taliban 173

Target, Mary 300n18
technophilia xvii
Thatcher, Margaret 10
"*Theorie der Halbildung*" (Adorno) 151
Theory of Communicative Action (Habermas) 99
ticket mentality 136–137, 149
Till, Emmett xxi
Todestrieb (death drive) *see* death drive (*Todestrieb*)
trans exclusionary radical feminist (TERF) 166
Transformations and Symbols of the Libido (Jung) 112n12
Transformations in Slavery (Lovejoy) 280
transitional phenomena 20, 292–294
trauma: collective 115, 122–124, 127; consciousness and 78; dream-work and 78; lack of empathy and 115, 122; phylogenetically inherited 79; transgenerational transmission of 123–128
Trotsky, Leon xvi, xxiii
Trump, Donald J.: authoritarianism and xxi, 2, 160, 162; fascist propaganda and 83; insurrection and 180n2; prejudicial forces and 120; pseudo-conservatism and xxiii
Truskolaski, Sebastian 109
Tutu, Desmond 271
Tuvel, Rebecca xxi

unconscious: affects and motives in 287; anti-Semitism and 134, 140–141; collective 198, 205, 213, 268; dream and 203–204; Freud on xviii, 14–16, 22, 33, 83, 86, 202; Fromm on 191, 198, 201–206; group formation and primal horde 83–84; Habermas on 15–16, 20; impressionability and 215; instinctual life and 4, 22; Jung on 99–100, 104, 202; Lacanian theory and 247, 254–255, 257; nonlinguistic 15–16; phylogenetic past and 75, 86, 88; prejudicial forces and 119–122, 128; sexuality and 186; social relations and 298, 301n31; somatic forces and 16; subconscious messaging and 214–217; symbolism and 203, 206; unconquered nature and 99–100

United States: anti-Black racism in 264–265, 276, 283; anti-Semitism in xiv, 133–134, 141, 213; collective psyche and 120, 213; consumer capitalism and 211–222, 228; lack of class struggle in 172; left-wing authoritarianism and xiv, 174, 180; personality type in 214–215; puritanism in 220–221; right-wing extremism and xiii, 120, 162; susceptibility to subconscious messaging in 214–217
universality principle 198, 204
universities: academic freedom and 162, 166–167; anti-Semitism and 168–171, 180; defunding of liberal arts in 151; equity, diversity, and inclusion (EDI) in 169–170; growth of management in xxii; left-wing authoritarianism and xxi–xxii, 166–169; self-censorship and xxii; student activism and xxii–xxiii, 164, 166, 177
Unmastered Past, An (Löwenthal) 176
UN Resolution 3379 174, 176, 181n8

virtue concept 212, 224–229
Von Mises, Ludwig 217

Waal, Frans De 193
Wallace, Edwin R. 47
Washburn, Sherwood 193
Weber, Max 33, 43, 95, 97
Weikart, R. 91n4
Weiss, Bari 268
Weiss, Hilde 160

Wellmer, Albrecht 21
White, John R. xx
Whitebook, Joel xx, 19–23
whiteness studies: critical theory and 264; impact of critical race theory on 266–267; Parasitic Whiteness and 277–282; psychoanalysis and 267–271, 274–284; psychopathy and 268, 274; racial essentialism and 272, 275, 283, 285; White unconscious and 268; *see also* critical race theory
White supremacy xiv, 169, 265, 267
Winnicott, Donald: on attachment 300n19; critical theory and 19, 118, 288; Honneth and 118, 288, 290, 294; object relations theory and 291; Stern and 297, 300n19; transitional phenomena and 20, 292–293
Wonders of Life, The (Haeckel) 72
Woods, Alexandra 276, 284
Wordsworth, William 58
working class xvi, xvii, 251, 261n16
World Conference Against Racism, Xenophobia and Other Forms of Intolerance (WCAR) 173

X, Malcolm 174

Yates, Frances 107

Zionism 173–179; *see also* anti-Zionism
Žižek, Slavoj 171–172, 258–259
Zupančič, Alenka 235

For Product Safety Concerns and Information please contact our EU
representative GPSR@taylorandfrancis.com
Taylor & Francis Verlag GmbH, Kaufingerstraße 24, 80331 München, Germany

www.ingramcontent.com/pod-product-compliance
Lightning Source LLC
Chambersburg PA
CBHW050527300426
44113CB00012B/1988